TCHAIKOVSKY
The Man and his Music

TCHAIKOVSKY

David Brown was born in Gravesend, Kent. A graduate of Sheffield University, he learned Russian during National Service, and taught in secondary modern schools before becoming music librarian of London University. In 1962 he moved to Southampton University, retiring as Professor of Musicology in 1989. After books on the English madrigalists Thomas Weelkes and John Wilbye, he focused on Russian composers, producing major studies of Glinka, Musorgsky and Tchaikovsky, the last (in four volumes) the largest life-and-works of a Russian composer ever published (as the official Soviet review acknowledged: 'Frankly we have nothing like it'). He has broadcast frequently.

by the same author

THOMAS WEELKES
JOHN WILBYE
MIKHAIL GLINKA
TCHAIKOVSKY (4 volumes)
TCHAIKOVSKY REMEMBERED
MUSORGSKY

TCHAIKOVSKY

The Man and his Music

David Brown

PEGASUS BOOKS
NEW YORK

TCHAIKOVSKY
THE MAN AND HIS MUSIC

Pegasus Books LLC
80 Broad Street
5th Floor
New York, NY 10004

First Pegasus Books edition 2009

Library of Congress Cataloging-in-Publication Data is available.

ISBN: 978-1-60598-017-1

10 9 8 7 6 5 4 3 2 1

Printed in the United States of America
Distributed by W. W. Norton & Company, Inc.
www.pegasusbooks.us

This book is offered to those who, though perhaps already familiar with this greatest of Russian composers, may welcome some company while extending further their experience of his music – but even more, perhaps, to those who, knowing little or nothing about classical music, may look for a listener's guide to some of the grandest and most moving experiences that music can offer.

Contents

The Nomad Years

The Celebrity Years

Appendices

List of Illustrations

Acknowledgements

For help in checking this book (as with my previous nine) I am very grateful to Elizabeth, my wife.

My thanks also to all the staff members of Faber involved in seeing this book out into the wider world.

A Personal Note

First, a thin slice of autobiography. In 1968 I was asked to write a book on Tchaikovsky. I declined: 'Not interested.' Then in 1971 came an invitation to contribute a 20,000-word entry on Tchaikovsky to a new edition of the very prestigious *New Grove Dictionary of Music and Musicians*. It was irresistible – and researching this shifted my whole view of this great Russian composer. Three years on, the publishers, Victor Gollancz, proposed a single-volume study of the composer, to take some four years. I accepted, though still with hesitation. But then Tchaikovsky himself took over. The contracted 150,000 words grew to 600,000; four years became sixteen, and a single volume became four. The result was the largest life-and-works of a Russian composer ever written anywhere – including Russia itself: as the official Russian review put it, 'Frankly, we have nothing like it.' Never had I realized how fascinating, how complex a man Tchaikovsky was – even more, how great and varied a composer, and just how much of his vast output I simply had not known. Tchaikovsky was, I discovered, one of the *true* giants of nineteenth-century music.

Making that study has been the richest and most privileged of the many experiences of my professional life. But events have moved on. During the past fifteen or so years the transformation of the totalitarian Soviet state into the democracy Russia is today has seen the abolition of censorship and, with the opening of archives shut for decades, secrets known to only a tiny handful even of Soviet citizens have now emerged into the public domain. Of no individual is this more true than of Tchaikovsky, and within this enriched perspective an urge to return to him has reawakened in me. My earlier four-volume investigation, with its very detailed scrutiny of each work, all illustrated by an abundance of music examples, had been directed primarily at fellow professionals and musically literate amateurs. Now this new volume is offered to readers of all ages who may claim little or no musical competence, merely an interest in knowing more of this Russian genius, in deepening their enjoyment of his music by reading about any piece they may choose, and in having their ears alerted to things that they might not have picked up intuitively.

But I have a further and rather special hope. In our country, where class teaching of music in schools seems so often to have dwindled or even collapsed, and where virtually the only music most young people encounter is pop, or its associated styles, I am dismayed at what a whole generation has been cheated of in cultural experience. I know very well what once was but is now lost, having started my professional career in the mid-1950s teaching for five years on Thameside in secondary modern schools, the 'dustbins', as they were sometimes called, for those who had failed the eleven-plus, and were now condemned to leave school at fifteen. Yet what response could sometimes be aroused in such kids! Listening to a piece of classical music was always part of a lesson (two 40-minute periods a week for every class), and what might catch the imagination of my charges could be surprising – and sometimes much at variance with the orthodoxy preached by teacher-training gurus. Just one instance. It involved a 3C class (thirteen- to fourteen-year-olds, some still illiterate) whom it was my fate one year to take last period on a Tuesday afternoon – a particularly low point of the week, since exhaustion had already set in, yet it was still a long haul to Friday afternoon. Sometimes I seemed to be getting to the end of the class early and a fairly substantial filler was required to achieve a decent proximity to four o'clock. I knew the question that would get the sort of answer I needed: what would *they* like to hear? 'Please, sir, can we have that cup music?' was the almost predictable response. No, not 'Nessun dorma' sung by Pavarotti (I am talking about 1955, not 1990); 'that cup music' was the Prelude to Wagner's opera *Lohengrin*, a musical vision of the Holy Grail gradually emerging into a great light, then receding into darkness. Eight and a half minutes of very slow music with no trace of a beat, no 'proper tune', the quietest of openings, which took nearly five minutes to get to a climax, and a long dying end that faded into nothing – yet they would listen, perhaps just dreamily, remaining quiet and certainly, in their own ways, attentive, even when I turned the old 78 rpm record over in the middle.

I learned early that many of our professional educationalists seemed to judge children and young people by their own inadequacies, under-estimating these youngsters' capacity to engage with often highly sophisticated musical experiences. So while I hope, of course, that all readers who follow me through these pages will find some interest and illumination in them, it will delight me above all if I can awaken a curiosity in some of those whom our degraded education system has cheated of the experience of classical music that they should have been offered, but who can still catch up on lost time, if they choose.

DAVID BROWN

A Note on Using this Book

As I have written in my Personal Note, I hope that this book will be read by anyone who has some interest in tracing Tchaikovsky's personal biography and discovering something of his major works, and where they fit in to his life. But my prime aim has been to provide a listener's guide to readers who may have little or no knowledge of musical theory and terminology, but who may wish to make closer acquaintance with a selection of Tchaikovsky's individual works. Especially I would wish to help those who seek a deeper knowledge of how Tchaikovsky mapped out these pieces, and of some of the procedures he used to create them, for I believe that, with this added knowledge to guide their ears, they may become conscious of things that can contribute richly to the listening experience, but of which they would otherwise have remained unaware.

The book can, of course, be read simply as a biography by omitting all the segregated discussions of individual works. As for the examinations of the music itself, these are done in clearly marked self-contained sections as each work crops up in the narrative. An introductory note in *italics* opens each of these sections, and I hope this will help the reader to decide whether he or she wishes to investigate that particular work, or to pass on. I have provided a specially detailed note on the second piece I have examined (the fantasy overture *Romeo and Juliet*) so that those who may never have attempted to approach music other than through what their ears have picked up may have some guidance on how Tchaikovsky assembled a piece. (Readers in this category should bypass the examination of the 1st Symphony on pp. 31–4; they can always return to this later, should they wish.) By this I hope to alert them to things that can be of real significance to the listener, but that might otherwise be missed. Before my examination of *Romeo and Juliet*, I have also briefly discussed listening strategies.

Tchaikovsky's output was huge, and it has been simply impossible to deal with every piece. I decided, sometimes very regretfully, to take virtually no account of his many songs and short instrumental pieces, nor to examine in any depth larger pieces that are universally agreed to be less than his best. I realize, of course, that the number of pieces individual readers will choose will vary enormously from perhaps just two or three up to, say, twenty or more; listening to the latter number might well be spread over many months, even years. I realize, too, that while some readers may want to choose for themselves which pieces they will listen to, most will wish to investigate only a selection of the most important works – say, six to a dozen – and to satisfy this preference I have set out below a series of Options. Such readers should select from Option 2's 'Top Dozen', or from Option 3, fixing on the 'Mixed Menu'. Others may want to have a wider range of choice. In an attempt to answer these varying demands, I have divided Tchaikovsky's works in three ways:

Option 1

Here I have assumed that my reader wishes to make his or her own selection of pieces, but would appreciate an indication of how strongly I would recommend each piece. I have therefore grouped the pieces into five categories, a work's placing signalled by the starring convention as each crops up for scrutiny in the main narrative (a bracket round the final star in some instances indicates that I have a certain reservation about my classification):

***** Top-priority pieces, discussed in detail (a dozen in all)
**** Major pieces, discussed in some detail
*** Important pieces, though usually less closely examined
** Pieces of interest, perhaps discussed in very general terms
* Pieces of some significance, but not discussed

Option 2

Here I have made a rather more precise selection specially for readers who know they will be wanting to listen to only a limited number of works. I have given first, in chronological order of composition, a 'Top Dozen' – but six of these also offer alternatives, which will, of course, be out of sequence. The point is that if, for instance, you want to tackle only one opera, I have named the two I consider to be the best – but very different – ones for you to make your own choice. If you decide you want to take an extra opera on board, you now know which one I would recommend. Likewise, you might want to stick with the piano for a second concerto, or you might prefer one with a violin. Then, if you should have also listened to all the alternatives in the 'Top Dozen' category, the 'Next Eight' gives you pointers to what you might then enjoy investigating; these appear in chronological order, with the exception of *Mazeppa*.

Top Dozen

Fantasy Overture: *Romeo and Juliet*
Symphony no. 2, *Little Russian*
Piano Concerto no. 1
Ballet: *Swan Lake* or *The Nutcracker*
Symphonic Fantasia: *Francesca da Rimini* or *The Tempest*
Symphony no. 4
Opera: *Eugene Onegin* or *The Queen of Spades*
Violin Concerto or Piano Concerto no. 2
Serenade for Strings or Suite no. 3
Manfred Symphony or Symphony no. 5
Ballet: *The Sleeping Beauty*
Symphony no. 6, *Pathétique*

Next Eight

String Quartet no. 1
Opera: *Cherevichki* or *Mazeppa*
Symphony no. 3
Rococo Variations, for cello and orchestra
Piano Trio
Fantasy Overture: *Hamlet*
String Sextet: *Souvenir de Florence*
Symphonic Ballad: *The Voyevoda*

Option 3

My third selection offers a series of mostly five- or six-a-piece menus for readers who may wish to investigate a particular kind of music. Two especially important pieces, *Romeo and Juliet* and the Sixth Symphony (*Pathétique*), are to be included, as the first and last items respectively, in all menus.

All Menus

(as opener and closer respectively)
Fantasy Overture: *Romeo and Juliet*
Symphony no. 6, *Pathétique*

Mixed

Piano Concerto no. 1
Symphony no. 4 or 5
Ballet: *Swan Lake* or Opera: *Eugene Onegin*
Violin Concerto
Serenade for Strings
Suite no. 3

Symphony/Concerto

Symphony no. 2
Piano Concerto no. 1
Symphony no. 4
Violin Concerto
Symphony no. 5
Piano Concerto no. 2

Literary Trail

Symphonic Fantasia: *The Tempest*
Symphonic Fantasia: *Francesca da Rimini*
Fantasy Overture: *Hamlet*
Symphonic Ballad: *The Voyevoda*
Manfred Symphony

Ballet/Opera

Ballet: *Swan Lake*
Opera: *Eugene Onegin*
Ballet: *The Sleeping Beauty*
Opera: *The Queen of Spades*
Ballet: *The Nutcracker*

Concerted Works

Piano Concerto no. 1
Rococo Variations, for cello and orchestra
Piano Concerto no. 2
Violin Concerto
Sérénade mélancolique

Chamber Works

String Quartet no. 1
String Quartet no. 2
String Quartet no. 3
Piano Trio
String Sextet: *Souvenir de Florence*

I am assuming that many readers will know nothing of musical theory, but would wish to gain some knowledge of such things as may be of use to the listener. All but one of the matters on which I make observations require simply attentive listening, and do not depend on any specialized technical knowledge. The one exception is the matter of key. Some readers will already be thoroughly familiar with key and its usage, but others will not, and I do not believe that any reader will lose out significantly by not wishing to extend his or her knowledge here. Others, however, will want to fill this gap, and so I have given some explanation of key in Appendix 2. More importantly, in Appendix 1 I have described as briefly as possible some of the main musical forms that constantly recur in classical music – sonata form and rondo, for instance. In Appendix 3 I have also supplied glossaries of technical terms and foreign words (most of them Italian) that are used in this book.

A Word on Russian Style

Russian Names

The Russian convention is to use three names. The first is the baptismal name (i.e. our Christian name); the second (the patronymic) indicates the name of the father; the third is the surname. However, gender comes into it, for the patronymic will normally have 'evna' or 'ovna' added in the case of a woman, and 'evich' or 'ovich' in the case of a man. As for the surname, a woman's will normally have 'a' added to it. However, where the male surname ends in 'y' (as in the case of 'Tchaikovsky'), the ending of the woman's surname will be 'aya'. Thus Tchaikovsky's mother's surname was 'Tchaikovskaya'.

There could be variants in the case of certain patronymics, and Tchaikovsky's father's baptismal name, Ilya, produced one such. Thus, while his composer son's fully transliterated name was 'Pyotr Ilich Tchaikovsky', his daughter's was 'Alexandra Ilinishna Tchaikovskaya'.

Russian Dates

In Tchaikovsky's time the Russians still adhered to a calendar that was twelve days behind that used in Western Europe, and this can cause some confusion (for instance, the Russian Christmas Day, according to our calendar, would have been on 6 January of the following year). I have adjusted all dates to fit in with the Western Calendar.

TCHAIKOVSKY
The Man and his Music

Prelude

I

Childhood 1:
Votkinsk

In August 1844 a governess of French extraction was in St Petersburg
seeking an appointment. Her name was Fanny Dürbach, and she was
twenty-two. At the same time a young Russian mother who was looking to engage just such a person was travelling to the Russian capital
with her eldest son, Nikolay. She had come from Votkinsk over eight
hundred miles to the east, where her husband was the mining engineer
in charge of the government iron works. The couple had three sons
and a daughter. The two women met and an agreement was reached;
Fanny would begin working for the Tchaikovsky family. And so a
rather apprehensive governess set out on a three-week journey with
her new employer. Some of her anxieties had eased as they progressed,
but how would she be received on arrival? Fifty years later she recalled
it all:

> During the journey we became so closely acquainted that when we
> reached the factory we were on thoroughly intimate terms. The
> kindness and courtesy of Mrs Tchaikovskaya and the good looks,
> even handsomeness, of Nikolay disposed me to my companions,
> while the meticulous good manners of the latter [Nikolay] were an
> assurance that the task before me would not be difficult. Yet, all the
> same, I was very uneasy. All would be well if, on my arrival, I had
> to deal only with Mrs Tchaikovskaya and her son – but before me
> lay acquaintance with people and a way of life that were completely
> unknown. And so the closer we got to the end of our journey, the
> more my concern and uneasiness grew. But when at length we
> arrived at the house, one moment sufficed to show that all my fears
> were groundless. A host of people ran out to meet us, there began
> rapturous embracing and kissing, and it was impossible to distin-
> guish family from servants in the crowd. All were made equal by an
> undivided, living joy; everyone greeted the return of the mistress of

the house with equal warmth and affection. Mr Tchaikovsky came up to me and, without a word, embraced and kissed me like a daughter. The simplicity and patriarchal character of his action at once set the stamp of approval upon me, and sealed me almost as one of the family. I had not just arrived; rather, like Mrs Tchaikovskaya and her son, I too had 'returned home'. Next morning I set about my work without the slightest agitation or fear for the future.

Among the throng that greeted Fanny was the couple's four-year-old second son, Pyotr Ilich Tchaikovsky, the future composer.

It was indeed a happy family within which Fanny would work. Ilya Tchaikovsky, Pyotr's father, came of a line with a strong military tradition, but Ilya had chosen differently, entering the School for Mining Engineers and qualifying with a silver medal. He would be three times married; by his first wife he had a daughter, Zinaida (born 1829). Soon after this her mother died, and in 1833 he married Alexandra (née Assier); the future composer was their second surviving child. Ilya was clearly a kindly, trusting man, gentle in manner, benign and sentimental. He had no particular interest in music: as a youth he had taken up the flute only to abandon it. But the theatre was a different matter; here he would readily give way to tears whatever the play, and this love of a world of the creative imagination helps explain why he would later support his second son's mature decision to seek a professional career in the sister art of music.

Pyotr's relationship with his father was easy but not particularly close. With his mother it was a very different matter. Though she would die when he was only fourteen, she would prove the most important woman in his whole existence, and to the end of his life each anniversary of her death brought a flood of treasured memories and painful emotions. She was half French, her father being an immigrant who had taken Russian nationality, married a local girl, and gone on to work as a customs official. Born in 1813, Alexandra scarcely knew her mother, who had died when she was only three, and at the age of six she had been placed in a school for orphan girls where she had received a good education, gaining a high competence in French and German, some skill in singing, and an ability to play dances on the piano. Ilya Tchaikovsky was eighteen years her senior. They would have six children who would survive into adulthood, of whom Pyotr (born 7 May 1840) was the second. He was preceded by Nikolay ('Kolya', born 1838), and followed by Alexandra ('Sasha', born 1842), Ippolit ('Polya', born 1843), and twins Modest and Anatoly ('Modya' and 'Tolya', born 1850).

As a person Alexandra was reserved, not given to open expressions of endearment, but conscientious and capable in all her domestic responsibilities. Modest Tchaikovsky (who scarcely knew her as a person, being only four when she died) later noted:

> From the testimony of people who knew her she was a tall stately woman, not particularly beautiful, but with an enchanting expression in her eyes, and looks that involuntarily drew your attention. Certainly all who knew her unanimously affirm there was something exceptionally attractive about her appearance.

More interesting, however, is Modest's record of his composer brother's special memory of her as 'a tall, rather ample lady with a wonderful expression, and hands which, though not small, were unusually beautiful'. Pyotr's noting of her hands seems particularly significant. For a young child, a mother's hands are the primary instruments of close physical contact – of touch, tenderness, caress, ministration, and protection. Given that the homosexual Tchaikovsky would, some thirty years on, contract a harrowingly disastrous marriage with a woman whom he would declare, within only days of the wedding, had become 'physically . . . totally repugnant' to him, this enduring memory of the one woman from whom he had clearly yearned desperately for intimate physical contact must seem all the more poignant.

Fanny's recollections of her four years as governess to the Tchaikovsky children were drawn from her by Modest in 1894, the year after his brother's death. Rarely can we get such precise and vivid glimpses into the very earliest years of a great composer-to-be. Though there had been no intention that Pyotr should become one of Fanny's charges, he begged tearfully to be allowed to join her two official tutees, Nikolay and Ilya's niece, Lidiya, one of his family dependents. He outshone them both. Within two years he could read French and German without difficulty (so we are told), and within a further year was writing sentimental verse in French, including a celebration of Joan of Arc, upon whom he would, thirty years on, compose one of his largest operas. In transcribing these juvenilia from Fanny's treasury,

Modest seems to have retained faithfully his seven-year-old brother's exact text, mistakes and all:

> L'héroïne de la France,
> On t'aime, on ne t'oublie pas,
> Heroïne si belle!
> Tu as sauvé la France,
> Fille d'un berger!
> Mais qui fait ces actions si belles!
>
> Barbare anglais vous ont tuée,
> Toute la France vous admire.
> Tes cheveux blonds jusquà tes genoux,
> Ils sont très *beau*.
> Tu étais si célèbre
> Que l'ange Michel t'apparut.
> Les célébres on pense à eux,
> Les méchants on les oublie!

Fanny used to call Pyotr 'le petit Pouchkine' after the greatest of Russian poets, Alexander Pushkin. There is no doubt that he became the favourite among her three pupils, and a tiny incident she recorded is a pointer to why this should have been, and to that sensitivity towards others close to him that would mark so much of his later life:

Once, during a break for recreation, he sat down before an atlas and examined it. Coming to a map of Europe, he suddenly began covering Russia with kisses, and then made as if to spit on the remaining portion of the world. I stopped him, and began explaining that it was shameful to behave thus towards fellow human beings who, like himself, addressed God as 'Our Father', that it was bad to hate fellow men because they weren't Russian, and that it meant he was spitting on me also, because I wasn't Russian. 'You don't need to scold me,' Pierre replied. 'Didn't you notice I had covered France with my hand?'

Fanny may have cultivated zealously her young charge's literary skills, but she clearly had little concern for his musical aptitudes. His first known attempt at composition had been made when his mother was on her trip to St Petersburg, Ilya writing to his wife that 'Sasha and Petya have composed a song, "Our mother in St Petersburg"'. But his musical education proper was probably initiated by the orchestrion (a species of barrel organ that could simulate quite elaborate orchestral effects) that his father bought soon after arrival in Votkinsk. Part of its repertoire proved especially crucial for the future composer, introducing him to the giant who would forever remain for him the greatest of musical geniuses, and to the opera that would always remain the greatest of all musical creations. As Modest put it:

> He was particularly captivated by the pieces of Mozart that it played. The composer himself [Tchaikovsky] repeatedly asserted that his passionate worship of that genius had its beginning in the unspoken delight, that 'holy rapture' which he'd experienced during his early childhood on hearing the orchestrion play Zerlina's aria, 'Vedrai carino', and other excerpts from *Don Giovanni*. Moreover, this orchestrion also acquainted him with the music of Rossini, Bellini and Donizetti, and it was probably from this that there stemmed that love of Italian music that remained with him all his life, even when the persecution of it was in full swing in serious musical circles during the 1860s and 1870s.

Even before having piano lessons Pyotr had begun picking out the orchestrion's tunes on the piano. Frustrated when his parents on occasion forbade him the instrument, he would continue fingering these tunes on some other surface, on one occasion practising so vigorously on a window pane that he broke the glass and cut his hand badly. This, Modest stated, was the moment that decided his parents he should have proper piano lessons. His teacher, a Mariya Palchikova, was competent, though her knowledge of the repertoire was limited, and within three years he could sight-read as well as she. Yet he remembered what he owed to her, for thirty-five years later, on receiving a letter from her revealing that she was in difficulties, he arranged for money to be sent to this woman to whom 'I am very, very indebted'. Such generosity, often anonymous, was to mark his later life.

It is no surprise that for a future composer improvisation was of as much importance as learning music by other composers, though the effect of this on him could be drastic, as Fanny recalled:

> After work or long periods of letting his imagination loose at the piano he was always nervy and edgy. On one occasion the Tchaikovskys had guests, and the whole evening was spent in musical

7

entertainments. Because it was a holiday the children joined the adults. Pierre was initially very lively and happy, but towards the end of the evening he became so tired that he went upstairs earlier than usual. When I went to the nursery some time later he was not asleep; instead, his eyes glistening, he was weeping agitatedly. When I asked what was the matter with him, he replied, 'Oh, it's this music!' But there was no music to be heard at that moment. 'Get rid of it for me! It's here, here,' said the boy, weeping and pointing to his head. 'It won't give me any peace.'

The creative gift of the future composer was, it seems, already precociously stirring.

2
Childhood 2:
St Petersburg

Sadly, the idyll with Fanny was about to end. Some fifty years later the governess herself would describe her four years with the Tchaikovsky family as the happiest of her life – and so, too, they would prove to be for the future composer. Her departure was, for him, cruelly abrupt. Though in 1848 Ilya retired from his government post with a pension, he still needed to work, for his growing family had increasingly to attend proper schools. Accordingly, he opened negotiations for a new appointment in Moscow; as for Fanny, she decided to remain in Votkinsk and find a position with another family. In October the moment came for the Tchaikovskys to move and, realizing how painful the break with Fanny would be, the parents arranged that she should slip away that very morning before the children awoke. The latter were distraught – above all Pyotr who, a year later, could still dissolve in tears on receiving a letter from her. Then further misfortune struck. Ilya's hoped-for appointment did not materialize, and within a month the family had moved on to St Petersburg, where Nikolay and Pyotr were promptly enrolled in the fashionable Schmelling School. The routine was gruelling, the academic day lasting nine hours with much homework to follow, and this told on Pyotr's health. Paradoxically it proved a blessing for him that he finally contracted measles, for his debilitated condition made a return to the school before June impossible, by which time the family had moved to Alapayevsk, where Ilya had secured a new post.

St Petersburg had provided Pyotr with two compensations: he had had some piano lessons with a very good teacher, and had been taken frequently to the opera and ballet. But Alapayevsk, like Votkinsk, was a provincial town, and even farther to the east. The pains of St Petersburg and of his illness had unsettled Pyotr to a degree that sometimes drove his mother to tears. Even his interest in music seemed to recede, and for pleasure he turned to reading – a diversion that would become a lifelong refuge. Chateaubriand's *Le Génie du christianisme* he found, unsurprisingly, beyond him, but Nikolay Gogol's fantastic tale, *Christmas Eve*, enthralled him; without knowing it, he had found a second subject on which, one day, he would compose an opera. The arrival of a second governess, Anastasiya Petrova, brought some stability into his world and set him on course for entry to a major school back in St Petersburg. Clearly he liked her, for in 1854 he would set her name on his earliest surviving composition, his *Anastasie valse* for piano.

We can only guess whether what also had unsettled Pyotr was awareness of the break with his family that this tuition would ultimately entail; what is certain is that, when the moment arrived, it could not have been worse. In May 1850 Alexandra, having given birth to her last children, the twins, set off within three months for St Petersburg where the ten-year-old Pyotr was to be enrolled in one of its best schools, the School of Jurisprudence. It would be two years before his entry into the main school, and meanwhile he was registered in the preparatory class, and lodged with Modest Vakar and his wife, old friends of his father. Significantly Ilya had shown his continued concern for his second son's main interest: 'Don't, of course, forget about his music either,' he had exhorted his wife. 'It would be wrong to abandon a good thing already begun.' But Ilya had already realized what the return of his mother to Alapayevsk would mean for Pyotr. In the event it proved traumatic – 'one of the most terrible days of my life', as he later told brother Modest:

> The incident took place at the Central Turnpike where it was usual to go at that time to see off those who were taking the road to Moscow [Modest recorded]. On the way there Pyotr shed a few tears, but the end of the journey seemed a long way off and, cherishing every second he could look at his mother, he appeared comparatively calm. But with actual arrival at their destination, he lost all self-control. Pressing himself against his mother, he could not bear to let her go. Neither caresses, consolings, nor promises of a quick return had any effect. He heard and saw nothing, seeming almost to become one with the beloved being. Force had to be used to tear the boy away from Alexandra Andreyevna. At last their efforts succeeded, she took her seat in the carriage, the horses started to move – and then, summoning up all his remaining strength, the

boy broke loose, and rushed after the carriage with a cry of mad despair, trying to grab hold of the footboard, the splashboard, whatever came to hand, in a vain hope of stopping her. Never in his life could Pyotr Ilich speak of that moment without a shudder of horror. The impression left by that first intense grief paled in comparison only with one yet more intense: his mother's death.

It would be nearly two years before Pyotr would see his mother again, and in the meantime he poured his feelings into letters home. Anniversaries brought bursts of nostalgia: 'Last week Advent began, and you, my Angels [his parents], will be fasting faithfully because, in those happy times when I was with you, you always did. And now I remember how joyfully we received the Christmas Tree from you. But I shan't be able to join in with Sasha, Polya, Malya, Katya and Mina. But at least I shall remember it.' In September 1851, however, his father resigned from his Alapayevsk post, his intention now being to bring the whole family back to St Petersburg. Yet it would be May 1852 before his parents at last arrived, a delight augmented by his success in the entrance examination to the School of Jurisprudence itself. Something of the new joyful – at times, exuberant – mood that now possessed him is underlined by one tale (for there are more of the same) from the following summer recorded by Modest. It is something of a surprise to learn that all his life Tchaikovsky delighted in practical jokes – as, for instance, on the occasion when Nikolay and another boy had perched themselves on a ladder to overhear Zinaida and two other girls who were confiding to one another their affairs of the heart, Pyotr engineered a drenching with cold water for the eavesdroppers in their turn. Modest (who thoroughly deplored such things) observed that his brother's delight in pranks like this was exceeded only by his pleasure in recalling them.

In the autumn Pyotr settled into his new school. The School of Jurisprudence had a good reputation, being a highly disciplined institution whose primary function was to provide a vocational training in law which facilitated entry into the civil service. Pyotr's relations with both the staff and his fellow pupils seem to have been good, all the surviving evidence pointing to him being well liked, though he also gained a reputation for his dishevelled appearance, the disorganization of his daily existence, and his forgetfulness. His one serious challenge to the rules was smoking, which was strictly forbidden.

Yet it seems doubtful that this was simply an act of bravado, or a means to create for himself the image of a daredevil; rather, it relieved inner tension. Whatever the case, tobacco became, as he later freely admitted, a lifelong addiction, not simply a pleasure. Significantly for the future, perhaps, the most important of the friendships he forged at school was with Alexey Apukhtin, who would become a noted homosexual and leading poet, at least six of whose texts Tchaikovsky would later set in songs.

As for music, he would owe little to what he learned at the school itself. His one family ally in music making was his mother's sister, Ekaterina, who would take him through the whole of Mozart's *Don Giovanni*, providing him with the greatest musical epiphany of his whole life. Equally important for his musical development were the three years of piano lessons that began in 1855 with Rudolf Kündinger, a young German pianist, whose brother, Auguste, also gave Pyotr a year's lessons in music theory. As for his own creative activities, the only surviving evidence from this period is the *Anastasie valse* for piano of 1854. His next extant composition dates from 1857 or 1858, and is **a song, 'My genius, my angel, my friend'**,** a modest drawing-room romance that shows a remarkable sensitivity in one so young, and which can still occasionally be heard in Tchaikovsky song recitals.

However, the event that would forever mark the 1850s for Pyotr was a family matter. In 1854 his mother contracted cholera. More than two years passed before he could bring himself to write to Fanny about what followed:

Finally I have to tell you of a horrible misfortune that befell us two and a half years ago. Four months after Zina's departure, Mama suddenly fell sick with cholera, yet though she was dangerously ill, she recovered her health, thanks to the redoubled efforts of the doctors. But this was only temporary, for after four days of convalescence, she died without having time to say goodbye to all those around her. Although she did not have the strength to utter a word distinctly, it was nevertheless understood that she wanted to take final communion, and the priest arrived in time with the blessed sacraments, for after taking communion she rendered up her soul to God.

The blow was shattering – all the more so for being so sudden. All his life Tchaikovsky would keep diaries, and an entry in 1877 says it all:

> Despite the triumphal strength of my *convictions* [that there is no eternal life], I can never reconcile myself to the thought that my mother, whom I loved so much, and who was such a wonderful person, may have disappeared for ever, and that I shall never again have the chance to tell her that, even after twenty-three years, I still love her . . .

Yet Pyotr was now well practised in living without his mother's presence, and he seems to have disciplined himself to adjust outwardly to the changed circumstances. To add to Ilya's loss of his wife was the gradual dispersal of various members of his family. Zinaida had recently married, his niece Lidiya was about to wed, and feeling unable to cope with all but the twins, he enrolled Sasha and Ippolit in boarding establishments. In this reduced domestic situation Ilya soon arranged for his favourite brother, Pyotr, to bring his wife, Elizaveta, to share quarters with him in St Petersburg. The future composer was fortunate in his aunt; she had no compunction about enjoying life's blessings to the full, seeing that her children learned to draw, enjoyed the best of literature, music and drama, and led a healthy social life. It made for a very congenial three years of joint living.

In May 1859 Pyotr graduated from the School of Jurisprudence, with the rank of titular councillor giving him a special eligibility for civil service employment. His childhood was behind him.

3

Civil Service:
Personal Matters – and Conservatoire

Modest aptly described his brother's career in the civil service in one word: 'uncomplicated'. In June 1859, now aged nineteen, Tchaikovsky began employment in the Ministry of Justice, and after two modest promotions, remained in the same grade until his resignation in May 1863. Tchaikovsky himself always claimed he had been a conscientious worker, though when asked sometime later what his actual duties had been, he confessed he could not remember. Absentmindedness had always been one of his failings, and it was even alleged that once, having stopped to talk to a colleague while carrying a document signed by his chief, he unthinkingly tore off and ate pieces of the paper so that it had to be recopied. Modest questioned the authenticity of this story, though he confirmed that, all his life, his brother would devour pieces of theatre programmes in this way. Certainly his civil service career was inglorious, and when he resigned we might suspect sheer boredom – or dismissal for incompetence – as the cause. In fact, the reason was far more positive – and cheering.

For also in 1859 in St Petersburg there had occurred another event whose consequences for Tchaikovsky would be momentous: the establishment of the Russian Musical Society (RMS). Though there had always been an abundance of folk music in Russia and also a long tradition of music for the Orthodox Church, the Russian musical tradition, as we in the West understand it, had been founded only in 1836 with the first performance of Mikhail Glinka's opera, *A Life for the Tsar*, the story of how a Russian peasant, Ivan Susanin, sacrificed himself to save the Tsar from marauding Polish troops. The opera's popular success was enormous, far greater than that of its successor, *Ruslan and Lyudmila*, a tale of heroism and enchantment based on a poem by Pushkin, and produced in 1842. Nevertheless, *Ruslan* was probably even more important for later Russian composers, for it contained music that was far more original and radical than that of its predecessor, bequeathing to Glinka's successors new styles and methods which they would avidly make their own. Without these two operas, together with the four short orchestral pieces which followed in the next ten years (the Valse Fantasie, the two Spanish Overtures and, above all, the orchestral scherzo, *Kamarinskaya*), Russian music would never have evolved quite as it did.

But if by the middle of the century all these pieces were in place, there remained the problem of building a proper structure for musical tuition and for the concert performance of orchestral music. This was where the pianist and composer, Anton Rubinstein (born 1829), stepped in. A Russian Jew with a brother, Nikolay (born 1835), who was also a pianist, Anton had by the late 1850s become probably the most famous of all living Russian musicians. An insatiable activist, he was already aware of the yawning gaps in Russia's musical world, and in 1859, and with the active support of the Tsar's German-born great-aunt, the Grand Duchess Elena Pavlovna, the RMS was founded to promote orchestral concerts conducted by Rubinstein, and – in the long run more important still – to establish classes in music theory. Not only had there never before been such classes in Russia; there was not even a textbook on harmony in Russian (it would be Tchaikovsky himself who, in 1871, would fill this gap). So successful were these new classes that within three years they had grown into the St Petersburg Conservatoire, with Rubinstein as its Principal, and some remarkably distinguished musicians among its staff. Meanwhile, in 1860, similar classes had been instituted in Moscow by Nikolay Rubinstein, and these likewise had so flourished that in 1866 a matching conservatoire would be founded in that city, with Nikolay as its Principal. Among its earliest staff would be a man who, only two and a half years earlier, had still been a civil servant – Pyotr Ilich Tchaikovsky.

Back in 1859, with school now behind him, Tchaikovsky was free to organize his leisure time as he chose. For the period immediately following his departure from the School of Jurisprudence we have to rely on Modest's memories, though since he was still only nine when his brother entered the civil service, his record is inevitably very circumscribed, and is certainly not scrupulously objective. Of all Tchaikovsky's siblings Modest would be the closest to him, no doubt because he, too, was homosexual. But there would also be tension in the relationship, mainly from Modest's side. The cause was clearly jealousy. Modest would aspire to be a playwright, but would enjoy little success (despite all his composer-brother's strenuous efforts on his behalf), whereas Tchaikovsky for the last years of his life would be fêted everywhere as the greatest of living Russian composers – as, indeed, after Tolstoy, the greatest of all living Russians.

For a moment we must turn aside from the main narrative to take account of Modest and his activities, and also of Tchaikovsky's sexuality. After the composer's death in 1893 Modest set himself to be curator of his brother's legacy, and especially of his letters to the family. Nervous about the effect on the composer's personal reputation – and perhaps, by association, on his own – if Pyotr Ilich's homosexuality became common knowledge, Modest suppressed and sometimes, certainly, even destroyed documentary evidence. Between 1900 and 1902 he would publish his three-volume life of his brother, packing it with quotations from his letters, over five thousand of which survive to this day, but carefully manicuring the texts to exclude anything that might point too markedly to his brother's sexual preference, and ensuring that his own narrative did nothing to hint at it. Certainly we now have nothing that points clearly to any homosexual initiation or involvement that might have occurred during Tchaikovsky's school years even though, as in any single-sex boarding school, there would certainly have been much heightened sexual curiosity and, at the very least, 'foreplay', both of an experimental and of a committed kind. The evidence of Tchaikovsky's homosexuality has been investigated exhaustively by Alexander Poznansky, an expatriate Russian scholar, now long resident in the USA. In very detailed research he has concluded that 'it is quite likely that the majority of Tchaikovsky's friendships at the school were erotically innocent, though several were still close in the "special" sense' – that is, what might more recently have been labelled as a 'mutual fixation'.[1] Sexually the most significant friendship begun by Tchaikovsky at the School of Jurisprudence was with Alexey Apukhtin. A prodigiously gifted boy, Apukhtin built for himself a reputation for brilliance and wit, as well as for a poetic gift that would gain him status as one of the most popular of late nineteenth-century Russian poets. His lifespan was exactly that of Tchaikovsky (born 1840: died 1893), and by 1853, when they were both thirteen, he and Tchaikovsky became close in a friendship that would last all their lives. Even while at school Apukhtin had dedicated

1 Alexander Poznansky, *Tchaikovsky: The Quest for the Inner Man* (London, 1993), p. 39.

three poems to his schoolfriend, and twenty years later a poem that recalled their schooldays together, dreaming 'of an ideal glory', and which then went on to review their subsequent lives, Tchaikovsky's with its personal pain and public praise, and Apukhtin's with its measure of relative obscurity, would reduce Tchaikovsky to tears. It was not to be an untroubled relationship, but Apukhtin's death only weeks before Tchaikovsky's own would strike him with uncommon force.

The image Modest conjures of his brother in the latter's post-school years is as sexually sanitized as it is, at times, personally resentful. From it we might gather that the newly emancipated Tchaikovsky, now with an income of his own, became something of a social butterfly, plunging into an empty-headed existence, dining out, going to dances, and becoming popular at parties for his readiness to provide piano improvisations for dancing. Tchaikovsky himself also claimed light heterosexual amours ('Recently I became acquainted with a certain Mme Gernkross and fell a little in love with the elder daughter,' he would write to Sasha in June 1861, for instance), and even aspired to become something of a dandy. In fact, this image might seem to hint at the kind of flamboyance typical of some of his gay friends and acquaintances. In addition, Modest particularly mentions his brother's developing friendships with Apukhtin and Piccioli, an Italian singing teacher, noted for using cosmetics and for his ostentatiously affected appearance. This is no proof of Piccioli's sexuality; in any case, he was married, though this was also true of many of Tchaikovsky's future homosexual friends.

Poznansky has observed that Tchaikovsky's 'demi-monde existence' during this social phase gave him a 'full opportunity to satisfy his secret desires', but that 'it seems unlikely that at this time he perceived his homosexual inclinations as uncontrollable or irreversible'.[2] Certainly there is no hard evidence of what he may or may not have done, though the one major biographical event of Tchaikovsky's first three post-school years seems to point, at the very least, to a very qualified view of homosexual engagement at this stage. In the summer of 1861 one of Ilya Tchaikovsky's friends, a certain Vasily Pisarev, needed an interpreter for a visit to Europe, and Tchaikovsky, with his secure French and at least competent German, obtained leave of absence

2 Alexander Pozansky, *op. cit*, p. 55.

from his civil service duties to be Pisarev's companion. This would be Tchaikovsky's first trip abroad, and he viewed the prospect with excitement. They set out from Russia in mid-July, Tchaikovsky noting the places where they stayed, including London, where they visited Westminster Abbey, the Houses of Parliament, the Crystal Palace (where he was overwhelmed by Handel's 'Hallelujah' chorus performed by 'several thousand voices'), the Thames tunnel (where he was nearly stifled), and the Cremorne Gardens. London itself he found 'very interesting, but the sun is never seen: it's always raining'.

But it was Paris that provided the greatest delight, and always would. The plan had been then to head for a Normandy resort where Tchaikovsky's cousin, Lidiya Olkhovskaya, was staying. Whether this intention was fulfilled is unknown; what is certain is that when Tchaikovsky returned to Russia in early October, he returned alone and in a state of shock. The letter he wrote to Sasha some weeks later points to the prime reason:

> If ever I committed any colossal folly in my life, then this journey is it. You remember Pisarev? Imagine that beneath that mask of *bonhomie*, from which I took him to be an unpolished but worthy gentleman, there are hidden the most vile qualities of mind. Up till now I had not suspected that such incredibly base persons existed on this earth.

The most plausible reason for Tchaikovsky's revulsion would seem to be that Pisarev had made an homosexual advance on (or even assault upon) him from which he had recoiled. Interestingly, this would seem further to support a view that the evolution of Tchaikovsky's sexuality had followed a course similar to that of another composer who, as it happens, was a great Tchaikovsky admirer: Benjamin Britten. As in Russia in the 1990s, so in the United Kingdom the veil would now be increasingly lifted on the intimate lives of dead homosexuals, and Humphrey Carpenter's account of Britten's sexual awakening reveals a late developer in physical maturation, sexual drive and sexual commitment. That Britten had long felt a strong attraction to young boys (but also to young girls), and sought their company, is certain, but with adults in 1936, the year in which he became twenty-three, an ambivalence remained, and he would note in his diary that 'life is a pretty hefty struggle these days – sexually as well. Decisions are so hard to make, & it's difficult to look

unprejudiced on apparently abnormal things'.[3] Also in 1936 the poet
W. H. Auden, also homosexual, who knew Britten well, both personally and as a creative collaborator, considered that he was still holding
back from full emotional commitment, and it seems it would not be
until June 1939, when Britten was twenty-five, that he would make a
complete sexual and emotional commitment when he began his lifelong relationship with the tenor Peter Pears.

Far more significant, however, than Tchaikovsky's account of his
European expedition was the information that he quietly slipped into
the course of his letter to Sasha: 'I have begun studying harmony, and
it's going extremely well. Who knows, perhaps in three years you'll be
hearing my operas and singing my arias.'

Exactly when Tchaikovsky had enrolled in the classes of the RMS is
unknown. Though after Paris he returned to his civil service post, even
for a while working more diligently in the hope of promotion and a
higher salary, his personal lifestyle was now changing. He had long
had a love of the theatre, and especially French theatre, which had
flourished in St Petersburg because, ever since the eighteenth century,
French had been a standard language of the aristocracy and upper
classes – and as for Tchaikovsky, he had long been drawn to it because
he was fluent in the language and because he was himself one-quarter
French. Yet even this slipped in his priorities: 'Two evenings a week
are taken up with lessons. On Fridays I go alternately to Piccioli's and
Mariya Bonnet's [both singing teachers],' he informed Sasha. 'On Sun-
days I'm at home. On Mondays I almost always play piano, eight
hands, at someone's home.' This would not have been simply to pass
a pleasant evening. Although Tchaikovsky's visits to see operas would
already have acquainted him with some of the customary operatic
fare, his knowledge of other musical genres, especially the symphonic
repertoire, would have been almost non-existent because of the
dearth of orchestral concerts. Hence he learned such music, as did
most musical enthusiasts before the gramophone-record industry
became properly established during the middle years of the twentieth
century, by playing symphonies and overtures in piano transcriptions,
often arranged for two players, but on occasion, as on Tchaikovsky's
Monday evenings, for four. (Even as recently as the late 1940s, at university my future wife and I still had to learn much of the standard

3 Humphrey Carpenter, *Benjamin Britten: A Biography* (London, 1992), p. 80.

orchestral and chamber repertoire by playing it in piano-duet transcriptions.)

Having attended the RMS classes for a year, in September 1862
Tchaikovsky enrolled in the newly founded St Petersburg Conservatoire, though still retaining his civil service post. His letters to Sasha
reveal how contented he was, now that he was on course for a profession in music. He had no illusions about the uncertainty that
might lie ahead:

> Don't think that I imagine I'll become a great artist. It's simply that
> I want to do that to which I am drawn. Whether I shall be a famous
> composer or an impoverished teacher, I shall still think I have done
> the right thing, and I shall have no painful right to grumble at Fate
> or at people.

Now frequenting the Conservatoire, Tchaikovsky found himself in
a substantial group of like-minded individuals within which it was
natural to begin building friendships. One of his fellow students in
particular, Hermann Laroche, would become a lifelong and loyal,
though in many ways problematic, friend. Though Laroche himself
would have little subsequent success as a composer, he would become
one of Russia's finest, most perceptive music critics, and a great sup-
porter of Tchaikovsky's cause.

Tchaikovsky had two main teachers during his three Conservatoire
years: Nikolay Zaremba and Anton Rubinstein. The former has been
much maligned by history as no more than a pedant with an implacably
blinkered view of musical technique and a comprehensive intolerance of
the trends that were now marking contemporary music. But such a
teacher could be invaluable in laying the foundations of a secure
composing technique, in that he demanded that all musical procedures
that were essential were thoroughly learned and practised, even
though the student might find some of them tedious – for a composer's
ability to compose is in direct proportion to his degree of control of
his musical materials and of their employment. It was Zaremba above
all who instilled in Tchaikovsky his self-discipline (as Tchaikovsky
himself readily acknowledged), and who laid the foundations of that
mastery of all aspects of musical technique which Tchaikovsky would
command more absolutely than any of his Russian contemporaries.

Rubinstein could hardly have been more different. Where Zaremba
preached the virtues of orthodoxy and correctness, Rubinstein applauded

fluency and imagination. Not that his own compositions had much of the latter, for Rubinstein's limited creative gift was for merely efficient, production-line products that would only occasionally rise above competent mediocrity; no one today need feel called upon to institute a Rubinstein revival. But that mattered not in 1862. What Rubinstein especially gave to the newly founded Conservatoire was the cachet of his name and the dynamism of his leadership – and for Tchaikovsky the stimulus of his enthusiasm and the indefatigable commitment that his authoritarian but supportive personality demanded not only of his students, but of himself. Something of the man and his method, and of what made him both liked and respected, comes through in an anecdote from one of Tchaikovsky's fellow students:

> Over and over again he [Rubinstein] repeated how harmful timidity was, advising that one should not stop over a difficulty but leave it and press on, accustoming oneself to write in sketches with indications of this or that form – and to avoid resorting to a piano. I remember on one occasion he came into Zaremba's room beaming all over and, taking Zaremba's arm, said, 'Come into my room. I'll acquaint you with one of Tchaikovsky's composition exercises.' Zaremba was about to resist, saying that he'd have to break off his own explanations when he'd barely started. 'No matter! I'll let you return straight away. Just listen to Tchaikovsky's assignment.' We, fifteen people in all, entered the hall in a merry crowd, where we found just two people, Tchaikovsky and [Gustav] Kross. Tchaikovsky had been set to write music to Zhukovsky's *Midnight Review*. I hated the very idea, observing that Glinka had written a romance on this text. 'So what? Glinka wrote his own music – and Tchaikovsky his own.' Tchaikovsky's piece turned out to be not a romance but an entire, complex picture having nothing in common with Glinka's composition. Tchaikovsky had written the piece in two days.

But there was a side to Rubinstein that divided him fundamentally from Tchaikovsky. So different in other ways from Zaremba, Rubinstein resembled him in being a musical conservative who accepted as a model nothing after Mendelssohn (died 1847) and Schumann (died 1856), and this would cause a major incident when Rubinstein was presented with Tchaikovsky's first composition of any serious interest

to us. In fact, Rubinstein would, for instance, conscientiously introduce his students to the latest additions to the mid-nineteenth-century
orchestra, but would then allow them to present nothing that went
beyond the classically styled orchestration of Mendelssohn.
Tchaikovsky, like any other eager young composer, was excited by
what was happening in the contemporary creative world, and the visit
of Wagner himself to St Petersburg in 1863 to conduct five concerts,
mostly of his own music, must have inflamed a natural impulse to use
all the latest orchestral possibilities as now revealed by Wagner. In
1864, when Rubinstein was confronted with Tchaikovsky's vacation
exercise, he would explode.

A whole bundle of exercises and compositions, some incomplete,
survive from Tchaikovsky's three years at the Conservatoire. Most are
of only documentary interest, though an Impromptu for piano, composed as early as in his second year, would be published as the second
of the two pieces comprising his opus 1. Yet even this gave not the
slightest warning of the prodigious piece he would produce during the
summer of 1864 – **the orchestral overture, *The Storm*,*** *(*) based on a
play by Alexander Ostrovsky (we in the West are familiar with the
outlines of its plot through Janáček's opera, *Kát'ya Kábanová*, which
takes its name from the play's central character). Rubinstein had prescribed a substantial orchestral piece as his pupil's vacation exercise,
and Tchaikovsky, deeply impressed by Ostrovsky's drama, opted to
make this the basis for his assignment. It proved to be a prodigiously
talented, if uneven, piece – and Rubinstein was initially furious at
Tchaikovsky's stylistic boldness. But then, clearly recognizing not only
the piece's promise for the future but also the level of attainment it
represented for the present, he decided to proceed gently, for nothing
must be done to undermine the confidence of such a student. Indeed,
Tchaikovsky himself would judge one theme worthy of resurrection in
a later work: now slowed to *Adagio cantabile ma non troppo* and
scored for muted strings, it would provide the first eight bars of
hushed music that both opens and closes the slow movement of his
First Symphony.

Little of the music that Tchaikovsky would go on to compose during his final year at the Conservatoire even hints at the creative personality so remarkably delineated in much of *The Storm*, though three
pieces deserve mention. One is an orchestral piece, *Characteristic
Dances*, which Tchaikovsky would later rehabilitate into his first

opera, *The Voyevoda*. But a greater interest attaches to the scherzo of a **Piano Sonata in C sharp minor**,** which, now scored for full orchestra, would provide the flanks of the third movement of Tchaikovsky's First Symphony (the central trio would, however, be new). As for the third piece, an **Overture in F**,** it was judged good enough by Rubinstein to be given a Conservatoire performance in November 1865 and, subsequently revised, it would provide Tchaikovsky with his first public success in Moscow, whither he would move in January 1866 on graduation from the Conservatoire.

Tchaikovsky's favoured haven for his summer break would for many years be Kamenka in the Ukraine. In 1860 his sister Sasha had married Lev Davïdov, who managed his family's estate at Kamenka, and by 1865 Sasha had already produced three daughters for whom Tchaikovsky would become very much a favourite uncle. His next major challenge was the composition of his graduation exercise. Only on 24 October was his task prescribed, with the examination itself to be a public performance a mere eleven weeks later. To be given Schiller's 'Ode to Joy' to set was a daunting challenge – but then, Tchaikovsky's treatment was bound to be very different from Beethoven's, and comparisons with the choral finale of the latter's Ninth Symphony would hardly seem invited. Knowing that the work had to demonstrate a command of conventional musical mechanisms and forms, Tchaikovsky was certainly not going to risk repeating the imaginative boldness of *The Storm*, and his *Ode to Joy* is of only documentary interest. He must have realized this and, unable to face the public scrutiny the occasion would bring, he absented himself. Rubinstein was furious, initially thinking he would withhold Tchaikovsky's diploma, but then relenting, and the truant graduated with a silver medal.

This accolade did not prevent one critic, a certain César Cui, from giving the cantata (and its composer) a blistering review:

> The Conservatoire composer, Mr Tchaikovsky, is utterly feeble. It is true that his composition, a cantata, was written under the most unfavourable circumstances: to order, to a deadline, on a given subject, and with adherence to familiar forms. Yet all the same, if he had any gift, then at least somewhere or other it would have broken through the fetters of the Conservatoire. To avoid saying much about Mr Tchaikovsky, I will say only that Messrs Reinthaler and

Volkmann [two contemporary minor German composers] would rejoice unutterably at this cantata, and would exclaim ecstatically: 'Our numbers have been increased!'

Cui's verdict would be a potent reminder to Tchaikovsky that there was a force other than the Conservatoire that was also driving Russia's musical destiny. Yet within some three years Tchaikovsky himself would find the very composers (Cui included) who represented this force of critical importance in his own creative world.

THE MOSCOW YEARS

4
Moscow Conservatoire:
First Symphony

'Nikolay Rubinstein's life was devoted to Moscow and inseparable from its history.'[1] Thus reads the first sentence of Nikolay Barenboim's biography of Anton's younger brother. Nikolay was born in the city, attended university there, and until his death in 1881 was at the very heart of its musical life. Six years younger than Anton, he trained as a pianist, though for a while he veered away from music, entering the Law Faculty of Moscow University; he then worked briefly as a civil servant, was married equally briefly, but finally returned to music to become a very successful piano teacher, establishing for himself a firm place in Moscow circles, both musical and social (he was also an inveterate gambler and nocturnal carouser). In 1860 he was responsible for founding the Moscow branch of the RMS. Though, like his brother, Nikolay was a truly virtuoso pianist, his style was very different and, unlike his brother, he composed very little (as he put it, Anton 'wrote enough for three'). And also unlike Anton, his tastes encompassed the very latest music, both as pianist and as conductor. Tchaikovsky would owe Nikolay an enormous debt for all the performances of his music (some premieres) that he gave over the next dozen or so years.

It was on Anton's recommendation that Tchaikovsky had been appointed teacher of music theory in the classes of the RMS's Moscow branch. On his arrival in that city on 18 January, Nikolay had within twenty-four hours installed him in his own home, and begun to assume charge of his social life, taking him to the theatre and opera, and introducing him to certain of the Moscow social elite, an activity Tchaikovsky clearly did his best to thwart. 'He's a very sympathetic man,' he wrote to his twin brothers three days after arriving, 'without any of his brother's certain inaccessibility. I occupy a small room

1 Nikolay Barenboim, *Nikolay Grigorevich Rubinstein* (Moscow, 1982), p.14.

27

alongside his bedroom and, to tell the truth, in the evenings when we go to bed at the same time (which, however, it seems will happen very rarely), I feel inhibited; I'm afraid the scratching of my pen will hinder him from sleeping (we are separated by a thin partition) – and meanwhile I'm frightfully busy. I scarcely ever go out, and Rubinstein, who lives a rather disorderly life, can't stop being amazed at my diligence.' But for all Rubinstein's 'disorderliness', his views on professional attire were strict. 'All my first month's salary will go on new clothes,' Tchaikovsky lamented to Anatoly. 'Rubinstein requires me to buy these, saying that my present ones are not decent enough for a professor of music theory.' But clearly recognizing Tchaikovsky's impecunious condition, his new chief contributed handsomely to the assembling of Tchaikovsky's personal wardrobe, and his sartorial principle was fully accepted: for the rest of his life Tchaikovsky would have a serious concern that his public attire should reflect the standards of taste and quality expected of his professional status.

There was much else to do. His teaching would start within only a few days (regular classes on Tuesdays and Thursdays at eleven o'clock), and there was much to prepare. Rubinstein naturally wished to exhibit the prowess of the latest acquisition to his staff, and accepted the Overture in F on condition Tchaikovsky revised it. Since this would be, in its way, another test piece, Tchaikovsky took this requirement very seriously, and the result made an excellent impression at the concert conducted by Rubinstein in March, where the applause was warm and unanimous. But, Tchaikovsky wrote to brother Anatoly:

Even more flattering to my self-esteem was the ovation accorded me at the supper which Rubinstein gave after the concert. I was the last to arrive, and when I entered the room exceedingly warm applause rang out, during which I bowed very clumsily in all directions, and blushed. At supper, after the toast to Rubinstein, he himself proposed a toast to me – again there was an ovation. I am writing this to you in such detail because this was virtually my first public success, and therefore very agreeable to me.

There were other good things. Tchaikovsky was totally inexperienced in group teaching, but his class consisted mainly of young women who, one supposes, must have been instinctively sympathetic to this amiable and seemingly very eligible young man, and after a fortnight he could report to Anatoly that 'my classes are going very successfully, and already I'm enjoying an unusually sympathetic relationship with the Moscow ladies whom I teach. Little by little my shyness has passed completely.'

Within a month of arriving in Moscow Tchaikovsky would meet three people who would remain lifelong friends. One was Nikolay Kashkin who, as a teacher of piano and music theory, would be a professor at the Moscow Conservatoire for three decades, though today he is better remembered for his fifty-two years as a music critic. Tchaikovsky was particularly indebted to Kashkin for the hospitality he and his wife provided for him, especially during his early Moscow months, and for the good advice on matters musical and non-musical for which Kashkin was noted. Kashkin's memoirs of Tchaikovsky are of much importance, though his memory was not infallible.

The second new acquaintance was Konstantin Albrecht. Of German extraction, Albrecht never properly mastered the Russian language, and his linguistic ineptitudes, especially with Russian verbs, were a constant source of amusement to his friends. (For centuries German colonies had been resident in some of Russia's great cities and had continued to use their native tongue, to the bewilderment of the natives: it is perhaps no accident that the Russian word for 'dumb', *nemoy*, spawned the Russian word for 'German', *nemets*!) Konstantin had a Teutonic instinct for order, which made him a splendid administrator in the Conservatoire, and he was also a fine cellist. Tchaikovsky had much personal respect for Albrecht, and much gratitude for his kindness.

The third lifelong friend was Pyotr Jurgenson, Tchaikovsky's main publisher, and a sorely needed manager of his financial affairs. Though Jurgenson was a businessman, there was an idealism to his publishing operations, for he declined to issue light music, concentrating instead on Western classics to be made available in moderately priced editions, and on new music by the best native composers. Jurgenson was to become not only Tchaikovsky's main and very supportive publisher, but a good friend and counsellor in his private affairs.

Once he had revised his Overture in F, Tchaikovsky was naturally eager to set about a major piece through which, as a newly professional composer, he would make his wider mark. The obvious choice was between an opera and a symphony. Rubinstein was in favour of the former, but Tchaikovsky rejected as bad all the libretti he gave him, and instead in March he set about his First Symphony. In early May he reported that it was going only sluggishly, that he was suffering from insomnia, and that his nerves were in a terrible state. But the public success of his Overture in F in May in St Petersburg under Anton Rubinstein raised his morale, stimulated his creativity, and by 19 June he had begun to score the symphony.

At the end of August, and with the scoring still incomplete, he showed the symphony to Anton Rubinstein and Nikolay Zaremba, who both condemned it roundly. This verdict, as well as the beginning of the Conservatoire term, may have decided Tchaikovsky to set the symphony aside for the moment, a break that would be extended by a commission from Nikolay Rubinstein to compose a **Festival Overture on the Danish National Anthem,****(*) to be played during the visit to Moscow of the Tsarevich (the eldest son of the current Tsar, and the heir to the throne) and his new Danish bride. Tchaikovsky was to prove himself a true professional in the creation and delivery of such functional pieces, which might have no further use after their original purpose had been served, and at his life's end he could still write that this Overture was 'very effective, I remember, and far better as music than *1812*'. Tchaikovsky decided to incorporate also the Russian national anthem to symbolize the union of the two realms, but this happy intention led to disaster and the cancellation of the official performance because, as one journal reported, our 'talented young composer for some reason took it into his head to set forth our Russian national anthem in the minor key, which completely transforms the character of this well-known melody'. All the same, the Tsarevich expressed royal gratitude for Tchaikovsky's effort by the gift of gold cuff-links with turquoises which the indigent Tchaikovsky promptly sold.

Nevertheless, despite this interruption, by the year's end a revised version of the symphony was ready, but it was a full year before it was given its official premiere in February 1868. Yet though Tchaikovsky could report to Anatoly that the symphony 'scored a great success, particularly the *Adagio*', fifteen years would pass before it was heard again, despite the score being published in 1874 after Tchaikovsky had made further revisions, especially to the first movement.

Symphony no. 1 in G minor (*Winter Daydreams*) * * *(*)

[Tchaikovsky's First Symphony is an immature work, though with some excellent music in it – but, taken as a whole, it is not a piece with which to start a first-time investigation of Tchaikovsky's music. However, the slow second movement is very beautiful, rich in melody, and makes a very worthwhile listening experience that really requires little preparation from me: whether you will find Tchaikovsky's heading for the movement ('Land of gloom, land of mists') convincing I leave you to decide. The scherzo that follows (taken over from the piano sonata of his student days) is also an approachable movement with a waltz at its centre. A glance at the observations below on these two movements may, of course, be helpful. Otherwise, pass on to chapter 5. For the sake of the widely experienced listener I have provided the following commentary.]

Mendelssohn's *Italian Symphony* (his Fourth) had been preoccupying Tchaikovsky as he set about his First Symphony, and the German composer's example may have persuaded him likewise to give his new creation a title: *Winter Daydreams* – though neither this, nor the individual labels he gave to the first two movements ('Daydreams on a winter journey' and 'Land of gloom, land of mists') provide any particular insights into their natures. Nor does this music need suggestions of an imaginative content in order to hold the listener's attention. Indeed, the first movement reveals not only a flair and inventiveness that already marks out Tchaikovsky as a really major composer discovering himself, but is, in some regards, a very innovative piece. In 1866 there were as yet virtually no Russian symphonies except Rubinstein's three examples, which were, in any case, situated squarely in the pre-1850 West European tradition of Mendelssohn and Schumann; otherwise there were only the still unperformed or in-progress first symphonies of Rimsky-Korsakov, Borodin and Balakirev. In his First Symphony, therefore, Tchaikovsky was truly a pioneer, but one determined to be himself and to confront some at least of the challenges the form could pose for a Russian composer; it is therefore worth pausing here to contrast briefly Tchaikovsky's approach at the opening of his first movement to that of a West European symphonist. Like many symphonic first movements, this is in sonata form.[2]

2 For a brief description of sonata form, see Appendix 1.

To generalize very freely (and perhaps somewhat dangerously), while a Western composer tends to think organically, a Russian composer tends to think decoratively, perhaps even in circles. To take, first, an example from Beethoven: his Third ('Eroica') Symphony. Two terse chords – and the first subject enters quietly, builds to a loud restatement – and then, through music which emerges seamlessly from the first subject's restatement, we are *moved on* to a new key and a new theme (the second subject) introduced by the woodwind; thus this process has been an evolving one. Now let's move to the corresponding section of Tchaikovsky's first movement. Here the two subjects are themselves very extensive (each lasting more than two minutes), and are self-contained as far as their material is concerned: each modulates, yet ends back in the key in which it began (i.e., it has gone in a circle), and there is no transition passage between them: all that separates the two subjects is a single repeated chord (more a punctuation mark – or a jolt – than a transition). An over-arching organic process has had no part in this exposition.

Nevertheless, the melodic quality of Tchaikovsky's two subjects is excellent, as is his treatment of them. As to what follows, the development (introduced by what sounds momentarily like an earlier version of the famous 'Valse des fleurs' from the ballet, *The Nutcracker*) builds efficiently to a formidable climax, and the lead to the recapitulation is a quiet, mysterious crescendo that might be a forewarning of the yet stranger one to come in the finale. Also arresting is the movement's extensive two-minute coda, which finally returns to the material and scoring of the symphony's opening, and fades into a last *ppp* chord.

But if the most remarkable movement of the First Symphony is the opening *Allegro tranquillo*, the most perfect is the slow movement. Maybe its title, 'Land of gloom, land of mists', can be seen as some sort of clue to its content, even though the opening eight bars, which also close the movement, had originally served to convey the heroine's 'yearnings for true happiness and love' in that precocious student work of 1864, *The Storm*, though its new slower tempo and re-scoring for muted strings transforms its character. Such a sustained flow of fresh, tender melody as fills out this movement (though its climax is powerful) needs little commentary; it is its own recommendation. Nor should we conclude that, because the workings of this music are less complex than those in the outer movements, it is more lightweight. It is not.

Though less impressive, the third movement contains some attractive music. In fact, the scherzo itself (that is, the outer portions) had been composed in 1865 during Tchaikovsky's last year at the Conservatoire as part of a piano sonata, but it sounds better as an orchestral piece. The central trio, newly composed, is a waltz. Tchaikovsky's unsurpassed genius for ballet music, and especially for the grand set-piece waltz, is universally acknowledged. Here was his first major venture into that dance, and his ability to extend his melody effortlessly, to vary it and build climaxes as landmarks that give it shape, truly makes this example worthy of its symphonic context; then, cunningly, Tchaikovsky starts to introduce the little rhythmic matrix of the scherzo itself and, in so doing, can slide almost seamlessly back into the expected repetition of that section to conclude the movement. But not quite, for there is another unexpected and very acceptable addition: while the timpani continue to reiterate the ubiquitous rhythmic cell of the scherzo, the main waltz theme slips in on the strings before gently allowing attention to return to the scherzo's main theme. A very deft composer is at work here.

The slow introduction to the finale is based on a folksong presented (after numerous false starts) by the violins. A return to the hesitancy of the movement's opening, followed by a powerful crescendo, an increase in pace – and a sturdy tune (the first subject) bursts in. Then an abrupt change – and a fugato,[3] based on the same tune, leads to the second subject – which turns out to be the folksong from the introduction, though now no longer brooding, but ebullient. If all had continued as it had begun, then all might have been well. But this movement uncovers Tchaikovsky's inexperience in producing a finale that unfolds with assurance to provide the culmination of a multi-movement piece. For some reason Tchaikovsky decided to build the central development as a full-blown fugue on a theme derived from the first subject, but the music becomes rhythmically stodgy. The coda is vigorous, very noisy, and overblown.

If it had not been for the so impressive achievements of this symphony's first two movements, the shortcomings of this finale would have been less noticeable. Nor did Tchaikovsky lose his pride in the whole work, for in 1874 he revised it, and in 1883, he could still write that 'although it is in many ways immature, yet fundamentally it has

---

3 For a description of fugue (fugato), see Appendix 1.

more substance and is better than many of my other more mature works'. Certainly his First Symphony merits the occasional performances it is at last receiving.

———

5
First Opera:
Enter Balakirev

Tchaikovsky would spend some twelve years in Moscow, abandoning the city only in the autumn of 1877 in the aftermath of his disastrous marriage. During this period he would produce a steady flow of compositions that would firmly establish his national status, and begin to make his name known abroad. To augment his income he took on work as a music critic, showing himself to be a thoroughly competent writer and a perceptive judge. He was capable of blistering condemnation when confronted by incompetence, observing of one singer that 'now in her stentorian voice she screams out some high note resembling the cry of some great owl, now she'll rattle out a low, almost bass note which makes your flesh creep, and all this out of time with the orchestra, extremely off key, wildly, eccentrically', yet also having sufficient objectivity to recognize the positive qualities in music even when it did not appeal to him personally. Other pieces seem to have simply bewildered him and, like so many composers past and present, he had his deaf spots. Beethoven overawed him, but not, for instance, for the overwhelming power with which his Ninth Symphony projected the blazing idealism of Schiller's 'Ode to Joy'; instead Tchaikovsky heard it as 'the cry of hopeless despair of a great creative genius who has irrevocably lost his faith in happiness, who has quit life for a world of impossible daydreams, for a realm of unattainable ideals'. He found special pleasure in French music (he was himself, of course, a quarter French), and Bizet's *Carmen*, which he first heard in 1875, would become for him the greatest of all operas – that is, after Mozart's *Don Giovanni*.

In his personal moments Tchaikovsky delighted in books. All his life he was a voracious reader, and not only of Russian authors; he was as attracted to French novels as to French music. Here he had no language problem such as confronted him with British authors, but the impression made upon him by Russian translations of writers such as

Thackeray, George Eliot and, above all, Dickens (early on in Moscow he had revelled in *The Pickwick Papers*) persuaded him to make efforts to learn English so that he could read their works in the original. Of native authors Pushkin received from him that special adoration which all Russians reserve for their greatest poet, and three of his four finest operas would be based on works by Pushkin. But Tolstoy, Turgenev, Dostoevsky and Gogol were also favourites. In later life he would often end the day by retiring to his bedroom with a book and wine, and read into the early hours.

Apart from the First Symphony none of Tchaikovsky's works from his first three Moscow years needs to be more than noted here. Clearly he had decided that he should launch his career as a composer by tackling the two main forms of mid-nineteenth century music: symphony and opera. The former had preoccupied him during most of 1866, but in the autumn this had been interrupted by the Danish Festival Overture; this commission discharged, he was now looking beyond the symphony to 'gently setting about an opera. There is hope that Ostrovsky himself will write a libretto for me on his play, *The Voyevoda* ["The Provincial Governor"],' as he confided to his brother Anatoly. The subject was a melodrama concerning an elderly and ruthless voyevoda who successively falls for two young women (one already married) and imprisons them, and of their respective partners' joint attempt at rescue, an attempt that is initially thwarted, but is then saved by the *deus ex machina* appearance of a replacement voyevoda.

Alexander Ostrovsky's nearly fifty plays were, as D. S. Mirsky noted, 'of unequal merit but, taken as a whole, doubtless the most remarkable body of dramatic work in Russian',[1] and the suggestion that such a celebrity should provide a libretto for a virtually unknown composer's first opera sounds implausible. Yet within little more than three months a libretto for Act 1 had arrived – a measure, surely, of the deep impression Tchaikovsky had already made on Moscow's creative community. Composition of *The Voyevoda* **(*) was begun in March 1867, but problems soon arose; initial progress was slow, then Tchaikovsky lost Ostrovsky's libretto and had shamefacedly to ask the dramatist to rewrite it, which the latter promised to do, but then delivered only belatedly. Nevertheless, Tchaikovsky pressed ahead as

1 D. S. Mirsky, *A History of Russian Literature* (London, 1968), p. 39.

best he could, finally devising most of the text himself, and adapting a number of extracts from compositions of his student years. *The Voyevoda* was first staged in February 1869 in Moscow, and appeared to be well received, with Tchaikovsky taking fifteen curtain calls. While there is no question that there are passages and moments in the opera that are thoroughly worthy of the mature Tchaikovsky, one suspects that the audience's enthusiasm sprang more from a wish to encourage a young and promising first-time opera composer than from the overall quality of what it was hearing, for the opera survived only four further performances, and Tchaikovsky himself later destroyed the score. (After his death the opera was reconstructed from the surviving vocal and orchestral parts.)

Yet *The Voyevoda* was not without its legacy. Huge chunks from it would provide much of Act 1 of Tchaikovsky's next surviving opera as well as passages elsewhere. A duet in Act 2 would, some dozen years later, become the basis for the broad string melody in the *1812* Overture. Even more, seven or eight years on, was *Swan Lake* a beneficiary, the entr'acte to the opera's Act 3 launching the ballet's final act, while the heart-wrenching music that had brought together the opera's lovers would also reunite Odette and Siegfried in preparation for the ballet's tragic ending. That Tchaikovsky could so early in his creative career compose such concentrated and characteristic music was a potent augury for his future.

Though it would become Tchaikovsky's normal practice to escape from Moscow during the summer vacation, in 1867, because he lacked the funds for a lengthy journey, he ended up having to spend the break with members of the Davïdov family at Hapsal (now Haapsalu) on the Estonian coast. Among the party was Vera Davïdova, Sasha's sister-in-law, who had fallen in love with Tchaikovsky. The latter was already aware of her feelings, and Hapsal had not been his first choice as a summer base, for he recognized that Vera's desires were a challenge to his sexuality, and that, try as he might, he had no capacity to reciprocate. As an honourable man he pitied her, but knew no kindly way of responding, hoping helplessly that her recognition of all his 'far from poetic qualities' would finally smother her feelings. It was, of course, a forlorn hope, as he would discover over the next two to three years. Yet this interlude did have one positive result – the composition of three piano pieces issued under the title *Souvenir de Hapsal*, the last of which, '**Chant sans paroles**',**(*) became the first of his compositions to achieve wide popularity. He inscribed all three to Vera, and she treasured his manuscript for the remainder of her days.

It has been too often assumed that, because of his sexuality (especially when it became public knowledge after the disaster of his marriage in 1877), Tchaikovsky was always a rather sombre, even dour person, and photographs of him mostly do little to dispel that image. Nothing could be farther from the truth, especially during his Moscow years. With people he knew and with whom he felt at ease, he could be very convivial, and he enjoyed eating out in company. During his civil service days he had participated in amateur theatricals and now, in Moscow, he could sometimes be induced to do the same. He was not above performing, as a prank, an elaborate deception. Sofiya Kashkina, daughter of Tchaikovsky's very close friend, Nikolay, recalled one such incident. Her father and Tchaikovsky attended a masked ball, having made a bet that each would not recognize the other. To disguise himself Kashkin shaved off his beard, and this was judged sufficient to mask his identity, a friend who had been let into the secret then introducing him as a visiting musician. The event began, but then –

the appearance of a very elegant, tall lady produced something of a sensation. She was dressed in an unusually luxurious domino [a loose cloak with a small mask hiding the upper part of the face] made of black lace, and was wearing diamonds and carrying a fan made, I believe, from ostrich feathers. As she began grandly walking around on the arm of one of the male partners, many recognized this domino as the only one of its kind, made to the order of a wealthy Moscow lady. Her husband, who was also at the masquerade, was very embarrassed. His friends had alerted him to her arrival – for earlier she had told him she had felt unwell and would not be going to the masquerade, and he had now begun flirting with a certain actress. He hastened to make himself scarce, someone else took over his lady friend, and the author of this rumpus continued calmly strolling past the dancers and the guests, who were happily chatting together. Several times she passed the table where Kashkin was chatting with some others – when suddenly, having turned so that Kashkin became visible to her from behind, she stopped, with a pronounced gesture struck herself on the forehead, and exclaimed, 'Idiot! Of course he would have shaved!'

38

The 'lady' had recognized Papa – and by the characteristic gesture the others had recognized Tchaikovsky. Their anonymity was broken, to the amusement of all.

Now for a time the main narrative will be abruptly broken as it moves some two hundred and fifty miles eastwards to Nizhni Novgorod, and takes a step backwards in time. The future composer, Mily Balakirev, was born in this city in 1837, and though only three years older than Tchaikovsky, he would become a powerful influence on the latter's creative career and music. As a boy Balakirev had piano lessons, but far more important would be his contact with a local teacher, Karl Eisrich, who was also the conductor of the local theatre orchestra which played at soirées at the home of Alexander Ulibïshev, a writer on music, best remembered for his three-volume biography of Mozart. Balakirev became Eisrich's assistant at these events, playing in chamber music, even conducting the orchestra in Beethoven symphonies and, through his ready access to Ulibïshev's library, being able to study and lodge in his excellent memory knowledge of a wide range of musical styles and procedures which he then applied in his own compositions. At sixteen he entered Kazan University to study mathematics, but two years later, in 1855, Ulibïshev took him to St Petersburg where he met Glinka, who was deeply impressed by the eighteen-year-old. 'Never have I met a man in whom I found views so close to my own on everything concerning music. He will in time become a second Glinka,' the grand old man of Russian music informed his sister, Lyudmila Shestakova, whom he instructed to entrust to Balakirev the musical education of her young daughter.

Two years later Glinka was dead, and Balakirev, just twenty, inherited his mantle. He wasted no time. He had already encountered César Cui, a fortifications engineer a year older than himself (and who would be blistering about Tchaikovsky's graduation cantata), and before the end of 1857 had enlisted an eighteen-year-old army officer, Modest Musorgsky. Starting with these two, Balakirev began assembling around himself a group of passionate music enthusiasts whom he proposed to turn into major composers. There being still no textbook on musical composition in Russian – as noted earlier, the first such would be provided by Tchaikovsky in 1871 – Balakirev taught mainly by playing and analysing works by major Western composers in piano-duet versions, then sending his 'pupils' away to attempt such pieces for themselves. Two more members were soon added to the group: a seventeen-year-old naval cadet, Nikolay Rimsky-Korsakov, in 1861, and the following year a young chemist who would become one of Russia's most distinguished scientists, Alexander Borodin. Though, technically, all but Rimsky would remain 'amateurs' in music, all grew as composers, and three at least – Musorgsky, Borodin and Rimsky-Korsakov – are now recognised as among the truly major figures of nineteenth-century music. Balakirev's catalytic powers were manifestly extraordinary: rarely can one man be credited with creating such a galaxy of great achievers.

Nor in fostering the fortunes of this group should the services of the Stasov brothers, Dmitri and more particularly Vladimir, be overlooked. True, Dmitri, a lawyer, had been one of the founders with Anton Rubinstein of the RMS, but he was not one-sided in his views. As for Vladimir, a senior member of staff of the St Petersburg Public Library, he was a writer whose interests were as varied as his productivity was vast. A passionate champion of all things Russian, he gave tireless moral support to Balakirev's group, dubbing them the *moguchaya kuchka* (the 'mighty handful'), and feeding them with ideas upon which they might create works. Without Vladimir Stasov, for instance, we would not have had Borodin's opera, *Prince Igor*, Musorgsky's *Khovanshchina* – nor, as we shall see, Tchaikovsky's symphonic fantasia, *The Tempest*, or his *Manfred Symphony*.

But the *kuchka* was by no means Balakirev's only field of enterprise. Alarmed by the increasing influx of a very conservative Western musical influence that he saw could result from the projects of the newly founded RMS, in 1862 Balakirev founded the Free Music School (FMS) to provide tuition in composition *gratis*, and also instituted a series of concerts that would introduce recent Western music, with composers such as Schumann, Berlioz and Liszt featuring prominently, as well as pieces by the younger generation of Russian composers, such as the *kuchka* itself represented. The Tsarevich Nikolay agreed to provide the royal patronage, thus balancing the cachet afforded the RMS by the Grand Duchess Elena Pavlovna.

All this had happened while Tchaikovsky had been a civil servant and then a student in the classes of the RMS. But throughout his Conservatoire years the fortunes of the FMS had flourished, and when in 1867 Rubinstein had resigned as conductor of the RMS concerts, Balakirev, of all people, had been invited to replace him, a year later also taking over the directorship of the FMS itself. Thus this tireless activist, only just thirty, had become the most powerful force in St Petersburg's music outside the opera houses. We know nothing of how Tchaikovsky viewed all these developments, but in January 1868, in connection with Berlioz's second visit to Russia as conductor, he certainly met Vladimir Stasov. The great French composer was now old and ailing, and though Tchaikovsky had strong reservations about some aspects of Berlioz's music, his admiration for the man and his implacable personal struggle for the cause of his art deeply touched him, and at a dinner at the Conservatoire he paid a wholehearted tribute to this visitor for whom he would retain a lifelong veneration. Then, hard on Stasov's heels, Balakirev arrived. For Tchaikovsky it would prove his most momentous encounter since, six years earlier, he had come under Anton Rubinstein's tutelage, for over the next two years Balakirev would be the most significant single factor in his creative life.

Approaching Classical Music – and Some Hints

There are three recognized branches of creative art: the visual, the literary and the musical, each with its own mode and speed of communication. Faced with a picture, we instantly take it all in. By contrast, a book requires time, yet it uses language we already know, and by its end we have totally absorbed its narrative. Classical music does not work like this. Certainly it has a language with its own special materials (melodies, rhythms and chords), a highly sophisticated grammar (harmonies and keys), and a great variety of structures (fugue, symphony and so on) – yet though we may know nothing of these matters, we can still enjoy, even be deeply touched by, a piece that is their product. Indeed, we know we have intuitively *understood* what we have heard if, for instance, when someone has played a wrong note, we can spot it. But this only identifies a negative fact; conversely, none of us can explain the positive fact that some pieces can have a very powerful, even overwhelming, effect on us. For my part as a writer, I may try to define the music's character by describing it as being 'tender', 'passionate', 'sprightly' and so on, and I expect many readers will sense what I mean. Thus I may point to things in the music that contribute to that consensus, and may sharpen my reader's response – yet I still cannot explain *why* it sounds thus. There are no magic aids, no short cuts to comprehension.

What I am really saying, I suppose, is that the only way you can get a clear view of a whole piece, and experience its full impact, is by listening to it – and *at least* several times until it has begun to be familiar so that you retain some sort of memory of it, some sort of grasp of its various sections and how these are set out. Music demands time (and perhaps some patience) – and between these hearings you will, I hope, find some useful pointers in what I have written about the piece in question (don't worry if you do not understand everything). Then if you have had enough of a piece for the moment, give it a rest – but try coming back to it sometime: I can tell you from experience how my refreshed ear can not only come to enjoy even more the piece as I already knew it, but also become aware of things I had never noticed.

By the way, there is one bonus the music-lover has that is denied the art enthusiast and the bookworm. The former can only imagine what he has seen, and the latter can only remember what he has read – but the music-lover can *re-create* what he has heard: he can at least whistle the tunes!

6
Aborted Marriage:
Romeo and Juliet

In early April 1868 Tchaikovsky visited St Petersburg. He had already begun a correspondence with Balakirev over his own *Characteristic Dances*, which Balakirev wished to include in one of his concerts; now he despatched the score, at the same time soliciting 'a word of encouragement', a request that drew from Balakirev a response couched in a mixture of deferential and authoritarian terms that would become very familiar to Tchaikovsky:

> Regarding the word 'encouragement', this I consider, as far as you are concerned, not only inappropriate, but also dishonest. Encouragements are only for the little children of art, whereas from your score I see you are, both in orchestration and technique, a fully fledged artist to whom only *strict criticism* and not encouragement is to be applied. When we meet in person I shall be very pleased to give you my opinion. It would be far better, when we are both in Moscow, to play through the piece at the piano and examine it bar by bar. Let us not substitute criticism for lively argument!

Whether Balakirev's intended autopsy materialized is unknown, though doubtless it would have been a challenging experience. But Tchaikovsky's first encounter with other members of the *kuchka* was heartening, and their reception of him cordial.

It was a very different atmosphere when he once again encountered Vera Davïdova. Evidently Tchaikovsky had said something that had encouraged her hopes that he might soon yield, and now he bitterly regretted it. Yet, curiously, at this very moment another women was entering his life with whom the seemingly impossible – matrimony – was actually planned.

Désirée Artôt was a Belgian soprano, thirty-two years old, and already enjoying a formidable European reputation, especially as an operatic actress. In April 1868 she arrived in Moscow with an Italian opera company, and was such a sensation that in the autumn the company returned. Tchaikovsky now made her acquaintance and the relationship developed apace. 'I've become very friendly with Artôt and am enjoying extremely marked favour with her,' he reported to Anatoly. 'Rarely have I met such a pleasant, intelligent and sensible woman.' In November he confirmed his admiration by composing and dedicating to her his **Romance in F minor, for piano, op. 5.****

Tchaikovsky was now involved for the first (and, evidently, the last) time in a relationship with a woman where it seems his sexual feelings may have been touched. Yet a strong suspicion remains that it was Artôt's extraordinary talent for portraying operatic heroines, rather than the woman herself, that had really captivated him. Whatever the case, the fact is that they soon discussed marrying in the following summer. It quickly emerged, however, that Artôt was not prepared to abandon her career, and Tchaikovsky's friends, led by Nikolay Rubinstein, were fiercely opposed to a marriage, arguing that he would become a kind of poodle trailing after her, and dependent on her. They need not have worried. By early January Artôt had gone off to Warsaw – and had promptly married a Spanish baritone! Nikolay Rubinstein broke the news to Tchaikovsky, making no attempt to hide his relief. As for the rejected bridegroom, he (as a friend who was present reported) 'didn't say a word; he simply went white and walked out. A few days later he was already unrecognizable; once again he was relaxed, at ease, and had only one consideration in the world – his work.'

Towards the year's end Tchaikovsky had to meet Artôt again when she came back to Moscow for performances of Auber's opera, *Le Domino noir*, with recitatives that Tchaikovsky had been commissioned to supply. He found his feelings ambivalent: 'This woman hurt me greatly, yet some inexplicable sympathy draws me to her to such a degree that I am beginning to await her arrival with feverish impatience. Woe is me! All the same, this feeling is not love.' Her hold on him would continue, and when she returned a month later to perform Marguerite in Gounod's *Faust*, Kashkin remembered that when she appeared onstage, 'Tchaikovsky hid himself behind his opera glasses and didn't remove them from his eyes until the end of the act, though he can hardly have seen much because tears, which he appeared not to notice, were streaming out from under the glasses.' Yet though the present relationship was certainly over, eighteen years on they would encounter each other again – with richly productive results, which we can still enjoy.

It is intriguing to speculate whether the substantial orchestral piece Tchaikovsky began in October and completed in December while his romance with Artôt was in progress was a wry comment on the affair, but there is no evidence that he was writing his **symphonic poem,** *Fatum (Fate)* **(*) to any programme. He was initially pleased with the piece when Nikolay Rubinstein conducted it in Moscow early the next year, but most of its materials are indifferent, some even banal – though there is one good string tune that unfolds promisingly, once the various fragments that make up the introduction are out of the way; indeed, Tchaikovsky would subsequently find a home for this in his opera *The Oprichnik*. But with the *molto allegro* introduced by the timpani the inventiveness slumps, and there is no identifiable structure to the piece. Tchaikovsky had dedicated *Fatum* to Balakirev, but some four weeks later, after conducting its premiere in St Petersburg, the latter had written privately to Tchaikovsky a savage but well-targeted criticism of his piece.

However, it was not Balakirev's nature to write off Tchaikovsky on the evidence of one inferior work, and his damning letter ended with an expression of confidence:

> I am writing to you with complete frankness, being fully convinced that you won't go back on your intention of dedicating *Fatum* to me. Your dedication is precious to me as a sign of your sympathy towards me – and I feel a great weakness for you.
>
> M. Balakirev – who sincerely loves you.

Tchaikovsky was too self-critical not to perceive the truth of Balakirev's verdict, and later he would destroy the score of *Fatum*. (The piece was reconstituted after his death from the parts used at the performances.) If the initial impact of Balakirev on Tchaikovsky's creative life had been negatively beneficial, its positive value would be brilliantly shown in another orchestral work that Tchaikovsky would set about before 1869 was out.

Yet it is a mark of Tchaikovsky's seething creativity, and of his ability to focus on the creative project in hand, that in the meantime, between January 1869, while awaiting the premieres of both *The Voyevoda* and *Fatum*, and July, when he was taking his summer break with Sasha and her growing family at Kamenka, he should have composed and scored a whole new opera, *Undine*. Its subject was taken from a short story by the German writer, Friedrich de La Motte Fouqué, and for which a libretto already existed: thus there would be no problems such as Tchaikovsky had endured with Ostrovsky over *The Voyevoda*. It told of a water nymph, Undine, who is loved and then deserted by a knight, Huldbrand. She drowns herself and, after Huldbrand's rekindled love has ended in his death, turns into a fountain. The opera completed, Tchaikovsky was frustrated by the delay in fixing a date for the premiere, then was told in November that it could not be mounted that season, and finally learned that it had been rejected as unsatisfactory. Like the manuscript of *The Voyevoda*, that of *Undine* was later destroyed by Tchaikovsky. Nevertheless, as with *The Voyevoda*, several pieces from it found their way into later compositions, notably a wedding march, which would provide the basis for the slow movement of the Second Symphony (*The Little Russian*), and the main theme of the final lovers' duet, which achieved universal fame by becoming the foundation for the great *Pas d'action* (with violin and cello solos) for Siegfried and Odette in Act 2 of *Swan Lake*, a scene that every ballet-goer adores.

In August, with *Undine* completed but its future unknown, Tchaikovsky returned to Moscow to find Balakirev in residence and about to make wearisome demands on his time. Yet it was, according to Kashkin, during one of the long walks on which Balakirev took Tchaikovsky that the former suggested a subject for an orchestral piece. The result was that on 7 October Tchaikovsky set about what would ultimately be his first masterpiece: the fantasy overture, *Romeo and Juliet*.

Yet it did not at first come easily, as Tchaikovsky admitted to Balakirev after a week's work. The old autocrat's response was exactly what might have been expected, and his interventions and Tchaikovsky's responses afford such vivid insights into the way great composers' minds can work that it is worth devoting significant space to it. Balakirev began by describing very specifically how he had tackled his own overture on another Shakespeare subject, *King Lear*:

First, after reading the play, I was inflamed with a desire to write the overture, but having as yet no materials, I fired myself by means of a ground plan. I projected a *maestoso* introduction, and then something mystical (Kent's prophecy). The introduction fades away, and there begins a stormy, passionate *allegro*. This is Lear himself, already uncrowned, but still a strong lion. The characters of Regan and Goneril also functioned as episodes, and finally the quiet and gentle second subject personified Cordelia. Further on came the development (the storm, Lear and the Fool on the heath), then the recapitulation of the *allegro*. Regan and Goneril finally get the better of him and the overture ends with a dying down (Lear over Cordelia's body). Then follows a repetition of Kent's prophecy, now fulfilled, and then a calm, solemn death. I'll tell you that at first, even with this plan, no ideas formed themselves – but then, afterwards, ideas did come and fit themselves into the frame I had created. I think this will happen to you also if you first *inflame yourself* with a plan. Then arm yourself with galoshes and a stick, set off for a walk along the boulevards – and I'm convinced that before you reach the Sretensky you'll already have some theme – or at least some episode. At this very moment, while thinking of you and your overture, I am some-how involuntarily fired, and I conceive that your overture must begin straight away with a fierce *allegro* with sword clashes like this: [here Balakirev jotted down four bars of vigorous music]. If I were composing this overture then, having inspired myself with this germ, I would let it incubate – or, rather, would carry it around deep within my brain, and then there would issue something alive and feasible like this.

Balakirev could not resist taking the matter further, making sugges-tions for a key scheme. And the strategy worked, for on 9 November Tchaikovsky replied:

My overture is progressing quite rapidly. The greater part is already composed in outline, and when it's crept out of my womb you'll see that, whatever else it may be, a large portion of what you advised me to do has been carried out as you instructed. In the first place, the scheme is yours: the introduction depicting the friar, the feud (*allegro*), and love (the second subject). Secondly, the keys are yours: the introduction in E, the *allegro* in B minor, and the second theme [in fact, two themes] in D flat.

Balakirev was, predictably, impatient to see what Tchaikovsky had already composed, promising to make no comment until the whole piece was completed. It was wise of Tchaikovsky to have limited his response, for even with no more than the four main themes, his St Petersburg mentor could not resist instant comment:

Because it's already finished I consider it permissible to give you frankly my opinions of the themes you sent me. The opening theme is not at all to my taste. Perhaps when it's fully realized it achieves some degree of beauty, but when written out unadorned as you have sent it to me, it conveys neither beauty nor strength, and doesn't even depict the character of Friar Laurence in the way required. Here there ought to be something like Liszt's chorales, with an ancient Catholic character. But instead your E major tune has a completely different character – the character of quartet themes by that genius of petty bourgeois music, Haydn, and which arouses a strong thirst for beer. As for your B minor theme [the feud music], this isn't a theme but *a very beautiful introduction to a theme*, and after the C major rushing about there is surely need for a strong, energetic melodic idea. I assume it is there. The second theme in D flat is very beautiful, though a bit overripe, but the first D flat tune is simply *delightful*. I play it often, and I want very much to kiss you for it. Here is tenderness and the sweetness of love. When I play [here Balakirev wrote out the broad love theme with its two-note 'sighing' horn accompaniment], then I imagine you are lying naked in your bath and that Artôt–Padilla herself is washing your tummy with hot lather from scented soap. There's only one thing I'll say against the theme; there's little in it of inner, spiritual love, and only a passionate physical languor (with even a slightly Italian hue) – whereas Romeo and Juliet are decidely not Persian lovers, but Europeans.

The first performance of *Romeo and Juliet* was conducted by Nikolay Rubinstein in Moscow in March 1870. Balakirev, having now seen the full score, wrote of the enthusiasm with which the *kuchka* had greeted the piece, and 'how delighted everyone is with your D flat bit [the love themes] – including Vladimir Stasov, who says: "There were five of you: now there are six!" The beginning and end are to be strongly censured', and required rewriting. Nevertheless, such was the enthusiasm of the *kuchka* for the piece that at their meetings Balakirev was always required to play it through at the piano, a feat he learned to perform from memory.

Tchaikovsky himself also remained ambivalent about his latest composition and in the summer of 1870 he revised it drastically, scrapping the whole slow introduction and opening its replacement (now in F sharp minor) with a chorale-like idea, exactly as Balakirev had prescribed. Much else was replaced, including almost the entire coda. In 1880 a final, much less drastic, revision produced the work's ultimate, and perfect, form.

Fantasy Overture: *Romeo and Juliet* * * * * *

[This is where readers unfamiliar with classical music should begin their investigation of Tchaikovsky's work. Though this is obviously a highly descriptive piece, Tchaikovsky effortlessly designed it in sonata form [see Appendix 1 for a description of this], and its various sections should not be, in the end, particularly difficult to identify. Above all, however, Romeo and Juliet *is a marvellously graphic and musically rich piece – on all counts, one of Tchaikovsky's greatest. But not only is it a very attractive piece – it is also a very substantial one, so if you are a (relative) newcomer to classical music, do not try to complete its examination at one sitting – unless, that is, you become instantly hooked on it. Classical music is often so rich in varied details that it may require several hearings before you can begin to feel really familiar with a piece, and even beyond this further hearings may reveal new treasures. You can, of course, simply play the whole piece a number of times until you feel comfortable with it, but I suggest you might adopt the following alternative strategy:*

1 *Listen to the lot – or at least a good portion of it. Have patience: it is lengthy (about 20 minutes), and don't worry if getting your head round this (or keeping your attention constantly focused) proves formidable – though there may already be some bits that have struck you.*

2 *Now read on through the following three paragraphs. The third deals with the work's slow introduction (about 6 minutes); listen to this, and try to pick out some of the things I have described in it. Pause when the feud music (noisy and violent) enters. If you think it will help, go back and listen again: things you missed first time round may now begin to become apparent.]*

Romeo and Juliet is such a masterpiece, and so characteristic of the mature Tchaikovsky, that it is worth examining it more closely than space will permit with most later pieces in this book. Like Balakirev with his *King Lear* overture, Tchaikovsky had composed *Romeo and Juliet* as a sonata structure. It may seem odd that a composer, when turning a stage play into a musical organism, should cast it in a form where the preordained course of musical events is unlikely to have any plausible parallel to the narrative sequence of the play. But the point of music by itself (i.e. not as in opera, where it is tethered to a text and the events onstage) is that it can concentrate single-mindedly on the essence of the play. More precisely, it can focus, on the one hand, on the prime players whose characters and emotional responses create the play's train of events and, on the other, it can suggest, either through graphic projection or by mood, the context in which they act and react. In fact, though music may conjure certain of the landmark events into which the characters are caught (here, for example, the skirmishes between the Montagues and the Capulets), we learn little from Tchaikovsky's music of Shakespeare's actual plot except that its outcome is catastrophic. Instead, Tchaikovsky encapsulates the two conflicting forces of the play (the love of Romeo and Juliet on the one hand, and the bitter mutual hostility of their families on the other) in two savagely contrasting kinds of music, then proceeds to a deeper exposure, but in *musical* terms, of these two fevered worlds and of the human consequences of their confrontation.

But there is a third factor in the story: Friar Laurence – and his role is very different. He is the activist who enables the course of love, but who stands outside the central conflict. Yet his presence must be clearly signalled, and so he is given his own musical badge, the dignified hymnlike theme that opens the work pointing to his priestly status and always retaining its stable identity, even when later we hear him desperately intervening in a forlorn attempt to calm and separate the warring clans.

Romeo and Juliet begins with a slow introduction so substantial that it is a very significant section in its own right. As already noted, the solemn initial theme introduces Friar Laurence, the string music that immediately follows suggesting, perhaps, a smothered restlessness, reinforced by the insistent dissonance marking the following *crescendo* which passes into a solemn, harp-decorated theme.

Tchaikovsky repeats all this, though rescoring it and starting in a different key. This ended, the action moves away from the uneasy calm of this introduction; the string music recurs, this time urgently and with a following powerful *crescendo*, then is heard again quietly as before, as though Friar Laurence is willing a return to the stability of his own world. It is not to be. A chord, first quiet, but then repeated with growing force and impetus – and the *Allegro giusto* feud music (the first subject, marking the beginning of the exposition) erupts from it.

Now investigate the next stretch from the beginning of the feud music (but again, perhaps, first have a look at the diagram of sonata form in Appendix 1). I suggest simply listening to the whole of the exposition (about 5 minutes), then track your way through it again, using the following commentary. Again, if you think it will help, listen to this section for a third time.

In the work's introduction, which we have just listened to, I sense that Tchaikovsky may indeed have been imagining an unfolding process, though emotional rather than graphic. Yet 'erupts' surely fits the feud music that has now arrived. This first subject is long enough to bring home the implacable aggression that marks this inter-family vendetta. Then the following increasingly calm transition prepares us for the new music (the second subject) to come, and for a total change of mood and climate: warm, secure, calm and reassuring. From the field of strife we have passed to the closet (or the balcony?) of love.

This is the second subject, which it would become quite normal practice for Tchaikovsky to build from two very distinct themes; *Romeo and Juliet* sets a precedent for this. Nevertheless, one reason for the pair here could be to present a broader perspective on one of the deepest of human experiences than would be possible through a single theme. And yet this duality also poses a question: are we to hear these two themes as complementary, the first spacious, ardent and conveying the warmth and strength of love, the second (on muted strings) intimate, delicate and breathing love's gentleness and tenderness? Or are they, in fact, separate representatives of the lovers themselves, the first of Romeo, full of masculine but tender ardour, the second of Juliet and her feminine adoration? The latter hypothesis will gain some support from their treatment in the recapitulation, where the themes' order is, unusually in a symphonic work, reversed, the feminine theme, now desperately agitated, coming first, the masculine theme spreading itself with an unexpected breadth and power that might suggest Romeo's implacable assertiveness in defence of his love until he is finally, but surely, overwhelmed. Yet in Shakespeare he did not die a violent death. Thus the question remains open, and each of us can make up his or her own mind.

The development is relatively brief (about 2 minutes), and it topples over into the recapitulation (where the feud music recurs). Since the work's main themes will now be becoming more familiar, perhaps it is a good idea to play on to the end of the recapitulation (that is, up to the silence that precedes the last stage (the coda) – about 4 further minutes on). Then, as before, go through all of this again, using the commentary.

The second subject has fully presented the lovers, the third party in the case, and the exposition has ended ravishingly with muted strings and low woodwind cushioning a gently rocking harp figure and brief, receding cor anglais phrases; now it is the development's concern to present the first stage in which the drama itself is played out. Here matters are clearly between the Friar and the two families, the former heard from the beginning against constant rumblings of dissent. Slowly but remorselessly the hubbub grows, the Friar shouting two final desperate appeals (his theme on trumpets), but to no avail, and the turmoil spills over into the recapitulation, introduced by the feud music exactly as it had appeared in the exposition, though here very much shortened. It is succeeded by the love music (the second subject), but now represented first by the second love theme (Juliet's?), this time not tenderly rapturous, but desperately agitated.

Whatever criticism may have been levelled at Tchaikovsky in the past, no critic has ever questioned his melodic gift. And if any doubters remain, then they should experience Tchaikovsky's exploitation of the broad love theme that will go on to dominate the recapitulation. In the first version it had already been spacious, but in the 1870 revision Tchaikovsky had extended it enormously, both in expressive range and in duration. The point at which his second revision begins is fairly easy to spot – it is where the grand melodic surge is suddenly softened, the theme dropping to the cellos before resuming its full-throated course, only to encounter the feud music, which grapples with it, swiftly achieving ascendency. This is where Friar Laurence attempts to intervene, but without success. The final catastrophe is embodied in the work's most brutal and violent climax, from which issues a descending line that tumbles to the bass of the orchestra and, after a brief but violent timpani eruption, expires.

Only the coda remains. Use the same double procedure as before.

After such turmoil, even silence seems eloquent as (I imagine) the two families stand, stunned by what they have caused. But then, to a muffled-drum rhythm suggestive of a funeral march, the twisting line resumes, but now given a rhythm – and we can hear that, extraordinarily but so aptly, it had already, even before the timpani eruption, been a broken, mutilated version of the broad love theme. A quiet hymnlike theme for woodwind and horns signals, presumably, Friar Laurence's benediction over the tragic lovers; then the opening of the broad love theme, its true character restored, rides majestically above a strong, darkly descending bass. An apotheosis of the lovers perhaps, it provides a final, perfect touch before six unsparing chords bring to an end one of Tchaikovsky's greatest masterpieces.

[None of the following examinations of individual works will offer as precise listening guidance as has been given in the case of Romeo and Juliet. *Nevertheless, I hope the experience of getting to grips with this piece will have helped you decide what are the most useful things* you *found in my method of approach (and what perhaps you found was not helpful: we all listen in our own ways) so that you can begin building/discovering the way* that suits you *for getting inside a classical piece and getting the best out of it.]*

———

First Quartet
and *The Oprichnik*

Romeo and Juliet was certainly a masterpiece, but it was only years later that it achieved the popularity it enjoys today – surely a reminder to us that works we may initially not connect with, even reject, may subsequently gain not only our acceptance but our affection. Nevertheless, the fact remains that Tchaikovsky's fame was first established by certain of his shorter pieces such as could be performed domestically, or in concerts involving only one or a very few performers. Here piano pieces were important, and so were songs. Of the former we have already noted the swift popularity gained by Tchaikovsky's 'Chant sans paroles', the last of the three pieces that make up *Souvenir de Hapsal*. If he did produce a set of pieces, it would usually comprise six items (the dog-loving Tchaikovsky once jokingly asserted this was prompted by the habit of a bitch he had owned of always presenting him with litters of six puppies). In December 1869, with the first version of *Romeo and Juliet* completed, he set about his first set of six songs, the final one of which quickly gained wide currency, and has remained ever since by far his most famous example of the genre. Outside Russia as late as 1943 the Welsh novelist and dramatist, Richard Llewellyn (best known for his play *How Green was My Valley*) used the English title of **the song, 'None but the lonely heart'**,***(*) as the title of a novel, and a year later it was employed for a film starring Cary Grant and Ethel Barrymore (also providing the theme tune). Unlike so many pieces by great composers that achieved a currency that their purely musical quality did not justify, 'None but the lonely heart' is one of its creator's finest songs. Its text was a Russian translation of one of Mignon's four songs from Goethe's *Wilhelm Meister* (oddly, Lev Mey, whose Russian translation Tchaikovsky used, had turned it into a song for a man). This agonized lament of the young Mignon at separation from her beloved had already engrossed earlier composers (Beethoven had set it four times, Schubert no fewer than six), and though Tchaikovsky's response was very different, it proved as perfect in its form as in its melodic distinction. 'None but the lonely heart' is a little masterpiece.

Tchaikovsky's personal life at this period had its strains. While these songs were being created Vera reappeared in Moscow, her passion for Tchaikovsky still lingering. Simultaneously Artôt returned to Moscow to sing in Gounod's *Faust*, and Vera attended a performance with Tchaikovsky and members of her family, but left before the end. All this, and the lukewarm reception of the first version of *Romeo and Juliet* at its Moscow premiere in March, decided Tchaikovsky that he needed a substantial break and in June, as soon as the Conservatoire term was over, he headed west to join his young friend, the eighteen-year-old Vladimir Shilovsky, in Paris. He would be away for some three months – though far from completely idle, for during extended stays in Bad Soden in Germany and Interlaken in Switzerland he completed his first, and most substantial, revision of *Romeo and Juliet*. September found him, with his morale restored, back in Moscow for the new Conservatoire session.

By now Tchaikovsky was thoroughly settled in Moscow. He had established a good circle of friends, was frequently invited to dine out, and enjoyed a rich cultural life of plays, concerts and operas. And early the following year he delivered the first substantial piece that would carry his name around the world. By 1871 his national fame had grown sufficiently for Nikolay Rubinstein to suggest that he should mount a concert devoted entirely to his own music. Tchaikovsky concurred; he was short of money, and such a concert might make a profit – but to make it really attractive, it should contain a completely new work. An orchestra would have been far too costly, but a string quartet made up of his professional friends was feasible. The result was Tchaikovsky's First String Quartet, begun in February for a concert scheduled for the end of March. The audience was gratifyingly large, and the event's prestige was heightened by the appearance of Ivan Turgenev, one of Russia's most famous and respected novelists.

'Chamber music' – that is, music for a small group of (usually) instrumental soloists, such as might be played in a room of a large house – does not feature very prominently in Tchaikovsky's output. Nevertheless, his three string quartets, Piano Trio (for violin, cello and piano), and string sextet (*Souvenir de Florence*) contain some excellent music. The form of most string quartets and quintets, etc., composed in the late eighteenth and nineteenth centuries (i.e. in the Classical and Romantic periods) paralleled that of the contemporary symphonies in that they were usually in four movements and normally employed the corresponding musical structures. Clearly a small group of instrumentalists cannot match the sheer power and variety of an orchestra, but what it can offer is intimacy and a greater refinement; also, on the assumption that the smaller audience is likely to be a more consistently committed and receptive one, the composer may be encouraged to present a musical experience that is more subtle and sophisticated, and sometimes even of a personal, perhaps almost confessional, nature.

There is, however, nothing of the latter quality in Tchaikovsky's first quartet, and from the circumstances of its composition, it cannot be expected that there would be. Instead it is a straightforward four-movement piece of great charm, vitality and inventiveness (especially in its rhythmic flexibility), and it contains the movement that would, more than any other, introduce his name to the rest of the world.

String Quartet no.1 in D major * * * *

[This is an engaging work, and a good first-time piece for those readers who are largely unfamiliar with the rather individual and slender sound of music for only two violins, a viola and a cello. It can fairly be described as a symphony for four soloists, and its form is pretty straightforward. But even if you do not go for the whole piece, listen to the slow movement, which has always been one of Tchaikovsky's most popular pieces.]

The quartet's first movement is in sonata form, and the boundaries between the chief components are mostly clear. It opens with a gently pulsing chordal idea; the beginning of the transition is marked by the intervention of melodic roulades that pass between the instruments (these will also be a prominent feature of the finale, and contribute to the work's sense of unity). The second subject is a new theme plainly presented, the ornamental lines soon reappearing and building to a powerful climax before the whole exposition is repeated (or should be: in recorded performances this is often omitted, presumably because the producers want to squeeze two quartets on to one CD). Though the development opens with the first subject unadorned, the ornamental lines quickly reappear, but now they home in on a little five-note scalic figure that not only dominates the whole development but persists in the first violin as a companion to the first subject when the recapitulation slips in on the three lower strings. In due course the second subject recurs, and a vigorous coda rounds off the movement. Only here does one suspect Tchaikovsky might have wished he had an orchestra at his disposal.

The scherzo and finale (movements three and four) are clear siblings of this first movement, their rhythmic characters equally attractive. The scherzo follows the usual ternary pattern of such movements at this time, the central trio ushered in by a slow trill on the cello. The finale is in sonata form, the second subject easily identified as the playfully repeated morsel against which a broad sustained melody, initially delivered by the viola, enters (again the repeat of the exposition may be omitted). Otherwise these movements require no further comment.

But the slow movement, the *Andante cantabile* built around a folksong that Tchaikovsky himself had noted down in 1869 from the singing of a peasant at his sister Sasha's home in the Ukraine, is a very different matter. Rendered into doggerel English that fairly matches the literary quality of the original words, the text runs thus:

> Upon the divan Vanya sat
> And filled a glass with rum:
> Before he'd poured out half a tot
> He ordered Katenka to come.

The folksong itself is a world away from this. It is, in fact, barely a quarter of a minute long, but within this tiny span it establishes a memorable individuality. Tchaikovsky forthwith repeats and then effortlessly extends it, returning to the original tune before continuing with a theme of his own creation over a four-note pizzicato ostinato from the cello. These facts observed, no further comment is needed, surely, on the rest of this simple and perfectly conceived movement. Certainly Tchaikovsky's contemporaries fell for it completely – and not only in Russia; constantly he was encountering it abroad, played by every sort of instrument and instrumental combination. This came to irritate him because the obsession with this particular movement was not matched by interest in his other, more important, pieces. But it did occasion one incident, the memory of which he treasured for the rest of his days – the occasion in 1876, when the colossus of Russian literature was alongside him during a performance of this *Andante*: 'Perhaps I was never so flattered in my life, nor was my pride as a composer so stirred, as when Lev Tolstoy, sitting beside me listening to the *Andante* from my First Quartet, dissolved in tears.'

––––––

The summer of 1871 was passed first at Kamenka. Sasha's family now presented Uncle Pyotr with a growing bevy of young nieces who could be enlisted into modest domestic entertainments, and this was probably the year in which he dreamed up a ballet for them to perform. He, of course, composed the music, but he also acted as choreographer, and years later one of his nephews recorded his part in the proceedings:

> The staging was done entirely by Uncle Pyotr. It was he who invented the steps and pirouettes, and he danced them himself, showing the performers what he required of them. At such moments Uncle Pyotr, red in the face, wet with perspiration as he sang the tune, presented a pretty amusing sight. But in the children's eyes he was so perfect in the art of choreography that for many years the memories of this remained with them down to the finest details.

Uncle Modest, who was also in residence, danced the Prince, and their eldest niece, Tatyana, was Odette – for it was in this tiny, unambitious domestic entertainment that the embryo was conceived of the most famous ballet in the world, *Swan Lake*. It would also prove to be the first of a whole series of theatrical enterprises at Kamenka, which would include Nikolay Gogol's hilarious play *The Marriage* and Molière's *Le Misanthrope*, Uncle Pyotr almost always acting as designer, producer, and prompter.

From Kamenka Tchaikovsky headed for the estate of a friend, Nikolay Kondratyev, at Nizy, some eighty miles north-west of Kharkov. Kondratyev was noted for his unfailing optimism, and Modest believed it was this capacity to see the bright side in everything that endeared him to Tchaikovsky. Here at Nizy Tchaikovsky completed his textbook on harmony commissioned by Jurgenson. On returning to Moscow in September he was at last able to detach himself from Nikolay Rubinstein and move into quarters of his own. Now needing a personal servant, he engaged Mikhail Sofronov, who had formerly been in the service of the violinist Ferdinand Laub, the leader in the recent premiere of Tchaikovsky's First String Quartet. Mikhail was joined – soon, it seems – by his teenage brother, Alexey, and when Mikhail and his master parted company in 1876, Alexey stayed on. It was the beginning of a lifelong relationship, Tchaikovsky becoming increasingly attached to Alexey, missing him greatly when circumstances caused significant periods of separation (he was especially distraught when Alexey was conscripted into the army for a time), being much concerned for his welfare, and placing great trust in him personally. The closeness of their relationship would become a source of deep jealousy among some of Tchaikovsky's relatives, and in his will Tchaikovsky would bequeath Alexey one-seventh of the capital from his estate, as well as furniture. In consequence, by selling his legacy the former servant was able to purchase Tchaikovsky's last home at Klin, which would become the Tchaikovsky Museum. Alexey would survive his master by thirty-three years, himself bequeathing to the Museum some scores of Tchaikovsky's music which he had concealed from Modest.

The generosity of his bequest to Alexey indicates the affection Tchaikovsky had developed for his servant, and raises the question of whether their relationship was entirely a business one. Certainly the very heightened tone of some of Tchaikovsky's letters reveal that the strength of his personal concern for Alexey was very great. Poznansky has pointed out that in Russia at this time servants could also become convenient sexual partners, and it seems plausible that Tchaikovsky did indeed seek sexual satisfaction from Alexey (who himself was very obviously heterosexual). As already noted, Alexey was in his midteens when he entered Tchaikovsky's life, a time when the teenage male seems to have been a particular preoccupation of Tchaikovsky. Another youth from this period was a certain Eduard Zak, in 1871 seventeen years old, to whom Tchaikovsky's brother, Nikolay, had been showing some kindness. Tchaikovsky himself knew the lad and became very emotionally involved with him, as is clear from the letter he sent to Nikolay in October:

> I beg you, old chap, to let him – and even order him – to travel to Moscow. In doing this, you'll give me great pleasure. I have missed him a great deal, and I'm fearful for his future. I fear that manual work will kill all higher aspirations in him. But whatever happens, it's absolutely essential that I see him. For God's sake, arrange it!

Zak did come to Moscow and associate with Tchaikovsky, but then two years later committed suicide. Yet he was not forgotten; sixteen years on Tchaikovsky could confide to his diary:

> How amazingly well do I remember him: the sound of his voice, his movements, but in particular the uncommonly wonderful expression at times on his face. I think I never loved anyone as much as he. My God, but what did they not say to me *then* – and however much I console myself, my guilt before him is terrible! And yet I loved him, and the memory of him is sacred to me.

The pain, the longing, the mysterious guilt which is clearly the consequence of some incident which was, presumably, homosexual, the ineradicable memory: all are there. And at the same time, in 1871, gossip about Tchaikovsky's relationship with the nineteen-year-old Shilovsky had been circulating. The latter had invited Tchaikovsky to spend nearly a month with him in Nice around the New Year – but no one must know about this, Tchaikovsky told brother Anatoly, 'and because in Moscow everyone (except Rubinstein) must think that I am going to Sasha's, please don't tell anyone'.

As it was, the break in Nice proved beneficial and, back in Russia, Tchaikovsky resumed work on a major project: the completion of his second opera, *The Oprichnik*, which he had begun a year earlier, and which is the first of his operas to have survived intact. In the West Tchaikovsky is not normally perceived as a composer much interested in opera. Only two – *Eugene Onegin* and *The Queen of Spades* – are regularly mounted outside Russia, but Tchaikovsky wrote eight others. In the later nineteenth century, with symphony concerts still being generally (and especially in Russia) neither as prestigious nor as numerous as they would later be, opera dominated the musical scene, and it was in the opera house that the composer could achieve supreme fame. Tchaikovsky was always on the lookout for viable operatic subjects. In early 1870, with *Undine* rejected by the Imperial Theatres, he projected *Mandragora*, an opera based on an idea from a certain Sergey Rachinsky, a botanist friend:

> A knight, rejected by his lady love, learns of the all-powerful mandragora, an enchanted root that may do the trick for him. At night he seeks it out in an enchanted garden; the mandragora bursts into flower, and the knight tears it out by its roots – whereupon it is

transformed into an enchanted beauty who immediately is enamoured of him. Turning herself into a page, she attaches herself to him, but he now falls in love with another woman, at which the unfortunate mandragora turns herself back into a flower.

Tchaikovsky actually composed a rather beautiful chorus of flowers and insects for the nocturnal garden scene of *Mandragora*, but then dropped the subject. Rachinsky promptly offered another, *Raimond Lully*:

Raimond, a Spanish knight, is so debauched that his lady love, Donna Inez, has sought refuge in a nunnery. During a chapel service Raimond bursts in (on horseback), scattering everyone except Donna Inez, who joins him in a duet, during which he is converted into a warrior missionary who sets out for Africa, only to be struck down by an old accomplice who is disconcerted by the improvement in his character. Meanwhile Donna Inez has also arrived in Africa to negotiate the freedom of some Christian prisoners; she just happens to be passing – so Raimond is able to die in her arms.

Tchaikovsky's brother, Modest, alleged the composer found this 'very interesting', but then rejected it. If we may feel that he would have been wiser to have accepted something other than the highly melodramatic subject he was about to settle on for his next opera, we can reflect that its plot was at least a vast improvement on either of the previous two. In fact, Tchaikovsky based *The Oprichnik* on a tragedy by a respected Russian playwright Ivan Lazhechnikov, set in the time of the sixteenth-century tsar, Ivan the Terrible. Ivan was, historically, a brutal ruler (though with contrasting bouts of extreme piety) who maintained a corps of personal bodyguards known as Oprichniks, and who were notorious for their atrocities. Tchaikovsky was his own librettist, and had begun composition early in February 1870. For a year progress had been slow and intermittent, and though the success of the concert devoted to his own works in March 1871 had fired his creativity, it was still May 1872 before all was done, and a further two years before the opera reached the stage.

The Oprichnik: opera in four acts * * *

[The Oprichnik may be safely left to those who like high-powered melodrama with music to match. However, do not judge the whole piece from Act 1, which is stuffed with music taken over from The Voyevoda *before Tchaikovsky destroyed the latter. But opera buffs should find plenty to enjoy in the later acts: there is some very good, sometimes very touching, music here. Other readers should move on to Chapter 8.]*

The plot of *The Oprichnik* is briefly as follows:

Act 1. Andrey and Natalya are in love, but the former's family has been dispossessed by Natalya's father, Zhemchuzhny, who demands she marries the elderly Mitkov. Natalya is dismayed. In despair, Andrey confides to his friend, Basmanov (already an Oprichnik), that he has decided to join the Oprichniks in the hope of getting justice through the Tsar himself. Alone, Natalya voices her yearning for Andrey. Her women enter and try to cheer her with a choral dance.

Act 2 Scene 1. The Boyarina, Andrey's mother, worries about Basmanov's influence on her son, despite the latter's reassurances. Andrey reaffirms his determination to remain virtuous.

Act 2 Scene 2. In the Tsar's mansion the Oprichniks are assembled. Vyazminsky, their commander and a deadly enemy of Andrey's father, is enraged to learn the Tsar will accept Andrey as an Oprichnik, but then sees in this a hope of getting his revenge. Andrey enters, and Vyazminsky administers the Oprichniks' oath to the young man who, if he should break it, will have to die – and only too late does Andrey discover that he will have to renounce even his mother and Natalya. He is already committed, but only after phases of terrible doubt does he finally and fully complete the oath.

Act 3. In a square in Moscow a crowd is lamenting its troubles, and the Boyarina voices her anxieties concerning Andrey. Natalya has fled from her father's house, and now pleads with the older woman for her protection. Zhemchuzhny enters with servants, and Natalya confesses her love for Andrey, the Boyarina interceding, though unsuccessfully, on the lovers' behalf. Andrey, Basmanov and the Oprichniks rush in and rescue Natalya. When Andrey confesses to the Boyarina that he is now an Oprichnik, she curses and disowns him in the most uncompromising terms. Basmanov counsels Andrey to go straight to the Tsar to gain release from his Oprichnik's oath.

Act 4. The Tsar agrees to this plea, and the wedding begins joyfully, Andrey pledging his undying loyalty to Ivan. But he is not to be released from his oath until midnight. Natalya remains uneasy, and while the wedding is being celebrated, a message arrives: Ivan demands to see the bride – but alone. Andrey curses the Tsar, is arrested, and Vyazminsky fetches the Boyarina. Through a window she witnesses her son's execution, and drops dead.

The Oprichnik is unblushing melodrama, and not a truly great opera – but neither is it a bad one. The overture provides a clear introduction to the three principal forces that drive the opera: the Oprichniks, who have a single collective function, and the two prime individuals – the Boyarina, and her son Andrey. Each in the opera has a personal theme, and after the overture's opening, which promises a turbulent tale to come, the Oprichniks' badge is heard, a terse, clipped theme which will become very familiar, once this group has presented itself at the beginning of Act 2 Scene 2. The woodwind theme that follows is the Boyarina's – the dignified melody which, in Act 2 Scene 1, had carried her exhortation to her precious son to practise resignation and virtue (note the instant rejoinder in the overture from the Oprichniks' theme, now muttered on pizzicato strings – a tiny harbinger of the conflict between good and evil which is what this opera is all about). The third theme follows forthwith – the fine violin melody is that to which Andrey will present himself before the Oprichniks in the oath scene, still unaware of the terrible dilemma he is about to face, and which will ultimately destroy him.

The first act is by far the weakest, for Tchaikovsky was intent on recycling as much as he could of his *Voyevoda* music, and some three-quarters of this act were adapted, or simply transferred bodily, from the earlier opera. Sometimes even the original text was taken over, and to accommodate all this, characters and elements of the new plot had to be distorted, with dismal consequences for the tale itself. Only the fine recitative and arioso for Basmanov (a 'trouser' role taken by an alto: presumably Basmanov is to be seen as very young), his ensuing exchanges with Andrey, and Natalya's splendid monologue of love (vintage Tchaikovsky, this!) were new.

From the beginning of Act 2 the whole level of *The Oprichnik* rises, and there will be very few transfers from earlier works. We encounter the Boyarina, the first of a succession of ill-starred women who would prove to be some of the most memorable creations in Tchaikovsky's subsequent operas. Whatever we may think of the dramatic hyperbole of *The Oprichnik*, the Boyarina comes over as a truly credible, and very Russian, woman: vulnerable because of her sex, yet courageous, patient in suffering, and possessed of a moral resolve that will make her prepared to curse to all damnation the son she loves for what she sees as his recourse to evil. From the aria that opens Act 2 we may gauge her troubled but dignified condition, then observe her moral firmness in her ensuing scene with her son. But if this has been a static one-to-one encounter, the next scene will be action packed. We meet the massed Oprichniks themselves with their commander, Vyazminsky, their music here overlaid with an ecclesiastical tone – for, like their master Ivan, they pretend to a religious devoutness, though even here there are also eruptions of their more truthful music of violence. Basmanov announces that Andrey's initiation into the Oprichniks' ranks is to take place, and Vyazminsky reacts with violent hostility, then shifts his ground as he sees how he can turn this to his own purposes. Andrey pleads his cause in a well-calculated aria (already presaged in the overture), and the initiation begins. What follows is powerful stuff, set in progress by the Oprichniks' terse theme, which will be a ubiquitous concern of the orchestra in what follows. The preliminaries over, Vyazminsky begins to administer the oath itself, the Oprichniks adding their collective voice. A brief abatement as Andrey realizes with horror that he must renounce both his mother and Natalya – but Vyazminsky demands obedience, and the Oprichniks remain adamant. More than once Andrey resists their demands (on one occasion, with Andrey rendered speechless by weeping, the orchestra has to act as his surrogate by recalling his pre-oath aria, while Vyazminsky mutters to himself gloatingly). Finally threatened by death if he will not accept the oath, Andrey yields. Whatever underlying reservations some listeners may have about the hyperbole and unashamed melodrama of this whole situation, there is no denying that Tchaikovsky's treatment (and pacing) of it was exactly what was required, right up to the final triumphal trumpeting of the massed Oprichniks' theme that brings the scene to the noisiest – and most audience-rousing – of conclusions.

To open Act 3, a chorus of the peasantry gives voice to its troubles, and prays to God for pity. The Boyarina laments her loneliness and her continuing anxieties concerning Andrey; a tiny chink of harmless mischief in an otherwise tormented world is provided by a bunch of urchins harassing her before being driven off by a group of men. The meeting between a desperate Natalya and a wise-counselling Boyarina consolidates further the latter's character, demonstrating that already Tchaikovsky can treat an intimate encounter such as this with a sensitivity that complements the panache with which he had handled the supercharged turmoil of the oath scene. Zhemchuzhny appears and Natalya begs to be heard, couching her appeal in the simplest possible terms which are reiterated exactly by the Boyarina, only to have her plea rejected.

What follows is a full-blown operatic finale – that is, an expansive movement concerned with some crucial incident marking a watershed in the plot, and in which the fullest-possible performing forces are mustered onstage to provide the opera's most grandiose display of stage spectacle and musical grandiloquence. It begins with the sounds of the Oprichniks' theme, signalling the approach of Andrey and his fellow Oprichniks. It might fairly be questioned whether Tchaikovsky was wise to use for a third time the music, to which both Natalya and the Boyarina had already pleaded with Zhemchuzhny, as the dressing for Andrey's plea to his mother to accept he is still the same son she had always known. Ignoring the urgent appeals of Basmanov and the Oprichniks that he should remember his oath to forsake his mother, he confesses he is an Oprichnik. The Boyarina's reaction is the most critical moment of the opera: to the insistent challenges of the Oprichniks' theme in the orchestra, she curses her son, then is led away.

The essential business of this Act being now over, the finale gets down to its real task – that is, to consolidate in both individual and corporate terms the supercharged dramatic atmosphere which the Boyarina's curse has fostered, and to reflect on its immediate impact and its consequences for the future. First the four principals – Andrey, Natalya, Basmanov and Zhemchuzhny – voice their individual reactions corporately in a quartet, to be in due course joined by the chorus, who reflect on the horror of the curse. It may be objected that, with such a multitude of voices simultaneously singing a variety of texts, no verbal sense can be grasped – though a skilful composer can ensure that, from time to time, certain crucial phrases from the individual participants can break the surface of the texture and be caught by the attentive listener. But in any case, by this stage we may fairly guess the matters and feelings that will be preoccupying the various participants, and the purpose of this vast ensemble becomes simply to give vent to the massed emotion these have engendered. This stage past, Basmanov takes the initiative; Andrey must beg the Tsar to release him from his vow. The chorus, now as much participants as observers, add their endorsement, and an even more prolonged ensemble rounds off the act.

It may be felt that the sheer scale that this finale attains was a miscalculation on Tchaikovsky's part – that he was guilty of overkill. It is indubitably a blockbuster, but there is no denying that it is also a powerful foil to the happier event that opens the last act. An audience of Tchaikovsky's time would have expected a liberal dose of dancing in an opera, and the entertainment attached to the wedding of Andrey and Natalya was a fair enough excuse for this, to which Tchaikovsky responded handsomely. True, this ballet clogs the action but, with the turbulence of what has gone before and the horrors that are to come, this period of respite has its positive side. Andrey now pledges undying loyalty to the Tsar, bids his comrades farewell (to which they respond) in one of the most indelibly Russian passages in the whole score (another appropriation from *The Voyevoda*), and reaffirms his loyalty to the Tsar (again his companions respond). But in the duet that ensues Natalya remains ill at ease, despite Andrey's reassurances, Tchaikovsky employing the main theme of his symphonic poem *Fatum* (withdrawn from circulation after Balakirev had condemned it), to set Natalya's troubled declaration of devotion. The guests' attempt at reassurance is ruptured by Basmanov's entry to forewarn of disaster, confirmed when Vyazminsky, with feigned affability, enters to deliver the Tsar's final requirement: to see the bride – and alone. In an ensemble Basmanov and the chorus beg Andrey to agree – and a finale evolves, involving all onstage. What follows is expeditiously treated: Andrey's defiance, Natalya's terror, the Oprichniks' theme increasingly assertive in the orchestra. Andrey is led away to execution and Vyazminsky leaves to fetch the Boyarina, her reappearance foretold in the orchestra by a portion of her exhortation to Andrey to submit to the will of God – and never to leave her. Even more expeditious is the end itself: the return of Vyazminsky with the Boyarina, her witnessing, through a window, the brutal act which destroys her, and the

Oprichniks (offstage) glorifying their Tsar to the theme that throughout the opera has constantly projected their true nature.

———

The premiere of *The Oprichnik* took place in St Petersburg in April
1874. Its reception was rapturous, and the opera was swiftly taken up
by other houses: by Odessa in August, Kiev in December, and by
Moscow the following May. It was Tchaikovsky's first great success,
and he might have been expected to revel in it. He did not. A fortnight
after the opening night he wrote to Modest:

> *The Oprichnik* torments me. This opera is so bad that I fled from all
> the rehearsals (especially those of Acts 3 and 4) so that I shouldn't
> hear a single sound, and at the performance I would willingly have
> vanished. Isn't it strange that when I had written it, it seemed to me
> initially such a delight. But from the very first rehearsal, what dis-
> enchantment! There's no movement, no style, no inspiration.

Tchaikovsky was too hard on himself and on the opera. But in recognizing that its subject was contrived – no more than a shock-horror
tale whose characters were caught up in extreme predicaments, and
whose consequent tensions and torments were designed simply to
manipulate audiences – he was pointing the way to his own future.
How much better in an opera to uncover the misfortunes, pains and
sorrows such as may arise in everyday life and afflict any one of us,
real people. Though some of his operas to come would contain tough,
sometimes harrowing situations, the ones that are most precious are
those that expose the sorrows (and joys) that we, as ordinary mortals,
can understand from our own observation and experiences. It is no
wonder that the Tchaikovsky opera that draws audiences again and
again is *Eugene Onegin*, Pushkin's tale of an innocent teenage girl who
is ultimately denied, by the chain of real-life circumstances and experiences into which she is caught, the love that would have given her
fulfilment and happiness.

8
High Nationalism:
Second Symphony and *The Tempest*

The broader pattern of Tchaikovsky's living during the summer of 1872 followed that of the previous year: first a visit to Kamenka and then, after two delightful days in Kiev with Modest, visiting friends and sightseeing, ten days with Kondratyev at Nizy and with Shilovsky at Usovo. But on leaving Usovo, Tchaikovsky was struck with disaster, prompting an episode he delighted in retelling for the amusement of his friends, though the joke was against himself. Arriving at the first staging post, he ate well; then, fortified by wine, and anxious to continue his journey, he demanded that the horses be harnessed. But the postmaster declared that this was impossible, and there followed a heated exchange, upon which Tchaikovsky called for the complaints book, signing himself 'Prince Volkonsky, gentleman of the Emperor's bed chamber'. Instantly an abjectly apologetic postmaster had had the carriage ready. It was at the next stop that Tchaikovsky discovered that he had forgotten to have his baggage loaded. Here the brothers' ways parted, and Tchaikovsky, not wishing to face the postmaster, sent an emissary to recover his possessions. But the postmaster insisted that its owner's eminence demanded that he should release the baggage only to 'Prince Volkonsky' in person. And so a very embarrassed Tchaikovsky was forced to make the journey himself. This time he dealt affably with the postmaster, finally enquiring his name. 'Tchaikovsky' was the reply. Mystified, Tchaikovsky suspected this was the postmaster's sharp-witted revenge. Enquiries revealed it was indeed his true name.

It was well that the baggage was recovered, for in it were the first sketches of Tchaikovsky's most important composition since *Romeo and Juliet*, his Second Symphony, the *Little Russian*, so called for its incorporation of three folksongs from the Ukraine (or 'Little Russia'). By now Tchaikovsky's dealings with Balakirev had also fostered contacts with the *kuchka* generally, and there began cautious relations with others in the group. In October 1871 Cui had published a gratifying article praising *Romeo and Juliet*, and Tchaikovsky had warmed to Borodin in particular as a man of 'gentle, subtle and refined nature' (as he recalled him in 1887 after Borodin's death). Of all Tchaikovsky's orchestral works, the *Little Russian* Symphony moved closest to the kind of musical world cultivated by Balakirev and his colleagues. It is also perhaps the most consistently joyful of all his non-operatic compositions, and this may be in part a reflection of his state of mind at this time. He had now completed *The Oprichnik*, and his personal disenchantment with that opera was still in the future. Anxieties over the Conservatoire's financial future had been relieved by a government grant, and Tchaikovsky's own salary had been increased by over a half, enabling him to move to a more comfortable apartment. In his now buoyant mood he gave every spare moment he could to the symphony. 'This work of genius (as Kondratyev calls my symphony) is close to completion,' he wrote in mid-November to Modest. 'I think it's my best composition as regards perfection of form, a quality for which I have not been conspicuous.' Three more weeks, and it was finished. That Christmas he introduced it to the *kuchka* in St Petersburg. Their response could not have been more favourable. 'I played the finale at a soirée at Rimsky-Korsakov's, and the whole company almost tore me to pieces in rapture – and Madame Rimskaya-Korsakova begged me in tears to let her arrange it for piano duet,' he further informed Modest. In February 1873, at an RMS concert in Moscow, it received its premiere, enjoying (so Tchaikovsky informed Vladimir Stasov) 'a great success, so great that Rubinstein wants to perform it again at the tenth concert of the RMS's season as by public demand. To tell the truth, I'm not completely satisfied with the first three movements, but "The Crane" itself [the finale, which employs most prominently a Ukrainian folktune with that title] hasn't come out so badly.' Two months later Rubinstein kept his promise, Tchaikovsky receiving an ovation after each movement, and a laurel wreath and silver cup at the end. Between these performances it had been introduced to St Petersburg; so popular was it that in May it was given for a third time in Moscow at a special RMS concert.

But before listening to the piece, a word of explanation. What we almost invariably encounter today as Tchaikovsky's Symphony No. 2, the *Little Russian*, is by no means the symphony as it was first heard. It was the opening movement that troubled Tchaikovsky, and seven years later he completely rewrote it, leaving only the slow introduction and coda untouched; at the same time, he made minor revisions in the remaining three movements. In fact, the original first movement had been a far more substantial and complex piece. As such, it balanced the finale well, and the comparatively lightweight slow movement provided the right degree of contrast to such a weighty utterance, such as is not required when the replacement first movement of 1879 is performed. Thus there were both gains and losses, a situation that still applies, whichever version of the symphony is played. Some of Tchaikovsky's contemporaries (including Sergey Taneyev, his former pupil – and, of all men, the one whose criticism of his own music Tchaikovsky valued most) were outspoken in preferring the original. For us, surely, the message is clear: both versions are valid, both are worth having, and which we prefer is our own business. But since the revised version is the official one that is still almost invariably played, that is the one that we will now investigate.

Symphony No. 2 in C minor (*Little Russian*) * * * * *

[The Second Symphony is one of Tchaikovsky's most approachable large-scale works – and especially the finale. It is no surprise it was so successful.]

Of all his large scale, multi-movement creations, the *Little Russian* Symphony is the most consistently accessible, and its structure one of the clearest. Moreover, it is such an engaging piece. The horn solo that opens the first movement's slow introduction presents the first of the symphony's three folksongs, and the tune is forthwith twice repeated intact, but with different backgrounds – a process that places it squarely in the national tradition initiated by Glinka. The scale of this introduction makes the conciseness of the following movement all the more striking, while the lucidity of the movement's material, the clarity of its outlines and its compactness makes finding one's way through it relatively easy. The first subject is a vigorous, bustling creation introduced by the strings; the second subject has two distinct themes, the first a gentle oboe melody, the second a generous but concise string tune (in fact, really a countermelody to the oboe tune, which is still present in the lower strings). But note also the fidgety little seven-note figure that unobtrusively punctuates both these tunes;

it will become far more prominent later. A sudden hush and a rather mysterious crescendo (the darkly rising bass is, in fact, the opening of the oboe theme, though now sounding very different), and the material from the energetic first subject resurges to round off the exposition.

Now the opening of the folksong from the introduction, partnered enthusiastically by the fidgety figure, returns to launch the development, which rapidly grows in complexity as the first subject asserts its right to be heard. Indeed, once that right has been claimed, it parades itself with increasing grandiloquence (and noise), leading us straight into the recapitulation. The latter is little more than a repeat of the exposition (with the expected adjustments of key), and though, towards its end, it might sound for a while as though the development will be rerun, it is not to be, and it is a brief return of the slow introduction's horn theme with one of its backgrounds that rounds off the movement.

The wedding march for the rejected opera *Undine* provided the main theme of the slow movement. It is a charming invention, heard over oscillating timpani taps, its delicacy making it thoroughly plausible as having once been the accompaniment to a nymph's nuptials. The movement is planned as a rondo (ABACABA, plus brief coda), the wedding march providing the A sections. The B sections (both absolutely identical) are marked by a simple dotted rhythm and are more expansive, while the central C section brings in the symphony's second folksong, sounding it four times to changing backgrounds before proceeding more freely. A delicate dying coda, incorporating tiny allusions to the B section's pervasive dotted rhythm, closes the movement.

The symphony's most arresting movement is its scherzo and trio, and the source for its special character may lie in Tchaikovsky's consolidating association with the *kuchka*. In 1869 Borodin's First Symphony had received its premiere, and Tchaikovsky's new acquaintance with the group, and their enthusiasm for *Romeo and Juliet*, would certainly have, in turn, drawn their recent works to his attention. In 1872 the relationship seemed to be thriving, and one wonders whether the scherzo of Tchaikovsky's Second Symphony would have come out quite the way it did if that of Borodin's First Symphony had not existed. What was so striking about Borodin's scherzo was its harmonic boldness – its spiciness, even pungency, and its quietly elemental rhythmic pulse. It had that very energy which the scherzo of Tchaikovsky's First Symphony, its rhythm confined within a single tiny cell, had lacked. And it is not just the rhythmic inventiveness that is so striking about Tchaikovsky's scherzo: constantly phrase lengths are being altered, fleeting melodic fragments may decorate the texture, even sometimes momentarily dislocate the momentum. Stop the music at any point and try to guess what will come next (if only what *sort* of music might come next), and you are likely to be wildly wrong – yet listen to the lot, and it sounds totally coherent. That is a mark of creative genius. As for the insistent quaver pulsing of the central trio, this provides the most extreme, but appropriate, of contrasts. The brief coda, like that in the First Symphony's scherzo, incorporates elements from both the scherzo and the trio.

However, it is the finale that is the real *tour de force* of the Second Symphony, and where Tchaikovsky's allegiance to the Glinka tradition is most complete. Here it is that the third folksong ('The Crane') comes into its own. First parading itself in a grandiose introduction (was this haunting Musorgsky's imagination when, two years later, he composed 'The Great Gate of Kiev' which so majestically rounds off his *Pictures at an Exhibition*?), it then declares its true and mischievous identity to launch the *Allegro vivo*, virtually monopolizing the next two minutes against a succession of varying backgrounds. So spacious a deployment leaves no time for a transition, and the very different second subject enters forthwith, its contrasting character nicely reinforced by a very abrupt and clear change of key. If its predecessor had been a merry Russian dance, this tune could almost be of South American provenance – for, with its slightly tipsy rhythm, it might be a lightly disguised, rather decorous rumba. But there is no containing its spirited companion, and it is the Russian tune that will soon monopolize the exposition's end.

All this has been dazzling, but it is eclipsed by what follows. The development is introduced by a series of widely striding notes, seeming to direct themselves whither they wish, like some sportive colossus. Against these the two subjects re-enter, and are taken on a bizarre journey, the second subject sometimes twisted in mid-course and even made to take on the personality of its boisterous companion. The trip becomes more heady, the excitement and turmoil ever greater. To change the metaphor: this is the strongest potion Tchaikovsky ever brewed. But when the recapitulation arrives, and firm ground is at last regained, it is the second subject that enters, Tchaikovsky having excised the first subject, with its further succession of changing backgrounds, in his 1879 revision (such a pity!). Further comment is unnecessary here. The recapitulation concluded, a brief recurrence of the striding theme, a single mighty stroke on the tam-tam, a moment of silence – and the *presto* coda brings the symphony to the most unbuttoned of conclusions.

————

As we have noted, Vladimir Stasov knew a great composer when he heard one, and during that evening at the Rimsky-Korsakovs' at Christmas 1872, when Tchaikovsky had roused the company to rapture over his new *Little Russian* Symphony, Stasov had talked to him about what the subject of his next composition would be. Within days he had come up with three proposals, of which two were by British authors: *Ivanhoe* by Sir Walter Scott and *The Tempest* by Shakespeare. Tchaikovsky reflected on these for a fortnight and then decided: for a second time it would be Shakespeare. But one point immediately troubled him:

> Does there need to be a tempest in *The Tempest*? That is, is it essential to depict the fury of the elements in a piece in which this incidental circumstance [the tempest] serves simply as the point of departure for the whole dramatic action? If a tempest is necessary, where should it go: at the beginning or in the middle? If it's not necessary, why not call the overture *Miranda*?

Stasov could not resist the opportunity this provided, and within a fortnight he had sent a programme for the whole piece. 'Should there be a tempest in *The Tempest*?' Tchaikovsky had asked. 'Of course there must be!' Stasov had replied:

> Certainly, certainly certainly! Without it the overture won't be an overture, and the whole programme will be changed! I have pondered every moment, both for their continuity and their contrasts. I had thought of presenting the sea twice, at the beginning and at the end – only at the beginning it would be *introductory*, quiet and gentle, and Prospero, uttering his magic words, would break the calm and raise a storm. But I think this storm should differ from all preceding ones in that it should begin *suddenly*, at full strength, in utter turmoil, and should not grow and arise *by degrees*, as normally happens. Let your storm rage and engulf the boat with the Italian princes in it, and let it immediately afterwards subside. And now, after this picture, let another begin – the enchanted island of wonderful beauty, and

Miranda passing across it with light tread, a creation of even more wonderful beauty – all sun, with a smile of happiness. A moment of conversation between her and Prospero – and immediately afterwards the youth, Ferdinand, who fills her with wonder, and with whom she immediately falls in love. I think a motif of someone who is falling in love, a substantial *crescendo* that bursts into bloom (this will be plainly drawn from the end of Shakespeare's Act 1) should exactly match the requirements of your talent and your whole nature. After this I would suggest the appearance of Caliban, a bestial and base slave, and then Ariel toying with the Italian princes: the inspiration for him is the lines which Shakespeare himself wrote at the end of the first act, to my mind a whole picture in themselves:

> Come unto these yellow sands,
> And then take hands:
> Courtsied when you have, and kiss'd –
> The wild waves whist:
> Foot it featly here and there;
> And, sweet sprites, the burden bear.

two strophes in all.

After Ariel, Miranda and Ferdinand should appear for a second time, but now at the height of their passion; then the majestic figure of Prospero, renouncing his magic power and sadly bidding farewell to all his past: finally a picture of the sea, now calm and quiet, lapping the desert and deserted island, while all the former brief inhabitants fly away in the boat to distant happy Italy.

Taking all this in order, I consider it quite impossible to omit the sea at the beginning and end, and to call the overture *Miranda*.

Tchaikovsky was delighted with Stasov's 'superb programme, enticing and inspiring to the highest degree', as he put it in his acknowledgement. But he did not intend to hurry and, in any case, an urgent (and lucrative) commission had intervened.

Tchaikovsky's **incidental music for Ostrovsky's The Snow Maiden****(*) is one of his least-known compositions. Two of Moscow's state-run theatres were the Maly ('Little') and the Bolshoy ('Big'), the former accommodating a dramatic troupe, the latter a Russian opera company and a ballet company. But as the Maly was closed for renovation early in 1873, it was decided that the drama company should move to the

Bolshoy and share in a new drama-music 'spectacular' involving all three companies. Ostrovsky was approached to provide the text, was enthusiastic, and chose as his subject the Russian folktale of the Snow Maiden who can survive only if her heart is never warmed by love. But, wishing to be as other girls, she enters the human world and innocently disrupts a wedding when the bridegroom falls in love with her. Accused of seduction by the bride, she is brought before Tsar Berenday and told she must marry. By now that is what the Snow Maiden herself also wishes but, being warmed by love, she is unprotected from the rays of the Sun God, and melts away. Tchaikovsky was commissioned to provide the music, composing it rapidly during March and early April. It comprised nineteen numbers incorporating at least a dozen folksongs and, though uneven in quality, some items are very attractive. Tchaikovsky's own verdict on it was affectionate: 'The Snow Maiden is not one of my best works, but it is one of my favourite offspring. I think the happy, spring-like mood with which I was filled at the time must be audible in the music.' If some enterprising choral-society-plus-orchestra (with, perhaps, a tenor soloist) should be seeking some effective but not very demanding material to complete a programme, then possibly a selection of pieces from Tchaikovsky's The Snow Maiden music might be worth investigating.

Having received 350 roubles for this Bolshoy commission, in June, after visits to Kondratyev at Nizy and sister Sasha and family at Kamenka, Tchaikovsky headed abroad. By now he was becoming something of a celebrity, and learning that Liszt, one of the most famed and respected of all contemporary musicians, had expressed a wish to meet him, he decided he would include Weimar, Liszt's current home, in his itinerary. But it was not to be. Instead he directed himself to Dresden, where he could enjoy the company of his publisher Jurgenson and his wife: then via Cologne to Zurich ('The Rhine falls are magnificent: Zurich's a charming place,' he noted in his diary), Berne, Vevey, Montreux and Geneva. Next Italy (Turin, Milan, Lake Como), but the heat drove him north to Paris, which was already his favourite European city. A week there, and his funds all but ran out – and so it was back to Russia. In mid-August he arrived at his final destination: Usovo. Here, on 19 August, now mentally refreshed – and undistracted by his often demanding host, Shilovsky, who was absent – he set to work on The Tempest.

'I cannot convey to you my state of bliss during these two weeks,' he would remember for his secret patroness, Nadezhda von Meck, in 1878:

I was in a kind of exalted, blissful frame of mind, wandering during the day alone in the woods, towards evening over the immeasurable steppes, and sitting at night by the open window, listening to the solemn silence of this out-of-the-way place – a silence broken only by some indistinguishable sound of the night. During these two weeks I wrote *The Tempest* in rough without any effort, as though moved by some supernatural force.

In fact it was composed in eleven days, though the scoring was delayed until after his return to Moscow in September.

The Tempest received its premiere that December in Moscow, with Nikolay Rubinstein conducting, and its success was sufficient to win it a second hearing before the concert season was over. But it was nearly a year before St Petersburg – and Stasov – heard it. The latter was in raptures:

What a delight your *Tempest* is! What an incomparable piece! Of course the storm itself is inconsequential and isn't marked by any originality, Prospero is unremarkable – and finally, near the end, there is a cadence just like something out of an Italian operatic finale. But these are three tiny blemishes. All the rest is wonder upon wonder! Caliban, Ariel, the love scene – all these have a place among the *loftiest* of musical creations. In both love scenes, what beauty, what languor, what passion! Then the magnificently wild, ugly Caliban, Ariel's miraculous flights and sporting – all these are absolutely capital! And, again, the orchestration in these scenes – wonderful! Both of us, Rimsky-Korsakov and I, send you our profound, most profound compliments.

Balakirev, too, approved, and even Cui, who had crucified Tchaikovsky for his *Ode to Joy*, his graduation exercise, was won over: 'a most fine, most impassioned, talented composition, wonderfully, sonorously and beautifully scored,' he wrote for his St Petersburg readership.

Symphonic Fantasia: *The Tempest* * * * *

[The Tempest *is not as consistently excellent a piece as* Romeo and Juliet, *but it offers some very good descriptive listening, and some of the other music, especially that which relates to the participants in the story, is superb.*]

As has been noted, back in January, when Tchaikovsky had voiced to Stasov some of his own uncertainties about *The Tempest*'s proposed content, he had prompted that old autocrat to an instant detailed prescription for the whole piece, and this now proved as profoundly important for Tchaikovsky as had Balakirev's for *Romeo and Juliet* (in fact, it is almost a programme note for what Tchaikovsky went on to create in his symphonic fantasia). Though both subjects were taken from Shakespeare, their natures were fundamentally different. *Romeo and Juliet* had been the precisely focused story of a feud between two families, and of the disastrous consequences for two young lovers who had dared to challenge that mutual hatred. Since this dual focus was so clear, it could be played out musically through the duality fundamental to sonata form, the two forces first presented as the two very contrasted subjects of a sonata movement, with Friar Laurence, the compassionate observer, in the preceding introduction; the development had then projected the conflict and the peacemaker's unavailing urgings as mediator, and the recapitulation the disastrous consequences of his failure, with the coda a tragic epilogue. But there was no such single, focused issue in *The Tempest*. Where *Romeo and Juliet* was a human drama of close engagement, *The Tempest* presented a world of both enchantment and humanity, inhabited by an exiled magician, a sprite, a grotesque, and two very human lovers, disparate beings caught into a fantasy plot with a variety of outcomes. Sonata form could not have worked here, and Stasov's very different programme focused on each of these elements in a series of separate, contrasted sections. Tchaikovsky accepted this scheme fully, but amplified it into a mirror structure so as to present a musically balanced whole:

The sea	Prospero raises a furious storm	Miranda and Ferdinand – love scene part I	Ariel	Caliban	Miranda and Ferdinand – love scene part II	Miranda and Ferdinand –	Prospero renounces his magic powers	The sea

As this diagram shows, the sea provides the flanks, Prospero's two crucial actions (the raising of the tempest, and his renunciation of his magic powers) are symmetrically placed, the lover's two scenes (their meeting, and their ultimate commitment) likewise. The portrayals of Ariel and Caliban provide the central pivot.

Russian composers have always had a special flair for the fantastic, whether visual or atmospheric, and Tchaikovsky's creative powers were fired to the full by this so diverse assortment of imaginative challenges. Navigating one's way through *The Tempest* raises few problems, each section being so vividly conjured or characterized. First the sea, still calm, though constantly in gentle motion with woodwind flickerings across its surface – but also awesome and vast, the background to a solemn brass phrase – Prospero's thematic surrogate, surely. The music gathers momentum, the magician thrice utters his incantation – and the tempest erupts and rages with intimidating violence, Prospero's phrase signifying his personal control of the elements. Next Miranda, her cello phrase sounding the more tenderly after the tumult, while the pauses, and especially the tremulous flutterings, reflect the nervousness of a girl who has never before seen any man, other than her father. Twice her cello phrase recurs, each time some of its intervals widened: her interest and assurance is strengthening – and then follows, surely, the broader, more masculine declaration of Ferdinand. This is exquisitely done. Now confidence and commitment grow, and the fading conclusion to this whole amorous episode is wonderful, especially for some of its harmonic touches.

The lovers have departed, we may presume, to be truly alone. Now it is the supernaturals' turn, Ariel fleet and fantastic – but it is the grotesque, blundering Caliban who is the more graphically projected, already displaying Tchaikovsky's gift for vivid caricature. At length we hear Prospero's impatience with Caliban asserting itself, and the lovers return, the nervous viola line underlining their still veiled but growing inner excitement. Again their love music dies away. But this is not the end, simply a moment of suspense before constraint suddenly vanishes, and a final, passionate commitment is made. And so a silence, a swift, frenzied string *crescendo*, and the love music bursts in again, *quintuple forte*, the loudest dynamic marking Tchaikovsky had ever written. Then we hear Prospero, in equally unequivocal terms, renounce his magic powers, and it is the sea music, this time finally fading into silence, that signals the disappearance of the mortals beyond the horizon, bound for their homeland 'in distant, happy Italy'.

The success of *The Tempest* at its premiere clearly raised Tchaikovsky's morale, and within little more than a fortnight he had begun his next major work, his Second String Quartet. Completed during January 1874, it was tried out at a soirée in mid-February, where the select listeners greeted it warmly (except, that is, for Tchaikovsky's old teacher, Anton Rubinstein, who happened to be present and had little sympathy with the direction his former pupil's music had taken), and it was received with equal enthusiasm at its premiere in March.

String Quartet no. 2 in F * * * (*)

[The Second Quartet will clearly be of interest to those readers who are drawn to chamber music. It is a less engaging piece than the First Quartet, and less characterful than the Third Quartet, still to come. Nevertheless, the slow movement is a substantial and particularly affecting piece. Chamber music buffs should pause here and, on the assumption that they are likely to be people who already have at least a fair knowledge of the quartet repertoire, I have set this one in a wider context, as well as examining the piece itself. But I recognize that the whole quartet will be of interest to only a small minority of my readers, but those who are interested in the slow movement should jump ahead to pp. 82–3, where I discuss this movement. Other readers can, of course, choose to pass on to chapter 9, which deals with one of the most unclouded – and, in some ways, most surprising – works Tchaikovsky ever wrote – and one of which, I imagine, few of my readers will ever have heard.]

Even allowing for the difference in medium, the style of Tchaikovsky's Second String Quartet could hardly be further removed from that of *The Tempest* – or, indeed, from that of his First Quartet. Though string quartets were being composed in Russia in the earlier part of the nineteenth century, they were neither plentiful nor in any way comparable with those of the contemporary Viennese classical tradition, and the quartet had remained a minority interest in Russian concert life up to Tchaikovsky's time. Fundamental to the quartet market were the often significant expatriate German communities in the larger cities, and to such connoisseurs of the great West European tradition a modest quartet such as Tchaikovsky's First must have seemed thoroughly acceptable, but unambitious. We can only guess that this provided a prime motivation for its very different successor. Larger in scale and more weighty in content, where the First Quartet had sought to entertain (in the best sense), the Second clearly aspired to emulate the scale and ambition of the great products of the German–Austrian school as represented by Beethoven. The first two bars of the slow introduction suggest a shift westward, for it has been observed that lurking distantly behind these is what is probably the most famous musical moment in all post-Beethoven nineteenth-century music: the opening of Wagner's great music drama, *Tristan and Isolde* (those readers who happen to know that opera will, I think, find it interesting to check this point for themselves). There are also some strange moments in some of what immediately follows; where may this music be leading? Yet we arrive soon on stable ground, for when, after a great flourish from the leader, the main body of the movement begins, we could hardly be in a more untroubling world. Instead, the insistence seems to be on fluency, clarity and balance in a movement of spacious dimensions and no expressive surprises.

And yet – after the so vividly contrasting turmoils and tenderness of *The Tempest*, can we recognize this as by the same composer? And if not, are we to judge this music as inferior? That depends. If we are listening for music that instantly says, 'Tchaikovsky!', and if we believe that this quality is essential before the piece can be rated as of supreme quality, we still need to be cautious, for not every piece that sounds thoroughly characteristic of Tchaikovsky is necessarily a masterpiece. The *1812* Overture is one of his most characteristic works, but it is not one of his greatest (though elsewhere I have defended it from the blanket denigration that it has often suffered), its blemish being primarily one of overstatement, especially towards its end. Tchaikovsky himself was often very aware of the shortcomings in his own pieces, especially in matters of form. As has already been noticed, with his very natural way of building his more ambitious symphonic pieces in expansive and highly focused stretches, one of his particular problems when using sonata form could be getting smoothly from his first to his second subject. (As he himself once frankly put it, 'My seams always show.') And it was probably an awareness that Beethoven's ability to compose truly organic transitions was one of that composer's strengths that made Tchaikovsky rein in his more rampant creativity in this new quartet, firmly containing his most natural impulses, and inventing music that was still original, but with the component parts rigorously proportioned to ensure a balanced and integrated whole.

To this end the melodic material of the Second Quartet's first movement is far less arresting, more concise and less self-assertive than we might have anticipated, thus facilitating far greater flexibility in what is built from it. In fact, the form of Tchaikovsky's first movement reflects closely the outlines of a typical Beethoven first movement. There are two subjects linked by a classically modelled transition, the proportions of the development and recapitulation also reflecting those of a typical first movement of fifty years earlier, and there is an expressive single-mindedness that is never waylaid by surprises: contrasts are there, but always only relative. While *The Tempest*, being written to a programme, was a piece pre-ordained to be a rich array of dazzlingly varied materials deployed in distinct, highly characterized, and very contrasted sections, the Second Quartet's first movement uses expressively modest, succinct materials to build an expansive, integrated experience rich in its detail, that is (and this is most important of all) greater than the sum of its parts. Commentators have sometimes referred to this process as 'an argument' (that is, as a coherently unfolding process), and it requires quiet, attentive listening.

Such is the condition I find of the Second Quartet's first movement; it wins my respect, but only a portion of my affection. However, the middle two movements, and especially the second of these, are rather different matters. Listeners confronting the second movement, the *Scherzo*, for the first time may be struck by its slightly tipsy gait. The vast bulk of music that we normally experience is written in bars of consistent length. But here Tchaikovsky mixes his bar lengths, using the same tiny 2+2+3-bar (that is, two two-beat bars, plus one three-beat bar: try counting through a bit of this) phrase length almost throughout, but occasionally stretching it to 2+2+2+3 – once, even to 2+2+2+2+3. It imparts a special character to this quietly engaging music, thrown into relief by the regular three-beat metre of the waltz-like trio.

After these two relatively detached (in the expressive sense) movements, the *Andante ma non tanto* slow movement strikes home the more powerfully. But while it is the succession of six plangent, silence-separated phrases that sets the tragic tone, it is the following four-bar phrase, each bar founded on the same tiny three-note drooping figure, that will prove by far the more important. This figure had been pre-echoed in both the third and sixth of those preliminary phrases, and it will be not only within the recurrences of this new phrase that it will be heard; it may crop up anywhere, becoming the nucleus of whole stretches of the movement (in all, it recurs over eighty times). One of the problems for any writer on music is to fix clearly for his reader the expressive character of a piece, and (this is the trickiest thing) to assess how much of its character has been objectively determined by its creator, and how much may be subjective. Some writers scorn the idea that such emotional self-confession can truly exist in music (music is out there – and that's that!), and unless we know (as we do in some instances) that the composer was consciously responding to some circumstance, great caution is needed. But there is in this seemingly pain-filled music an intensity – indeed, an obsessiveness – not previously displayed anywhere in Tchaikovsky's music, though this intensity will become a familiar element in some of his works to come. Whatever the case, this drooping figure recurs time and again in this movement with, finally, an almost lacerating insistence, and especially after the central section has produced the whole quartet's dynamic *fff* climax; then finally, after a portion of the central section, now *pp* and *tranquillo*, has brought some ease, this morsel, so tiny but so telling, will also, three-fold and *ppp*, bring a kind of peace at the movement's end.

This movement has brought into Tchaikovsky's work for the first time an element that may be autobiographical, not in the sense of reflecting a particular incident or relationship, but rather a prevailing inner mood or reaction. It is significant, perhaps, that in the autumn of 1873 Modest noticed his brother's fits of depression becoming longer, stronger and more frequent, and that in December he had confessed to a sense of personal isolation. Yet his next major composition after this quartet would be not only one of his finest, but one of his most unclouded. Nor does he let this slow movement provide the Quartet's final mood, for the *Finale* returns to the style of the first movement. As was not uncommon in finales of classical quartets, this one makes no attempt to outdo that movement either in expressive ambition or in its scale (rather less than half that of the first movement); instead it provides a lively culmination and exit to the whole piece. It is cast as a rondo (ABACABA), the melody of the B section the one lyrical element in an otherwise bustling piece, the C episode a constant rattle of semiquavers, with the A theme used on its final recurrence as the subject for a fugue leading into an unexpected rerun of the B theme, then an ebullient coda.

———

9
Two Contrasting Masterpieces: *Vakula the Smith/Cherevichki* and First Piano Concerto

In 1872 the Grand Duchess Elena Pavlovna created a competition for an opera on a libretto by Yakov Polonsky, drawn from Gogol's story, *Christmas Eve*. The prize was 1,500 roubles, with a guarantee of performance at the Maryinsky Theatre. The administration was entrusted to the RMS, but the Grand Duchess's death early the following year disrupted progress, and the closing date was settled as 1 (by our calendar, 13) January 1875, though finally it was revised to seven months later (1/13 August 1875). Tchaikovsky had read Gogol's story when he was only nine, but its magic remained for him, and he determined to enter. With the completion of his Second String Quartet in January 1874 he had to direct his attention to the impending production of *The Oprichnik* but, as has been noted, he turned violently against that opera, so much so that on 25 April, the day after its premiere, he fled to Western Europe. His mood was dreadful. After a day in Venice ('a city as gloomy as if it were dead') he headed for Rome, which he found lifeless, though some of the historical remains interested him, and in the Vatican, St Peter's basilica ('that triumphal summit of human genius') overwhelmed him. Thence to Naples, where he made the obligatory round of tourist visits, though only the ruins of Pompeii really intrigued him: 'I made the tour first with the inevitable guide, but later I detached myself and went round the whole town again, but now alone, going into nearly every house, surrendering myself to dreams, and trying to imagine to myself life in this place that was buried alive.' But underneath, thoughts of *The Oprichnik* haunted him, and his longing for Russia grew – not for St Petersburg and that hateful opera, but for Moscow where, in any case, he should have been teaching. Passing through Florence, by mid-May he was back home, his spirits much improved. On 13 June, immediately after the Conservatoire term ended, he directed himself to Kondratyev's at Nizy, intent on setting about *Vakula the Smith*, as the opera would be called, without delay, for still he thought the earlier closing date applied.

His working conditions at Nizy were ideal:

> I get up at six-thirty, drink five glasses of mineral water, the first at seven. From tea at nine until midday I read and play the piano (mainly Schumann): at noon lunch, work from then until three – that is, composing *Vakula*: from three to five the first session of bezique (to which I have taken a great liking), then a bath and dinner: after dinner a walk by myself, lasting about two hours, then I sit outside in the porch: at nine tea, and soon after that a second session of bezique, and at eleven or eleven thirty bedtime. This routine has been going on essentially unchanged for a fortnight.

In fact, so entranced was Tchaikovsky by Polonsky's libretto that within six weeks composition of the whole opera was virtually completed, and within three further weeks it was scored, the whole operation having taken no more than ten weeks. Over the next three weeks he spent some time getting it into its absolutely final form. This done, he promptly despatched it to the RMS.

All entries to the competition had to be submitted anonymously, and Tchaikovsky chose 'Ars longa, vita brevis' as his mark, though he must have realized that his identity could not remain unknown, for Rimsky-Korsakov, one of the judges, would recognize his handwriting. But in any case, desperate to see a production of his new creation in which he felt such pride, he had soon approached the chief producer at the Maryinsky to have it mounted ahead of the competition. Worse still, he then allowed the overture to receive a concert performance, conducted by Nikolay Rubinstein, another of the judges. By now he should have been expelled from the competition. Yet he was not and, in May 1876, with the judgement still not yet made, he offered to play *Vakula* through to Rimsky at the piano; even worse, in mid-October, Rimsky himself *wrote* to Tchaikovsky that he 'didn't doubt for a moment but that your opera will get the prize'. Perhaps it was to save some of the embarrassment the judges must have felt over these monstrous irregularities that their verdict noted that Tchaikovsky's opera was 'deemed worthy of the prize not as *relatively the best*, but as the *only one* that measures up to the artistic demands of the competition'.

Vakula was produced in 1876. During rehearsals the enthusiasm was enormous, but the opera's reception was disappointing. Yet despite muted audience response, it played to good houses, and was revived in each of the following three seasons. Tchaikovsky was quick to spot what he thought was amiss: as he put it, it would have been better if 'I had restrained more my purely musical inspiration, and been less forgetful of the conditions required for that *theatrical and scenic effectiveness* peculiar to the operatic style'. And so in 1885 he drastically revised the opera, renaming it *Cherevichki* (after the high-heeled boots worn by Ukrainian women).

Cherevichki (the version we shall examine) was first heard in 1887, conducted by Tchaikovsky himself. Still the audiences seemed merely respectful – yet still Tchaikovsky remained philosophical: 'For the moment the opera rouses interest rather than affection. I think that *Cherevichki*, like *Eugene Onegin* [Tchaikovsky's most popular opera], will be performed without much audience clamour – but that, little by little, people will come to love it.' Sadly, he would never see this himself.

Cherevichki: opera in four acts****

[*First, I will claim that* Cherevichki *is as fine as any of Tchaikovsky's operas 'in its own way'. That last remark is critical, and it is only that the very special character of the piece will not appeal to all music-lovers that I have not given it a five-star rating. No piece could be further removed from the real-life dramas of his later operas,* Eugene Onegin *and* The Queen of Spades, *where painfully real human beings are caught into situations of terrible torment which we can instantly understand, and which thus can touch us very directly and very deeply. However,* Cherevichki's *setting is an imaginary Ukrainian village; its characters are peasants or supernaturals (and there's a devil in it, too), and the tale is a comic fantasy. Though it contains some very powerful music, mostly* Cherevichki's *strengths lie in the wonderfully vivid and precise way in which Tchaikovsky catches the world, the actions, and the personalities of his simple characters in music which matches them so perfectly, subtly, sometimes so touchingly, sometimes so comically: imagine a scene in which there is a quintet for an attractive woman (a witch) and her four would-be lovers (three of them concealed in large jars, so that they each have to pop their heads out of the top when required to sing), and you get a taste of what is in store. This opera really needs to be seen staged, which only happens very rarely. But with the libretto in front of you,* Cherevichki *can make excellent listening if you have a taste for such things.*

Cherevichki is what we might classify as a comic fantasy, but in its imaginary world there are human beings, especially the two lovers, who feel human emotions that are as painful as those in real life. The plot has more funny detail than can be set out here:

Act 1 Scene 1. *A street in Dikanka on Christmas Eve.* Solokha – a witch, and also the mother of Vakula (his DNA must be interesting!) – muses how she might ensnare a man. The Devil, looking like any ordinary human – though with mini-horns and, like Solokha, with a tiny forked tail – surprises her from behind and pinches her bottom. They tease each other and a comic love scene develops. Finally Solokha disappears into her cottage. Alone, the Devil reveals his fury with Vakula, who has painted a picture of him in the church which makes him look ridiculous, and which makes the other devils laugh at him. In revenge he raises a great storm so that Chub, father of the beautiful Oxana, will not be able to get to the inn; this will make it impossible for Vakula to visit his beloved. The Devil follows Solokha into the cottage and both, now in their supernatural forms, fly out of the chimney and up to the moon. But when Chub and his friend Panas emerge from Chub's cottage, they somehow grope their way to the inn.

Act 1 Scene 2. *Chub's cottage.* Oxana, alone, is admiring herself before her mirror, and singing about a young girl who longs for love. Vakula enters and she demands impatiently why he has not made the trunk he has promised her. He replies that it is nearly finished, and all he wants now is to gaze at her, and talk. He breaks into a passionate declaration of love, but she rejects him, and exits. Chub enters, so covered with snow that Vakula does not recognize him, and ejects him. Oxana reappears, Vakula discovers his mistake, and is crestfallen. Oxana pretends to love another young man. Vakula becomes increasingly distressed: 'You're not a girl – you're a snake in the grass,' he shouts, and rushes out. Alone, Oxana is contrite, and when revellers enter, she will not join in. They leave, and she admits to herself her love for Vakula.

Act 2 Scene 1. *Solokha's cottage.* Solokha enters as the Devil emerges from the stove. She has had a hectic night, and her broomstick's been broken. The Devil flirts with her, she says she is weary, but still joins in a gopak (a lively, two-in-a-bar dance). A sudden knock at the door. The Devil is worried: it is the Mayor who, when drunk, keeps crossing himself, which the Devil finds disconcerting. The Devil hides in a coal sack, and the Mayor enters. He flirts with an unwilling Solokha – but suddenly yet another knock is heard, the Mayor hides in a second sack, and the Schoolmaster enters. Solokha reproves him, especially because he is married; he sings a ditty in praise of her – but suddenly another knock is heard. The Schoolmaster hides in a third sack, and Chub enters. He is warmly received, a little love scene develops – but suddenly yet another knock is heard. Chub hides, but in the sack already occupied by the Schoolmaster. All four heads poke out of the sacks and, with Solokha, join in a quintet. The heads all disappear as Vakula enters. Left alone by Solokha, he decides to take the sacks to his smithy. Singing of his passion and pain, he mechanically loads them (expressing surprise at their weight), then leaves.

Act 2 Scene 2. *A street in Dikanka.* Girls and lads approach, singing: the old folk join in. Oxana and Odarka, another girl, appear. Vakula enters with the sacks, and Oxana torments him. Spying Odarka's cherevichki, Oxana wants a pair for herself, and Vakula offers to procure them – but Oxana wants a pair belonging to the Tsaritsa [the Tsar's wife]: if he can get them, she will marry him. The young people leave to play snowballs. Alone, Vakula gives voice to his desperate longing for Oxana. Re-entering, Oxana repeats her condition, but the crowd soon take Vakula's part, and Oxana realizes she may have gone too far. Vakula, carrying the sack containing the Devil, leaves with the young women. The young men notice the wriggling in the remaining sacks, untie them, and the Mayor, the Schoolmaster and Chub jump out. The first two leave abruptly, but Chub good-naturedly turns their mishap into a joke.

Act 3 Scene 1. *Moonlight on a river bank.* A distant lament from rusalkas (water nymphs) disturbs a grumpy woodgoblin. Vakula enters with the sack, and again laments. The Devil jumps out of the sack and demands Vakula's soul in return for getting Oxana for him. But Vakula outwits the Devil, who concedes defeat, and promises him anything he wants. 'Take me to the Tsaritsa,' Vakula commands. In an aerial flight on the Devil's back he is whisked off to St Petersburg.

Act 3 Scene 2. *A reception room in the royal palace.* The Devil flies in with Vakula. Some Cossacks, who have been summoned to the Tsaritsa, enter. Vakula asks to join them, they reply that their business is private, but the Devil points out, enigmatically, that Vakula's presence might help them. The Cossacks learn that they are to be taken to the Great Hall.

Act 3 Scene 3. *The Great Hall*. A grand polonaise is in progress. The Prince enters to report a great victory, and delivers an ode written to glorify the event. A minuet begins, and the Cossacks are told that their petition will be answered. One of the Cossacks nudges Vakula to make his request for the Empress's cherevichki. General amusement – but a servant is sent to bring them. Vakula is overwhelmed. More dancing: a Russian dance, and a Cossack dance. The Prince invites all guests to see a play. The Devil reappears, and bears Vakula back towards the Ukraine.

Act 4. *A sunny Christmas morning in Dikanka*. Solokha and Oxana are bewailing Vakula's disappearance. Villagers emerge from Mass. Oxana cannot be persuaded to go with them to the Christmas feast, and goes out, weeping. Chub enters and invites the men to feast at his house, looks round for Oxana, and is cross she is not there. Suddenly Vakula is seen approaching. The crowd question him, Solokha greets him, and goes in search of Oxana. Vakula begs Chub's pardon for throwing him out of his own house. Chub forgives him, and asks what he wants. 'Oxana' is the answer, of course. The young men support Vakula, Chub agrees and, as Oxana enters, Vakula offers her the cherevichki. 'I don't need them . . . I don't want them . . . without them I'm . . .' she stutters. Chub gives the couple his blessing and orders the kobza players to praise them. All join in.

Each of Tchaikovsky's operas begins with the expected overture, but these display much variety. Those to *Eugene Onegin* and the one-act *Iolanta* are the briefest (a mere two and a half minutes each), that to *Cherevichki* the longest. It is, in fact, a full sonata-form movement (with slow introduction) founded on three themes from the opera. The introduction introduces us to a portion of Oxana's Act 1 aria, a flow of fresh and free-ranging melody that will catch the excitement of a young woman who has awakened to her own attractiveness and foreseen its power, which she will so thoughtlessly misuse. The sprightly music of the first subject is the gopak from early in Act 2, a piece for the opera's two supernaturals. The fourth principal is Vakula himself, presented in the broad string melody that comes next (the second subject): this young man sounds strong, trustworthy and emotionally generous.

Folksong stylizations (that is, tunes composed to sound like folk-songs) can turn up anywhere in *Cherevichki*, as can the genuine article. When the curtain rises Solokha introduces herself with a true folk-song, and her comic scene with the Devil is delightful (note how judicious and sensitive the orchestral scoring is here, and in so much of the opera). But if we should think all the supernaturals' music will be thus, the storm that the Devil conjures disabuses us; you may be able to out-wit him, but clearly he can also command awesome forces, and the melody that rides through the ensuing storm is one of Tchaikovsky's strongest. Panas's and Chub's blizzard-ridden search for the village inn gives us our first sight of the opera's rougher peasantry; then the storm abates and we are led, via an orchestral transition, into Oxana's room for the second scene.

Now the two arias anticipated in the Overture will be amplified, Oxana's into one of self-revelation, Vakula's into a fervent confession of love. To get the best from this opera it is really necessary to follow a translation of the libretto, not only to understand what is going on, but also how tactfully pointed is so much of Tchaikovsky's music. This whole scene is beautifully handled. But whereas this scene is much concerned with a very sensitive human relationship, it will be the lively characterization and humour that, above all, will mark the first scene of Act 2. Again Solokha and the Devil get matters moving with a bout of teasing leading to the gopak from the overture, but the following episode of Solokha with her would-be lovers is yet more entertaining. The latter enter in turn, the Mayor first (portly and pompous), the Schoolmaster next (an unfaithful, creepy little bore, who insists on singing a rather awful, gawky song), and then Chub (unpolished, hardly eloquent, but good-humoured), the man Solokha is after. As for the quintet that, with heads poking in turn out of the sacks, follows – this is hilarious, and a further confirmation of Tchaikovsky's very real sense of humour. And at the other expressive extreme, the sorrowful yet dignified melody that Vakula sings as he leaves with the sacks is mint Tchaikovsky.

So far *Cherevichki* has been mainly concerned with the principal characters in one-to-one encounters, and the chorus's role has been small. That is now to change, as we learn from the very elaborate chorus of mutual greeting that launches the second scene of Act 2. This is, at least in part, determined by an opera audience's expectations not only of the sound of massed voices, but also of spectacle. And the action gathers pace and energy, Oxana increasingly carried away by her very public taunting of Vakula and her demand that he obtain the Empress's cherevichki, with the chorus prominent both as sonorous background and, in their corporate exchanges with the solo singers, as participants in the action. Then, to balance the huge opening ensemble, all culminates in a finale, an abrupt pause in the action to crystallize the feelings of those present. It is set off by a heart-broken Vakula, soon joined by a desperately repentant Oxana, the chorus adding their weight, fearful of what Vakula might do. There is a studied formality about all this which has resonances from a more Western operatic tradition – which, in turn, brings home just how original a piece of work *Cherevichki* otherwise is. But a touch of humour rounds off the scene.

However, as stage spectacle this will be topped by the pomp and splendour of the Empress's court in the third scene of Act 3. But first the plot's thread must be spun further. In Act 3's opening scene an offstage five-beats-to-the-bar chorus of water nymphs, their sultry tone suggestive of an oriental provenance, upsets a tetchy wood goblin, establishing a hauntingly melancholy tone for Vakula's entry with his Devil-occupied sack. Vakula's fine aria reaffirms his despondent condition, but his fortunes quickly take a turn for the better, and the aerial ride from the Ukraine to St Petersburg (five hundred miles at least, surely) is accomplished to the lively sounds of an orchestral gopak, and is clearly ultra-supersonic, to judge from its brevity. If the 'cherevichki' scene had brought forward the chorus, what now follows is dominated by the ballet. After Vakula's encounter with the Cossacks, a huge orchestral build-up prepares for a magnificent choral–orchestral polonaise to abet the stage spectacle. At the opposite extreme is the decorous offstage minuet, especially significant as the first of a whole series of rococo (that is, late eighteenth-century) pastiches that would appear in Tchaikovsky's work over the years, prompted by his reverence for 'the divine Mozart'. Against this background Vakula's business is transacted, and the official ballet resumes with a Russian Dance and Cossack Dance, and ends with the second aerial ride.

Act 4 finds us back in Dikanka where the story began, and a whole world away from what we have just heard. Now the responses roused by all that has gone before are exposed and resolved, beginning with Solokha's and Oxana's plangent, heartfelt lament at Vakula's disappearance, and ending with Vakula's stammered apology to Chub for his misdemeanour in the first scene (the orchestra recalling his Act 1 declaration of love, thus uncovering the deeper motivation behind his present words); this is followed by Oxana's tearful acceptance of the cherevichki, backed with gentle irony by the music to which she had once so brutally challenged Vakula to obtain them. The final celebration of happiness is launched by the lusty music that had ended the overture.

Vakula/Cherevichki is unique among Tchaikovsky's operas, and this may partially explain successive audiences' muted response. *The Oprichnik*, a conventional melodrama, had been taken up quickly by other opera houses, largely because of its sensationalism and matchingly supercharged music. But *Vakula* (as it then was) was too far removed from conventional reality, its characters, though beautifully etched, too plebeian, and the tale it tells too unassuming to rouse audiences, the happy charm of its ending incapable of manipulating the listener as could the shock-horror conclusion of *The Oprichnik*. Yet, taken on its own terms, *Cherevichki* makes for an evening that is not only amusing but also rather touching. Above all, it is rich in musical inventiveness, in its freshness and sureness of dramatic touch, and in its conjuring of a gallery of real characters, even down to the most minor roles. Tchaikovsky himself never lost faith in this opera; indeed, as his brother Modest later recorded, 'he always retained a particularly soft spot for *Cherevichki*, and until his death remained convinced it was the best of his operas.'

Tchaikovsky's own account of Nikolay Rubinstein's reaction when he played over to him his new First Piano Concerto will already be well known to many Tchaikovsky aficionados. It is not certain exactly when Tchaikovsky set about his most famous and finest concerto, though it was within only two months of putting the finishing touches to the first version of *Cherevichki*, and the new piece was completed within a further seven weeks. Tchaikovsky's hope was that Nikolay would give the first performance in the New Year, and at the beginning of January he introduced the concerto to him. Tchaikovsky's account of what ensued was penned to Nadezhda von Meck some three years later. Having played through the first movement, Tchaikovsky awaited Rubinstein's reaction:

Not a single word, not a single comment! Rubinstein's eloquent silence had tremendous significance. It was as though he was saying

93

to me, 'My friend, can I talk about details when the very essence of the thing disgusts me?' I fortified my patience, and played on to the end. Again silence. I got up and asked, 'Well?' It was then that there began to flow from Nikolay Grigorevich's mouth a stream of words, quiet at first, but subsequently assuming more and more the tone of Jove the Thunderer. It appeared that my concerto was worthless, that it was unplayable, that passages were trite, awkward and so clumsy that it was impossible to put them right, that as composition it was bad and tawdry, that I had filched this bit from here and that bit from there, that there were only two or three pages that could be retained, and that the rest would have to be scrapped or completely revised. 'Take this, for instance – whatever is it?' (at this Rubinstein played the passage concerned, caricaturing it). 'And this? Is this really possible?' – and so on, and so on. I can't convey to you the most significant thing – that is, the *tone* in which all this was delivered. In a word, any outsider who chanced to come into the room might have thought that I was an imbecile, an untalented scribbler who understood nothing, who had come to an eminent musician to pester him with his rubbish. I was not only stunned, I was mortified by the whole scene.

I left the room and silently went upstairs. I could say nothing because of my agitation and anger. Rubinstein soon appeared and, noticing my distraught state, drew me aside into a distant room. There he told me again that my concerto was impossible, and after pointing out to me a lot of places that required radical change, he said that if by such-and-such a date I would revise the concerto in accordance with his demands, then he would bestow upon me the honour of playing my piece in one of his concerts. '*I won't change a single note*,' I replied, '*and I'll publish it just as it is now!*' And so I did!

As far as we know Tchaikovsky was true to his word. Nevertheless – and perhaps very significantly – when the concerto was first performed in October, it was not in Russia nor even in Europe, but in Boston, USA: if there was to be a disaster, then at least it would be far from home. The soloist was Hans von Bülow, one of the great pianists and conductors of the later nineteenth century, who reported a resounding success, further performances even gaining an encore for the finale. The Russian premiere, in St Petersburg, followed a month later. Within three weeks Moscow had heard it, with Taneyev as soloist, and with – of all people – Nikolay Rubinstein conducting. Clearly the latter had begun revising his opinion; indeed, he subsequently learned the piano part and became one of the concerto's strongest advocates.

Piano Concerto no. 1 in B flat minor * * * * *

[There is no need for me to commend the First Piano Concerto to Tchaikovsky-lovers, and it is a must for those who, as yet, may be unfamiliar with it.]

To describe a concerto as a symphony for orchestra, but with a high-powered soloist, is an over-simplification, though there is a strong overlap between the two forms. The concerto, as we know it, was firmly established by Mozart in the late eighteenth century and con-solidated by Beethoven in the early nineteenth. It differed from the symphony most obviously for its three instead of four movements, the absent one being the minuet (or scherzo) and trio which, both in style and form, would have fitted uncomfortably into a work where the confrontation between a heroic soloist and the orchestral mass was absolutely fundamental. That said, there are many similarities between the nineteenth-century concerto and symphony. Each nor-mally begins with a fast movement based around sonata form, and ends with an often even faster movement with a rondo structure, while between these two there is a slow movement of a more lyrical charac-ter. In general terms this is the pattern of all three of Tchaikovsky's concertos – two for piano, one for violin – though both piano concer-tos contain significant deviations from this norm, and in the case of the First Piano Concerto we are immediately confronted with one of these deviations. Many critics have commented (and some censoriously) on the huge opening tune that runs for some three-plus minutes, which is a clear ternary structure, which makes it an enclosed section, suffi-cient in itself: none of it is ever heard again, and it is linked to the main body of the movement by a sustained and very functional transition. Only then does the first (and comparatively *very* trivial) Ukrainian folksong dart upwards to provide the official first subject. Yet in fact, this great thematic gesture has contained thematic particles that will provide tiny building blocks in subsequent themes; thus there is a truly organic linkage with what follows, albeit a very veiled one. Moreover, despite all the surprise, even bewilderment, that has been expressed about this grand initial flourish, no critic seems to have condemned it with much conviction, and the present writer, who has known this concerto for some sixty-five years, is certainly very happy to leave things as they are. In any case, can you really imagine beginning the concerto with the Ukrainian folktune?

In fact, Tchaikovsky's First Piano Concerto incorporates three existing tunes. Two are Ukrainian folksongs, the first mentioned above (little more than a brief melodic tag noted down by Tchaikovsky himself at Kamenka) launching the first subject of the first movement, the second serving as the main theme of the finale. However, the third, which is the foundation of the central section of the concerto's slow movement, was a French popular song of the time, 'Il faut s'amuser et rire', and was said to be a familiar item in the repertoire of Désirée Artôt. It is well established that some composers have used musical 'ciphering'[1] as a discreet way of incorporating into a piece of music either some hidden programme or a tribute to some particular person(s), and elsewhere I have presented a case for the presence of this song being part of a private 'memoir' concealed in this concerto, and prompted by Tchaikovsky's recent affair with this Belgian opera singer.[2]

Finding one's way through what follows on the concerto's massive introduction is not difficult, the whole movement being cast in sonata form, though with two clear, but easily identifiable deviations. As in *Romeo and Juliet*, the exposition contains three clear themes. Obviously Tchaikovsky himself had to extend and supplement the tiny Ukrainian folktune, and it proves to be merely the launch pad for a substantial ternary structure (for future reference, note how the presentation of the Ukrainian tune is varied when it recurs to complete the ternary form; it is at this point that the movement's recapitulation will begin). There is no formal transition, and

1 For an explanation of ciphering, see Appendix 2.

2 Readers interested in this should, if possible, consult my *Tchaikovsky: A Biographical and Critical Study*, vol. 2: *The Crisis Years* (London, 1982), pp. 23–4, [in the paperback reprint of this mammoth four-volume study, *The Crisis Years* makes up the second half of vol. 1, titled *To the Crisis, 1840–1878*]. The 'Désirée Artôt' cipher used to open the second subject of the first movement (D flat–A–[B flat], the final B flat being the most natural resolution after these first two notes) evidently determined the very unusual key (B flat minor) in which the concerto is set.

the second subject's initial tune is first assigned to the woodwind (again, note how effectively its opening bar had already been twice inserted just ahead of this – that is, into the end of the first subject; far from there being a separate transition, the two subjects are actually overlapped). This is then repeated by the piano, and the gentle third theme (that is, the second limb of the second subject) is presented on muted strings. But the exposition is not yet over, for the woodwind theme returns, now with soloist and orchestra collaborating to build a very powerful climax. Yet again, however, the tumult subsides, the gentle third theme recurring, though this time it will become overlaid with exquisite piano figuration, which finally passes into silence.

Now follows the concerto's first major deviation from the symphony's normal route – the large, purely orchestral *tutti* that launches the development section. First almost stealthily picking up the gentle theme and then (but only briefly) the first subject, it steadily builds to a powerful climax, at the height of which the soloist abruptly takes over, but quickly reintroducing a calmer mood, then ruminating on the remaining so-far-untreated woodwind theme. However, the thematic basis slyly begins to change, and when the orchestra re-enters for a tight dialogue with the piano, their discussion is based on a new idea. And when the recapitulation arrives, only a portion of the exposition is rerun, the final muted string tune being omitted altogether – for what intervenes is the second of the concerto's major deviations: the cadenza.

A main feature of any concerto is obviously the brilliance and versatility of the soloist, and this is evident throughout in what the composer himself prescribes. But the idea that *every note* of a concerto should be predetermined was a relatively recent development. In Mozart's concertos, for instance, certain places, designated cadenzas, were specified where the soloist might improvise, the most significant occurring towards the end of the first movement, between the recapitulation and the coda. The moment for beginning the cadenza was carefully prepared, the orchestra ending on a sustained chord that was obviously not the conclusion of the piece; the soloist would then improvise (though one wonders whether the 'improvisation' might on occasions have been carefully practised), ending with a trill that could be sustained as long as it took the orchestra to collect themselves, ready to take over and round off the movement.

Beethoven, who was himself a famed improviser, allowed this free practice in all his solo concertos except the last, the 'Emperor' Concerto, and later composers, though they might retain the cadenza element, nearly always composed it themselves – Mendelssohn in his Violin Concerto and Grieg in his Piano Concerto, to name but two well-known examples (Brahms's Violin Concerto is a rare, belated instance of the soloist still being free to 'do his or her own thing'). In fact, Tchaikovsky would increasingly incorporate cadenza-like slabs of music for the soloist into his later concerted works, but he always specified exactly what should be played, as in the case of his First Piano Concerto. Here the cadenza is a very substantial piece, and it leads quietly into the so-far-missing muted string theme (now on flute and clarinet) on which the coda centres, though with increasing energy and volume.

This is quite certainly the finest – and by far the largest – first movement Tchaikovsky had yet composed. Twice as long as the parallel movements of the first two symphonies, it is marked by excellent melodic material, by unfailing inventiveness (think only of the one-and-a-half-minute first subject he manages to generate out of a five-second folksong), and by a resourcefulness in applying that material to build a twenty-minute structure that is as splendidly balanced as it is sure-footed. The remaining two movements make no attempt to match this – but do they really need to? True, later in the nineteenth century it would become a more regular practice to make the finale of a symphonic work the weightiest movement – yet Tchaikovsky's great classical predecessors, Mozart and Beethoven, had so often made their finales lighter in tone, and perhaps briefer, than their opening movements. In fact, even taken together, the remaining two movements of this concerto occupy less time than did the first movement. Gentle lyricism is the prevailing mood of the outer sections of the *Andantino semplice* (which steals in so quietly with eight *pianissimo* pizzicato chords that you may easily miss them if not fully attentive). The flute theme is as lovely as it is simple, but is still strong enough to sustain the flanks of this ternary movement. By contrast, the central section, marked *prestissimo*, is founded mainly on the playful tune associated with Désirée Artôt, but this is preceded (and will be followed) by a scampering section for the piano made up of minuscule fragments that flash by so fleetly that there is little time to make out their individual identities, for all their fine clarity. But in fact we have already heard some of these, though I am sure most listeners will have missed them –

as I confess to having done until after *very* many hearings. The movement had opened with two statements of the main theme, the second by the piano – but now note the following tiny, slender figures which had been gently introduced by woodwind and pizzicato strings, and then repeated by the piano; it is these, now played many times faster, that we are hearing again to provide the opening bars of the *prestissimo*.

The lyricism of the slow movement yields abruptly to the dynamism of the finale. Tchaikovsky wastes no time in this *Allegro con fuoco*; though it is only a third of the length of the great first movement, it will compensate through sheer energy. But energy alone is not enough. The concerto had opened with a massive movement, often of great grandeur; somehow this finale must, by its ending, have recaptured something of that monumental element to ensure some expressive equilibrium. Yet the finale opens in its own particular world. A brief orchestral salvo – and the piano introduces the second of the concerto's Ukrainian folksongs, then builds from it, this section ending with a rumbustious orchestral *tutti*. The piano forthwith re-enters to provide a dazzling link to the movement's second main idea, a broad lyrical theme which is first presented quietly by the orchestra, then built on by the piano; a short link leads straight back to the Ukrainian folksong. So far it seems we have been listening, unsurprisingly, to the first sections of a compact sonata rondo (that is, the ABA, with links between these components), but if it maintains this line, will not the movement, by its end, have sounded almost dismissive? In fact, Tchaikovsky does at first, though in a very businesslike way, pursue the sonata rondo track; however, this completed, we are suddenly moved on to a new, unheralded stage, the piano pouring out a deluge of semiquavers, against which the orchestra quotes snatches of both the Ukrainian folksong (on woodwind), and of the broad lyrical theme (on strings). But abruptly the piano falls silent, the orchestra focuses on elements of the Ukrainian folksong (and the tripping idea) – but then the opening four notes of the broad lyrical theme, quiet at first, are heard on the massed violins rising in stately, unbroken steps ever more inexorably. A great climax, a torrent of double octaves from the pianist – and the majestic second theme celebrates its unchallenged supremacy at length, endowing the concerto's end with a grandeur that magnificently balances, some forty minutes

on, that great maverick theme that had launched this whole masterpiece.

––––––––

One of Tchaikovsky's best-known works is his Violin Concerto, composed in 1878, but there are two other violin-and-orchestra pieces,
much less ambitious, that remain virtually unplayed, yet worth the
occasional hearing. This is particularly true of the first, the *Sérénade
mélancolique*,*** composed in February 1875 for the virtuoso
Leopold Auer, though for some reason the violinist delayed its premiere, and it was only two years later that Adolf Brodsky introduced
it to the wider world, Auer himself first playing it publicly some ten
months later. It is a very attractive piece, with clear evidence that
Tchaikovsky's creative memory was still haunted by the two masterpieces that had occupied him during the preceding year, for its very
first sounds are taken straight from Oxana's challenge to Vakula in
Act 2 Scene 2 of *Vakula/Cherevichki*, while a melody in the piece's faster
central section echoes the French chanson of the Piano Concerto's slow
movement. The *Sérénade*'s full title prepares us for the elegiac mood of
the soloist's opening, though the *Vakula* melody infiltrates the centre
of this spacious theme, and the memory of Artôt's chanson helps
prompt a livelier central section. This is music to be listened to, not for
any epic experience, but simply for the pleasure afforded by the unfaltering loveliness of its melody. Let us never despise such unpretentious
pieces!

10

Towards an Epoch-making Ballet: Third Symphony, Third Quartet – and *Swan Lake*

Tchaikovsky was good with words. He was an indefatigable correspondent, his five thousand surviving letters, which fill fifteen volumes in the Russian edition, are often very lengthy, especially when he is writing to those of his family to whom he felt closest, and they are very well written, as were the reviews he wrote for the Russian press during the three years when he was regularly active as a music critic. Back in 1871 he had produced his *Guide to the Practical Study of Harmony*, the first composition manual to be published in Russia, and he now followed this up with another volume, *A Short Manual of Harmony Adapted to the Study of Religious Music in Russia*, which had been requested by the Synod of the Russian Orthodox Church, and which Jurgenson published in 1875. Tchaikovsky had completed this earlier in the year, once he had finished composing the First Piano Concerto. When relatives or friends needed support Tchaikovsky was ever quick to respond if he could. On the more personal front he propped up Modest, who had also begun a career as a critic, but who was now suffering a bout of self-doubt. 'Perhaps you haven't a first-class talent for writing, but you have a positive aptitude, taste, and you have that *understanding* which Laroche so values in you,' brother Peter wrote. '*Understanding* is a great thing; sometimes very intelligent people lack it. Because of your understanding you will never write anything cheap or false.' Wise words. He also supported Laroche himself, who had been a colleague at the Moscow Conservatoire since 1867, and whose wife was now terminally ill with consumption. As a last resort Laroche had taken her to the mineral springs at Aachen, but there was also a young family whom he had to leave behind. It was a very distressing situation, and Tchaikovsky helped in arranging for one of their children to travel to Aachen to bring some comfort to his dying mother. Coincidentally, in 1887 Tchaikovsky would himself make the very same journey, and endure three dreadful weeks at the bedside of his terminally ill friend, Kondratyev, in what seems, from the evidence of Tchaikovsky's private diary, to have been a virtually solo vigil. Difficult Tchaikovsky may have been in some of his relationships, but when it came to supporting a dear friend, relative, or even someone he barely knew but whom he could truly help, he could be unstinting in giving of himself to a degree that I imagine few of us could claim to match.

Tchaikovsky had hoped to begin his summer break with a brief trip abroad, but lack of funds forestalled this, and towards the middle of June he set out for Shilovsky's estate at Usovo. His creative urges were restored, and within days he had set about a new symphony, 'doing a bit at a time', as he wrote to the Sofronov brothers. 'I don't sit over it for hours on end, and I'm walking more. Nothing's changed here. Even the dogs are the same, and they chase after me to go for a walk.' Yet despite Tchaikovsky's current relaxed lifestyle, the symphony was wholly sketched and partially orchestrated by mid-July, when he moved on to Kondratyev's estate at Nizy. Remaining there ten days, he then directed himself to Verbovka, another of the Davïdov estates near Kamenka, where Sasha and her family were spending the summer, together with Tchaikovsky's father, and brother Anatoly. To have so many of his close family about him made for a very pleasant stay. A fortnight later his Third Symphony was complete.

Symphony no. 3 in D ＊＊＊＊(＊)

[This, sadly, is an uneven symphony – though this does not mean that it does not contain very good music. The outer movements do not represent Tchaikovsky at his best, but the middle three movements (and especially the central Andante elegiaco*) are excellent, and well worth investigating.]*

'As far as I can see this symphony presents no particularly successful ideas, but in workmanship it is a step forward. I am satisfied above all with the first movement and the two scherzos.' This was Tchaikovsky's own verdict after it had received its premiere in November. In fact, the Third Symphony is the least satisfactory of his mature examples (that is, not counting the First), and the clue to this is contained in his second sentence. Perhaps the root cause lay in

Nikolay Rubinstein's reaction to his most recent symphonic piece. The First Piano Concerto's opening movement had been by far the most impressive and boldest Tchaikovsky had so far composed – yet it had been mercilessly trashed by the one man from whom Tchaikovsky could have expected a highly professional, balanced judgement. Though, of course, Nikolay Rubinstein later recanted very publicly of his error, in the summer of 1875 the concerto remained unplayed, and Tchaikovsky, for all his vehement rejection of Rubinstein's verdict, had clearly been questioning within himself whether there might be grounds for such criticism. Whatever the case, Tchaikovsky's own stated satisfaction with the Third Symphony's first movement seems extraordinary. True, it bears all the hallmarks of orthodox symphonic correctness, yet it contains some patches of the most stolid, least characteristic music he ever composed. He seems to have attuned his creative ear to the more recent West European symphonic tradition, specifically to Schumann, and even more specifically to that composer's own Third Symphony (very unusually composed in five movements – as is, significantly, Tchaikovsky's Third), and to have adjusted, even suppressed, his own musical language to accommodate material from which to manufacture a 'politically correct' first movement. But not all is lost. The slow introduction is fine, and in the three-theme exposition the second theme is very attractive and the third vivacious; it is in the first subject, rhythmically stodgy despite its energy, that the seed of the movement's problem is sown, for it will become more and more assertive in the repetitious, heavy-handed development, and annex much of the movement's overblown coda.

Yet elsewhere in the Third Symphony there is some excellent and thoroughly characteristic music. In the central slow movement especially – and Tchaikovsky was right to take pride in the two lighter movements that enclose it. He marked the first of these *Alla tedesca* ('like a German dance'), but, it being by Tchaikovsky, we would probably immediately identify it as a waltz which we would expect to be as masterly in its breadth as it is inventive in its detail. Indeed it is: the main section does truly feel like a single integrated span, even though it is built from several ideas. In the movement's central trio orchestral colour and delicate textures are the most striking features (some may feel that already they can sense the world of *The Nutcracker*, though this ballet was still some fifteen years away in the future). Note in particular how deftly Tchaikovsky reintroduces the movement's main theme before the trio's chatter has completely faded. Note also the lengthy, fading coda that follows the repetition of the first section – and particularly the way Tchaikovsky twice vastly elongates the first two notes of each of the final two waltz phrases to bring an extra touch of fading finality. This is a delicious movement. So, too, is the fourth (actually labelled 'Scherzo'). Here orchestral colour applied to flying fragments and tiny interjections from elsewhere in the band make up most of this music; only at the end does a solo trombone presume to present a quietly determined melody to bring this section to earth. The movement also has a trio, and its provenance is surprising: Tchaikovsky adapted it from the orchestral prelude to his Peter the Great Cantata of 1872, a routine commission of mostly functional music which need not concern us here. Note the single unbroken horn note that runs through this entire section (it has, of course to be shared between two overlapping players), and around which the sprightly, ex-cantata phrase, which is exchanged between woodwind and strings, seems to dance, though firmly anchored. There is a coda also to this scherzo, and this reminds us of the middle section before a tiny flourish of fleet scamperings rounds off the movement.

When Tchaikovsky came to create the ravishing *Andante* that is the very heart of the Third Symphony, was he again touched by the magic of Usovo, as he had been two years earlier when composing *The Tempest*? And did a memory of how Berlioz had opened (and closed) his *Scène aux champs*, that was the very heart of his *Symphonie fantastique*, also haunt Tchaikovsky as he opened (and closed) this movement, which is the very heart of this symphony? It could well be. And it was surely a specific memory of his earlier Usovo creation that conditioned the enchanting melody that follows, for it seems to grow straight from the lovers' music in *The Tempest*, though without the unbridled passion of Shakespeare's pair. This is one of Tchaikovsky's most beautiful tunes, launching one of his most beautiful slow movements, a piece that draws in the listener through its loveliness, both impassioned and serene, in a way that surely renders further comment unnecessary. If I had to choose a piece by Tchaikovsky as one of my desert-island discs, this could certainly be among the candidates.

I cannot say that of the Third Symphony's finale, however. It is a polonaise – a grand rondo movement with an A theme that is certainly imposing, but with a rather dreary B theme and, towards its end, an efficient but faceless fugue before the B theme recurs in preparation for one of Tchaikovsky's noisiest codas. Significantly, perhaps, the Third Symphony is by far the least played of his six mature examples (this number includes the magnificent *Manfred Symphony*). It is so sad that, consequently, the central three movements – above all, the *Andante* – are so infrequently heard in our concert halls.

In mid-December the distinguished French composer Camille Saint-Saëns visited Moscow. He gave two concerts, Tchaikovsky attending both and being much impressed. He met Saint-Saëns, and found him as congenial as his music. There is no doubt Tchaikovsky calculated that cultivating a good relationship with the French composer might, in turn, help his own cause with French audiences, but the two men's personalities were compatible, sufficient for them to indulge in a little impromptu clowning. Modest, who chronicled the incident, was the only witness: 'As young men,' he remembered,

> both had not only been attracted to the ballet, but also had some natural skill for that sort of dancing. And so, on one occasion, wishing to show off their art to each other, they performed on the stage of the Conservatoire's main hall an entire little ballet, *Galatea and Pygmalion*. The forty-year-old Saint-Saëns was Galatea and performed the role of the statue with remarkable assiduity, while the thirty-five-year-old Tchaikovsky took upon himself the role of Pygmalion. Nikolay Rubinstein provided the orchestra.

Quite apart from the comic aspect of this caper itself, it furnishes further evidence that, even when the clouds were gathering in Tchaikovsky's inner world, he retained a relish for fun and humour. Certainly within two years the storm would break, and Tchaikovsky would be plunged into the most agonizing phase of his whole life. As for the relationship with Saint-Saëns, this proved fleeting. On New Year's Day 1876, immediately after the French composer had left Russia, Tchaikovsky and Modest set out for Western Europe, and within three weeks were in Paris – yet Tchaikovsky expressly requested those who knew where he was to keep this a secret, and he deliberately avoided meeting Saint-Saëns. When they would subsequently meet face to face, 'they were as strangers, and such they always remained,' Modest remembered. This would not be the only hot–cold relationship in Tchaikovsky's life.

However, this visit to Paris did afford Tchaikovsky one of the most decisive musical experiences of his life when, on 20 January, he attended a performance of the opera *Carmen*. It was less than a year since Bizet's masterpiece had received its premiere, and within three months of that event Bizet himself was dead. Such a poignant occurrence had fanned interest in the opera itself, but it is unlikely that this played any significant part in Tchaikovsky's response, Modest later recording that he had never seen his brother so taken by a piece from a contemporary composer, *Carmen* becoming (and remaining) second only to Mozart's *Don Giovanni* in his love and esteem. Indeed, it would condition some of his own work, deciding him (so Modest wrote) that his own next opera should likewise be on a real-life subject from modern times. Not only did it contribute to his choice of Pushkin's *Eugene Onegin* the following year; music taken from *Carmen* would be a material and pointed, though secret presence in his next symphony, the Fourth. This would be in the future, however, and it does not appear that the opera had anything that could have conditioned the piece that Tchaikovsky had begun even before his return to Russia in early February: his Third String Quartet.

When Tchaikovsky's first two string quartets had been given their premieres, the first violin had been Ferdinand Laub, a Czech violinist with a distinguished international career, who had been one of Tchaikovsky's colleagues at the Moscow Conservatoire since its opening in 1866. But in March 1875 Laub had died suddenly, and Tchaikovsky had resolved to honour his memory in his next string quartet; thus it is no surprise that the Third Quartet is imposing, and that its prevailing (though not exclusive) tone is elegiac. It is a huge work, matching in size the First Piano Concerto, but it took barely a month to complete. Only a fortnight later it was heard for the first time, and its impact was colossal, repeat performances following quickly. 'It pleased everyone very much,' Tchaikovsky could inform Modest. 'During the *Andante funebre e doloroso* [the slow third movement] many, I am told, were in tears. If this is true, it's a great triumph.' It is no surprise that, when Tchaikovsky died, it was this quartet that was chosen as tribute to its composer in memorial concerts in St Petersburg, Moscow and Kharkov.

String Quartet no. 3 in E flat minor * * * (*)

[The Third String Quartet is the most impressive of Tchaikovsky's three – and especially for its elegiac slow movement. A piece of very high quality and maybe something of a challenge to the listener's attention span, this Quartet is perhaps a piece for the more experienced listeners – though the slow third movement is worth hearing for itself alone.]

Clearly a work of this size, but without the decibels and high drama of the earlier piano concerto, is a challenge, especially since the prevailing mood of the massive first movement is not broken by those clear contrasts and easily recognizable landmarks that, with a little familiarity, can help the listener to orientate himself or herself through a large-scale movement. But to those whose temperament is for reflective, intimate and deeply felt experiences, Tchaikovsky's Third Quartet can be richly rewarding. The slow introduction begins quietly and rather haltingly, but this leads into a spacious, and very beautiful, melody for the first violin, a pointed choice of instrument, surely, in this tribute to a great violinist and close friend. It is a melody that becomes even more intense when the cello repeats it, the first violin soon resuming with a free countermelody. All finally fades to insistent echoes of this great theme's opening, and the faster main movement begins. It is, as expected, in sonata form, the first subject a close relative of the phrase that had opened the whole work, the second subject a sort of wistful waltz. Locating yourself in what follows is not easy, though the exposition/development and development/recapitulation boundaries are marked by passages of more hushed music. But my advice is 'just listen', for what follows in this nearly twenty-minute movement consolidates very single-mindedly the prevailing mood of what has gone before until, finally, the great melody from the introduction returns to set the seal on this monumental conception. There has been, however, one curious incident. In the recapitulation, between the two official subjects, there was a third theme not heard before, nor ever recurring. Was this some tune from elsewhere, which Tchaikovsky especially associated with Laub? We shall probably never know.

Such a consistently sustained experience demands some sort of relief, especially since the third movement will focus yet more pointedly on the funeral ritual itself. The scherzo that separates these two movements seems simply a punctuation mark, no more than a quarter the length of the first movement, but affording a break sufficient to make the return to grievous matters the more poignant. There is, indeed, something almost raw about the music that opens the third movement, *Andante funebre e doloroso*, a sort of halting funeral march interspersed with sounds of anguish, and which in due course will lead into a graphic but hushed evocation of the solemn chanting of a funeral choir, punctuated by the intonings of the priest (what the viola plays here is on a monotone, but with the note lengths very precisely prescribed to match exactly the real-life delivery of the liturgy by the officiating priest). This merges seamlessly into a melody shared by violin and cello, and as beautiful as that which had provided the whole quartet's introduction. Here is the work's expressive heart, yet it has its own centre when the funeral march of the opening breaks in before the violin/cello melody (with the viola now having a share) resumes. What follows retracks through earlier music, and it is with a benediction from the choir and priest, and an ascent heavenwards (surely?) that the movement closes.

After such a mighty utterance the finale might initially strike, both in character and length, as dismissive; rather, it is surely a celebration of gratitude for Laub's life. In any case, the quartet's specific memorial purpose is not forgotten, for just before this vigorous and very Russian music has run its course the pace slows, and the pizzicato chords of the first movement's slow introduction return. But the wisp of cello melody that follows is not what we heard then; in fact its four notes trace exactly the pitch contour that may be ciphered[1] (1) from Laub's first name. Thus the dedicatee's identity is, it seems, indelibly stamped on this memorial work. This accomplished, however, the movement (indeed, the whole quartet) proceeds to a most joyful conclusion.

———

Back in June, as Tchaikovsky had been about to leave for Usovo, a proposal had arrived from the Imperial Theatres. Because he had already decided to compose his Third Symphony, this new commission had to wait, and it might have been thought that exhaustion from labour on the symphony would have enforced a creative rest, once

1 For an explanation of musical ciphering, see Appendix 2.

that was completed. Nothing of the sort. In mid-August, within days of finishing the symphony, Tchaikovsky set to work, and within a fortnight two acts were sketched of one of his most famous, and certainly most innovative, works: the ballet *Swan Lake*.

The ballet in Russia had had a long and, in many respects, distinguished history well before 1877, when *Swan Lake* was first mounted in Moscow's Bolshoy Theatre. However, what had given Russian ballet its quality was what happened onstage, not in the orchestral pit. Though ballets such as the ever popular *Giselle* had reached Russia in the 1840s, the great bulk of music for the Imperial Ballet in Moscow was still being provided by local composers who had neither the talent, nor the encouragement from their masters, to produce other than functional music to support the dancers. It was still the normal practice in the 1870s to employ such composers, even though Delibes's *Coppélia*, produced in Paris in 1870, had set a precedent for ballet music of an altogether higher quality. Tchaikovsky evidently did not know this ballet when composing *Swan Lake*, and even those in the Moscow audience who might have seen *Coppélia* would have been unprepared for some of what Tchaikovsky challenged them with in *Swan Lake*. In fact, as music for ballet, *Swan Lake* was, as a revolutionary conception, second only to Stravinsky's *Rite of Spring* of nearly forty years later. No ballet score had ever contained such rhythmically complicated music, and the challenge this presented to the dancers was so enormous that, even before the premiere, pieces by other composers were being slipped in. Press reaction was mixed, but mostly unfavourable. Yet the audience response was evidently good, and over the next six years the ballet was performed forty-one times (an unusually high score), though all the time the substitutions continued until one-third of Tchaikovsky's own music was gone. In 1883 it was withdrawn from the repertoire, evidently because the scenery had disintegrated. It was never again heard in Tchaikovsky's lifetime.

And that might have been that. But in 1895, two years after Tchaikovsky's death, his brother Modest, together with the great choreographer Marius Petipa, and the infinitely less great composer Riccardo Drigo, devised a new version of *Swan Lake*, Modest rewriting the scenario, Petipa choreographing it afresh, and Drigo meddling in the music, deleting some numbers, truncating others, changing their order and adding three piano pieces by Tchaikovsky, which he orchestrated. The most serious single mutilation was to give the story a happy ending. However, whatever outrage may be felt about this reworking, it proved enormously successful, laying the foundations for that overwhelming popularity *Swan Lake* enjoys today. For that we must, of course, be grateful. Nevertheless, the 1895 revision, and especially the reordering of so much of the music, produced in places a dramatic mutilation that is insupportable. In much of the score Tchaikovsky had composed his music specifically for certain dramatic passages or moments, and the resiting of these is always damaging, and sometimes grossly inept, because the music is entirely inappropriate for the stage action. In recent years there have been productions in which the original scenario and Tchaikovsky's own score have been used, but these have seemed powerless to oust the travesty version. However, we are concerned in this book only with authentic Tchaikovsky, and since the various complete recordings of *Swan Lake* are always (it seems) of the original score, it is this that will be investigated here.

Swan Lake: ballet in three acts * * * * *

[Swan Lake *is the most popular of all ballets. The music by itself is very accessible, and with CDs that band the separate numbers clearly it should be possible to link the successive dramatic incidents with the relevant music. Those interested primarily in the best passages musically should pay special attention to Acts 2 and 4.]*

Like an opera, a classical ballet has a scenario divided into acts, and these are subdivided into mimed action sections (*scènes*), danced action scenes (*pas d'action*), and sections of formal dancing (*valse, pas de deux*, etc.). The following summary of the plot omits much action detail.

Act 1. *A splendid park. Scène* (no. 1): Prince Siegfried and his friends are drinking wine. Peasants congratulate him on his coming of age. His tutor, Wolfgang, tells them to dance for the Prince's amusement. *Valse* (no. 2): The peasants dance. *Scène* (no. 3): The Princess arrives. Her son must marry; reluctant to do so yet, he nevertheless asks her whom he should choose, but is told he must do that for himself from among the beauties at the grand ball tomorrow night. The Princess leaves. The Prince is depressed but his friend Benno consoles him. The drinking resumes. *Pas de trois* (no. 4) (six dances) and *pas de deux* (no. 5) (four dances) for peasants. *Pas d'action* (no. 6): The tutor gets drunk, arouses amusement, pirouettes, then falls over. *Sujet* (no. 7): It grows dark. *Goblet Dance* (no. 8). *Finale* (no. 9): A flock of swans appears in the sky. Benno urges the Prince to shoot; the tutor tries to dissuade him. But when the tutor leaves, the Prince, with Benno, hurries off in pursuit of the swans.

Act 2. *A wild mountainous place. Scène* (no. 10): orchestral prelude. *Scène* (no. 11): A flock of swans, led by one with a crown on its head, is swimming on a lake. The Prince spots a swan, prepares to shoot, but the swans disappear. Odette appears and tells her tale. Her mother, a good fairy, had fallen in love with a knight whose mistreatment of her had caused her death. Odette's father had married again, neglected her, and her wicked stepmother had almost destroyed her. Her grandfather had then taken her in, but so grief-stricken had he been for his own daughter's death that his tears had formed a lake, into the depths of which he had taken Odette. Now he has given her freedom to be herself, and now she and her friends, turning themselves into swans, enjoy that freedom. But her wicked stepmother, turning herself into an owl, haunts her. Only if Odette marries will her stepmother's power over her disappear. The Prince begs forgiveness. *Scène* (no. 12): A flock of swan-maidens appears and they reproach him. He throws away his weapons. Odette reassures him. *Danse des cygnes* (no. 13): The Prince falls in love with Odette (the fourth and fifth of the seven dances being, respectively, the famous cygnet dance and the *Pas d'action*, with violin and cello solos). Odette promises to return the next night. *Scène* (no. 14): Odette and the swans disappear into the ruins. A flock of swans swims out on to the lake. Overhead a great owl flaps.

Act 3. *A luxurious hall in the Princess's castle, ready for a feast.* *Scène* (no. 15): Wolfgang gives orders, guests appear, the Prince and Princess with pages, dwarfs, etc. *Danses du corps de ballet et des nains* (no. 16). *Scène* (no. 17): A trumpet call announces the entry of new guests, including an old count, his wife and daughter. Their daughter dances a waltz. Another trumpet call: the same routine is repeated. All dance a large-scale waltz. *Scène* (no. 18): The Princess asks her son which of the maidens has pleased him; he replies none. Suddenly a trumpet call announces the entrance of Baron Rotbart with his daughter, Odile, who, the Prince immediately notices, looks exactly like Odette. *Pas de six* (no. 19) (a series of six dances): Odile dances and the Prince in due course joins her. A suite of four national dances follows: *Danse hongroise: Czardas* (no. 20); *Danse espagnole* (no. 21); *Danse napolitaine* (no. 22); *Mazurka* (no. 23). *Scène* (no. 24): The Prince asks Odile to dance a waltz with him, and kisses her hand. The Princess announces Odile will be the Prince's bride. The stage suddenly darkens; an owl's cry is heard, Rotbart's disguise falls away, and he is seen as the devil he is. Odile laughs, and a frantic crowned swan appears at the window. In horror the Prince rushes out of the castle. General confusion.

Act 4. *Entr'acte* (no. 25). The scene is as in Act 2, at night. *Scène* (no. 26): Odette's friends wonder about her disappearance; meanwhile they teach the cygnets to dance. *Danse des petits cygnes* (no. 27). *Scène* (no. 28): Odette rushes in and unburdens herself of her grief; they reassure her the Prince is coming, and withdraw. Thunder rumbles. *Scène finale* (no. 29): The Prince rushes in, begging forgiveness, but Odette says she has no power to grant this. She rushes towards the ruins, but he detains her: she shall be his for ever. He tears the crown from her head and flings it into the lake, which is now overflowing its banks. A screeching owl flies overhead, with Odette's crown in its talons. Odette falls into the Prince's arms and they disappear beneath the water. The storm abates. In the moonlight the swans appear on the lake.

Swan Lake is a tragedy in which evil (Rotbart/Odile) overwhelms good (Odette/the Prince), yet cannot thwart the triumph of love over hate. The short orchestral prelude presents the opposing sides, a gracious theme on the oboe (very much Odette and the swans' orchestral surrogate) introducing music characteristic of the swans, the violent music that follows forewarning of the evil forces that will finally seem triumphant. But when the curtain rises it is a very light and untroubled world that we enter. In the *scènes* the course and character of the music is determined by the events that are happening onstage, and the bustling, cheerful music that follows the raising of the curtain complements the revelry of the Prince and his friends, the less hectic woodwind tune that follows introducing the peasants and the various bits of action that follow before they begin their waltz. The latter proves to be a very substantial movement (some eight minutes long), made up of a number of different tunes shuffled together to provide background for a pleasantly decorative stage spectacle, all rounded off by an expansive and sonorous coda. For a ballet audience of 1877, when set-piece dances were the priority, this must have admirably satisfied that requirement. But dramatically it is a miscalculation, clogging the action before it has barely started; nothing like this would happen thirteen years on when Tchaikovsky, his fame now giving him a formidable personal authority, came to compose *The Sleeping Beauty*.

In the *scène* (no. 3) the action resumes, the build-up to the Princess's appearance appropriately grand, her entry itself marked by a trumpet fanfare, her consultation with her son by quieter, more intimate music; her exit is less ceremonial – and then a return to their consultation music, but now with a nervous additional contribution from flute and oboe, signifying that the Prince is reflecting joylessly on her command, though the resumption of the act's opening music indicates that more serious matters are again set aside. Beyond this point, and up to the flurry of excitement occasioned by the above-stage appearance of the swans, the music consists entirely of dances. The peasants have ten in a row, six nicely varied ones making up the *pas de trois*, the second of the four *pas de deux* dances being a particularly beautiful violin solo that would display the talents of the orchestra's leader, who could well have been a player of international stature (in St Petersburg the current court violinist who discharged this duty was Leopold Auer, one of the most noted violinists of all time). Presumably designed for a beautiful ballerina to display her charms, it is by far the largest and most arresting piece in this series of mainly relaxed or extrovert pieces – though pieces that still, when compared to similar examples by mere artisan composers, have a distinction and a quiet inventiveness that lifts them decisively above the merely routine.

The incident of the drunken tutor is backed by comparatively quiet music in the *pas d'action* (no. 6) – until the ending, that is. The *sujet* (no. 7) provides a tiny atmospheric interlude before the polonaise-style *Goblet Dance* (no. 8), a large-scale set piece that symmetrically counterbalances the grand waltz near the act's opening, is set going. But the *finale* (no. 9) will be no formal rounding of the act. It introduces the ballet's most famous swan theme (clearly a sibling of the melody that had opened the whole work: significantly, Tchaikovsky assigns both to the oboe). And just as the scenario now leads the Prince and Benno towards the swans' domain, so a repetition of this music will announce their approach before the curtain rises again on Act 2 .

Act 1 had been well stuffed with decorative dances with little or no relevance to the main plot; Act 2 has far fewer, and those it does have are either fundamental to the plot, or have at least some relevance to it. The *scène* (no. 11), which opens proceedings, is action packed. The Prince enters in pursuit of the Swan/Odette, spots her (sudden loud chords), prepares to shoot (pizzicato strings), but the Swan vanishes and the earlier music resumes. Next Odette appears as herself (new oboe theme), and in due course begins her story (new, more agitated music after four detached notes). Soon the owl appears (four very loud detached chords, followed by agitated music). The music dies away into a long-held single note – and Odette sets out what will release her from her bondage ('With my marriage . . .', as a little rubric in Tchaikovsky's score indicates). A silence – and with the new *scène* (no. 12) the other swans appear. They are nervous of the Prince, but Odette reassures them (a new, quieter theme, again on the oboe), the Prince decisively throws away his weapons and Odette reassures him in his turn (high woodwind music).

Now formal dancing takes over (no. 13). First a massed waltz, then a solo for Odette, graceful at first, but ending excitedly (showing off to the Prince?), and then the massed waltz again, to be followed by possibly the most famous dance of the whole ballet: the cute little dance for the cygnets. This could hardly have been in greater contrast to what will follow: the very heart of the ballet, the great *pas d'action*, in which Odette and the Prince play out their courtship, and seal their love. The substantial introduction, largely a grand harp cadenza, precedes the dance itself, which opens with a solo violin unfolding one of the loveliest, tenderest melodies Tchaikovsky ever composed – one that had, in fact, been composed eight years earlier as the main theme of the love duet in his opera *Undine* but which he had subsequently destroyed. There follows a nervous, lightly throbbing interlude, and then a further violin solo, this time marked by upward-flying scales, joyous and bright. Again the nervous interlude, again a portion of the upward-flying music, again the nervous interlude – but only a fragment this time, for the lovers, it seems, urge a return to that wonderful tune that had initiated their courtship. This time they make it a duet, a solo cello taking the tune while the violin unfolds a new countermelody above, a perfect collaboration between two people in perfect harmony. It only remains for a lively coda to round off this magnificent musical celebration of young love.

What can follow this? No more needing to be said, Tchaikovsky wastes no time. The main waltz theme is heard once more, rounded off by a short coda, and the swans disappear into the ruins to that same great tune that had concluded the first act and ushered in the second.

Act 3 dispenses with a formal orchestral introduction, and the curtain rises promptly (no. 15) on the final preparations for the banquet at which the Prince is to be offered new choices of bride. Like the first act, this will have a high proportion of decorative dancing, and the introductory dance (no. 16) proves most interesting for the dwarfs' dance that provides its middle section. In the *scène* (no. 17) trumpets herald the first batch of guests (an old count, with his wife and daughter) who are introduced, bow, the daughter then dancing a short waltz with a partner; this ritual is twice repeated for a second and third trio of guests, though the waltz is different for the first of these last two; the third waltz is then very substantially extended by the corps de ballet. This done, the Princess asks (*scéne*, no. 18) her son for his view on the maidens he has seen, but she is interrupted by a fourth fanfare, though what now follows will be very different. Baron Rotbart and his daughter Odile (customarily costumed in black to distinguish her from Odette, but danced by the same ballerina) enter to disruptive sounds, with agitated references to the now familiar swans' theme. During the following dances the Prince first observes Odile, then joins in. To fall in love he must, I suppose, be given some time, but the seduction itself comes surely in the second dance, for which the pace suddenly slows. From its beginning there is something slightly sultry about this, but this is as nothing compared to what follows when gently throbbing strings take over, to be joined, during a remorseless crescendo with a quickening pulse, by brash wind and brass solos, and then thudding bass drum, all finally at maximum volume. Putting it rather crudely: Julie Andrews has become Shirley Bassey! And the instant shift to very quiet, yet still not quite 'safe' music is brilliantly calculated. Incidentally, in the revised *Swan Lake* of 1895, where does this unashamed vamp music turn up? To back the lacerating reunion of the lovers in Act 4, just before the ballet's catastrophic end. Well, I suppose Tchaikovsky didn't always get it right!

Sadly, after this the remaining four dances, for all their individual attractiveness, seem otiose. Even more so are the four national dances that follow, well characterized as they are. In performance it is not until some 25 minutes after the dance of seduction that the real action is resumed with a *scène* (no. 24 – and a return to the music of the Princess's earlier questioning of her son in no. 18). This time the Prince goes to dance with Odile to the same short waltz to which successive suitors had danced at the act's opening, and then kisses Odile's hand: the act of betrothal. Instantly the music becomes more agitated, growing in volume. Then suddenly the room darkens and, to the swans' theme, now at its loudest and most frantic, Odette appears at the window (another ballerina doubling for the real Odette). Rotbart's ruse has succeeded, and the scene ends in the noisiest confusion.

With Act 4 we return to the swans. They and their world have already drawn from Tchaikovsky the ballet's most consistent music, and the final act will maintain this consistency, culminating in what must surely have been, in 1877, the most powerful climax yet composed for any ballet. It is also the most concise act, shorter in fact than the string of decorative dances that had filled out the middle of Act 3. But it opens quietly with an *entr'acte* (no. 25) that, some eight years earlier, had served in exactly the same relative location in the opera *The Voyevoda*. There is urgent anxiety in the music that opens the following *scène* (no. 26) where the swans fret over Odette's disappearance, but Tchaikovsky's broader strategy soon becomes clear: better to continue at some length with a melancholy restraint that will make the impact of the cataclysmic events to come the more powerful. And so the swans give the cygnets a lengthy and unhurried lesson (no. 27), a telling foil to the precipitate reappearance of Odette.

From that point (no. 28) dramatic tension is never lost, and is sometimes almost unbearable. Odette's narration (the quieter music that follows) has pathos in plenty, but is broken by the first sounds of the gathering storm (timpani roll) and an awesome crescendo. At its peak the Prince himself rushes in, and the *scène finale* (no. 29) begins (this entry tune, as strongly contoured as it is concise, is yet another *Voyevoda* orphan). It is to the sound of the swans' theme, its former serenity now undermined by a nervous accompaniment, that the Prince begs forgiveness, and at the moment Odette gives him her hand and the newly rising storm overwhelms the couple, the swans' theme on full orchestra will finally be presented in the brighter major key, celebrating the triumph of love, even though it has ended in the lovers' deaths. And the ballet's ending will present another

ambivalence. Love triumphant, whatever the immediate consequences, cannot but bring joy – but the world goes on as before and
will continue thus as memories of Odette and the Prince first fade,
then vanish. And so the final sounds support the reappearance of the
swans on the lake, doing what they had always done, and would
continue to do. It does not make for a cosy ending, but it is surely
one more powerful (and more truthful?) than the trite 'ever-after'
outcome that was foisted on the ballet when Tchaikovsky was no
longer present to protest.

––––––

Swan Lake was the first momentous step in establishing
Tchaikovsky's reputation as perhaps the greatest-ever ballet composer: certainly no one has been greater than he. But it also represented a
very significant moment in the evolution of Tchaikovsky's own creative world. One of the dramatic themes that will recur again and
again in his subsequent works is that of the young woman who is condemned to suffer, even to be destroyed, by (as Tchaikovsky would
have put it) the workings of Fate – that is, each is caught into a trail of
mishaps or events over which she has no control and which bring
inescapable unhappiness, misery or even death. Odette in *Swan Lake*
is but the first example of this. In his operas, there will be Tatyana in
Eugene Onegin, Joan of Arc in *The Maid of Orleans*, Mariya in
Mazepa, Nastasia in *The Enchantress*, Liza in *The Queen of Spades*.
Not all these operas are of supreme quality, but it is noticeable that, so
often, the best and most moving music (sometimes music among the
very best Tchaikovsky ever wrote) is drawn from him by such characters, as we shall hear when we reach the first, *Eugene Onegin*, probably his finest opera.

Tchaikovsky did not always aim to produce masterpieces, nor did
he feel any professional or, indeed, moral pressure always to hit the
high ground. He had no contempt for what might be the functional
rather than the inspirational, and though he would take on certain
commissions simply because he was short of funds, that did not mean
that he was any less diligent in offering the best that was in him. It was
while he was in the throes of creating *Swan Lake* that he also produced a set of modest piano pieces, some of which still remain among
his most widely known works.

The Seasons: twelve pieces for piano * * *

[This is Tchaikovsky's most famous work for piano composed for adults, and presents us with twelve splendid examples of what the 'artisan' in Tchaikovsky could create. They are mostly charming, unpretentious pieces (though some are quite challenging technically) which, as a set, have never really caught on in this country. Rather a pity!]

In December 1875 Tchaikovsky was approached by the editor of a well-known periodical, *Nuvelliste*, to compose a series of twelve monthly supplements for the 1876 issues. The result was what we know as *The Seasons*, though a more accurate title would be 'The Months of the Year'. Kashkin recorded that Tchaikovsky, fearful that he might forget to discharge his monthly chore, instructed Alexey, on a certain day each month, to remind him of his duty, whereupon Tchaikovsky would compose the required piece at one sitting. That Tchaikovsky was capable of this feat is perfectly plausible, but the surviving correspondence with the editor of the periodical indicates that all the pieces were completed by May 1876. Shortage of funds may have made Tchaikovsky especially expeditious.

The Seasons may be little more than a series of salon pieces targeted on amateur pianists (though some items present formidable technical challenges), but they should not be scoffed at. *January: By the fireside* is notable for some of its harmonic touches (and its central section anticipates one of the most famous of all Tchaikovsky's melodies, as we shall later hear), and the rumbustiously rattling *February: Carnival* surely reflects the celebrations before the season of Lent closes in. The twitterings in *March: The lark's song* have much charm, and *April: Snowdrops* is a lightly disguised waltz. *May: May nights* is a dreamy nocturne, though with an animated centre. No doubt because of its distinctive tune, *June: Barcarolle* has always been one of the most popular of the series. *July: Reaper's song* may suggest initially repetitive scything, but this gives way to celebration which will be joyfully reinforced in *August: Harvest time*. Two pieces are strikingly pictorial: *September: The hunt* echoing with horn calls, and *November: The troika* with merry jingling bells. In the intervening, lightly melancholy *October: Autumn song* Tchaikovsky added a tenor melody to counterpoint the main tune: could this have been fathered by the great *pas d'action* with violin and cello obbligati in Act 2 of *Swan Lake? December: Christmas* – well, Tchaikovsky was simply incapable of writing a dull waltz. If composing these pieces had been currently good for his pocket, they would, at this time, have done as much good in spreading his name through the humbler households of Russia.

————

11
Towards the Crisis:
Francesca da Rimini

For ten years Tchaikovsky had been based in Moscow, establishing himself in the city both as teacher and member of the community, and building a reputation that was spreading beyond the boundaries of Russia itself. Of his private activities during this period we have little precise information, especially on those relating to his sexuality. Now, however, it is clear that, being fully adult, he was participating in the homosexual subculture that existed in Moscow, as in other Russian cities. As has already been noted, such activities were also, it seems, a factor in his domestic life, and there was clearly a strong homosexual element in some of Tchaikovsky's other friendships – with the young Vladimir Shilovsky, for instance – and especially with some of his nearer contemporaries such as Nikolay Kondratyev. Investigating the details of such relationships is not to the point here: suffice it to say that the tensions between Tchaikovsky's homosexual drives and his wish to establish a heterosexual image that would silence gossip, of which he had good reason to believe he had become subject, would now grow inexorably and tormentingly.

Certainly for the whole of the coming summer break of 1876 Tchaikovsky remained restless and often depressed, and in this condition it seems major composition was impossible. Instead, he wandered from place to place. First to Nizy, where he found the riotous indiscipline of Kondratyev's servants so outrageous that within three days, and after a blazing row with Kondratyev himself, he had fled to Sasha at Kamenka, only to find that his sister was absent. Vienna was next, and thence to the French spa of Vichy, where he intended to take the waters. The latter proved beneficial to his physical health, but he hated the town itself. 'Accursed, loathsome, revolting Vichy!' as he exploded to Anatoly. 'Everything has conspired to make my stay intolerable – the bustle, the crush for every glass of water at the spring, the total absence of any natural beauties but, most of all, the *loneliness* – all this poisons every moment of my life.' To Modest he wrote in similar vein: 'The melancholy that consumes me is the more terrible because those three days I spent with you in Lyons are so clear in my memory.' Yet what had begun during those three days would have seismic consequences for his own future, for in Lyon he had encountered a seven-year-old deaf mute, Kolya Konradi, who would unwittingly be a significant factor in driving him towards the most critical single act of his whole life.

It was back at the beginning of 1876 that Modest had decided to become tutor to Kolya, and the lad's father had forthwith arranged for Modest to undertake a course at an institution in Lyon that specialized in a method for teaching deaf mutes to speak. Having left Vichy for Lyon and Modest, Tchaikovsky now met Kolya, and with the newly qualified Modest and a governess for Kolya, he set out for Palavas-les-flots, a resort on the south coast of France. It proved a disastrous choice. Palavas was dreary, the local water was polluted, and all but Tchaikovsky, who had brought a supply of Vichy water with him for personal use, now became ill. It fell therefore to Tchaikovsky to care for Kolya, and this he did with exemplary zeal, as Modest recalled:

> He was attentiveness, patience, gentleness itself in his handling of this deaf and dumb boy who was himself nervy, fidgety, able only with great difficulty to express himself to those around him. The mutual adoration of two friends, which had already established itself before this, now became even stronger. I can truly say that this relationship with a boy who at that moment was entirely dependent upon him, this role as head of the family which for a short time had fallen to his lot, showed Pyotr Ilich a way out of the melancholy that was tormenting him, out of the 'loneliness' of his recent years.

It cannot be doubted that there was a strong homosexual undercurrent in Tchaikovsky's feelings towards Kolya, though erotic urges were surely blended with a genuine paternal feeling which made him long for a family of his own within marriage. Among his homosexual friends there were ones who exemplified this dual situation, and by the summer's end, now back in Russia, he had come to a fateful decision. On 31 August he wrote to Modest:

> I am now living through a very critical moment in my life. When an opportunity occurs I'll write to you about it in rather more detail,

but meanwhile I'll simply say: *I have decided to marry.* I cannot avoid this. I have to do it – and not just for my own sake, but also for *you*, and for Tolya, and for Sasha, and for all those I love. For *you* in particular. And you, Modya, need to think seriously about this.

The course towards disaster had been set.

The letters Tchaikovsky exchanged with his twin brothers, Modest and Anatoly, at this time make both fascinating and disturbing reading. Sometimes he seemed to shrug off the self-evident problems and tensions marriage would bring for him, at others the turmoil and the pain he was enduring breaks through with irrepressible force. Sasha was clearly horrified at her brother's declared intention, and Modest did all he could to dissuade him. Tchaikovsky's reply to the latter is the most eloquent and perhaps most revealing testimony to his now dreadful inner state:

> I've lost your letter, and I cannot reply point by point to your arguments against marriage. I remember that many of them are unsound; many, on the other hand, coincide completely with my own thoughts. You say that one shouldn't give a damn for what people say. This is true only up to a certain point. There are people who cannot despise me for my vices simply because they began to love me when they still didn't suspect that I was, in fact, a man of lost reputation. For instance, this applies to Sasha. I know that she guesses *everything* and *forgives* everything. Many other people whom I love or respect regard me in the same way. Do you really believe that the consciousness *that they pity and forgive me* is not painful to me when, at bottom, I am guilty of nothing! And is it not a terrible thought that people who love me can sometimes *be ashamed* of me! But, you know, this has happened a hundred times, and it will happen a hundred times more. In a word, I should like by marriage, or by a generally open liaison with a woman, to stop the mouths of various contemptible creatures whose opinion I do not in the least respect, but who could cause distress to people close to me. In any case, do not fear for me, dear Modest. The fulfilment of my plans is not nearly as close as you think. My habits have become so hardened that it's impossible to discard them like an old glove. And besides, I am far from possessed of an iron character, and since my

letters to you I have already three times given way to the force of natural inclinations [participated in a homosexual act]. Thus you are completely right in saying in your letter that, despite all one's vows, it is not possible to restrain oneself from one's weaknesses.

All the same, I am standing by my intentions, and you may be sure that, one way or another, I shall carry them through. But I shall not do this suddenly or hastily. In any case, I do not intend to take a *yoke* upon me. I shall only enter a legal or an extramarital union with a woman if I can fully guarantee my peace and freedom.

While it is certainly true that some of Tchaikovsky's compositions are indelibly stamped with something of the particular joy or torment he might have been himself experiencing at the time of their composition, he stated bluntly that he was quite capable of detaching himself from his current mood, and composing a piece that might seem a very denial of that condition. Only three days before writing this letter Tchaikovsky, at Nikolay Rubinstein's request, had set about a piece for a charity concert in aid of victims of the war that had broken out between Turkey and Russia's fellow Slavs in Montenegro and Serbia – a war into which it seemed Russia might herself be drawn. Not normally a political animal, Tchaikovsky nevertheless experienced a surge of patriotism, and within five days an eight-minute **Slavonic March** *** was not only composed but scored. At the concert a month later it created a sensation. As one person present recorded: 'The rumpus and roar that broke out beggars description. The whole audience rose to its feet. Many jumped on to their seats: cries of *bravo* and *hurrah* were mingled together. The march had to be repeated, after which the same storm broke out afresh. Many in the hall were weeping.' No piece demonstrates more powerfully Tchaikovsky's super-professionalism in responding to commissions. The Slavonic March is not a great piece, but it is a prodigiously well-targeted one. Adapting three Serbian folktunes, and incorporating a portion of the Tsarist national anthem in the middle in preparation for a full-blown restatement before the final furore-prompting coda, it is no surprise the piece was rapturously received, and it merits the occasional performance it still receives today.

Though on leaving Palavas Tchaikovsky headed first for Paris, he remained there only briefly, for he had to discharge a commission that he had accepted before leaving Russia. This was to write five articles for a Russian journal on the opening of Wagner's brand-new opera house at Bayreuth with the first ever complete performance of Wagner's mammoth *Ring* cycle, comprising four of his operas (*Das Rheingold, Die Walküre, Siegfried* and *Götterdämmerung*). And so, after Paris, he headed for Bayreuth. He found a number of his friends and acquaintances there (Nikolay Rubinstein, Cui and Laroche among them), loathed the town, bewailed the crowds that packed it for the occasion and thus made finding food difficult, and judged the new opera house 'more like a huge booth put up hurriedly for some industrial exhibition'. He tried to visit Wagner but couldn't, and breathed a sigh of relief when it was all over and he could go home. Yet – how could he have turned down the opportunity to be present at what would prove to be the century's greatest single musical event, presenting probably the most massive musical conception ever in a purpose-built opera house? In fact, Tchaikovsky found the four operas themselves a test of endurance; he thought there were some wonderful moments between long tedious stretches, and it was with relief that he finally quit Bayreuth. Yet despite this, he could not altogether escape the power of Wagner's music (as he himself admitted), and there is no doubt that his next orchestral piece would not have come out quite the way it did if he had not had the Bayreuth experience.

Tchaikovsky had first considered composing an opera on the tragedy of Francesca da Rimini, as related in Dante's *La Divina Commedia*, in 1875, and it was among the various suggestions Modest had proffered when Tchaikovsky had been in Vichy, though this was to have been an orchestral piece. It was during the train journey on leaving Palavas for Paris that Tchaikovsky re-read the pitiable tale of Francesca, and resolved to take up Modest's suggestion, though it was not until October, immediately after completing the Slavonic March, that he set about the piece, composition being completed in three weeks, and the scoring finalized in November. He felt well pleased with the result, as did the audience at the premiere in March 1877.

Francesca da Rimini: symphonic fantasia after Dante*****

[Francesca da Rimini *will have a special appeal to those who like tempestuous music, though perhaps the finer part is the central portrayal*

*of Francesca and her sad fate. The first two of its three sections are
large, but they are well worth the patient attention they may require.]*

We are fortunate that Tchaikovsky set out on his manuscript score a full
programme for the piece, prefacing it with some lines from Dante which
he had already quoted to Modest from Vichy:

Nessun maggior dolore,	There is no greater pain
Che ricordarsi del tempo felice	Than to recall a time of happiness
Nella miseria . . .	In a time of misery . . .

Dante, accompanying the shade of Virgil, descends to the second
circle of hell's abyss. The air here is filled with groans, wails, and
cries of despair. In the sepulchral gloom a storm blows up and rages.
Furiously the hellish whirlwind races along, bearing in its wild
whirling the spirits of mortals whose reason in life was clouded by
amorous passion. From the countless human souls spinning there,
Dante's attention is specially drawn to the two lovely shades of
Francesca and Paolo spinning in each other's embrace. Shocked by
the soul-searing sight of these two young shades, Dante summons
them and asks them to relate the crime for which they had been prescribed so terrible a punishment. Dissolving in tears, the shade of
Francesca tells her sad tale. She loved Paolo, but was, against her
will, given in marriage to the hateful brother of her beloved, the
hunchbacked, deformed, jealous tyrant, Rimini. The bonds of a
forced marriage could not drive from Francesca's heart her tender
passion for Paolo. Once they were reading together the romance of
Lancelot. 'We were alone,' Francesca narrated, 'and were reading
without apprehension. More than once we blanched, and our confused gazes met. But one instant destroyed us both. When, finally,
the fortunate Lancelot gained the first kiss of love, he, from whom
nothing will now separate me, kissed my trembling mouth, and the
book that had revealed to us for the first time the secret of love fell
from our hands.' At that moment Francesca's husband had entered
unexpectedly and killed both her and Paolo with blows from his dag-
ger. And, having said this, Francesca was again borne away in the
embrace of her Paolo by the furiously and wildly raging whirlwind.

What better to guide the listener through a piece than the words of
the composer himself? *Francesca da Rimini* is planned as a massive

ternary structure and the first two of the three individual sections are very extensive, but when music is so consistently alive as here, experiencing it is time well spent. Straight away we are plunged into the inferno itself (here especially there is some definite legacy from the Bayreuth experience). The wailings and torments of the damned find graphic representation in the brass, and the grim descending scales of the bass strings, backed by trombones, tuba and bassoons, signify the presence of an implacable fate (there will be more of this in the following pages). The moaning winds begin to stir, gathering themselves to produce a tempest of awesome force and duration. But ultimately these die away, and we pass from the turmoil of the elements to the travails of two human lovers caught for all eternity into an embrace which, in the whirlwinds and chaos of hell, allows no place for the joys of love. The tender clarinet theme (surely Francesca herself) leads into a marvellously spanned violin melody of love and longing, one of Tchaikovsky's strongest themes: note how it finally dissolves into a tiny three-note figure shared alternately between clarinet and violins/violas, and which continues as companion to Francesca's theme when this whole two-theme section is repeated, now differently scored (and note how, when Francesca's theme is heard for yet a third time (on the cellos), it will take a new melodic course). But then this theme yields place to the most fragile music of the whole piece, a nervously pulsing melody for cor anglais, then oboe. This, surely, is Francesca's narration, the brief harp arpeggios that punctuate her breathless phrases seeming to confirm her fragility and essential innocence (is not this passage perhaps a little akin to some of the music which, so recently, had been drawn from Tchaikovsky by Odette, another fragile victim of fate?).

There is no need to particularize further. Francesca's theme will return quietly yet again; the love music erupts and builds with enormous strength, horn fanfares signal the approach of Rimini himself, the lovers are despatched, the storm music (truncated) resumes, and the coda ends with a brutally reiterated chord, as had Tchaikovsky's earlier masterpiece of tragic love, *Romeo and Juliet*.

––––––

Fundamentally *Francesca da Rimini* was very different from both *Romeo and Juliet* and *The Tempest*, for where the former had been a drama and the latter a panorama, *Francesca da Rimini* was really a portrait in music set against a nightmarish background; it is Francesca's story, Paolo merely a passive presence. And in centering on the young woman who endures misfortune at the hand of fate, Tchaikovsky had begun building the line he had initiated with Odette in *Swan Lake*.

However, the work that followed hard on the heels of *Francesca da Rimini* could hardly have been in greater contrast. That tempestuous, heart-rending and pathos-filled piece had been completed in mid-November, but before 1876 was out, Tchaikovsky had also finished another substantial piece, his **Variations on a Rococo theme, for cello and small orchestra**. It had been commissioned by Wilhelm Fitzenhagen, a German cellist who, since 1870, had been a colleague at the Moscow Conservatoire as well as the cellist in the first performances of all three of Tchaikovsky's string quartets. The two men clearly had a good personal relationship, but the early history of these variations is one of the most unfortunate among all of Tchaikovsky's works, for until 2004 they were available only in a grossly bowdlerized edition. The original orchestral score and performing material would not be published until 1889, and in the meanwhile Fitzenhagen had been performing the Variations, scoring an especially great success with them at the Wiesbaden Festival in 1879, after which Liszt, who was present, showered praise on him. Fitzenhagen reported this to Tchaikovsky, and one sentence of his letter is crucial: 'So greatly did I please that I had three recalls, and after the *Andante* Variation (D minor) I received thunderous applause.'

Unlike present-day concert etiquette, it was quite normal for a nineteenth-century audience to applaud a particularly impressive moment in a performance even though the music was still in progress – and since these variations are often seamlessly linked together by a solo passage for the cellist, this must, to us, seem even more odd. Fitzenhagen had discovered that the elegiac D minor variation gave him his greatest personal success: the trouble was it was only the third of the eight variations, and he wanted his greatest in-performance applause to come much later. Having commissioned these Variations, Fitzenhagen now seems to have assumed he had a proprietary right to them, and he did not flinch; he shifted the D minor variation to seventh place. But, he then decided, this required some reordering of the other variations, even that one variation should be dropped altogether. However, it was only in 1889, when the full orchestral score was about to be published, that Tchaikovsky seems to have woken up to what Fitzenhagen had done. His reaction was recorded by Anatoly Brandukov, who had studied under both Fitzenhagen and Tchaikovsky at the Moscow Conservatoire, and who, on a visit to Tchaikovsky, found him

> very upset, looking as though he was ill. When I asked, 'What's the matter with you?' Pyotr Ilich pointed to the writing table and said, 'Fitzenhagen's been here. Look what he's done to my piece – he's changed everything!' But when I asked what action he was going to take, Pyotr Ilich replied, 'The devil take it! Let it stand as it is!'

And so it remained until, in 1941, the original version was played at a concert in Moscow. But still it did not catch on, and it was not until 1979 that it was first heard in public in the UK when Raphael Wall-fisch played it in a broadcast performance. Since then, though some other cellists had taken up the original version, Wallfisch was unable to find a publisher until 2004. Now, however, all the performing material is available, and it is only a matter of time before Fitzenhagen's travesty is finally consigned to the dustbin of history.

Variations on a Rococo theme: for cello and small orchestra * * *(*)

[The Rococo Variations present few problems to the listener. It is a very relaxed but still high-quality piece. As noted above, until very recently it has been heard only in a mutilated form, but the Variations have now been published in their original form and will certainly, in due course, oust the bowdlerized one. The pioneer recording by Raphfael Wallfisch of the authentic version may still be available; otherwise check the record catalogue.]

Many listeners are inclined to believe that the variation form is a lowlier genre than is, say, the symphony, concerto or quartet. At one level it does make for much easier listening, since each variation is relatively brief, self-contained, and the sustained concentration required by a symphonic movement is not demanded. But with some variation sets it is, and that is certainly true of the Rococo Variations – if you are to get the full experience out of the work. Rococo is a style term applied to some kinds of later eighteenth-century classical music composed in a relaxed, graceful style, but for Tchaikovsky it meant more specifically (though true only up to a point) 'in the style of Mozart'. Certainly the orchestra in his Rococo Variations is scaled down to Mozartian proportions (six wind instruments, plus strings), and the theme, though original, is 'Mozartian'. However, if Tchaikovsky had gone on to compose the following variations in the style of his idol, they would probably have been of merely curiosity value. But he did not. Though always careful that we should never completely lose a sense of the borrowed-style theme as the original ancestor of each variation, Tchaikovsky otherwise allowed his own inventiveness free rein, sometimes (as in the above-mentioned D minor variation, for instance) simply reflecting initially the general pitch contour of the theme and its phrase structure, but then allowing his own melodic gift to complete the variation in a style entirely his own. The variations tend to grow organically, and twice Tchaikovsky even inserts the theme's little woodwind coda into the variation itself. The seventh, penultimate variation is a three-minute *valse triste* that takes us to the remotest stylistic boundary of the set before the final variation-plus-coda brings us back towards the relatively relaxed world in which the whole piece had started. The Rococo Variations may make for easy listening – but remain truly attentive: only then will Tchaikovsky's quiet but abundant inventiveness and mastery of musical space begin to become apparent. None but a truly great composer could have written this (seemingly) unpretentious piece.

––––––

The number of truly great creative artists living and working in Russia during the second half of the nineteenth century, and whose work is still alive today over a century on, is remarkable. In music there was Borodin, Balakirev, Musorgsky, Rimsky-Korsakov – and, of course, Tchaikovsky; in literature there was Dostoevsky, Turgenev, Chekhov – and, of course, Tolstoy. All were at least greatly respected in their own lifetimes, but the last was revered. Tolstoy's massive novel *War and Peace* is, I suppose, reckoned as the pinnacle of Russian prose literature (certainly no other work is placed more highly), while *Anna Karenina* is rated among the greatest tragic love stories of all time. Tchaikovsky, a voracious reader, was ambivalent about some of Tolstoy's work, heavily criticizing *Anna Karenina* when it first appeared in the mid-1870s, but later conceding its greatness. Already by 1876 Tolstoy was, to some, 'a demigod' (as Tchaikovsky himself put it), and in that year Tchaikovsky at last came face to face with this colossus. This was at a soirée at the Conservatoire in honour of Tolstoy, and on the programme was Tchaikovsky's First String Quartet, the *Andante cantabile* of which reduced the honoured guest to tears, as we have already noted. Ten years on Tchaikovsky could still recall the occasion, and the deep pride he had felt at Tolstoy's reaction. The two men would go on to spend several evenings together, gifts were exchanged, and Tolstoy sent Tchaikovsky some folksongs which he might use. But this gift did not draw the gratitude Tolstoy had expected, for the folksongs had been badly transcribed, and Tchaikovsky's one surviving letter to Tolstoy offsets an expression of genuine veneration for the writer with a frank rejection of the folksongs in this condition: 'They have been noted down by an unskilful hand, and contain no more than vestiges of their former beauty.' Indeed, it seems that talking with the man had brought some disenchantment – that there was a prosaic side to Tolstoy. And so Tchaikovsky avoided further encounters with the great man, content to retain, uncompromised, his unbounded reverence for Tolstoy the writer. The two men never met again.

And again as 1876 drew to a close, another relationship, whose future significance Tchaikovsky could never have envisaged, began. Among the Conservatoire students in Tchaikovsky's class in music theory was a young violinist, Iosif Kotek, with whom he had developed a strong bond. Then, also in 1876, a wealthy widow wrote to Nikolay Rubinstein in the hope of finding a young violinist who might join her household to play violin and piano music with her. The salary was very generous. Since she travelled much, there was also a good chance of seeing something of the world, and since she had a large family to occupy her there was also a reasonable expectation of much free time for private practice. Rubinstein suggested Kotek, and an agreement was made. The widow was already familiar with some of Tchaikovsky's music, had been much attracted by it, and now she made a formal approach to Tchaikovsky: would he make violin and piano arrangements of some of his pieces for her sessions with Kotek? Again, the remuneration would be very substantial. Kotek interceded, Tchaikovsky responded readily, and the finished work was despatched.

A letter of thanks came promptly:

Allow me to convey to you my sincerest gratitude for such a swift execution of my request. To tell you how much delight your compositions afford me I consider out of place because you have not been accustomed to that kind of praise, and the worship of a being, in music as insignificant as I, might appear to you simply ridiculous, and my enjoyment is so dear to me that I do not wish it to be ridiculed. Therefore I will only say, and I ask you to believe this literally, that with your music I live more lightly and more pleasantly.

Accept my sincerest respect and sincerest devotion.
NADEZHDA VON MECK

Tchaikovsky's reply was equally prompt:

I am sincerely grateful for all the kind and flattering things you have been so good as to write to me. On my side I will say that, for a musician amid obstacles and failures of every kind, it is comforting to think that there is a small minority of people, to which you likewise belong, who love our art so sincerely and warmly.

Sincerely devoted to you and esteeming you.
P. TCHAIKOVSKY

With these two notes began one of the most famed, extensive and extraordinary correspondences in the whole history of Western culture. For Tchaikovsky's future, both material and creative, its importance can hardly be exaggerated.

12
Two Women: Marriage

Nadezhda von Meck was nine years older than Tchaikovsky. As a child she had become a very competent pianist with a good knowledge of the repertoire. Then at sixteen she had been married off to a twenty-eight-year-old railway engineer, Karl von Meck, and a rapid succession of children had followed. Nevertheless, Nadezhda proved a feisty wife; domestic demands did not weaken the energy with which she exerted pressure on her husband to find a partner with capital, and join the boom in building the Russian railway network. Karl was persuaded, and during the 1860s he amassed a great fortune. But in 1876 he died suddenly, and with seven of her eleven children still living with her, Nadezhda concentrated on her business affairs and on the education of those of her still-dependent offspring.

On receiving the violin–piano arrangements she had requested from Tchaikovsky, she wrote a note of acknowledgement in which her impassioned feelings at this new relationship and her longing for the exchange of inner confidences are already clearly evident:

> There is much, much that I would wish to write to you, when the opportunity occurs, of my imaginary relationship with you, but I am afraid of intruding upon your so limited free time. I will say only that this relationship, however abstract it may be, is precious to me as the best, the highest of all feelings of which human nature is capable.

Tchaikovsky's reply said exactly what she had wanted:

> I know you rather better than perhaps you think. If, one fine day, you would be so kind as to favour me with a written account of those many things you would wish to say, then I should be extremely grateful to you.

This was enough for Nadezhda to drop all reserve, and her reply is almost a declaration of love. She begged a photograph of him, waxed rapturous over *The Tempest*, the first of his works she had heard ('for several days I was as one delirious, and I could do nothing to free myself from this state'), confessed she had already tried to discover everything she could about him, then ended with the condition that she wished should regulate their relationship:

> There was a time when I very much wanted to meet you. Now, however, the more I am enchanted by you, the more I fear acquaintance – I feel I would not be in a condition to begin talking with you – although if we should unexpectedly meet face to face anywhere, I could not behave towards you as to a stranger, and I would hold out my hand to you, though only to press yours – but I would not speak a word. Now I prefer to think of you from a distance, to hear you in your music, and to feel myself at one with you in it.

Her view of Tchaikovsky was, of course, a fantasy. But Tchaikovsky's reply was, in its own way, equally extravagant, all the more remarkable for coming from a man who was normally an exceptionally private being:

> You are quite right, Nadezhda Filaretovna, in supposing that I am in that condition to understand fully the peculiarities of your spiritual organism. I dare to think that you are not mistaken in believing me close to you as a person. Just as you have tried to listen to judgements made by the public on me, so I on my part have not missed any opportunity for learning details of you and your mode of living. I have always been interested in you as a person whose moral temper has many features in common with my own nature. There is certainly one trait that draws us together which is that we both suffer from one and the same illness. That illness is misanthropy – but misanthropy of a particular kind, at the root of which there is absolutely no hatred and contempt for people. Persons who suffer from this illness have no fear of that injury which can come from the machinations of someone who is close: instead they fear that disenchantment, that yearning for the ideal that follows upon every intimacy. From what I have said above, you will easily understand that I am in no way surprised that, loving my music, you are not attempting to make the acquaintance of its author. You fear you will not find in me those qualities with which your imagination,

being inclined to idealize, has invested me. And you are quite right. I feel that, on closer acquaintance with me, you would not find that correspondence, that complete harmony between the musician and the man, of which you dream.

And so began a correspondence that would spread over some thirteen years, producing well over a thousand letters, some very lengthy, and which, when published, would fill three very large volumes. For both correspondents it was at once a solace and a safety valve; for us this legacy is a priceless source of insight into Tchaikovsky's inner world. Nor would Nadezhda exist for Tchaikovsky merely as a fantasy (even mother) figure; she would also become a vital enabler in his day-to-day life. Yet in all this time they would meet but once, and that by an accident such as both had made every attempt to avoid. Not a word was exchanged; she seemed confused, did not 'hold out her hand to him'; he merely raised his hat, and then passed on. Nevertheless, they sought something that might, vicariously, consummate their relationship and, to this end, they engineered meetings between various of her sons and of Tchaikovsky's nieces (Sasha's daughters). In 1884 the chemistry worked, and Nikolay von Meck married Anna Davïdova.

Antonina Milyukova was nine years younger than Tchaikovsky, and had been a piano student at the Conservatoire. Tchaikovsky had been totally unaware of her existence until May 1877, when she wrote to him, declaring she had been in love with him for some years. This letter has disappeared, as has Tchaikovsky's reply, which clearly had discouraged her from any hope of a favourable response. But her second letter, dated 16 May, is extant. She noted that Tchaikovsky had told her to master her feelings, but she now made it clear she could not. 'Wherever I may be, I shall not be able to forget you or lose my love for you,' she had continued. 'What I liked in you when I first came to know you I can no longer find in any other man. Indeed, in a word, I do not want to look at any other man after you.'

But, unable to control herself, before the day was out Antonina had written a second letter which is a rising torrent of emotion and, by its end, near hysterical:

I see that my letters are already becoming wearisome to you. But will you really break off this correspondence with me, not having seen me even once? No, I am convinced you will not be so cruel.

After your last letter I loved you twice as much again, and your shortcomings mean absolutely nothing to me. Perhaps if you were a perfect being I would have remained completely cool towards you. I am dying of longing, and I burn with a desire to see you, to sit with you and talk with you. There is no failing that might cause me to fall out-of-love with you.

Having today sent a man to deliver my letter to you, I was very surprised to hear you had left Moscow, and longing descended upon me even more. I sit at home all day, I pace the room from corner to corner like some crazy thing, thinking of that moment when I shall see you. I shall be ready to throw myself on your neck, to smother you with kisses – but what right have I to do this? Maybe, indeed, you take this for effrontery on my part. I can assure you I am a respectable and honourable woman in the full sense of the word, and I have nothing that I would wish to conceal from you. My first kiss will be given to you and to no one else in the world. Farewell, my dear one! Do not try to disillusion me further about yourself, because you are only wasting your time. I cannot live without you, and so maybe soon I shall kill myself. So let me see you and kiss you so that I may remember that kiss in the other world. Farewell.

Yours eternally,
A. M.

Tchaikovsky enquired about Antonina from his friends who might know her, but discovered nothing favourable. Yet he had already, before ever he had met her, declared an irrevocable intention of marrying, and now Fate was presenting to him his predestined bride. He would go through with it: he had to. But a second factor must have long been troubling him: how would his new 'best friend', Nadezhda von Meck, respond to all this? In what is one of the most pain-filled of all his letters, on 15 July, two months on and only three days before the wedding itself, he confessed all. In the end, he had agreed to Antonina's request that he should visit her:

Why did I do this? It seemed to me now as though some force of Fate was driving me to this girl. When we met, I again explained to her that I entertained nothing but sympathy and gratitude for her love. But when I had parted from her, I began to think over the thoughtlessness of my conduct. If I did not love her, if I did not wish to encourage her feelings, then why had I visited her, and what would be the consequence of all this? From the letter that followed upon this I concluded that if, having gone so far, I were suddenly to turn away from this girl, then I would make her truly wretched, would drive her to a tragic end. Thus I was faced with difficult alternatives – either to preserve my own freedom at the price of this girl's death (*death* is not an empty word here; she does indeed love me to distraction), or *to marry*. I had to choose the latter course. The decision was supported by the fact that the sole dream of my eighty-two-year-old father and all my relatives is that I should marry. And so, one beautiful evening, I went to my future wife, told her openly that *I did not love her*, but that, whatever befell, I would be a staunch and faithful friend. I described to her in detail my character – my irritability, volatile temperament, my unsociability – finally, my circumstances. After this I asked her whether she still wanted to be my wife. Of course her reply was in the affirmative. I cannot convey to you in words those terrible feelings I went through in the days that followed immediately upon that evening. Having lived thirty-seven years with an innate aversion to marriage, it is very distressing, through force of circumstances, to be drawn into the position of *a bridegroom* who, moreover, is not in the least attracted to his bride. I must change my whole way of life; I must do my best for the peace and well-being of this other person whose fate is joined to mine – all this is not very easy for a bachelor who has become inured to being self-centred. To enable me to change my outlook, to get myself accustomed to looking to my future calmly, I decided still to hold to my original plan, and still to go off to the country for a month. And so I did. The quiet of country life in a circle of very nice people and amid *delightful* natural surroundings had a very wholesome effect upon me. I decided that I would not evade my destiny, and that there was something fateful in my encounter with this girl. Besides, I know from experience how it often happens in life that what frightens and horrifies sometimes proves beneficial – but also, of course, that, contrariwise, what you have striven after in the hope of bliss and happiness, can end in disappointment. If it is to be, let it be!

This letter is terrible to read; indeed, the dogged determination with which this hapless man propelled himself towards certain disaster might appear bizarre, were it not so appalling. Only on the eve of the wedding did he write to Sasha, and the horror in prospect for Tchaikovsky himself was compounded not only by his manifest fear that his bride would be rejected by Sasha's family, but by his own self-evident view that she was unworthy of them; worst of all, it is clear by now that, for all his claims to 'love' her, she was actually becoming repugnant to him. One can only guess at the shock his letter must have given Sasha, for his misery seeps out even more chillingly than in his letter to Nadezhda von Meck:

Any day now will be celebrated my marriage to a young woman, *Antonina Ivanovna Milyukova*. While giving you this news, I shall for the moment refrain from describing my bride's qualities since, except that she is a thoroughly respectable girl and loves me very much, I still know very little about her. Only when we have lived together for some time will the facets of her character reveal themselves to me with complete clarity. I shan't bring her to see you at Kamenka until I'm no longer shocked by the thought that my nieces will call her *auntie*. At the moment, although I love my bride, it still seems to me a little impertinent on her part to have become aunt to your children, whom I love more than any other children in the world.

I have spent a month not far from here in the country at the Shilovskys'. I needed to stay there, first to begin my opera, secondly to acclimatize myself to the thought that I'm getting married. The proof that I'm taking this important step not frivolously but with deliberation is shown by the fact that I spent this month very calmly, and composed a whole two-thirds of an opera.

That Tchaikovsky could have given his mind to such a project while in his present emotional turmoil may seem extraordinary. In fact, the opera proved to be one of his supreme masterpieces, as will emerge.

The wedding took place on 18 July. One of Tchaikovsky's colleagues, Dmitri Razumovsky, Professor of the History of Church Music at the Conservatoire, officiated. Anatoly was the only family member present; he and Kotek were the witnesses. Neither of Tchaikovsky's friends, Albrecht and Kashkin, knew of the wedding. Razumovsky realized the strain the event would put on Tchaikovsky, and nursed him through the ceremony as best he could. 'But, all the same, I remained a sort of bystander until the moment when Razu-movsky, at the conclusion of the ceremony, made Antonina Ivanovna and me kiss,' Tchaikovsky remembered to Kashkin. 'Then a kind of pain gripped my heart; I was suddenly seized with such emotion that, it seems, I wept. But I tried to gain control of myself, and to assume an appearance of calm.'

Two days later, and now in St Petersburg with his wife, Tchaikovsky poured out to Anatoly a detailed account of the wed-ding-night train journey he and Antonina had made to St Petersburg:

When the carriage started I was ready to cry out with choking sobs. Nevertheless, I had to occupy my wife with conversation as far as Klin in order that I might earn the right to lie down in my own arm-chair when it was dark, and remain alone, by myself. At the second station after Khinok, Meshchersky [one of Tchaikovsky's old friends from the School of Jurisprudence] burst into the carriage. When I saw him I felt that he had to take me elsewhere without delay. This he did. Before beginning any sort of conversation with him I had to give vent to a flood of tears. Meshchersky showed much tender sym-pathy, and did a lot to prop up my fallen spirits. When, after Klin, I returned to my wife, I was much calmer. Meshchersky arranged that we should be accommodated in a sleeping compartment, and after this I slept the sleep of the dead. The remainder of the journey after I woke up was not particularly awful. What I found most comfort-ing of all was that my wife didn't comprehend or even notice my ill-concealed anguish. Now and always she appears to be completely happy and contented. She is in agreement with everything, and con-tented with everything. We stayed at the Hotel Europa – very good, and even luxurious. I went off to have a bath. We dined in our own room. In the evening we took a carriage to the islands.

We have had conversations which have still further clarified our relationship with each other. *She is positively agreeable to every-thing, and will never want more. All she wants is to cherish and care for me.* I have retained for myself complete freedom of action. After taking a good dose of valerian, and begging my upset wife not to be upset, I again slept the sleep of the dead. Sleep is a great benefactor. I feel the time is not far distant when I shall *finally* compose myself.

And what, indeed, is there to grieve for? I have guaranteed my freedom of action to such a degree that, as soon as my wife and I have got used to each other, she will not constrain me in anything. *She's a very limited person*, but this is even a good thing. An intelligent woman might instil fear of herself in me; I stand so far above this one, I am so superior to this one that at least I shall never be frightened of her.

The nightmare of his new marital status – and not merely the physical aversion he felt towards Antonina, but also the contempt he was developing for her – make for appalling reading. He admitted Antonina did what she could to be a good wife, but in the daylight world of non-marital life, he discovered they had nothing in common – and that she did not know a note of his music. If, when they were out walking, he met a relative or friend, he could not bring himself to admit that Antonina was his spouse. He introduced her to his father and his third wife, Lizaveta:

Papa is enchanted by my wife, which was to be expected. Lizaveta Mikhailovna was very sweet and attentive, but several times I noted tears in her eyes. My perspicacious and dear stepmother must have guessed I was living through a critical moment of my life. I confess all this was painful to me – that is, Papa's display of affection and his endearments (the very opposite of my coldness towards my wife), and Lizaveta Mikhailovna's perspicacity. I am indeed living through a painful moment in my life, but I feel that, little by little, I shall grow accustomed to my new situation. It would be an intolerable sham if I were to deceive my wife in anything, and I have warned her she can count only on my brotherly love. Physically my wife has become *totally repugnant* to me. Yesterday morning, while my wife was taking a bath, I went to Mass at St Isaac's Cathedral. I felt a need to pray.

Before the week's honeymoon was over, he felt obliged to have a gathering of some of his friends. It brought on a fit of despair. 'The crisis was *terrible, terrible, terrible*,' he wrote to Anatoly. 'If it had not been for my love for you and others close to me bearing me up in these *intolerable spiritual torments*, then it might have ended badly, i.e. with illness or madness.'

Back in Moscow he visited his wife's family and was repelled by them. However, a brief escape was in prospect, for Antonina had agreed he could visit the Caucasus spa of Essentuki. On the way he would call in on Kamenka, and ahead of this he tried to reassure Sasha. 'I already love my wife, but how immeasurably distant is this love from that which I entertain towards you, my brothers, Lev, your children!!!' he wrote. There was certainly no joy for her to be found here.

On 7 August Tchaikovsky set out for Kiev, where he paused to write to Nadezhda von Meck, detailing the horror he had endured, and trying to put the best face he could on the future. Whatever her feelings had been, she had answered his pre-marital letter with an extravagant approval of his decision, and the warmest of good wishes for his future, ending with the most fulsome reaffirmation of her admiration and friendship. Yet it is difficult to believe that she had received his latest news without reflecting that the course of events would not be unfavourable to her future relationship with Tchaikovsky himself. His final sentence surely now confirmed this for her. All was as before – perhaps even more so: 'Nadezhda Filaretovna, I bless you for all that you have done for me. Farewell, my best, my inestimable friend.'

In the end Tchaikovsky never reached Essentuki. Instead he spent the following month or more with Sasha and her family. Immediately, it seems, his depression lifted, and he joined in the familiar corporate life of Kamenka. But on 23 September he was back in Moscow for the new Conservatoire term. The next day he wrote to Anatoly:

> My wife met me. She, poor thing, has suffered many painful moments in arranging our apartment pending my arrival. It's very elegant, nice, and not without luxury. Naturally you'll want to know how I feel. Tolya, allow me to pass over this in silence. I'm distressed: that's all I'll say. But, of course, this was inevitable after the abundance of happiness I experienced at Kamenka. I know that I'll still have to have patience, and then calm, contentment and – who knows – perhaps even happiness will come bit by bit.

Tchaikovsky's friends were naturally curious about Antonina, and Jurgenson arranged a dinner at his own home so that they might meet her. She was predictably ill at ease, and her husband constantly chimed in after her, completing what she might have wished to say when she had faltered. Nikolay Rubinstein observed later that she was pretty, behaved nicely, 'but is not particularly winning; it's as though she is not a real person, but some sort of confection'. For most of his friends that was the first and last time they would meet Antonina. The Conservatoire term was now imminent, and when it began, Tchaikovsky gave his classes punctiliously, but promptly disappeared, and became increasingly difficult to talk to.

Kashkin many years later recorded Tchaikovsky's own account of the final crisis. Though he wrote it out in the first person, and its literal accuracy must be treated with reserve, there is no reason to doubt the substance of what he wrote:

> During the day [Tchaikovsky said] I still tried to work at home, but in the evenings it became intolerable. Not daring to go off to a friend or even to the theatre, I set off each evening for a walk, and for several hours wandered aimlessly through the distant, out-of-the-way streets of Moscow. The weather had become gloomy and cold, and at night there was a slight frost. On one such night I came to the deserted bank of the River Moscow, and there entered my head the thought that it would be possible to kill myself by contracting a chill. To this end, unseen in the darkness, I entered the water almost up to my waist, and stayed there until I could no longer endure the bodily ache produced by the cold. I came out of the water with a firm conviction that, either from pneumonia or some respiratory illness, I should die. At home I told how I had taken part in a nocturnal fishing expedition, and had fallen into the water by accident. However, my health showed itself to be so sound that the icy bath had no consequence for me.

This desperate stratagem having failed, a more direct plan was needed, and Tchaikovsky forthwith contacted Anatoly in St Petersburg, urging him to send a telegram over the name of Eduard Nápravník, the conductor at the Imperial Theatres, requiring Tchaikovsky's presence in the Russian capital in connection with the forthcoming revival of *Vakula the Smith*. Anatoly acted immediately, Tchaikovsky scrawling a hasty note to Albrecht giving him the news, and promising he would be back in Moscow the following Tuesday.

He did not return. Anatoly met him at the station, could barely recognize his brother, and took him to a hotel, where his nerves gave way. A psychiatrist declared a complete change of environment was essential, and that there could be no question of him ever living with Antonina again. Anatoly hastened to Moscow to set his brother's affairs in some sort of order, and arranged a meeting with Antonina, Rubinstein accompanying him to ensure that she was told the full truth. Antonina invited the two men in, and listened while Rubinstein set out the position with a bluntness that made Anatoly cringe. She then invited the two men to take tea. Rubinstein excused himself, and Antonina accompanied him to the door. Returning with her face beaming, she observed: 'I never expected Rubinstein would take tea at my home today!' Anatoly was dumbfounded by the insensitivity and incomprehension this exposed in Antonina. Returning to St Petersburg, on 13 October he took his brother away for a long convalescence in Western Europe. Tchaikovsky's marriage was over.

13
Two Masterpieces:
Fourth Symphony and *Eugene Onegin*

It might seem surprising that, while Tchaikovsky was passing through one of the most agonizing phases of his whole life, he should have been able to compose at all. It must seem all the more surprising, therefore, that the two pieces he conceived during all this turmoil are among his greatest works. But it will not, perhaps, be surprising to learn that both pieces are indelibly marked by elements from his own experience during these dark months. None of the first movements of his preceding symphonies had given warning of the scope, scale, sheer intensity, even violence, of the first movement of his Fourth Symphony. Later he even assigned the whole symphony a detailed programme, with clear autobiographical resonances. Perhaps we may feel sceptical as to whether such a detailed programme was literally guiding him during the process of composition, or whether it was really a post-compositional metaphor of his own emotional experience while composing the piece. But there is one bit of secret but irrefutable evidence that I have discovered within the symphony itself that points to the fundamental factor that underlies the first movement, and is the driving force of the whole piece.

One lesson I learned very early on as a researcher was to take account of anything, even a tiny – even trivial – detail, that seemed at least a little unusual, and the discovery I now describe sprang – but only in part – from noting the key in which Tchaikovsky set his Fourth Symphony: F minor (four flats). Now, one of the things that marks out large-scale late eighteenth- and nineteenth-century works for orchestra is that they are almost all set in keys with no more than three sharps or flats. In only three other cases among Tchaikovsky's two dozen or so large-scale orchestral works did he break with this practice (in the symphonic poems *The Tempest* and *Hamlet*, both also set in F minor, and the First Piano Concerto, set in B flat minor –

though there is a possible secret non-musical explanation for this last choice[1]). As noted earlier, Tchaikovsky had been overwhelmed by Bizet's opera *Carmen*, when he saw it in Paris early in 1876 and, it seems, especially by its ending in 'the death of the two leading characters whom an evil destiny, Fate, has brought together and driven, through a whole series of agonies, to their inescapable end', as he put it. And within the opera itself there are two critical and fateful moments that create or portend this outcome, and both are set in the same key, F minor. One is the entry of Escamillo, the tore-ador and agent of Fate, who will displace the young soldier, Don José, in Carmen's affections, thus setting in train the events leading to the opera's fateful ending with the murder of Carmen by Don José. The other is the moment when Carmen reads her fortune in the cards, and learns that she is fated to die. But Tchaikovsky's Fourth Symphony is also about Fate (we have Tchaikovsky's word for this) and is also in F minor, and what Tchaikovsky clearly did, in order to create the restless theme that would launch the main body of his first movement, was write out the pitches of the first four bars of the Toreador's entrance aria and the first two bars of Carmen's reading of the cards (some thirty pitches in all); that done, and using a very different pace and style from Bizet's, and employ-ing a totally different rhythmic manner of his own, he 'fabricated' from this trail of pitches, with the absolute minimum of deviation, his own theme for the Fourth Symphony's first movement. It is surely one of the most extraordinary thematic transformations in the whole history of Western music – and a timely reminder to us that, though 'inspiration' can be an almost involuntary process, as Tchaikovsky himself experienced many times when he found he barely had time to set down on paper the torrent of ideas that his brain seemed effortlessly to be creating, 'inspiration' can also come from an initial, hard-headedly conscious effort. In fact, as we shall see in a later chapter, Tchaikovsky himself would vouch for the need at times for dogged slog before 'inspiration' would present itself.

But what this derivation from *Carmen* does confirm is that Tchaikovsky did indeed see Fate at the very heart of this new sym-phony. Precisely when he started composing it is unknown. In a letter

1 For some explanation of this last instance, see Chapter 9, page 96, footnote 2.

to Nadezhda von Meck in mid-May 1877 he wrote that he had begun it 'as far back as the winter', that three movements were complete, and the finale under way. Certainly the sketches were finished in early June, and already he had decided to dedicate it to his patroness. She, however, was reluctant to see her name on the title page, and proposed the inscription: 'To my friend'. This was insufficient for Tchaikovsky, and he amplified it: 'To my best friend'. We can hardly believe she would have been displeased.

Work on bringing the symphony to its final form now ceased, and it was only in January 1878 that it was fully scored. Yet in February in Moscow it had already received its first performance. Tchaikovsky was still recovering in Western Europe from the trauma of his marriage, and was not present. However, none of his Moscow friends seemed willing to comment on the piece, and after a month of such silence he could contain himself no longer. The bitter reproof he addressed to Taneyev drew a swift reply, but one written with the honesty typical of Tchaikovsky's former pupil. Tchaikovsky recognized this, was not offended by Taneyev's general remarks, and expressed gratitude for his forthrightness. But one comment did sting him. 'One of the symphony's failings with which I shall never be able to reconcile myself is that in each movement there is something that recalls ballet music,' Taneyev had written.

Tchaikovsky's response is worth quoting at some length, for it gives a very clear insight into how he could view a symphony, and what he felt was appropriate content:

I simply do not understand what it is that you call ballet music. Do you understand as ballet music every cheerful tune that has a dance rhythm? If that's the case, you must also be unable to reconcile yourself to the majority of Beethoven's symphonies, in which you encounter such things at every step. I can only suppose, therefore, that the *ballet-like* bits of my symphony that displease you do so, not because they are *ballet-like*, but because they're bad. As for your observation that my symphony is programmatic, I completely agree. The only thing I don't understand is why you consider this a defect. I fear the very opposite situation – that is, I would not wish symphonic works to come from my pen which express nothing, and which consist of empty playing with chords, rhythms and modulations. Of course my symphony is programmatic, but this programme is such that it cannot be formulated in words. Ought not a symphony – that is, the most lyrical of all musical forms – be such a work? In essence my symphony imitates Beethoven's Fifth – that is, I was not imitating its musical thoughts, but its fundamental idea. Do you think there is a programme to the Fifth Symphony? Not only is there a programme, but in this case there cannot be any question about its efforts to express itself. I'll add that there is not a note in this symphony (that is, in mine) which I did not feel deeply, and which did not serve as an echo of sincere impulses within my soul.

All very fascinating, *but* – the detailed programme that Tchaikovsky had confided to Nadezhda von Meck some weeks earlier seems to fly in the face of this statement that its programme could not 'be formulated in words'. Which should we believe: the letter to Taneyev, or the programme disclosed to Mrs von Meck? In fact, the truth probably lies somewhere between the two. The sheer drama of the Fourth Symphony, and our knowledge of the circumstances within which it was written, make the presence of an autobiographical strand seem highly plausible, and there is, of course, the secret but explicit connection with Bizet's *Carmen*. Tchaikovsky's preamble to his patroness suggests he is experiencing some ambivalence about the programme he is about to set down for her:

In *our* symphony there *is* a programme – that is, it is possible to express in words what it is trying to say, and to you, and only to you, am I able and willing to explain the meaning both of the whole and of the separate movements. Of course I can only do this in a general way.

Then, having described the whole programme, sometimes in great detail, Tchaikovsky ends by again cautioning his patroness not to take everything too literally:

For the first time in my life I have had to put into words and phrases musical thoughts and musical images. I have not succeeded as I ought. I was terribly depressed last winter when I was composing this symphony, and it serves as a true echo of what I was going through at that time. But it is merely *an echo*.

Symphony no. 4, in F minor *****

[This is the most formidable work we have so far encountered, and the examination of it will be correspondingly extensive. But it is such an impressive, if challenging, work that I make no apology for allocating such space to it. In the following investigation details of the von Meck programme are set out (in italics), for many listeners will, I am sure, find them useful when encountering, perhaps for the first time, the vast and complex experience afforded by the first movement in particular. Do not expect this very large movement to disclose all its riches on first (or, indeed, second) hearing, especially if your background experience of classical music has not been extensive (or has barely existed). But it is, I assure you, worth persisting with.]

The Fourth Symphony opens with a strident horns-plus-bassoons call: *This is Fate, that fateful force that prevents the impulse to happiness from attaining its goal, which hangs above your head like the sword of Damocles. It is invincible, and you will never overcome it.*

Those readers who may know something of Wagner's great *Ring* cycle will probably sense that memories of Tchaikovsky's recent Bayreuth experience haunt this opening – but then, the epic tale told in *The Ring*, and which ends disastrously, is also a saga about Fate. However, Tchaikovsky's introduction dies to nothing, and the main movement begins with the theme synthesized from *Carmen*: *Fate is invincible, and you will never overcome it; you can only reconcile yourself to it, and languish fruitlessly.*

The space occupied by this first subject is vast. Beginning quietly, almost wearily, and with a constant, slightly limping gait, it unwinds seamlessly, becoming more insistent (*the cheerless and hopeless feeling grows yet stronger and more burning*) – yet some three minutes on, though now *fortissimo*, it is the same theme's opening (and back in F minor) that rounds off the section. The bonds of Fate remain unbroken.

Is it not better to turn away from reality and submerge yourself in daydreams? Accordingly, there is now an abrupt change to new music (the transition to the second subject) and a shift in tone, for a tripping clarinet theme (the second subject, first theme) is about to enter, the miniroulades that round off each phrase echoed by other wind instruments.

O joy! There appears a sweet and gentle daydream. Some blissful, radiant human image beckons you away. Indeed, this is very relaxed.

And note the gently rocking melody that soon enters as background, becomes increasingly assertive, and then in due course reveals itself as the second subject's second theme.

How good this is! How distant now sounds the obsessive first theme of the Allegro [the first subject]. *Daydreams little by little envelop the soul completely. Everything gloomy, joyless is forgotten. There she is, there she is – happiness!* The violin theme rocking above gentle timpani strokes is certainly far removed in mood from that which had opened the exposition. And note the new woodwind theme that answers the violins' phrases: it is, in fact, none other than the opening of the *Carmen*-derived first subject transformed, its gloom now lifted. The attainment of happiness seems complete.

Yet there is soon a mounting unease as the pace quickens, a trenchant new theme enters, and the first subject increasingly asserts itself until the symphony's opening Fate theme erupts on the trumpets. *No! these were but daydreams, and Fate wakes you from them!* Not only the exposition, but also its seeming optimism is now in the past.

Tchaikovsky was the most self-critical of composers, and a remark in his letter to Taneyev is worth noting. Writing of the development section about to come, he noted that it was the one portion about which he 'did not feel deeply, and which did not serve as an echo of sincere impulses within my soul. The exception is perhaps the middle of the first movement – in which there are contrivances, seams, glueings together – in a word, *artificiality.*'

Tchaikovsky did himself much less than justice. Writing of the remainder of this first movement (including this development), he made no attempt to provide any detail: *Thus all life is an unbroken alternation of hard reality with swiftly passing dreams and visions of happiness. No haven exists. Drift upon the sea until it engulfs and submerges you in its depths. That, roughly, is the programme of the first movement.*

Nor was there any point in fleshing it out, for what he had been revealing in his programme were, in fact, the significances of each of the four main ingredients (the introduction, and the exposition's three themes); now it will be the structural principles and practices of sonata form that will determine the main outlines of the rest of the movement: thus (for instance) the expected recurrences of the subjects in the recapitulation have nothing to do with Tchaikovsky's programme, but everything to do with sonata form. But, if not actually amplifying, everything that remains does consolidate the experience that has gone before.

So what of this development? It is, of course, a section that the composer may evolve as he chooses, and is, in fact, magnificently constructed (I use the word deliberately), returning first to the *Carmen*-derived first subject, now subdued, fidgety, nervous, but growing in strength until it is joined by a violin theme made from a brief sustained phrase that is seamlessly repeated again and again, each time a note higher. The intensity and volume grow awesomely, to be capped by a twofold trumpeting of the Fate theme that had launched the symphony, now engaging in implacable conflict with the first subject. Rarely has a composer suggested more vividly not only the violence of conflict but also its chaos and confusion. Nor, when the first subject emerges, *fff* and seemingly triumphant, is it unchallenged, for trombones and tuba insert a sustained line that rises beneath it in measured steps, then falls away as (it seems) the conflicting forces sink back, exhausted.

That eruption of the first subject had marked the beginning of the recapitulation. But to have repeated the subject in full, as in the exposition, would have been unbearable (and, frankly, tedious), and Tchaikovsky passes almost dismissively to the second subject's tripping theme, and thence to an abbreviated restatement of the section ushered in by the gently rocking string theme. There should be little difficulty in identifying this.

Yet there will be a new turn of events by way of the coda. The Fate theme bursts in as before – now to be answered by a new, hymnlike tune (signifying, perhaps, a mood of resignation that is the best hope that Tchaikovsky's programme could offer?). Yet beneath this there persist restless memories of the *Carmen*-derived first subject, and it is with this theme, again *fff,* that this magnificent movement ends.

I doubt any symphonic first movement (not even that to Beethoven's Ninth) had welded such varied materials into so bold, massive, and wide-ranging an experience as that afforded by the first movement of Tchaikovsky's Fourth. After such a stupendous experience, respite is essential, and the two central movements provide this admirably, though Tchaikovsky would not have us believe that all will necessarily be brightness and light:

The Symphony's second movement expresses another phase of depression. This is that melancholy which comes in the evening when, weary from labour, you are sitting alone. You take a book – but it falls from your hand. There comes a whole host of memories.

It is both sad that so much is now past and gone, yet pleasant to recall your youth. You both regret the past, yet do not wish to begin your life again. Life has wearied you. It is pleasant to rest and look around. You remember much. There were happy moments when young blood boiled, and life was satisfying. There were also painful moments, irreparable losses. All this is now somewhere far distant. It is both sad, yet somehow sweet, to immerse yourself in the past.

There is no need here for the kind of detailed commentary which the preceding movement would have tempted anyway, even if Tchaikovsky's own programme had not existed. The flowing oboe theme that opens this quite extensive *Andantino in modo di canzone* is testimony to Tchaikovsky's ability to build a tune that immediately engages the attention despite using only one note value throughout (but listen to how the oboist often phrases the tune in little two-, three-, or four-note groupings, thus giving it a gentle rhythmic life). This melodic world is broadened a little by the new theme that the violins introduce (now with some variety of note values), but this is so natural a companion to the oboe theme that the movement's first three-plus minutes become in effect a single melodic span which brings a stability and equilibrium that is a perfectly calculated contrast to the tempestuous issues of the first movement. Nor is there much shift in melodic style in the central section, though its pace becomes slightly quicker and its dynamic level higher. And though the opening theme returns to complete this ternary-structured movement, it is by no means a literal repetition of the first section, for some new melodic material is interpolated. There has been nothing perfunctory in Tchaikovsky's approach to this charming, perfectly calculated movement.

The shift in this second movement into a brighter, less troubled world is taken decisively further in the third movement. Its title, *Scherzo: Pizzicato ostinato*, points only to one element in this movement's most distinctive feature: its exploitation of the contrasts between the light, sprightly spatterings of plucked strings and the bright, sometimes almost shrill sounds of the woodwind – and, later, the quiet clipped chords of the brass. This is a delightful confection, the three sound worlds being each introduced with its own material, and then juxtaposed, sometimes in dizzyingly swift alternations. It makes for a marvellously witty movement, exquisitely realized, and totally original.

But when the decision on which this movement is founded – that is, to exploit colour contrasts between three different instrumental families – was so much a purely musical one, the listener must wonder whether Tchaikovsky's alleged programme here was really an afterthought, devised to satisfy his patroness. Indeed, his first sentence seems to support this:

> The third movement expresses no definite feeling. It is made up of capricious arabesques, of the elusive images that rush past in the imagination when you have drunk a little wine and experience the first stage of intoxication. Your spirit is neither cheerful nor yet sad. You think of nothing; you give rein to your imagination – and for some reason it begins to paint strange pictures. Among these you suddenly recall a picture of drunken peasants and a street song. Next, somewhere in the distance, a military procession passes. This movement is made up of completely disjointed images which rush past in your head when you have fallen asleep. They have nothing in common with reality; they are strange, wild and disjointed.

The programme for the fourth and final movement is more plausible:

> If within yourself you find no reasons for joy, look at others. Go among the people. Observe how they can enjoy themselves, surrendering themselves wholeheartedly to joyful feelings. A picture of the people's festive merriment. Hardly have you managed to forget yourself, and be carried away by the spectacle of others' joys, than irrepressible Fate again appears and reminds you of yourself. But others do not care about you, and they have not noticed that you are solitary and sad. O, how they are enjoying themselves, how happy they are that all their feelings are simple and direct! You have only yourself to blame; do not say that everything in this world is sad. There are simple and strong joys. Rejoice in others' rejoicing. To live is still possible!

We can only guess whether Tchaikovsky's programme here was truly his own, or whether he had recycled it from a passage in the recently published novel *Anna Karenina*, where Tolstoy describes Levin's feelings as he watches some peasant women singing joyfully as they pass him by. Certainly the movement's initial explosion (I have seen an audience jump with surprise at this finale's first chord) suggests joy; significant, too, is the Russian folksong, first introduced immediately after the opening flourish, only to be overwhelmed as the earlier music of irrepressible ebullience is resumed. Then abruptly the folksong re-enters, is heard three times more to differing backgrounds, then again becomes drawn into the general mood of 'the people's festive merriment'. For a third time the folktune is granted its own space: again more changing backgrounds, more ebullience – and then, peremptorily, the symphony's opening theme enters. But this time Fate does not prevail; as the programme declares, 'Rejoice in others' rejoicing. To live is still possible!', and it is with a return to the high spirits of the movement's opening that this truly monumental symphony concludes.

The creation of the opera *Eugene Onegin* overlapped with that of the Fourth Symphony. On 25 May Tchaikovsky visited a friend, the singer Elizaveta Lavrovskaya, at her home, and the conversation turned to possible subjects for an opera. After Lavrovskaya's husband had made some inept suggestions, Lavrovskaya herself suddenly mentioned Pushkin's verse novel, *Eugene Onegin*. 'The idea seemed to me wild, and I didn't reply,' Tchaikovsky wrote to Modest five days later:

> Afterwards, while dining alone at an inn, I recalled *Onegin*, fell to thinking about it, next began to find Lavrovskaya's idea a possibility, then was carried away by it, and by the end of the meal had made up my mind. Straight away I ran off to track down a copy of Pushkin's work. I found one with difficulty, set off home, read it through with delight, and passed an utterly sleepless night, the result of which was a scenario for a delightful opera on Pushkin's text.

All this was happening, of course, during the earlier weeks when his relationship with Antonina Milyukova was evolving, and the facts recorded in what now follows fill out the conspicuous gap in the narrative set out in Chapter 12. Tchaikovsky's choice would result in his greatest opera, and it would also have an immediate and fateful consequence for his relationship with Antonina Milyukova, who had already written her first letter to him ahead of his decision to compose *Eugene Onegin*. Pushkin's masterpiece is the tale of a teenage girl, Tatyana, who falls in love with a young worldly man, Onegin, writes a letter confessing her love, but is rejected by him. Some years later he returns, sees the mature Tatyana, who is now married to an elderly and adoring husband, and falls in love with her. He forces a meeting on her but, confessing she still loves him, she refuses to be unfaithful and, though distraught, rejects her would-be lover.

What had particularly drawn Tchaikovsky to this subject was the moment when Tatyana writes her confession of love to Onegin. Years later he told Kashkin what had then happened:

> I began to write the letter music, succumbing to an invincible spiritual need to do this, in the heat of which I forgot about Miss Milyukova. Being completely immersed in composition, I so thoroughly identified myself with the image of Tatyana that she became for me like a living person. I loved Tatyana, and was furious with Onegin, who seemed to me a cold, heartless fop. Having received a second letter from Miss Milyukova, I was ashamed, and even became angry with myself for my attitude towards her. In her second letter she complained bitterly that she had received no reply, adding that if this letter suffered the same fate as the first, then the only thing that would remain for her would be to put an end to herself. In my mind all this tied up with the idea of Tatyana, and it seemed to me that I had myself acted incomparably more basely than Onegin, and I became really furious with myself for my heartless attitude to this girl who was in love with me. Because her second letter included Miss Milyukova's address, I forthwith set out thither, and so began our acquaintance.

On 1 June Tchaikovsky had his first meeting with Antonina, proposed marriage at a second meeting a day or two later, completed the sketches of the Fourth Symphony, and on 10 June set out for the estate of Konstantin Shilovsky, Vladimir's brother, at Glebovo.

It must seem extraordinary that Tchaikovsky, once he knew there was no chance of direct contact with Antonina, could seem to put all thought of her out of his mind, for it would be the same when he escaped to Sasha's home at Kamenka after his marriage. As for his working conditions at Glebovo, they were ideal, he told Modest:

> I have at my disposal an entire, superbly furnished house. When I'm busy no one, not a single human soul except my servant Alyosha, ever puts in an appearance, and, most important of all, I have a piano whose sounds don't reach anyone except Alyosha when I'm

playing [Tchaikovsky was also in the habit of singing loudly when composing]. I get up at eight, have a bath, drink tea (alone), and then busy myself until breakfast. After breakfast I take a walk, and again work until dinner. After dinner I go for a lengthy stroll, and pass the evening at the big house. There are hardly any guests – in a word, it's very peaceful and quiet here. The locality is delightful in the full sense of the word. However, what's terrible is the weather: it's so cold that there's a daily morning frost.

By virtue of the above, my work is going forward rapidly, and if nothing makes me budge from here before August [Modest still knew nothing of his brother's marriage plans], then I should certainly have managed to sketch the whole opera. But I shall probably leave here in the middle of July. I have to spend several days in Moscow with Kotek, then go to Sasha, where I hope to see you, and then go abroad.

Tchaikovsky left Glebovo on 14 July, only four days before the wedding, and with two-thirds of *Onegin* already composed. He may have done a little more work on the opera at Kamenka in August and September, but it was not until February 1878 that it was at last complete.

Tchaikovsky had composed his new opera *con amore*, and he was desperate to have it staged. Even before it was completed he was trying to persuade Nikolay Rubinstein to produce and conduct Act 1 and the first scene of Act 2 at the Moscow Conservatoire, using colleagues and students. He sent the score of these four scenes to Rubinstein, who expressed warm approval of the music, but argued against a premiere with Conservatoire students. Tchaikovsky was not to be persuaded. What he needed was not elderly stars, but good young singers who could act, a chorus who would not behave 'like a flock of sheep' – and Rubinstein himself to prepare and conduct the opera. If the opera could not be produced this session, he was ready to wait until the next. In the end he got his way, and in March 1879 it was mounted at the Maly Theatre, using Conservatoire forces, and with Nikolay Rubinstein in charge.

Recognizing that, in many ways, *Eugene Onegin* was very different from the usual run of operas, Tchaikovsky insisted it should be described as 'Lyrical Scenes in three acts'. He knew, too, that it would not answer conventional audience expectations, and that there was high risk in daring to use one of the best-loved classics of Russian literature; indeed, Modest, who attended the premiere, reported that he heard the word 'blasphemy' muttered more than once in the theatre that night. Nevertheless, there were ovations after each scene, and the press was largely favourable. Above all, Tchaikovsky was touched by the unanimous enthusiasm of his Conservatoire friends. Yet though in the wider Russian world *Onegin* was heard on occasion in the early 1880s, it was not until the Imperial Opera mounted a production in St Petersburg in 1884 that it began to achieve the success that has made it, today, the most popular of all Russian operas.

Eugene Onegin: lyrical scenes in three acts *****

[Eugene Onegin is one of Tchaikovsky's supreme masterpieces. I find it an almost painfully moving piece, and this not only because of Tchaikovsky's superb music: though it has its grand scenes with high drama, it is also a very intimate piece. Indeed, three of its seven scenes involve only two people onstage, and I find quite extraordinary the intensity with which Tchaikovsky focuses upon the fraught personal situations that are played out in these scenes. The Queen of Spades, another Pushkin-based opera, has a subject with more sweep and its story is more overtly 'dramatic'. I love it – but if I had to keep just one of them, I know which one it would be. Indeed, Eugene Onegin is one of the trio of works by Tchaikovsky that I would choose to keep if (heaven forbid!) I were forced to sacrifice all except three of his compositions.]

Each of Tchaikovsky's seven scenes presents only one incident from Pushkin's verse novel, but Tchaikovsky felt he could safely confine himself to these, for a Russian audience would know the full story and be able to place them in context. Few readers of this book will have that advantage, however, and so I supply, in italics, a brief summary of what Tchaikovsky excluded from his scenario, both before the curtain rises and between the scenes:

Eugene Onegin epitomizes Russian youth of the 1820s (that is, of Pushkin's own time). Well educated and popular, he becomes bored with the empty life of St Petersburg high society, and decides to try the country way on an estate he has inherited from an uncle. But he finds satisfaction only in the company of a neighbour, Lensky, an eighteen-year-old just returned from a German university, and untarnished by the tawdry ways of Russian high society. Lensky is betrothed to Olga Larina, younger daughter of a neighbour. Olga is an extrovert in contrast to her elder sister, Tatyana, a private individual with a passion for novels. One evening Lensky introduces Onegin to the Larin family.

Act 1 Scene 1. *The garden of the Larins' house.* Mrs Larina and the family nurse, Filipevna, are chatting while Tatyana and Olga can be heard singing a duet in the house. Peasants enter and present Mrs Larina with a ceremonial sheaf; they sing a lively song, and dance for her. Olga and Tatyana appear, and the former comments on her sister's dreamy nature, as opposed to her own extrovert personality. The peasants are given wine, then leave, together with the nurse. Asked whether she is ill, Tatyana attributes her pallor to the novel she is reading. The nurse rushes in to announce the approach of Lensky with Onegin. Tatyana's mother prevents her daughter from leaving. Onegin is introduced, and Mrs Larina leaves the four young people to themselves. They join in a quartet in which each voices his/her initial reaction to their present situation, Tatyana instantly revealing that she sees Onegin as predestined for her. They pair off, Onegin commenting on Tatyana's limited world, she admitting she reads and dreams much. They retire, and Lensky can reaffirm his love for Olga. Mrs Larina and the nurse re-enter and note Onegin's and Tatyana's continuing absence. The couple return, the nurse perceiving that Tatyana is already besotted with Onegin. She shakes her head doubtingly as she re-enters the house.

Act 1 Scene 2. *Tatyana's room.* Tatyana is ready for bed, but cannot sleep. At Tatyana's request, the nurse tells of her own arranged marriage, but sees Tatyana is not listening. Tatyana confides that she is in love. She asks for pen and paper, then dismisses the nurse. Now alone, she gives vent to her excitement, settles down to write to Onegin, tears up her first attempt, then begins again, stopping periodically to read over and comment on what she has written, or simply to reflect. Dawn breaks as she finishes. The nurse reappears, and Tatyana begs her to send her grandson with the letter. But to whom? 'To Onegin!' she cries. The nurse, hesitantly, leaves with the letter, and Tatyana sinks back in thought.

Act 1 Scene 3. *Another part of the Larins' garden.* A women's chorus is heard offstage. Tatyana enters precipitately: Onegin is coming, and she is fearfully agitated. He arrives and addresses her 'quietly and with a certain coldness'. Listing the various reasons why he should not marry her, he urges her to exert more self-control. Tatyana is humiliated. The offstage women's chorus is heard again. Onegin offers Tatyana his arm, and she takes it mechanically. They leave.

Onegin does not revisit the Larins until Lensky persuades him to attend the celebration of Tatyana's name-day. Meanwhile in a nightmare Tatyana has a premonition of trouble between Lensky and Onegin.

Act 2 Scene 1. *A room in the Larins' house.* A dance is in progress. Onegin is dancing with Tatyana, and Lensky with Olga. Sour comments are made about Onegin by some of the guests, especially female. Bored, and annoyed by Lensky inviting him, Onegin flirts with Olga while dancing a waltz. Lensky reproaches her, but she deliberately tries to make him more jealous. Monsieur Triquet, a French guest, sings a song in praise of an embarrassed Tatyana. The dancing resumes with a mazurka. Onegin sits with Olga, Lensky standing behind them. Onegin dances briefly with Olga, then pretends to have only just noticed Lensky, and asks why he is not dancing. A quarrel begins, Lensky becoming increasingly heated. The other guests notice, and Lensky publically rejects Onegin as his friend. Onegin tries to calm him, but Lensky 'demands satisfaction'. Mrs Larina is appalled, and Lensky leads off a huge ensemble, everybody reflecting on the terrible turn of events. But then the turmoil resumes, increasing until Lensky hurls the ultimate insult: 'You are a dishonourable seducer!' 'Be silent, or I'll kill you!' Onegin retorts. He throws himself on Lensky, but the guests separate them. Tatyana bursts into tears. Lensky turns to Olga, shouting, 'Farewell for ever!', and rushes out. Olga faints.

Act 2 Scene 2. *Early morning on a river bank.* Onegin is late and Lensky and his second are awaiting Onegin's arrival. Meanwhile Lensky sings of his lost happiness, his fate in prospect, and his longing for Olga. Onegin arrives. As their seconds discuss arrangements, Lensky and Onegin ponder the fateful situation into which they are now caught, but from which they cannot escape. The pistols are loaded, the signal is given, Onegin fires, and Lensky falls dead. Horrified, Onegin buries his face in his hands.

Onegin quits the area; Olga marries a lancer, and leaves too. On an evening walk Tatyana comes upon Onegin's empty house. The house-keeper gives her permission to enter and read in Onegin's library. Its contents, and his annotations in his books, give Tatyana insight into Onegin's character, and disenchantment ensues. 'Is he no more than some worthless shadow?' she asks herself.

Mrs Larina takes a reluctant Tatyana to Moscow in the hope of finding a husband for her, and she is paired off with an elderly general, Prince Gremin. Meanwhile a still tormented Onegin has been travelling. Finally he arrives in St Petersburg where Tatyana, now two years married, is a noted beauty.

Act 3 Scene 1. *A side-hall in a mansion in St Petersburg.* A bored Onegin watches the other resplendent guests dance. Tatyana enters with her husband, Onegin recognizes her, and Tatyana, left for a moment by her husband, enquires who the stranger is. Discovering his identity, she tries to hide her agitation. Prince Gremin tells Onegin that Tatyana is his wife, and Onegin admits that he already knows her. Gremin sings of his love for Tatyana, then reintroduces Onegin to her. Tatyana quickly pleads fatigue, and she and Gremin depart. Alone, Onegin confesses aloud his love for her.

Onegin writes three times to Tatyana, but receives no answer. Finally he bursts in on her in her home.

Act 3 Scene 2. *The drawing room in Prince Gremin's house.* An agitated Tatyana enters, holding a letter, and weeping. Onegin appears and falls on his knees. She signals him to rise, and recalls his earlier rejection. Onegin admits how mistaken he had been, but she questions bitterly whether he is now pursuing her because of her new wealth and rank. Onegin makes further protestations of love, and Tatyana tearfully reflects on the happiness that might have been: however, her fate has now been sealed, and she orders Onegin to leave – though finally confessing she still loves him. But she frees herself from his embrace, declaring she will remain faithful to her husband, and now bids him farewell for ever. In despair, Onegin flees.

Devising an opera libretto is not simply a matter of stringing together the words that the characters speak to one another, and then letting the composer dress them with appropriate music. First the structure of the whole plot needs to be decided, and these structures can be of very different types. For Mozart's four-act *The Marriage of Figaro*, for instance, Lorenzo da Ponte provided Mozart with a libretto where event piles on event, each actor spinning his or her dramatic thread which constantly intertwines with those of the other participants, thus weaving the fabric of the tale; only at the opera's end are all the threads drawn together and tied. Such a scenario is organic – that is, in a state of constant evolution. Tchaikovsky's *Eugene Onegin* is the very opposite, more like a strip cartoon, where each picture depicts an incident in the tale, sometimes with large narrative gaps between (over two years between Scenes 5 and 6, for instance), but such as the spectator can fill in for himself. Thus there is very little action in each scene of *Onegin* (indeed, as already noted, in three of its seven scenes only two people are involved), for Tchaikovsky's prime concern was with his characters as human individuals, focusing on their words, actions, reactions and emotions, and catching these into music of such insight, eloquence and expressive directness that we are drawn into their joys, predicaments and sorrows, empathizing with them, and bearing away memories of a very *human* tale, told with sometimes almost painful eloquence.

Dramatically the most complex scene of *Onegin* is the opening one, for here we first meet the characters in their particular world, and begin to grasp certain of the tale's bases, who the characters are, and what are their feelings and motivations. We can also now begin to see why Tchaikovsky, who had intended to use Konstantin Shilovsky as his librettist, finally did the job himself; only he knew what he needed. After the short, but wonderfully expressive orchestral prelude, based on a tender melody whose recurrences in the opera suggest it is Tatyana's theme, representing her as still the young, innocent woman, the opera opens unexpectedly with what is really a quartet. But this is a highly unconventional one because the participants are in separate pairs doing different things, and two of them cannot even be seen, only heard. The two older women's conversation while engaged in the most mundane of domestic activities (making preserves) tells us much about the unsophisticated lives they lead and about the relaxed, homely world into which Onegin will bring such chaos and misery; meanwhile, the offstage singing of a charming sentimental song gives us an insight into their recreational life. The peasants arrive (we must remember that *Onegin* is set in a time when the peasants were still the property of their masters; it was not until 1861 that the Russian peasantry was emancipated), and we see the good relationship which the

Larins clearly have with their 'slaves'. The two girls emerge, and we discover how different they are from each other. Though Tatyana is the first to speak, it is Olga whom Tchaikovsky then brings forward, furnishing her with an aria that reveals a straightforward, cheerful being (Tchaikovsky himself described her as 'very insipid') who lightly mocks her sister's taste for romantic novels. While Olga is extrovert, gregarious and superficial, Tatyana is introvert, reclusive, with a sensitivity to deeper issues. Note how much more expressive than Olga's was the music, already heard in the orchestral preamble, with which Tatyana had briefly introduced herself. There is great excitement as Lensky is seen approaching with Onegin; the introductions made, the chemistry between the four young people quickly becomes apparent during the quartet in which they join. This very economical movement bonds them, yet Tchaikovsky ensures that some of their individual, self-revealing words can escape from the corporate sound, thus enabling us to catch a little of each one's thoughts. Take the very first sounds of the quartet, Onegin's quiet mini-solo before the others join in: 'Which one is Tatyana?' he asks Lensky – already she has roused his curiosity. And note how Tchaikovsky places Tatyana on the top of the ensemble, her crucial words ('I know this is the one . . .') delivered more slowly and clearly so that we may catch them above the babble of the others.

The quartet over, the couples pair off, Lensky and Olga chattering easily, a lofty Onegin addressing a still totally bemused Tatyana before they go off. Now it is Lensky's turn to reveal himself in a declaration of love as generous as any woman could wish: first adoring, then impassioned and finally tender, it is a natural complement to Olga's earlier aria.

As the evening draws in, Mrs Larina and the nurse come out on to the terrace. Onegin and Tatyana return, the former still singing exactly the same music as he had first addressed her with, but now giving Tatyana the benefit of a bit of his family's history. We may easily guess who has done all the talking. They pass on to the terrace, leaving an anxious nurse to follow, shaking her head thoughtfully as echoes of the prelude's main motif return in the orchestra, passing to a final chord, reiterated at different levels, first ascending, then descending and leaving, perhaps, a sense of something still not finally settled.

With Scene 2 we pass straight from the panorama of the Larins and their world to the real concern of the opera: the fate of Tatyana – for it is she, not Onegin, who is Tchaikovsky's true preoccupation. It is her theme, introduced in the opera's Prelude and recurring in Scene 1, that reflects her mood as she sits in silent thought before her mirror (but note the orchestra's exquisite opening music which, sadly (for us), will never return: could anything express yearning more perfectly?). The nurse's music is markedly plainer and, as Tatyana questions her about her early years, dominates the opening stretch until she realizes Tatyana is no longer listening – and Tatyana confesses she is in love. The change of tone is as sharp as it is abrupt: a wonderfully spanned love theme that owes its effect as much to the harmonies Tchaikovsky gives it as to its own intrinsic quality. In a moment this love theme will return quietly in the orchestra, Tatyana will ask for pen and paper, dismiss her nurse – and the Letter Scene, perhaps the most famous scene in all Russian opera, will begin.

This great monologue is so rich in shifting emotions, detailed action, and pointed music that, in this present book, a comprehensive commentary could become burdensome. It is a scene to be experienced above all in the opera house, but since most readers will hear it at home from a recording, supplied with a translation, I will comment only on certain very special moments. As Tatyana finds herself alone, her love theme is heard for a third time, but is swept aside by a burst of exultant joy, for now she can give free vent to her feelings. Nevertheless, this outburst is short, and her special theme returns as, thoughtfully, she focuses on the matter to hand: her letter to Onegin, confessing her love. She sits, writes a little, but then tears it up. A few instants of hesitation, and she begins a second time.

This was in fact the point at which Tchaikovsky began composing *Onegin*, for it was not unusual for him to set about an opera at some crucial moment that particularly moved him. The text he uses is mostly Pushkin's own. His music may reflect Tatyana's physical actions as much as her inner condition. First an orchestral passage to accompany her silent writing, the nervous pulsing perhaps mimicking the tiny movements of her quill pen – and then the same passage again as she reads back aloud what she had written. But, in sharp contrast, comes new, hesitant music as she reflects anxiously on what she is doing. Her writing resumes to the same music as before, again she reads back, again hesitation: could there be another man predestined for her? Her doubt is only momentary. No, she cries – and the abrupt change of music reflects her new decisiveness before she goes on to reflect raptly on Onegin, then return to reality, and to her new resolve.

Yet there is still to be a final moment of doubt: 'Are you my angel and protector, or are you a vile deceiver?' she asks herself. On a very personal note, I will say that this so simple passage is, for me, almost the most nakedly expressive Tchaikovsky ever wrote. The agitated music has slowed, there has been a long pause, and the oboe has entered with the simplest of melodies – just six stepwise descending notes with a single magical change of harmony in the middle, answered by a gentle, twisting horn phrase. (I remember, some sixty years ago, hearing this on a Proms broadcast, and going to the piano to try to work out what this change was, the first time, I think, that a piece by Tchaikovsky had really gripped me.) It is, I suppose, its very simplicity that makes it so telling, but also the way Tatyana returns to it insistently as though her doubts nag and nag; that six-note descending phrase is, indeed, *her* Fate theme. But no! 'So be it! From now I entrust my fate to you!' she cries – and the music moves on, now incorporating a portion of her personal theme, followed by a full-throated, defiant delivery of her Fate theme when, come what may, she commits herself to Onegin. Quickly concluding her letter while the orchestra blares out, almost defiantly, her Fate theme, she seals it. But, as her final words tell us, doubts remain: 'I have finished it! It is terrifying to read it through, and I am dying with horror and shame. But your honour is my guarantee, and it is to *that* that, boldly, I entrust myself.'

Dawn is already breaking, and the orchestra reflects the sunlight flooding in as Tatyana draws back the curtain. A shepherd's pipe is heard and, as Tatyana's thoughts turn to her new commitment, the love theme is heard reflectively from a solo cello, and the nurse's theme signals her quiet re-entry. Tchaikovsky wastes no time on the final section. A somewhat bemused and troubled nurse is entrusted with the letter, and the love theme, now vastly expanded, swells in the orchestra before fading into nothing.

Scene 3 takes place some days later. Presenting only one incident, it is the shortest of the opera – indeed, shorter than Tatyana's great monologue in the Letter Scene. But it is as carefully conceived. The offstage women's chorus that opens and closes it might be heard as merely gratuitous decoration. It is not, for the joy of these peasant girls, playfully planning to lure some young man, then tease him, is in ironic contrast to the painful encounter that they flank. Tatyana's agitation is to be expected – but what of Onegin's reaction? In opera we can readily recognize the kind of music that reflects joy or sorrow, and connect it with what we see onstage. But does the string theme that marks Onegin's entry tell us anything? Is it, if anything, simply a dignified gesture, devoid of any particular 'expressive' quality? Yes, it is – and that is just the point. Listen to the music that had introduced Onegin in the first scene after the abrupt silence that had followed the Larin family's agitation at his imminent appearance: that brief theme, too, was simply a visiting card, revealing nothing of the man it introduced. But, most significant of all, listen to the music that will mark his appearance in the Duel Scene. Not only is Onegin about to face possible death: he is late for the appointment – yet even here the brief tune that marks his actual moment of entry (assuming the producer observes exactly Tchaikovsky's stage directions) shows no loss of poise, no embarrassment, no sign of feeling anything. (Is this not what, in Pushkin's novel, Tatyana would sense and comment on after visiting Onegin's library: 'Is he no more than some worthless shadow?') And this is the man who, in this garden scene, loftily and without experiencing any emotion himself, is about to dismiss her letter; note how formal everything he says sounds, how steady his vocal line is, untroubled by any touch of emotion (and note how different will be his entry in the opera's final scene). It is easy to dismiss this garden scene as merely a necessary link in the story. It is not. Tchaikovsky is as revealing here as anywhere in the opera.

Scene 4, the dance at the Larins', is the first of the opera's two spectacle scenes. It is very carefully schemed, beginning with carefree celebration, ending in total disaster. The orchestral introduction returns to the music to which Tatyana had concluded her letter to Onegin – virtually the only musical sign of her presence in the scene for, though there in person, she will not sing a note by herself. A grand choral–orchestral waltz launches the party, a splendid example of Tchaikovsky's flair for the extended dance. Musically this is a very carefully schemed scene, this dance and the later mazurka providing a lively, carefree background against, and between which, the contrasting trail of events that leads to the party's catastrophic end can be set. Bored by the parochial occasion to which Lensky has brought him, Onegin steals Olga for a dance, and she is only too ready to flirt. The dance ended, Lensky is reproachful, and his pain and anger begin to rise when Olga shows no repentence; indeed, she wilfully accepts Onegin's mischievous invitation for the next dance. But for the temperature to rise further at this stage would be premature, and to relax the tension Tchaikovsky inserts Monsieur Triquet's tribute to the person whose name-day celebration this is: Tatyana. Triquet is one of those cameo parts which occur elsewhere in Tchaikovsky's operas, and of which he was a master. Small as it is, it requires a good actor-singer to pull it off, but the fact that Triquet is a Frenchman (his couplets are based on a romance by a French composer, Beauplan) whose command of Russian is imperfect presents a ready-made opportunity for a light touch of parody. The tension relieved, the corporate festivities resume with an even livelier mazurka. Once again Onegin dances briefly with Olga, returns to where Lensky stands – and the next, and more serious stage in the altercation between the two men unfolds, their raised voices at last catching everyone's attention, and stopping the dancers in their tracks. Now the latter are drawn into the drama, assuming their group role, both as spectators and commentators. Onegin tries to calm the situation, but to no avail, and when Lensky 'demands satisfaction', Mrs Larina tries to intervene, and there begins a formal operatic finale, all participants pausing to voice their particular views and responses to this catastrophic turn of events. Besides providing what is likely to be, in decibels at least, the most imposing musical event of the scene, this finale will provide a double jolt: first an abrupt halting of the action, and then, after a span of reflective stasis, a violent outburst at the sudden intrusion of a critical and shocking factor. And so Lensky leads off this finale with the saddest – and most restrained – of utterances (thus ensuring the maximum potential for a growth in volume), Onegin and Tatyana in turn join in with their own thoughts, and finally Olga and Mrs Larina, plus the chorus. But when Lensky denounces Olga, all restraint instantly disappears, and the ensemble explodes. At any one moment five different texts are perhaps being sung, and the listener will probably be unable to distinguish any of them. No matter: the mood is universal for whatever personal reason, and only Onegin's violent attack on Lensky and the latter's agonized farewell to Olga both rupture, but also heighten, the corporate expression of horror with which the scene ends.

It might be argued that Scene 5, where the duel takes place, is yet a fourth scene for only two characters, since the other two participants are merely very minor appendages to Onegin and Lensky, with only minimal vocal contributions from one of them. Dramatically the duel itself is all that matters, but Lensky's predicament (and Onegin's late arrival) provided the most natural of opportunities for him to voice his thoughts and feelings, which must be sharply focused, considering that he may (and, indeed, *will*) be dead within a matter of minutes. His aria is a testament to love, one of the largest set pieces of the opera, but one that I would not wish to shorten for anything, and whose depth of feeling is so self-evident that it needs little commentary here – except for one particular point. The descending opening phrase of the aria is, believe it or not, Tatyana's Fate theme from her Letter Scene, though now in a minor, not major key: yet through this simple adjustment, and its new presentation, Tchaikovsky has transformed it into something quite new, though it still bears the same expressive message as in Tatyana's scene (I once encountered a professional tenor who admitted he had sung this aria without ever noticing this relationship). Nor does the treatment of the duel itself, so vividly presented, require further comment, except for one point. Just before it is fought, the two combatants, 'not looking at each other', voice their identical pain-filled reflections on what has happened, and what they are about to do, and Tchaikovsky gives them a canon – that is, both sing exactly the same music and the same words, but Onegin starts just behind Lensky, and thus they can never fall into unison and be reconciled. And so the duel is fought, Lensky dies, and his aria's 'fateful' opening phrase is his requiem.

Scene 6, set in a St Petersburg ballroom, may be grander than the scene at the Larins', but it is shorter, for it does not trace a dramatically evolving situation, but simply records the occasion when Onegin and Tatyana renew acquaintance. Like the earlier scene, it begins with a formal dance, though not a country waltz this time, but a grand cosmopolitan polonaise. Onegin stands apart, apathetically watching the dancers, and not only his demeanour and his words but also his music indicate he is a changed man. The tone is different, the self-confident flow has gone, his phrases are more broken, more agitated, there is more tension in them, and in the harmonies too. A lively *écossaise* (a Scottish dance) interrupts his soliloquy, and then the arrival of Prince Gremin and his wife is announced to the background of a gentle waltz. Once again we encounter a new character who, like Monsieur Triquet, has a single aria, and is never seen or heard again.

Gremin's outpouring of mature love and devotion to his adored wife, Tatyana, is one of the finest solos in the opera and, delivered personally as it is to Onegin, can only intensify the latter's pain. Gremin reintroduces Tatyana to Onegin while the orchestra quietly remembers her love theme from the Letter Scene, telling us that, despite her outward self-control, an old emotion has instantly stirred. She extricates herself by pleading fatigue, and Onegin, with mounting excitement ('Can this be the same Tatyana . . .?') recognizes he is in love, ironically to the very same music to which, alone in the Letter Scene, Tatyana had first confessed *her* love for him. As he rushes off a second ebullient *écossaise* concludes the scene.

There are few operas that are rounded off more intimately yet, in the end, more powerfully than Tchaikovsky's *Eugene Onegin*. Does the opening of the orchestral introduction distantly echo Gremin's aria, that song of devoted love from the man who torments Onegin because he presents the obstacle to his happiness, and Tatyana because she is irrevocably tied to him? The accompaniment becomes increasingly agitated, and Tatyana rushes in with a letter from Onegin in her hand. A double memory of the Fate theme (Onegin had also sung exactly the same version on his appearance in the Ballroom Scene), then a memory of her own, most personal theme, followed by a frenetic outburst from the orchestra to introduce Onegin, who also runs in, pauses to look at the weeping Tatyana, then falls on his knees before her. How things have changed! This final scene is full of reminiscences: in a moment, as Onegin begs for her pity, the orchestra will quietly – and very ironically – play that melody to which, in the garden, he had once so blandly told her that 'dreams and years cannot return'. There is no room to enumerate all such pointed, often bitter allusions here, but with the text before you, the expressive precision of this music can be all the more appreciated. Yet I will mention just two instances. First: that moment when, after Onegin has made his first desperate plea to her, Tatyana weeps, the music quietens, and a ghost of the Fate theme is twice heard, a prelude to one of the most moving passages in the opera. Second: when, having roundly condemned Onegin and begged him to leave, Tatyana suddenly, in the tenderest of terms, admits 'I love you', and Onegin perceives a glimmer of hope – only, of course, to be disabused when Tatyana repeats adamantly that she still cannot give way. At first Tchaikovsky had planned to end the opera with the entry of

Gremin, which would naturally have finished the matter. But that might have left a suspicion that, but for this intervention, Tatyana might have yielded. As it is, we know that it was her decision, and hers alone, to reject Onegin.

A personal recollection. Some years ago I was asked by Covent Garden to talk to teachers who were to bring some of their charges to a special matinee performance of *Eugene Onegin*. One of my bonuses was two tickets to the matinee itself. The cast was that which would have given the evening performances: Mirella Freni was Tatyana, and Wolfgang Brendel was Onegin (and still the best I have ever seen or heard). The organisers had placed myself and my wife in the Royal Box (Her Majesty would not, of course, be attending) which provides the clearest possible view of the whole house, and there was something unnerving in seeing the place packed with children, some seeming almost dangerously young, and hopelessly outnumbering their minders. How would they react to such a long, personal, intimate story, with music of such sophistication? I need not have worried. The only moment when there was a minor disturbance was in the Duel Scene: a slight titter (clearly a nervous release) was heard after the shot was fired. So caught up were these youngsters that in the final scene they applauded the entrances of both Tatyana and Onegin! There must be something very special about Tchaikovsky's *Eugene Onegin*.

————

THE NOMAD YEARS

14
The Russian Refugee:
Violin Concerto

The debacle of Tchaikovsky's marriage had created a deluge of rumours in Moscow, and an urgent damage limitation exercise was mounted by his family and friends. A tale was put about that the couple were to be reunited in Berlin, and this required Antonina's immediate removal from Moscow. Accordingly she was given money by Rubinstein and Anatoly, then packed off to Odessa, where she seems to have disappeared. Realizing what mischief she could create on the loose, Sasha had instantly headed thither, run Antonina to earth, then borne her off to Kamenka where she could be supervised. Since it was recognized that Tchaikovsky's absence was going to be prolonged, some explanation was needed. The Paris International Exhibition of 1878 provided the answer. A Russian musical delegate would be required, and Tchaikovsky's 'honeymoon' could be extended until it was time to take up this responsibility. Accordingly the appointment was sought and made. This posting would also provide subsistence. Meanwhile Rubinstein had arranged for the Conservatoire to continue paying a proportion of their absent professor's salary. At this moment of crisis, Tchaikovsky had very good reason for gratitude not only to his family, but to his friends.

Yet the most significant intervention at this time came from an outside quarter. Tchaikovsky had finally to tell Nadezhda von Meck of the collapse of his marriage. Her private joy might easily be guessed; Tchaikovsky was now emotionally dependent on her more than ever, and to bind him yet more tightly, she sent him one thousand francs to clear his debts, promising a future monthly allowance of fifteen hundred francs. Her offer was very tactfully put: 'Perhaps I am not a person who is intimate with you,' she wrote:

but you know how I love you, how I wish you the best in everything. You know how many happy moments you afford me, how deeply

grateful I am to you for them, how necessary you are to me, and how
for me you must be exactly that which you were created to be. Consequently I am not doing anything for you, but everything for myself.
And if I were to need something from you, you would do it for me,
wouldn't you? So this means we are quits – and so do not prevent me
from giving my attention to your housekeeping, Pyotr Ilich!

Tchaikovsky's gratitude can readily be imagined, and her allowance,
continued over the next twelve years, would give him financial security,
free him from his Conservatoire chores, and enable him to channel all
his energies into composing.

So far the day-to-day thread in Tchaikovsky's biography has been
notable for its very lack of anything notable. Schoolboy, civil servant,
Conservatoire student, Conservatoire teacher – each stage has followed
naturally and smoothly. For a while, all that is now to change, and
biographical detail will proliferate, sometimes recording a frenzy of
activity precipitated by his overwrought condition, the legacy of his
marital disaster. On leaving St Petersburg, Anatoly took his distraught
brother first to Berlin, then Geneva, finally settling for the next three
weeks for the quiet of a pleasant lakeside pension in Clarens, a tiny town
on the north bank of Lake Geneva. Yet even here there was one factor
that soon became oppressive. 'Mountains are very fine,' Tchaikovsky
wrote to his old colleague, Albrecht, 'but it's very difficult for a Russian
to stand their overwhelming grandeur for long. I'm dying for a plain, for
a boundless, distant prospect, for an expanse of open country, and for
wide horizons' – in other words, something like the Russia he knew.
Having received news of his patroness's generosity, he could move on,
and it was to Paris that he and Anatoly directed themselves. Now he
could also afford to summon his valet, Alexey, from Russia.

This was the good news: the bad concerned Antonina. She was still
at Kamenka and Tchaikovsky feared that she might be poisoning his
family's view of him. She wrote him wild letters, sometimes accusing
him, at others cajoling him; worst of all, he was in terror that she
might reveal publicly his sexual orientation. Modest and Sasha were
now hoping for a reconciliation, but Tchaikovsky was adamant that
this could never be. 'Even if you are right that she is good-hearted,' he
wrote:

even if I am guilty all round because I have not known how to
appreciate her, even if it's true she loves me – yet live with her *I cannot,*

cannot, cannot. Demand of me any satisfaction you will for her: when I return to Russia I'll give her two-thirds of my earnings, I'll hide myself in any backwater you like, I'm prepared to become a beggar – but, for God's sake, never hint to me that I should return to Antonina Ivanovna. In a word, in the fullest sense of the expression, *I do not love her!*

From Paris the brothers moved on to Italy. Two days in Florence – and then it was Rome. If Tchaikovsky had seemed to be on the road to recovery while in Switzerland, there had now been a relapse. 'I literally cannot bear any noise. Both yesterday in Florence and here today, every sound tears at my nerves. The mass of people moving through the narrow streets begins to irritate me so much that each stranger who comes towards me appears to be a rabid foe.' He had asked for the Fourth Symphony material to be forwarded to him in Rome, but apparently it had not arrived, and he would have to wait. Moreover, in a fortnight Anatoly had to return to Russia. To fill the time he visited the Vatican, St Peter's and the Colosseum, mainly to please Anatoly. Tchaikovsky was never particularly drawn to the visual arts, but one statue did hold his attention; that of the dying gladiator in the Capitol – much finer, he felt significantly, than the statue of Venus.

After three days the Fourth Symphony package was found (it had been mis-shelved), and they could leave Rome for Venice. Here his mood improved. Venice was a quiet, traffic-free city, and he loved the very narrow streets, especially in the evenings when the shops were lit by their gas lamps. He would remain nine days, scoring a little more of *Onegin*. He planned to part from Anatoly in Vienna, where he would also meet Alexey, and then he might return to Venice with his servant. In Vienna he had the delight of Kotek's company, too. However, the return to Venice was not the pleasure he had anticipated. His mood had changed, and he drank heavily to drown his sorrows. Yet the most disturbing evidence of his condition was found in his personal library after his death. It was a copy of three tragedies by Euripides, translated into Latin, in a very rare edition that had been published in Antwerp in 1581. Inside, in Tchaikovsky's own hand, was written: 'Stolen from the library of the Palace of the Doges in Venice on 15 December 1877 by Pyotr Tchaikovsky, court counsellor, and professor at the Conservatoire'.

Now at last, however, his depression truly began to lift. Alexey's cheerful personality helped, and finding he could resume productive work on the Fourth Symphony led to the establishment of a daily routine: rise at eight, drink tea, work till eleven, eat, walk with Alexey until one or one thirty, work till five, dinner, a walk by himself till eight, then tea. His voracious appetite for late-night reading had returned (among his current books was Thackeray's *Pendennis*). The news from Kamenka was cheering, too. By now his family had had their fill of Antonina, and she had been conducted back to Moscow, this reassurance being buttressed by letters from both Sasha and Lev making it clear he was redeemed in their eyes. Then Albrecht reported that Tchaikovsky's Conservatoire colleagues were enchanted by the first act of *Onegin*. Best of all, Modest informed him that he and Kolya would leave Russia on 1 January for San Remo on the Mediterranean coast, where Tchaikovsky could join them. Their accommodation being not yet fixed, Tchaikovsky hastened to San Remo to seek lodgings, and then use the time before their arrival to complete the symphony.

Instantly there came the official notice of his appointment as a delegate to the Paris Exhibition. Now having Nadezhda von Meck's generous allowance, Tchaikovsky wished to be rid of this commitment, especially when he learned all that would be required of him, which included residence in Paris. Forthwith he withdrew his acceptance, pleading that he was in no condition to take up the appointment. Rubinstein, who had arranged it for him, was understandably furious, and both Kashkin and Albrecht added their voices to his. The storm clouds raised by the affair took a long time to disperse.

The five and a half weeks spent in San Remo proved of great therapeutic benefit to Tchaikovsky. He had reservations about San Remo itself, and especially its olive-covered hillsides. But there were walks or donkey rides into the hills and along the beach, there was an opera house, and Kolya's speech was improving. If the lad came to talk and ask questions when he was working on the symphony's score, Tchaikovsky was always happy to suspend work. At San Remo he also completed *Onegin*. Though always, it seems, short of money (and Nadezhda von Meck came to his rescue several times during this period), his own generosity was well in evidence. Back in Moscow he had committed himself to helping a young violin student, Alexander Litvinov, through his studies, and he insisted on pursuing this to the end – just one of many such financial interventions he would make for impecunious students. As for his marriage, he insisted that the responsibility for this having taken place was his alone, that Antonina was blameless, and he proposed reflecting this in his alimony settlement – as long as she would leave him and his relatives alone. But when Jurgenson, who was handling the matter, commented on Tchaikovsky's generosity, the latter's reply uncovered a less charitable motive: 'Only with money can I buy myself the right to *despise* her as much as I *hate* her!'

On 19 February Tchaikovsky and his companions left San Remo. Looking back over the previous seven months, he found he could detach himself from what was now past. As he wrote to Anatoly:

> Only now, when I am completely recovered, have I learned to relate *objectively* to everything that I did during my brief insanity. That man who in May took it into his head to marry Antonina Ivanovna, who during June wrote a whole opera as though nothing had happened, who in July married, who in September fled his wife, who in November railed at Rome, and so on – that man wasn't I, but another Pyotr Ilich.

Florence was their ultimate destination but passing through Pisa they paused to see the sights and climb the leaning tower for its spectacular view. On his previous visit to Florence Tchaikovsky had found the city hateful, and he interpreted his very different reaction this time as confirmation of his recovery. Even more cheering was to discover that his creative gift was reviving, for on the second day he composed a completely new song, a grim, powerful setting of a poem by Mikhail Lermontov, Pushkin's great contemporary (like Pushkin, also dying young in a duel). 'The love of a dead man'** was not only a totally new composition: its quality was first rate.

A second song resulted from a small incident that gives us graphic insight into Tchaikovsky's inner sexual world. On his recent visit to Florence with Anatoly, Tchaikovsky had heard Vittorio, a boy of about eleven who sang to his own guitar accompaniment. 'His voice was marvellously rich, with a finish and warmth that one rarely encounters in professional artists,' he had written to Nadezhda von Meck. Now, with the help of a local inhabitant, a meeting with the boy singer was arranged. 'The man was there, and a group of other men were also awaiting me with curiosity,' he wrote to Anatoly:

In the centre of this was our boy. The first thing I noticed was that he had grown a little and that he was *beautiful*, whereas before he had seemed to us to be plain. Because the throng was still growing and it was a crowded spot, I set off a little in the direction of the Cascino. On the way I expressed doubt as to whether it was truly he. 'When I sing you'll know it's me. The last time you gave me a silver half-franc piece.' All this was spoken in a wonderful voice, and penetrated to the depths of my soul. But what became of me when he sang? It's impossible to describe. I do not believe that you get greater pleasure when you are listening to the singing of Panayeva [a singer for whom Anatoly currently had an unrequited passion]. I wept, I broke down, languished with delight. Besides the song which you know, he sang two new ones, of which one, 'Pimpinella', is delightful.

Two days later he saw the boy again. 'He appeared at midday *in costume*,' Tchaikovsky continued:

Only then did I examine him. He is positively *beautiful*, with an inexpressibly sympathetic look and smile. He is better when heard in the street than in a room; there he is cramped, and doesn't fully open up his voice. I wrote down all his songs. Then I took him off to be photographed.

Tchaikovsky had arranged to meet Vittorio again in two days for more songs, but the latter did not appear, pleading a sore throat. Presumably to consolidate for himself a memory of this encounter, Tchaikovsky made an arrangement of one of Vittorio's songs, 'Pimpinella', not hesitating to improve the tune a little, add a third verse of his own, and give it a piano accompaniment.

By early March, their finances being virtually exhausted, Tchaikovsky and his companions bade farewell to Florence and settled into the pension at Clarens. It now had an added attraction for him – that it was reasonably accessible from Berlin, where Kotek was studying with the great violinist, Joseph Joachim. Within days of arriving Tchaikovsky had begun a major piece, his one and only mature **Piano Sonata** * *(*). There are divergent views about the quality of this work, and my personal opinion is that it is, of all Tchaikovsky's large-scale compositions, perhaps the dullest. Tchaikovsky himself admitted that it was not the product of inspiration so much as of fabrication, and I find it mostly stodgy and lifeless, for all its grandiloquence. But some take a different view, so readers who investigate it and decide I have got it wrong can know they have supporters among other professionals. However, on the day after Tchaikovsky had begun the sonata, Kotek had arrived from Berlin with a pile of recent publications which he and Tchaikovsky instantly set about investigating. Among these was Édouard Lalo's *Symphonie espagnole*, in effect a five-movement violin concerto, its music deliberately impregnated with musical echoes and manners from Spain. Tchaikovsky was instantly captivated by it; as he wrote to his patroness, 'In the same way as Delibes and Bizet, Lalo does not strive after profundity, but he carefully avoids routine, seeks out new forms, and thinks more about *musical beauty* than about observing established traditions, as do the Germans.' He laboured one more day on the sonata, but admitted that inspiration did not come. Thus the urge to direct his creative energies into composing a piece to match Lalo's proved irresistible, and in Kotek he had to hand the ideal consultant on the solo violin part. Instantly abandoning the sonata, Tchaikovsky set about his own violin concerto.

Setting the Violin Concerto alongside its exact contemporary, the Piano Sonata, prompts a question: how could two symphonic works, so intertwined, be so different in quality, the sonata so stodgy and dull, the concerto so fresh and fertile. The speed with which the latter was written was prodigious. The first movement took a mere five days, the finale only three. And when Modest reinforced Tchaikovsky's own reservations about the original slow movement, within twenty-four hours its replacement had been composed. There can be little doubt that Kotek provided the spur to Tchaikovsky's inspiration in this concerto. A year earlier the twenty-two-year-old had been a student in Tchaikovsky's class at the Conservatoire, and Poznansky's assertion that, though himself heterosexual, Kotek was also, as least briefly, Tchaikovsky's lover is plausible. Certainly Tchaikovsky was unusually devoted to the young man. But it was an uneasy relationship. Kotek's attitudes and behaviour could be sources of annoyance to Tchaikovsky, most recently his over-willingness to continue living at his father's expense. Yet the acrimonious moments this precipitated could make even sweeter those phases when they were in harmonious accord. Just such a phase was surely this interlude in Clarens, releasing briefly those creative forces which had brought into being the Fourth Symphony and *Eugene Onegin* ahead of his marriage.

Tchaikovsky had at first intended to dedicate the Violin Concerto to Leopold Auer, one of the most eminent violinists of his time. But Auer had procrastinated in performing it, and it was first heard in Vienna in December 1881, with Adolf Brodsky as soloist. It produced one of the most notorious verdicts in the history of music journalism when Eduard Hanslick, one of the most famed and influential critics of his time, declared that the concerto was made up of music in which you 'hear how it stinks'. But under the continuing advocacy of Brodsky, to whom it was finally dedicated, the concerto rapidly acquired great success. Auer later excused his delay by claiming that he had wished to make revisions to the solo part, but had been unable to find time. In fact, when Auer finally paid attention to the concerto, he went much further, excising whole chunks of the first movement, and it was in this degraded form that for many years the concerto was played. It is important to note this here, since some early recordings may still be current that use Auer's emasculated edition. Nowadays few violinists would dream of using (or daring to use) it.

Violin Concerto in D *****

[The Violin Concerto is one of Tchaikovsky's most engaging works, yet do not underestimate it (as I confess I once did). No work of Tchaikovsky relies as heavily as this concerto on his melodic gift, and it never fails him. This is one of the great violin concertos.]

On the face of it, the Violin Concerto is one of the least sophisticated of Tchaikovsky's symphonic pieces, and it certainly contains none of the novel structural adventures of, say, the First Piano Concerto. But why should it? Certainly a piano offers the composer far wider possibilities than a violin, for it can present harmony as well as melody, enabling him to make it a more equal and flexible partner to the orchestra. But where a violin scores is in its far greater melodic potential. Like a singer, it delivers melody that is unbroken sound, allowing for all sorts of inflections within a melodic line (and even within a single note) in a way that the piano cannot match, and by skilful use of the bow a violinist can completely alter the tone colour of a melody. It is melodic potential that is one of the great strengths of Tchaikovsky's concerto. Its first movement's application of sonata form (as applied in a concerto movement) is straightforward. First a fairly brisk introduction, which hints at the first subject to come; then the violin introduces itself, and leads us into the exposition, where the instrument is not only very rarely silent, but is almost always centre stage, eloquently delivering the melodies Tchaikovsky has composed for it, or dazzling with virtuosic figuration. As in so many of Tchaikovsky's expositions there are three tunes, the first an invention of great charm, the second more sprightly and leading on to a brief burst of fireworks as a foil to the third (*con molto espressivo*), a tender invention that spreads itself vastly, never faltering, and building to an expansive climax to round off the exposition. It is difficult to over-praise the achievement of this great melodic expanse (if you happen to know Tchaikovsky's inspiration, the *Symphonie espagnol*, compare Tchaikovsky's exposition with the parallel stretch of Lalo's first movement, and I think the former's greater melodic richness will become even more apparent).

As expected, an orchestral *tutti* marks the entry into the development. This is the first time since the concerto's very opening that the orchestra has been allowed centre stage, and it is a substantial passage. The soloist goes on to offer a variation on the first subject, which is then extended – after which the orchestra returns, rather surprisingly perhaps, with a second ritornello. But the reason soon emerges: Tchaikovsky is going to follow the precedent of another of the most famous violin concertos, that of Mendelssohn, and insert his cadenza not near the movement's end, but before the recapitulation. Thus this ritornello has been a punctuation mark as well as a grand build-up to that passage in which the soloist can be in the spotlight unchallenged. As in the Mendelssohn concerto, the cadenza leads straight into the recapitulation, which follows the same course as the exposition (though there are variations of detail along the way), and passes into a substantial and brilliant coda. If, after hearing the concerto's first two or three minutes, we anticipated that because it sounded less grand this first movement would be shorter than that of the First Piano Concerto, we would be wrong; its performance time (and that of the whole concerto) fully matches that of the earlier concerto – yet it can sustain our interest just as much.

In the remaining two movements Tchaikovsky's Russian voice is suddenly in evidence. He labelled the slow movement *Canzonetta* (literally 'a little song') and it was the most consistently melodic movement he had composed since the *Andante cantabile* of his First String

Quartet. But this time all the melody is Tchaikovsky's own. A wind introduction sets the tone, and the hauntingly Russian flavour of the violin melody that follows is very marked; it has a gentle melancholy about it which is perfectly complemented by the more impassioned tone of its companion to follow. No movement could be more unfussy or speak more directly to the listener. Now the introduction slips in on the strings beneath the soloist (this is so furtively done that it is easy to miss it), who returns us to the first theme, after which the woodwind introduction both closes the movement and provides the first part of a transition to the finale. It seems extraordinary that all this was composed in a single day.

There is no break between the *Canzonetta* and the finale, and this reinforces the extreme contrast in mood between the two movements. The finale, as Russian as the second movement, though now possessed of tremendous vitality, is surely some rural folk scene, the soloist now a folk fiddler (though prodigiously talented!), first tuning his instrument, testing it, then launching into his first item. While this one has enormous energy, his second is earthily robust, its sturdy double pedal (the two-pitch 'drone' that persists beneath) suggestive, perhaps, of peasant bagpipes. Tchaikovsky dwells on this theme, decorating it with different backgrounds, then suddenly slowing it to suggest, perhaps, a more tender, feminine persuasiveness. I cannot guess what (if anything) may be represented by the courteous dialogue between oboe, clarinet and bassoon, but do we need to decode this when the music itself, just as music, is so infectious that we succumb to it anyway? This movement is its own advocate, among Tchaikovsky's own compositions the closest in spirit to that magnificent finale of his Second (*Little Russian*) Symphony.

That said, perhaps we have a clue to the deeper motivation of these last two so contrasted, yet so Russian movements.

―――――

By now Tchaikovsky had been in voluntary exile from Russia for some six months, and his letters home had been increasingly filled with expressions of longing for his native land. Only six days after completing his Violin Concerto, he was on his way home. But he returned to Russia a very anxious man, and his initial encounter with the frontier staff did nothing to raise his spirits. First there was a drunken gendarme, then a custom's official who charged him extortionate duty for a dress he had bought for Sasha, and finally another gendarme who seemed suspicious of him and delayed letting him through. Then there was the train journey: dirty railway carriages – 'Yids with that poisonous atmosphere which accompanies them everywhere' (despite his admiration for the Rubinstein brothers, Tchaikovsky had a streak of anti-Semitism in him) – a train full of typhoid victims, another with young recruits off to fight in the current Russo-Turkish war: all this depressed him. And how would he be received at Kamenka? In the event, his family's greetings could not have been warmer or more reassuring. Sasha had tactfully prepared a peasant cottage for him some way from the main house where he could be alone if he wished. 'My cottage is arranged very conveniently and comfortably,' he reported to his patroness. 'They have even got me a piano, and put it in the little room alongside my bedroom. Working will be good for me.' He set himself to complete the Piano Sonata, and then produced a clutch of piano pieces, though none of them is of real significance – at least, as far as the larger ones are concerned. But another set, the humblest that Tchaikovsky ever composed, does still have some very real interest for us today.

As his relationships with his nephews and nieces had long shown, Tchaikovsky had a natural ability to get on with children: think only of that little ballet he had created for them seven years earlier, and which would be the seed of *Swan Lake*. Now some of Sasha's children were well of an age to be playing the piano, and it was no doubt this that decided Uncle Pyotr to compose his **Album for Children: 24 Easy Pieces (à la Schumann)** **(*)**, completing them all within four days. His model was not Schumann's well-known *Scenes from Childhood* (*Kinderszenen*), which was a highly sophisticated presentation of experiences and incidents of childhood viewed from an adult perspective, but that same composer's *Album for Young People*. Yet whereas Schumann here had presented a course of forty-three pieces of increasing difficulty composed for his growing family, Tchaikovsky's *Album for Children* was simply a collection of charming morsels for young (and not so young) pianists at an early stage, and for those among my readership who are simply listeners, this set will be of little interest. However, for those who are also pianists, even though they would confess their skills to be limited, this set could be a real gift. What marks off Tchaikovsky's pieces from so much of the elementary piano fodder of our time are those special touches which may initially be something of a challenge: patches of striking harmony that present some reading (and sometimes fingering) problems, and unexpected phrase structures that present problems of timing. But all such things, though they may demand a bit of extra patience before they are absolutely right, will have their reward.[1] Many of the pieces have titles that are imaginative pointers to how they should be played. A number are arrangements of existing tunes, some Russian, but others from both France and Italy (including one from the repertoire of Vittorio, the Florentine street singer). Others are dances. But some of the best music (and, admittedly, some of the trickiest) is to be found in the character or descriptive pieces: for instance, in the sprightly galloping of the little horseman (no. 4) and the brisk marching of the wooden soldiers (no. 5), in the sad portrait of the sick doll (no. 7), and in its solemn funeral (no. 8). At the other extreme is the peasant trying out his accordion (no. 13), which seems finally to get stuck on two chords, and the portrait of the grotesque witch, Baba Yaga (no. 20). Elsewhere there are some pretty twitterings from a lark (no. 22). The set had opened with a morning prayer, and it is in church that it closes (at least it did in the original published edition: no. 24).

Now that Tchaikovsky's marriage had disintegrated, Nadezhda von Meck made a further offer to him which would bind him yet closer to her: she invited him to stay on her extensive estate at Brailov in the Ukraine at a time when she would be away. Thus he would come to enjoy – and share – a very real part of her world. To ensure everything would be to his liking she gave instructions to her staff that the guest was to have absolute freedom, be obeyed in everything and be left undisturbed: Alexey would be the intermediary between them and his master. The staff were told nothing of the guest's identity, and they would finally conclude that he must be the fiancé of one of her daughters. Tchaikovsky took up residence at the end of May, and though he enthused unconditionally to his patroness about Brailov, he was more reserved to Modest. The house was splendidly furnished and comfortable, and there were some excellent musical instruments, but he found the estate itself less attractive. Nevertheless, walking in the surrounding countryside was a great pleasure, and he discovered a nunnery with a good, musically literate choir where he was able to attend ser-

---

1 An edition of *Album for the Young* (edited by Howard Ferguson) is published by the Associated Board of the Royal Schools of Music. The above numbering follows that of this edition, except for the final item.

vices. He also developed a passion for collecting mushrooms. Best of all, perhaps, Brailov provided a relaxing environment in which he could work. As a gift for his absent hostess he composed two pieces, *Scherzo* and *Mélodie*, for violin and piano, which, together with a violin–piano transcription of the rejected slow movement of the Violin Concerto (now labelled *Méditation*), he left behind him as a token of thanks. The collective title he gave the three pieces must have added to her pleasure: *Souvenir d'un lieu cher* ('Memento of a beloved place'). In addition, he composed a set of six songs, op. 38, including two of his finest examples, '**Don Juan's serenade**',*** a splendidly rumbustious summons to the Don's Nisetta to appear on her balcony, and, in total contrast, a haunting waltz song, '**Amid the din of the ball**',*** in which the singer remembers the happy voice, but sad eyes, of a beautiful woman glimpsed across a crowded ballroom.

However, Brailov also saw the birth of a set of pieces quite unlike anything Tchaikovsky had yet composed, and which would have a profound consequence for the future of Russian church music. The initiative had come from Tchaikovsky himself back in February, when he had enquired of Jurgenson whether he would be interested in publishing some small pieces of church music or, preferably, a setting of part of the liturgy of the Russian Orthodox Church. Evidently the matter was discussed further, for by the time of his Brailov visit, Tchaikovsky could outline to Nadezhda von Meck the present situation. He conceded that some of the current composers of Orthodox church music were worthy artisans, 'but,' he added:

> how little is their music in harmony with the Byzantine style of our architecture and icons, and with the whole structure of the Orthodox service. Did you know that the composition of music for the church is a monopoly of the Imperial Chapel's musical establishment, which jealously guards this monopoly, and flatly refuses to allow new attempts to set sacred texts? My publisher, Jurgenson, has found a means of getting round this strange law, and if I write something for the church, he will then publish it abroad.

Having at Brailov sketched an unaccompanied choral setting of the Liturgy of St John Chrysostom (the main service of the Russian Orthodox Church), and completed it in August, Tchaikovsky now found Jurgenson in a more confrontational mood: he would challenge the Imperial Chapel's monopoly head on, and issue Tchaikovsky's Liturgy in Russia. As expected, on publication all copies were seized by the Director of the Imperial Chapel and a legal battle was joined. The case lasted over two years until, in 1881, judgement was given in favour of Jurgenson. From now on, the composition and publication of church music in Russia was open to all, and Tchaikovsky's Liturgy of St John Chrysostom could find a rightful place in church services.

Music for the Russian Orthodox Church

[To Western ears at least, Russian Orthodox church music has an esoteric character, and is likely to be of interest to only a minority of my readers. Nevertheless, some consideration should be given to it, though I shall be breaking the chronological sequence by taking account here of all three of Tchaikovsky's contributions to Russian church music.]

The Liturgy of St John Chrysostom*** is the form of Mass most widely used in Eastern Orthodox Churches, and a substantial proportion of it is devoted to dialogue between the officiating clergy and the choir. A body of traditional chants had evolved for this, and Tchaikovsky used these chants scrupulously, furnishing them with the simplest of homophonic (that is, chordal) accompaniments. The result was an enormous amount of functional music; our main interest, however, lies in the half-dozen texts for which he composed free settings. These include the Creed, the Lord's Prayer, and *Cherubim's Song*, the last the most substantial of all. In fact, though Tchaikovsky was free here to do as he liked, he gave the first two of these and a fourth piece, *Praise ye the Lord*, simple chordal accompaniments, but in *Thee we hymn* and *Meet it is indeed*, he allowed himself more freedom, in the latter using gentle imitation and, in the former, antiphonal rejoinders (that is, one vocal line briefly dialogues with another). On the page all this may appear to be music that will have little more impact than a traditional hymn sung in one of our churches, but in practice the effect can be very different. It is music that often demands a far more measured style of performance than we would accord a hymn tune, and at that slower speed its very simplicity informs it with a magisterial dignity, especially if a performance covers a very wide dynamic range (as one of my students observed after participating in a performance of

Thee we hymn: 'The earth moved!'). But the most elaborate piece is *Cherubim's Song*, with its independent, hushed, awesomely slow opening that is the most powerful of foils for the blaze of antiphonal sound that follows. The first section returns as before; there is an Amen, and then a complete change of manner incorporating a fugal-style passage so redolent of baroque music that, as used here, it is almost uncomfortable (or so, I confess, it is to me). But wait until you have heard it for yourself, for there are now some very good performances by Russian choirs available on CD.

Tchaikovsky would make two more sorties into the world of Orthodox church music. In 1881 he would turn his attention to another Service, the **All-Night Vigil**,** in which he tried more deliberately to escape the 'excessive Europeanism' that had been audible in some of his settings in the Liturgy. In the All-Night Vigil he was far less a composer than an arranger, for now he was faced with a huge body of traditional chants, and he saw his role to be mostly that of providing these chant melodies with simple note-against-note harmonizations. Only rarely did he allow his added alto, tenor and bass parts some real independence so as to produce something that sounds like real composition. However, while the All-Night Vigil may be of interest only to those who are particularly drawn to the inner world of Russian Orthodox church music, the **Nine Sacred Pieces****** for unaccompanied chorus, which Tchaikovsky composed in 1884–85, are free compositions with a wider appeal, and contain some very fine music. The three *Cherubim's Songs* are very impressive, and especially the third, where the normal treble, alto, tenor and bass lines are all divided into two, thus producing an eight-part texture which can have a particular weight and sonority. This splendid piece achieved considerable popularity in Russia, and this gave it some seminal importance in the evolution of later Orthodox church music. An equally impressive piece is another eight-voice composition, *Bliss I chose* (to give it a rather awkward English title), a more freely composed piece which reinforces even more one's regret that Tchaikovsky did not venture into this type of composition more often. Some of this music possesses a mystic aura and a special kind of grandeur quite different to anything I have met in our Western tradition – but seek out recorded performances by native Russian choirs; I have tried conducting English choral groups in this music, and our tradition and temperament are simply too different for us to do it real justice. Anyway, Russian choral singing is nearly always something rather special.

———

Tchaikovsky had now been back in Russia for some seven weeks. So far he had avoided Moscow, and he dreaded the moment when he would have to confront his long-term colleagues. He need not have feared, for they obviously welcomed him warmly. As for the matter of the Paris Exhibition, Rubinstein seems to have concealed any residual anger at Tchaikovsky's default. Now, with the promise of generous monetary help from his patroness if a reasonable settlement could be agreed with Antonina, it seemed that a satisfactory outcome to his divorce proceedings could be in sight. But it required more co-operation from Antonina, and Jurgenson agreed to deal with her on Tchaikovsky's behalf. Thus Tchaikovsky spent only three days in Moscow before, on 16 June, heading for Kondratyev's estate at Nizy.

In three months the new Conservatoire term would begin, and it was assumed Tchaikovsky would return to his duties. It was not a prospect he relished, and what marks his behaviour during these months is its restlesssness. In a matter of only days he had once again fled from Nizy and its disordered servants, and headed for Kamenka. Only here, or at the neighbouring family estate at Verbovka, could he find peace, revelling in the company of those closest to him, joining in their corporate life, and seeming for a time able to blot out all thought of the trials and tensions besetting his wider world. At Kamenka he could shoot ducks or bustards with neighbours, roam the countryside with the Kamenka dogs, compose at leisure, be alone when he wished, then join in the family recreations, playing the piano for dancing, and participating fully in their more ambitious entertainments. A letter to Modest provides a vignette of his lifestyle. All sorts of relatives had assembled at Kamenka, and been drawn into proceedings:

> During the last week I've transformed myself completely into some sort of Goddess Diana. I go hunting every day. On Sunday there was a big shoot with Vishnitsky, Volokhov, Roman, Tikhon, etc. Quite a lot were killed – but I, as usual, just *banged away*. Rehearsals for our performance [of Gogol's play, *The Marriage*, which Tchaikovsky was producing] started yesterday. Lev doesn't want Tanya to play the matchmaker, and Sasha Peresleny has taken her role. Dima, for want of anybody else, is playing Yaichnitsa. Vladimir Andreyevich

declined to take part in the performance. Besides *The Marriage* we're putting on two scenes for Tanya and Sasha: (1) the scene of the two women from *Dead Souls* [by Gogol], and (2) the scene of the two women from [Molière's] *Le Misanthrope*. Yesterday's rehearsal showed that Natalya Andreyevna will be delightful, but her delivery is a bit monotonous. Sasha plays the matchmaker superbly. Though Kolya Peresleny over-acts, he still isn't bad as Zhevakin. Tolya plays Podkolesin very respectably. Biryukov didn't know his lines.

The day before yesterday we went to the Verbovka wood to collect mushrooms. We found aspen mushrooms in such quantity as I have never before seen anywhere. The same day Sasha went with the three youngest children and Miss Eastwood [the English governess at Kamenka] to the Rayevskys', and had a whole series of adventures. On the return journey they were overtaken by a storm. Sasha was almost killed by the horses, they were all drenched, somehow or other got back to Kamenka, and arrived here when it was already late evening, where they found us all in a terrible state.

The dramatic performances took place a week later. To make a good audience, peasants from the estate were invited: Tchaikovsky was the prompter.

Tchaikovsky remained over seven weeks with Sasha and her family. By then feeling the need for solitude after the populous family life at Kamenka, on 23 August he installed himself at Brailov. His patroness had a splendid library, and he buried himself in her books, sometimes squatting on the floor for hours, engrossed in reading. He often went for walks accompanied by an army of dogs. But the urge to compose would not be quieted. 'This morning I wanted so much to sketch an orchestral scherzo that I could not resist it, and spent a couple of hours working,' he confided to his patroness. It marked the beginning of his First Suite for orchestra. But after a week at Brailov he had had enough of solitude, and he again directed himself to Verbovka where, within only days, he had sketched three further movements. Wanting to visit St Petersburg before settling back in Moscow for the new Conservatoire session, on 9 September he set out for the Russian capital. But on the way to Kiev he chanced on a scurrilous newspaper report. 'At one point the article talks about professors' *love affairs* with girls,' he wrote in alarm to Modest, 'and it adds at the end: "*Love affairs of a different sort also go on at the Conservatoire, but of these, for a very understandable reason, I will not speak"* – and so on. It's clear what he is hinting at.'

This decided Tchaikovsky: he would resign his professorship – not immediately, because that would cause chaos, but at Christmas. But he would now depend on his patroness's continuing bounty, and she had to be informed. So he wrote to her, detailing the reasons for his decision: the offensive newspaper article, overhearing (so he claimed) strangers in a train talking about his marriage and his madness, Rubinstein's despotism, and the oppressiveness of the Conservatoire. 'And so, my friend, what would you say if I were to quit the Conservatoire? I am going to Moscow and I shall try to accustom myself to it. But I must know for certain how you regard this. Not for anything in the world would I wish to act other than according to your counsel and instruction. Please give me your answer.' Of course he knew what it would be.

Tchaikovsky's decision merely exacerbated his aversion to the Conservatoire. He returned to Moscow, term began, and he felt worse still. After a week he poured out his feelings to Anatoly:

I'm utterly dispirited and regard everything around me with cold loathing. Moscow is thoroughly offensive to me. I try to avoid all society and all encounters with people. Everybody I see I find intolerable, and this includes Kashkin, Albrecht, Jurgenson and Laroche. I go straight to my class when I arrive, and I leave forthwith after the class, trying not to talk with anybody or encounter anybody. To various greetings such as 'Hello!', or 'Who's that I see?', I respond with a sweet-and-sour face, and immediately rush off in another direction. I walk for a couple of hours, and go home to dine.

There was one good thing, however: Antonina was keeping to the rules of the financial arrangement made with her, and seemed to have left Moscow.

Rubinstein having returned to Paris, it would be early October before Moscow saw him again, and so negotiations about Tchaikovsky's resignation could not be opened. When Rubinstein duly reappeared, there was a dinner in his honour, and in his first speech he heaped praise on Tchaikovsky for the international reputation he was building for himself, adding how fortunate the Conservatoire was to have such a celebrity on its staff. But there was a double edge to this accolade: Tchaikovsky felt he would have to postpone his resignation until the following summer. However, the very next day the matter was taken out of his hands. For all the prestige that Tchaikovsky brought to the Conservatoire, Rubinstein realized he could no longer detain him, and between them the two men devised a strategy that would allow Tchaikovsky to leave unobtrusively at Christmas: Taneyev would be invited to undertake a temporary piano class, and when Tchaikovsky slipped away, Taneyev would take his place. 'I shall go off to the country as though on family business,' Tchaikovsky explained, 'and from there I'll write and say I cannot return because of illness.' The same day he heard that his patroness fully approved his intentions.

However, Tchaikovsky then saw the opening that would enable him to leave before the year's end: why should not Taneyev also take over his theory class ahead of December? Straight away he informed Rubinstein that he would be leaving at the end of the week. On 19 October he took his last ever class. The next day he dined with his friends: Rubinstein, Kashkin, Albrecht, Jurgenson and Taneyev. 'Despite all my joy at my longed-for freedom, I experienced some sadness at parting from the people among whom I have lived for more than twelve years,' he would confess to Mrs von Meck three days later. 'They all seemed very grieved, and this touched me.' But already, on that day of farewell, he had enthused to her unreservedly on the prospect before him. 'Yesterday I gave my last lesson. Today I leave for St Petersburg. Thus I am a *free man*!'

15
Personal Freedom –
and Creative Trough

The narrative is about to quicken, for where Tchaikovsky would now settle was a matter entirely in his own hands, and he could remove himself whenever he chose if he found the environment growing uncongenial, or simply wanted a change of scene. Thus it might have been expected that, relieved of the personal tensions that had sprung from his disastrous marriage, and with a more than adequate lifestyle assured by his patroness's allowance, works would have flowed freely from him. Indeed they did, and the quantity is impressive; the problem is sometimes their quality. In technique they are as fluent as ever – but sometimes almost too much so. There is a detachment about some of them, an absence of that so precious personal element, of that edge, that sense of striving that truly excites, and sometimes disturbs; at their best they are like images, beautiful in concept and executed immaculately – but only passive, not living organisms. Not until 1885, when he settled into a dacha near Klin, some fifty miles outside Moscow, did he rediscover that stability that would enable his creativity to operate freely and fully as it had done before Antonina had entered his life. True, in the intervening years there would be at least two notable exceptions where some human element, one from real life, the other from fiction, really touched his creativity. The first was the death of a close colleague, the second the predicament of a young woman and her elderly husband as told in one of Pushkin's great narrative poems. These, together with the Second Piano Concerto, will receive closer attention. Nevertheless, that said, there is still much very acceptable music to be found in the compositions of the next five years, and they make generally easier listening than have some of the masterworks already examined, and some to come.

Such a one is his First Orchestral Suite. Tchaikovsky had begun sketching it back in August while still with his family at Kamenka, but its completion was delayed for a year, mainly because he was uncertain about the overall effect of what would be a very substantial piece, matching the Fourth Symphony in performance time (about forty minutes). In addition, while presenting a wide variety of styles and moods, it had to add up to a coherent, satisfying experience, and this caused Tchaikovsky much difficulty.

Suite no. 1, for orchestra * * *

[This, the first of Tchaikovsky's three true orchestral suites (the fourth is a series of orchestrations of pieces by Mozart), is the least important, though the little Marche Miniature *is very engaging.]*

A suite may be simply a selection of, say, half-a-dozen pieces extracted from a larger composition, and chosen primarily for their popularity, real or potential (Tchaikovsky's *Nutcracker Suite* is a famous example). But historically the suite has at times existed as a form in its own right. Probably the most famous suites are those composed by Bach in the late baroque period (the first half of the eighteenth century) – namely, his French and English Suites for keyboard. These are made up mainly from dances of the time (allemandes, courantes, sarabands and gigues especially). Tchaikovsky's four orchestral suites are, by contrast, a very diverse bunch. Nevertheless, the first does reveal Bach as a formative influence, for it opens with an introduction and fugue, and closes with a gavotte, a baroque dance. Yet there is little risk that any listener already familiar with some baroque music will believe that these pieces could credibly be by Bach, even though Tchaikovsky's fugue is clearly of an 'academic' nature, for its climax steps right outside baroque practice. It is the only movement that may present a challenge to the listener, following on a very spacious and, later, portentous slow introduction (the baroque equivalent of a prelude). However, the constant recurrence of the fugue's subject gives the whole piece a very precise focus, and it culminates in a very powerful, very nineteenth-century climax – though its end will, in fact, prove to be quiet.

The remaining five movements are built mainly from fairly self-contained sections shuffled in various ways, their orchestration exploiting especially the colour contrast between the wind and the strings.

Nowhere does Tchaikovsky's melodic gift ever fail him, even though the expressive temperature is never really high. The *Divertimento* (no. 2) could perhaps have been fairly labelled *Valse*. Tchaikovsky seems to give the solo clarinet at this movement's opening the task of 'discovering' the first tune – and note also the charming chattering of the three flutes a little later (anticipating their use in the famous *Mirlitons' Dance* in *Nutcracker*: older readers may also recall a once famed 'fruit and nut-case' TV commercial). The *Intermezzo* (no. 3) is more restrained, its main theme (in fact, a very slow 'ghosting' of the first movement's fugue subject) alternating with a broad, sustained melody, all deployed in a five-section ABABA structure, but with a climax after the fourth section and a quietly arresting rewriting of the fifth. But the *pièce de résistance*, though by far the shortest movement, is the cute *Marche Miniature* (no. 4). Scored for the upper woodwind, with only very discreet contributions from the violins, plus triangle and bells, it is an irresistible confection that would have fitted perfectly into the *Nutcracker* to come. After this the *Scherzo* (no. 5) may lose out a little – but it was the first number to be composed, and perhaps Tchaikovsky had not then discovered exactly what kind of piece he was trying to create for this suite. As for the final *Gavotte*, here Tchaikovsky was deliberately choosing to model himself on a stately baroque dance, but his music has nothing to do with Bach style; indeed, in its discreet piquancy, it could perhaps be an ancestor of that famous gavotte to come some thirty-eight years later in Prokofiev's *Classical Symphony*.

But how is Tchaikovsky to finish some forty minutes on after so much different music? His solution is simple: slip seamlessly back into the fugue music from the first movement, though this time rounding it off triple forte.

———

On resigning from the Moscow Conservatoire Tchaikovsky had headed for St Petersburg, remaining some three weeks with the intention of going on to Clarens. But his patroness was now in Florence, and had suggested he should spend some time there; she would make all the arrangements he required, and defray all his expenses. This was very acceptable in principle, but Tchaikovsky's reservations began to build once he had installed himself, for her behaviour seemed to suggest she wanted their relationship to be less distant. They exchanged letters every day, and though, in order that they should not accidentally come face to face, she gave him a timetable of her regular routes and outings, he sensed that she might be moving towards a face-to-face meeting with him. She asked him to see where she was staying, and the following day he saw her pass his own villa. Then she invited him to inspect hers when she was absent. But he declined. 'All this makes me feel less than free and, to tell the truth, in the depths of my heart I very much wish she would leave Florence,' he confided to Anatoly. It was worse a few days later when he went to the theatre and saw she was also there. 'This embarrassed me, just as her proximity in general also constantly embarrasses me. For instance, every morning I see how, when she passes my villa, she stops and tries to see me [fortunately she was very short-sighted]. How ought I to behave? Go to the window and bow? But in such circumstances, should I not also call out from the window: "Hello!"?' Finally she suggested he should postpone a visit he intended to make to Paris until February, when she would also be in the French capital; she would then provide an apartment for him, and make all arrangements. This was simply too much, and he declined this proposal emphatically, declaring that he could not put off his visit. Yet when she left Florence ahead of him, his own reaction surprised him. 'I feel a great longing for her. I pass her uninhabited villa with tears in my eyes,' he confided to Modest. 'What had at first embarrassed and confused me now forms a subject for the most sincere regret.' It had become truly a relationship that he both loved yet feared.

When Tchaikovsky had told his patroness that he could not delay his visit to Paris until her own arrival there in February, he was speaking the truth, for he was now embarking on a major new piece. Back in November, while browsing through Lev's library during a brief stay at Kamenka, he had come across a translation of Schiller's drama, *Die Jungfrau von Orleans*, had skimmed through it, instantly decided it should be the subject of his next opera, and within three days of his arrival in Florence had set about *The Maid of Orleans*, as it would be called. He devised his own libretto from Schiller's play, and so overwhelmed was he by the subject, and so full of ideas, that he had a nervous reaction and had to break off composition. But in any case, before proceeding further, he needed to discover what other literary sources might have relevance to his project, and France was most likely to provide these. Accordingly, at the end of December he set off thither. But having scoured Paris for materials relating to Joan, he concluded that Schiller's play would still be his best source, though he would also borrow bits from other writers. Moving on to Switzerland, he settled into his favourite hotel in Clarens on 11 January; the following day he set about his new opera in earnest.

The speed with which Tchaikovsky composed *The Maid of Orleans* was prodigious. His routine was as ordered as ever. 'I drink morning coffee with a light breakfast. A walk while my room is being cleaned,' he told Anatoly. 'Composing the opera until lunch at 1 p.m. After lunch a long walk. On returning, reading, and writing the *libretto* for tomorrow's work. At 8 p.m. supper with tea. Then letter-writing and reading. At 11 I go to bed.' Yet within fourteen days half the opera was sketched. Four days' break, and he was back at work; five more days, and something like three-quarters of *The Maid of Orleans* was drafted. When the opera's vocal score (that is, the voice parts, with the orchestral part arranged for piano) was published, all this would fill some three hundred pages. Looking back on what he had done, he wrote to Modest, 'In general I am pleased with myself – but I am a bit tired' – surely an understatement.

In mid-February, after some five weeks, it was with much sorrow that Tchaikovsky left Clarens, and especially the Pension Richelieu and the Mayor family who ran it. As he wrote to his patroness, 'It is very nice to know that there is a corner of Western Europe where I shall always be received with joy, care, and friendliness, where my habits and requirements are well known, where they always manage to arrange it so that, while I'm there, I feel I am at home.' As usual, during all this labour he had found some diversion in reading, and his current preoccupation had been *Little Dorrit*. About the British generally he currently felt very badly, for he was still outraged by Britain's part in the recent Russo-Turkish war. But his delight in Dickens's novel moved him to cast a crumb of redemption. 'Dickens and Thackeray are about the only people I forgive for being English,' he declared to Anatoly. 'One must add Shakespeare, but he lived at a time when that vile nation was less ignoble.'

After Clarens Tchaikovsky returned to Paris, and it was there on 8 March that *The Maid of Orleans* was drafted down to the last detail. Paris was, of course, a centre of fashion, including menswear, and Tchaikovsky indulged himself. 'I walk along the streets in a new grey coat (*demi-saison*) with a most elegant top hat, showing off a silk shirt front with coral studs, and lilac-coloured gloves. Passing the mirrored piers in the Rue de la Paix or on the boulevards, I invariably stop and admire myself. In shop windows I also observe the reflection of my elegant person.' But his expenditure had been indiscreet, and on leaving Paris, his remaining funds would get him only to Berlin. Here he tried to extract money due to him from Jurgenson, but the despatch of this from Moscow was delayed, and finally Kotek, with whom he was lodging, had to pawn his own watch. In desperation he telegraphed his patroness for an advance on his allowance. She replied by return, and he could at last head for St Petersburg.

As in 1878, Tchaikovsky passed most of the spring and summer of 1879 on country estates: Brailov, nearby Simaki, Nizy – and, of course, Kamenka. His preoccupation was scoring *The Maid of Orleans*, and preparing the vocal score. He took great pleasure in the first of these operations. 'It is difficult to convey the delight you experience when an abstract musical idea takes on a real form as the result of its assignment to this or that instrument or group of instruments,' he told his patroness. 'If not the most pleasant, it is one of the pleasantest moments in the compositional process.' Tchaikovsky was now taking longer over orchestration, studying in particular Wagner's scoring in his opera, *Lohengrin*, since, however unpalatable he might find so much of Wagner's actual music, he recognized that the German was a master of operatic orchestration. Whereas it had taken Tchaikovsky about three weeks to score *Vakula*, *The Maid of Orleans* took some four months.

The premiere of *The Maid of Orleans* took place in St Petersburg on 25 February 1881. The cast was good, and with Nápravník as conductor, cuts and revisions were required which probably helped the opera's fortunes, for it is still second only to Tchaikovsky's later *The Enchantress* in length. The staging and production were very different matters. Funds being short, there was no special scenery, some used was inappropriate, and the costumes were threadbare: 'wretched, grubby and pitiful' was how Tchaikovsky himself described it all to his patroness. The opera's initial success was not maintained, and it was revived in only one more season, never again to be heard in Russia in Tchaikovsky's lifetime.

The Maid of Orleans: opera in four acts * * *

[The Maid of Orleans, *for all its scale and grandeur, is not one of Tchaikovsky's better operas. It is a grandiose piece, clearly written to match some of the blockbusters being composed for West European opera houses. Despite one very fine scene (Joan's narration) and some good love music, only those readers really dedicated to opera are likely to revel in this one.*]

The Maid of Orleans is in three acts, divided into six scenes. Its plot is briefly as follows:

Act 1: *A country setting.* Thibaut, Joan's father, rebukes some girls for singing when France is in a dire state, and all their futures uncertain; he wishes Joan to marry Raymond. Joan struggles with inner feelings, realizing she has a different destiny. The offstage glow of a fire and a tocsin indicate the approach of the English enemy; a crowd enters, and prays for deliverance. Bertrand, a peasant, reports French defeats, and that Orleans is besieged. Joan tells the crowd to wipe their tears, prophesying that an armed maid will lead a victory at Orleans. She declares to a bewildered crowd that the English commander, Salisbury, is dead. A soldier rushes in to report that this is true. Joan exhorts the people to pray, and leads off a hymn for victory. All leave except Joan, who bids a sad farewell to her native region and childhood companions. As daylight fades and Joan is suddenly bathed in bright moonlight, an offstage women's chorus tells her to don the armour of battle, and to shun earthly love. Joan struggles against this call but, seeing her destiny is inescapable, she pledges herself to her mission.

Act 2: *A hall in the palace at Chinon.* The French King and his mistress, Agnès Sorel, listen to a choir of minstrels, but finding this melancholy, the King summons his gypsies, dwarfs and tumblers to raise his spirits. A ballet. Dunois, a knight, describes the French predicament, and Agnès leaves, saying she will give all she has to the King's cause. Dunois reproves and then exhorts the King when the latter declares he would abdicate for love of Agnès. Dunois prevails, and the two men resolve to lift the siege of Orleans. A further defeat is reported, and Dunois upbraids the King for now deciding to withdraw across the

Loire. Alone, the King despairs; even Agnès's re-entry with a promise of everything she has cannot revive him. A love duet. Trumpets herald the approach of Joan, and Dunois announces a French victory. The Archbishop relates how, as defeat seemed imminent, a maid had rushed in, rallied the troops, and routed the enemy; she had promised to lift the siege of Orleans. Joan enters. A series of tests directed by the King confirms her miraculous status, and she begins her narration. A shepherd's daughter, she had had a vision of the Virgin, who had disclosed that a sword predestined for her was on the grave of St Catherine at Fierbois. All accept Joan as divinely led, the King entrusts his army to her, and the Archbishop blesses her. Joan also demands a white banner with a purple stripe. Dunois leaves to collect Joan's predestined sword. All leave after the King.

Act 3 Scene 1: *A place near a battlefield*. Lionel, a follower of the treacherous Duke of Burgundy, rushes in, pursued by Joan. She falls on him, tears the helmet from his head, but is struck by his appearance. She spares him, and signals him to flee, but he scorns escape. She tells him to kill her – and he is perplexed. Mutual attraction develops into an impassioned duet. Dunois is seen approaching, and Joan again tells Lionel to flee. Instead Lionel offers Dunois his sword. Dunois reports a great French victory. Joan collapses, and is seen to be wounded. Supported by Lionel and Dunois, she leaves.

Act 3 Scene 2: *The square before Reims Cathedral*. A coronation cavalcade enters, led by Joan and the King, and goes into the cathedral. Thibaut and Raymond emerge from the crowd, and Thibaut, who sees his daughter as having renounced God, declares he must save her, even if she is to be reduced to ashes. The procession emerges from the cathedral. The King praises Joan as the agent of victory, but Thibaut steps forward and denounces her as the devil's agent. The crowd is outraged. As for Joan, she feels guilt at her love for Lionel, and remains silent when Thibaut challenges her virtue. Bewildered, the King and the crowd pray God to reveal the truth. Lionel steps forward as Joan's champion: an enormous clap of thunder. Thibaut denounces her: again thunder. The Archbishop confronts her: thunder. The crowd turns on Joan, but the King assures her of a safe conduct. All leave except Joan and Lionel. Joan rejects Lionel, and rushes out. He follows.

Act 4 Scene 1: *A wood*. Joan remains torn between her divine mission and her love for Lionel. She longs for him, and he enters. They embrace. Love duet, interrupted by angels' voices. Joan tears herself away, and is transfixed by the choir. English soldiers are heard approaching. She urges Lionel to flee. The soldiers enter, Lionel confronts them, and falls dying. Joan kisses him, and predicts they will meet in heaven. She surrenders to the soldiers.

Act 4 Scene 2: *A square in Rouen*. An unsympathetic crowd hears the approach of the procession bringing Joan. It enters, Joan clearly fearful; the crowd now pities her. 'Give me a cross!' she cries, and a soldier fashions one out of two twigs. Joan is bound to the stake, and the pyre is lit. As the flames mount, Joan cries out for acceptance into heaven. Offstage chorus of angels. Joan declares 'with an expression of joy on her face' (*sic!*), 'My suffering is at an end!'

The Maid of Orleans is a piece for opera buffs. It marked a new direction in Tchaikovsky's handling of opera, and the reason for this is clear. All four of his preceding examples had been on Russian subjects, but with *The Maid* he was clearly targeting the international opera scene. Joan of Arc was French, and her story was universally known in Europe; likewise, Tchaikovsky was self-consciously adopting the manners of European grand opera: a powerful subject, strong (melo)drama, spectacle scenes and choruses, massive scale – all these characteristics employed to achieve the maximum impact. But with these as the guidelines, there was little room for that wonderful, so human quality that had made for many of the best moments in his earlier operas – in, for instance, such a contrasting pair as *Vakula* and *Onegin*.

But there are some points that *are* worth noting here and, more important, some good, even excellent things in *The Maid*. The overture is largely drawn from material in the following drama – but note the lengthy flute solo that links it to the first scene: the flute was a symbol of innocence, and doubtless this solo is connected with the country maid who will go on to drive the epic events to come. The girls' chorus that opens Act 1 has great charm (and sounds, frankly, much more Russian than French), and the scene and trio that follow offer a splendid instance of Tchaikovsky's professionalism: the singer's line clear, inventive enough to sustain our interest, and the orchestra the most sympathetic and unobtrusively varied companion. When dialogue becomes more impassioned, the orchestra will respond appropriately with a more heightened accompaniment, and the dramatic pace never falters. But this is efficient heightened prose, the fluency unfailing; speaking personally, I can admire it all, but I am not drawn into it, as I am so often in *Onegin* (and it must be said that the theme that runs through the hymn is far from one of Tchaikovsky's best). Tchaikovsky himself seems truly touched only when Joan is finally alone and can reveal her ambivalence to her calling, her pain at what she will have to sacrifice in order to obey her God-given call. Here the melody now extends itself more freely, there are some lovely individual touches, and the offstage celestial voices are strikingly handled – though perhaps some readers will agree that the act's last stages are rather stiff.

But the most precious music of the opera (for me) will come near the end of the following act. Set in the French court at Chinon, it opens with the opera's obligatory dose of ballet. If the theme of the chorus of minstrels sounds familiar to some readers, they are probably right: it is a French tune, 'Mes belles amourettes', which Tchaikovsky had also used the previous year in one of his *Album for Children* pieces. Required to produce ballet music, Tchaikovsky always rose to the occasion splendidly, and the energy and impact of the opening *Gypsy Dance* is exceeded only by that of the final *Tumblers' Dance*. By contrast, the *Dance of the Pages and Dwarfs*, which precedes the latter, is a minuet, one of Tchaikovsky's rococo pastiches. The love scene between the King and Agnès has much to commend it, especially its rapt conclusion. Yet the best stretch of Act 2 is the scene between the King and Joan, and especially Joan's following narration. This is the jewel of the whole opera. Here there is no formality or gratuitous grandeur, but a simple account of a wondrous experience from a young woman who can speak with unaffected eloquence of earthly things and heavenly visions through music that touches the listener more deeply than all the heightened rhetoric of the finale that follows.

The first scene of Act 3 consolidates the impression that Tchaikovsky was more truly engaged by the individual predicaments of his players than by the grand, sometimes seismic events in which they are caught. This is a love scene, though its battlefield context is unusual. But while we may be sceptical about whether mutual love can spring up between two characters who, only moments before, had been trying to kill each other, I think we can accept that, given that a love scene was now required, Tchaikovsky rose to the challenge; indeed, I have to say on a personal note that, returning to this music after a good many years,

I am again struck by how fine it is. The preliminaries that signify the offstage battle, followed by the fraught entry of the two combatants, are handled, as expected, with workmanlike efficiency – but it is with Lionel's so quiet expression of incipient love for his young and beautiful captor that the music fills out with genuine tenderness and musical richness, bearing witness to Tchaikovsky's personal engagement with the predicament of this young woman who will, like Tatyana before her, become a victim of Fate because of love. There is, indeed, some great music here.

Act 3's second scene could hardly provide a greater contrast. This is the pivot on which the whole tale turns, but it is also the most unabashed spectacle of the whole opera. From the portentous introduction and the march to which the crowd add its glorifications of the King and Joan, all is played out at length to produce the maximum effect. And once the procession has disappeared into the cathedral and the foreground drama unfolds further onstage, a backstage organ reminds us that a solemn service is proceeding within the cathedral. Further comment is unnecessary here; the whole scene is designed to rouse an audience, not to address its inner sensibilities. Suffice it to add that Tchaikovsky rises to all the histrionic demands of the situation, but the scene's success (or otherwise – as at the first production) depends as much on the designer and the scale of the theatre's resources as on the composer.

This is certainly not true of Act 4's first scene. While the first scene of Act 3 had presented the burgeoning of love, this one deals with its joys and torments. The turbulent orchestral introduction, followed by Joan's agonized weighing of the conflicting demands of love and duty, makes a powerful foil to the quiet rapture she will share with her beloved after he appears. There are two love themes, the first (on Lionel's sudden appearance) full-blooded and passionate, the other tender, quietly ecstatic – music that is the more striking because there is nothing like it elsewhere in the opera: this love scene is beautifully managed. But the heavenly voices from the opera's first scene are heard and the rapture is broken, offstage trumpets signal the approach of English soldiers, Lionel dies defending Joan, and the latter is led away in chains.

I could well do without the final scene, but I suppose the last incident in the drama had to be presented. This execution scene is little more than a tableau, with only one significant incident, which, for obvious reasons, can be no more than a grotesque parody of the real-life event (here only made worse by Joan's eyes-heavenward declaration, added in an attempt to sanitize it). All that this scene required was a solemn march laced with appropriate comments from the crowd, followed by agitated music and celestial choir to back the final obscene act. To say that all this is little more than orchestral wallpaper would be unfair, but it is purely functional. Perhaps, however, this makes us the more grateful for the admirable, sometimes moving music in some of what has gone before.

———

One of the problems for writers on Tchaikovsky before the repeal of censorship in Russia in the 1990s was to define clearly his sexual behaviour. Alexander Poznansky was one of the first Western-based scholars to capitalize on this new freedom, and among his discoveries in the archives at Klin (Tchaikovsky's final home and now the Tchaikovsky Museum) was a letter to Modest that included an account of a one-night stand in late February 1879, when Tchaikovsky was in Paris putting the finishing touches to *The Maid of Orleans*. At last, in Tchaikovsky's own words (as translated by Dr Poznansky), we had a description of such an assignation, and of his own subsequent reaction to the incident. The degraded condition in which the young man lived shocked him:

> A bed, a pitiful little trunk, a dirty little table with a candle-end, a few shabby trousers and a jacket, a huge crystal glass, won in a lottery – those make the room's only decorations. Yet it did seem to me at that moment that this miserable cell is the centrepiece of the entire human happiness . . . There occurred all kinds of *calinerie* [tenderness] as he put it, and then I turned frantic because of amorous happiness and experienced incredible pleasure. And I can say in confidence that not only for a long time but almost never have I felt so happy in this sense as yesterday.[1]

The next morning his reaction to the experience was very different:

> I woke with remorse and a full understanding of the fraudulence and exaggerated quality of that happiness I felt yesterday and which, in substance, is nothing but a strong sexual inclination based on the correspondence with the capricious demands of my taste and

1 A. Poznansky, *Tchaikovsky's Last Days: A Documentary Study* (Oxford, 1996), p. 21.

on the general charm of that youth. Be that as it may, this young man has *much good* at the root of his soul. But, my God, how pitiable is he, how thoroughly debauched! And instead of helping him to better himself, I only contributed to his further going down.

As I noted earlier in this book, Tchaikovsky's sexuality has long been (and, perhaps, still is) a subject provoking sometimes violent dissent. I therefore leave each reader to draw his or her own conclusions from these two extracts.

16
Confidences with His Best Friend:
Second Piano Concerto

It must already be obvious that Tchaikovsky's relationship with his secret patroness was extraordinary, and one that some would say, probably unfairly, 'could have happened only in Russia'. But, strange as it may seem to our West European eyes, it did happen, and its consequences for music (and therefore for us) were incalculable. Without Nadezhda von Meck Tchaikovsky's existence during the whole of the latter half of his composing years would have been very different – above all, far less productive because of the necessity of earning his own living. But we do not have to thank his patroness only for the works we would otherwise have been denied; their huge correspondence is a mine of information about Tchaikovsky's attitude to other issues, other composers, to music generally – above all, to the workings of his creative mind, both conceptual and practical. So, for a while, we shall break the chronological narrative, and uncover some of the insights that these letters afford.

It was back in his first peripatetic year after his disastrous marriage that Tchaikovsky began providing his patroness with his views on, and reactions to, a variety of personal matters. Concerning religion, he had passed beyond inherited belief, could find no sense in the Christian doctrine of retribution after death, and could not accept the concept of eternal life. But the Orthodox Church was part of the Russia he loved, and he still was drawn to its rituals. He held the Orthodox Mass (the Liturgy of St John Chrysostom) to be 'one of the greatest of artistic works', but the service that really gripped him was the All-Night Vigil on the eve of Easter Day.

> To direct myself on Saturday to some small, ancient church, to stand in the semi-darkness filled with the smoke of incense, to delve deeply within myself in search of a reply to the eternal questions: *to what purpose, when, whither, why?* – to waken from my reverie

when the choir sings, 'Many a time from my youth have they afflict-
ed me', and to surrender myself to the captivating poetry of the
psalm, to be filled with a certain quiet rapture when they open the
central doors of the iconistasis and there rings out, 'Praise God from
the heavens!' – O, I love all this passionately. It is one of my greatest delights!

Manifestly it was not the hard doctrine that claimed him; it was the
aura of mysticism that enveloped it.

Tchaikovsky's response to her round question: 'Pyotr Ilich, have
you ever loved?' seems direct enough, but deftly evades the dangerously specific, instead deflecting attention to the expression of love in
his music:

> You ask, my friend, whether I am familiar with *non-platonic love. Yes
> and no*. If you phrase the question somewhat differently, that is, if you
> ask, have I experienced complete happiness in love, then I will reply:
> *No, no, no!* Yet I think the answer to this question is contained in my
> music. If you ask me, do I understand the full power, the full bound-
> less strength of that feeling, then I will reply: *Yes, yes, yes!* – and again
> I will tell you that more than once have I tried lovingly to express in
> music the torment and, at the same time, the bliss of love. Whether I
> have succeeded I do not know – or, rather, I leave others to judge. I
> totally disagree with you when you say that music *cannot convey the
> all-embracing characteristics of the feeling of love*. I believe quite the
> contrary – that *music alone* can do this. You say that here *words* are
> necessary. O no! It is precisely here that words are not necessary – and
> where they are ineffectual, the more eloquent language, that is, music,
> appears in all its power.

As for the intrusive question his patroness was really asking, I doubt
she was any the wiser.

More interesting are his comments on his Russian fellow composers. These were written in December 1878, when Tchaikovsky
probably felt some estrangement from a real world that was still
theirs, but also perhaps harboured some jealousy that they were still
functioning in it when their professional competence was so inferior to
his own. Rimsky-Korsakov, the one of their number who had tried to
repair this deficiency, and who had turned to Tchaikovsky himself
when trying to strengthen his own technique, comes off best:

All the latest St Petersburg composers are a very talented lot, but all of them are infected to the core with the most frightful conceit and a purely dilettantish confidence in their superiority over the rest of the musical world. The exception among them in recent times is Rimsky-Korsakov. He is just as self-taught as the others, but he has made a complete about-turn. His nature is very serious, very upright and conscientious. When he was a very young man he fell into the company of people who first assured him that he was a genius and, second, told him there was no need *to study*, that training kills inspiration, dries up creativity, and so on. Korsakov is the only one of them to whom, some five years ago, the thought occurred that the ideas preached by the Balakirev circle had, in fact, no foundation. I have one of his letters from that time. It deeply touched and amazed me. He had become profoundly despairing, then asked what he had to do. Of course he had to study. And he began to study. During one summer he wrote countless contrapuntal exercises and sixty-four fugues, ten of which he promptly sent me to look over . . .

Perhaps we may detect in this last phrase the main reason why Tchaikovsky was so disposed towards Rimsky. As for others of the St Petersburg bunch –

Cui is a talented dilettante. His music has no originality, but is elegant and tasteful. *Borodin* is a professor of chemistry at the Medical Academy. Again he has talent, even a strong one, but it has perished through neglect because of a blind *fate* which led him to a chair of chemistry instead of into the living profession of music. Thus he has less taste than *Cui*, and his technique is so weak that he cannot write a single line without outside help [simply not true]. *Musorgsky* you rightly call a hopeless case. In talent he is perhaps superior to all the preceding, but his nature is narrow-minded, devoid of any urge towards self-perfection, blindly believing in the ridiculous theories of his circle and in his own genius. In addition he has a certain base side to his nature which likes coarseness, uncouthness, roughness. He flaunts his illiteracy, takes pride in his ignorance, mucks along anyhow, blindly believing in the infallibility of his genius. Yet he has flashes of talent which are, moreover, not devoid of originality.

Finally Tchaikovsky homed in on the group leader to whom he himself owed so much:

> The most important personality of this circle is *Balakirev*. But he has fallen silent after doing very little. He possesses an enormous talent which has perished because of certain fateful circumstances which have turned him into a *religious fanatic*, whereas formerly he had long vaunted his disbelief. Now he is constantly in church, fasts, bows to relics, and does nothing else. Despite his colossal endowment he has done much harm. For instance, he destroyed Korsakov, having assured him that training was harmful. He is the general inventor of all the theories of this strange group which unites within itself so many undeveloped, undirected, and prematurely blighted talents.

This blistering indictment of Balakirev was, of course, wild, and grossly unfair. No one knew better than Tchaikovsky himself the huge benefit that could come from that old autocrat's often blunt and sometimes tactless directives and interventions – but also encouragements. It is a verdict that tells us more, perhaps, about Tchaikovsky himself than about his target. Yet there are some perceptive points in his verdicts, in particular, his assessment of Cui and, more surprisingly, of Musorgsky, for the latter's music demonstrated almost everything that would have irritated, even repelled Tchaikovsky, the ultimate professional among Russian composers: Musorgsky's technical roughness, even illiteracy (as Tchaikovsky would have perceived it), and inability to maintain a large-scale musical structure. Yet Tchaikovsky still rightly could recognize Musorgsky as perhaps the most talented of the group (though I personally would give Borodin equal billing).

But most precious of all are Tchaikovsky's descriptions of his own compositional processes, and of that elusive but most essential of all factors: inspiration. No other composer, to my knowledge, has ever written in such detail or so vividly about this mysterious phenomenon. He cannot, of course, take us inside the actual experience of inspiration – into how the musical ideas materialized in his conceptual faculty, and how he transferred these into the complex of notes, rhythms, harmonies and structures that these abstract ideas finally took, and which we hear. But what Tchaikovsky writes gets us about as close as would be possible to 'feeling' what it must be like to be a creator at the moment of 'conception', and then 'gestation'. So what is the experience of 'inspiration' like?

The *seed* of a future composition usually reveals itself suddenly, in the most unexpected fashion. If the soil is favourable – that is, if I am in the mood for work, this seed takes root with inconceivable strength and speed, bursts through the soil, puts out roots, leaves, twigs, and finally flowers: I cannot define the creative process except through this metaphor. All the difficulties lie in this: that the seed should appear, and that it should find itself in favourable circumstances. All the rest happens of its own accord. It would be futile for me to try and express to you in words the boundless bliss of that feeling which envelops you when the main idea has appeared, and when it begins to take definite forms. You forget everything, you are almost insane, everything inside you trembles and writhes, you scarcely manage to set down sketches, one idea presses upon another.

Sometimes in the middle of this enchanted process some jolt from outside suddenly wakens you from this somnambulistic state. Somebody will ring, a servant will enter, the clock strikes and reminds you that you have to go about your business. These breaks are painful, inexpressibly painful. Sometimes inspiration flies off for a while, and you have to go in search of her, sometimes in vain. Very frequently you have to resort to a completely cold, intellectual, mechanical process. Perhaps this is why you can find moments in even the greatest masters where organic cohesion is lacking, where a seam shows, where there are bits of the whole which are artificially stuck together. But there is no other way. If that state of the artist's soul which is called *inspiration*, and which I have just been trying to describe to you, were to continue unbroken, it would not be possible to survive a single day; the strings would snap and the instrument shatter into smithereens. Only one thing is necessary: that the main idea and the general contours of the separate parts appear not through *searching* but of their own accord as the result of that supernatural, incomprehensible force which no one has explained, and which is called *inspiration*.

However, Tchaikovsky knew well from experience that not all works were blessed with a conception and gestation such as is described above. After all, the whole musical language through which inspiration found its embodiment was a very rational and systematic one with its own very strict and complex set of rules; if these were violated, the offence would become apparent (put simply, if a wrong note is played, even a listener who admits to complete ignorance of musical theory will know). And so Tchaikovsky moved on from this description of the ultimate state for which the composer longs to a more down-to-earth situation where, say, the composer has accepted a commission which has to be fulfilled and perhaps performed within a certain period. But it should not be assumed that such a piece would necessarily prove to be an inferior piece:

> Very often it has happened that a work belonging to the *second* [that is, commissioned] category has turned out to be completely successful despite the fact that the initial stimulus to its appearance in this world came from outside – while, conversely, a piece that I had thought up for myself has, because of secondary circumstances, been less successful. These secondary circumstances, upon which depends the state of mind in which a work is written, have great significance. Complete calm is necessary for the artist at the moment of creation. In this sense artistic creation is always *objective*, even when it is musical creation. Those who think that the creative artist at the moment of *emotional excitement* is able, through the resources of his art, to express what he feels are mistaken. Both sad and joyful feelings express themselves always, one might say, *retrospectively*. Having no reason to be happy, I can fill myself with a happy creative humour and, conversely, in a happy situation produce a piece that is imbued with the most gloomy and hopeless feelings. In a word, the artist lives a double life: that common to mankind, and that of the artist, and sometimes, moreover, these two lives are not congruous. However this may be, I repeat that, for composition, the most important condition is the possibility of separating oneself, if only for a while, from the cares of the first of these two lives, and devoting oneself exclusively to the second.

Tchaikovsky then moves on to describe how he would set about a work that had been commissioned, and where he has to find his own way towards getting started. For such works –

> *Sometimes* you have to *attune yourself*. Here you very often have to overcome laziness, reluctance. Then certain things happen. Sometimes victory comes easily, sometimes inspiration slips away, eludes you. But I consider it is the *duty* of an artist never to give

way, for *laziness* is a very powerful human trait. For an artist there is nothing worse than to give way to this. You cannot simply wait. Inspiration is a guest who does not like visiting those who are lazy. She reveals herself to those who invite her. *You must, you have to overcome yourself.*

I hope, my friend, that you will not suspect me of vainglory if I tell you that my appeal to inspiration is rarely made in vain. I can say that that power, which above I called a capricious guest, has now for so long been familiar to me that we live inseparably, and she only flies away from me when, in consequence of circumstances which in some way or other are oppressing my more public life, she feels herself superfluous. Yet scarcely has the cloud dispersed, and she is there. Thus, if I am in a normal state of mind, I can say that I am composing every minute of the day, whatever the circumstances. Sometimes I observe with curiosity that unbroken labour which, of its own accord and irrespective of the subject of conversation in which I am engaged, or of the people with whom I find myself, goes on in that region of my head which is given over to music. Sometimes this is some preparatory work, that is, finishing off details within the accompaniment of some already planned bit, while on another occasion a completely new, independent musical idea appears and I try to retain it in my memory. Whence all this comes is an impenetrable secret.

Next Tchaikovsky describes how he sets about writing down his ideas:

I write my sketches on the first piece of paper that comes to hand, sometimes on a scrap of music manuscript paper. I write in a very abbreviated form. A melody can never appear in my head without its harmony. Both these musical elements, together with the rhythm, can never be separated from each other, that is, every melodic idea carries its own implicit harmony, and is unfailingly furnished with its own rhythmic structure. If the harmony is very complicated, then in the sketches I may happen to notate details of the part-writing. If the harmony is very simple, then sometimes I set out only the bass; sometimes I figure it [i.e., use a system of numerals to indicate the accompanying harmony], but on other occasions I do not outline the bass at all – I remember it. As for instrumentation, then if I have in mind the orchestra, the musical idea appears already coloured by this or that scoring; sometimes, however, when I am scoring, my first intention is changed. Words can *never* be written after the music, for as soon as music is being composed to a text, then that text draws out an appropriate musical expression. You can, of course, attach or fit words to a trivial tune, but when the composition is a serious one, such a matching of words is unthinkable. In exactly the same way you cannot write a symphonic work and afterwards seek out a programme for it, for here again each episode of the chosen programme elicits a corresponding musical illustration.

This phase of the work, that is, sketching, is very pleasant, absorbing, at times affording utterly indescribable delights, yet at the same time is accompanied by anxiety, by a certain nervous excitement. During this phase you sleep badly, sometimes you forget completely about food. On the other hand, the realization of the project and its execution are carried out very peacefully and calmly. Scoring a work which is already ripe, and which has been completed in my head down to the finest details, is very enjoyable.

You ask whether I keep to established forms. Yes and no. Certain kinds of composition imply the observance of a familiar form – for instance, *the symphony*. Here, in general outlines, I keep to the form established by tradition, but only in general outlines, that is, in the sequence of the work's movements. In details you may diverge as much as you wish if the development of the idea in question demands it.

Talking with you yesterday about the compositional process, I expressed myself inadequately about the work phase in which the sketch is brought to fulfilment. This phase is of capital importance. What was written in the heat of the moment must subsequently be critically scrutinized, amended, supplemented and, in particular, abridged in the light of structural requirements. Sometimes one has to do oneself violence, be merciless and cruel to oneself, that is, cut off completely bits that had been conceived with love and inspiration. If I cannot complain of poverty of fantasy and inventiveness, I have, on the other hand, always suffered from an inability to produce a finished form. Only by dogged labour have I managed to make the form of my compositions correspond more or less to the content. In the past I have been too casual, insufficiently aware of the full importance of a critical scrutiny of the sketches. Because of this the *seams* were always noticeable in my work, there was a lack of organic continuity in the sequence of the separate episodes. This was a major defect, and only with the years have I begun little by little to put this right. But my works will never be *models of form*, for I can only improve, not completely eradicate, the essential characteristics of my musical organism.

All this is so precious. It provides us with vivid insights into what it feels like – and takes – to be a great composer during the creative act itself, and then into the uncompromising way Tchaikovsky himself was prepared to endure even the self-inflicted pain of destroying something conceived with love simply because it did not fit into the final scheme. It scotches the old, patronizing view, still prevalent in my youth, of Tchaikovsky as a composer with an easy flair for rousing us with less than first-rate ideas, of manipulating us – a creator, therefore, of questionable integrity. Nothing was further from the truth, and now, at last, we have come to recognize this. Tchaikovsky was, quite simply, a tremendous working professional, endowed with one of the greatest creative gifts of the whole nineteenth century, yet ruthlessly and tirelessly self-critical in revising and reworking what he had produced so as to present it to us in the most perfect form possible for our never-ending enjoyment.

Ever since he had quit Russia in October 1877 in the wake of his marital disaster, Tchaikovsky had pursued a rootless existence, but by the spring of 1879 Kamenka was becoming increasingly his base, and it was here that he would spend most of the summer. His income now allowed him to contribute more to the cost of his living there, and he could ask for accommodation that suited his own wishes, install his personal belongings, feel free from the constraints and courtesies expected of a guest, and organize his existence as he chose. Clearly the domestic life at Kamenka could be lively, but in his new semi-independent state he could observe with amused detachment the personality clashes between the female members of the household. Here there were clearly strains. His elder nieces were now in their mid- to late teens, and Tchaikovsky himself would experience the temperamental challenges they presented on the two occasions when Sasha and Lev were absent, and he found himself in charge of the female menagerie. But mostly he could view these problems objectively, and even with relish – as, for instance, when the arrival of a new French teacher raised the hackles of the two incumbent governesses.

As he wrote to Modest:

> Mademoiselle Gautier is forty and a bit, her appearance is plain
> but not unpleasant: to wit, she has a good complexion, a slightly
> snub nose, and very kind eyes. She dresses well. *She eats with her
> knife!!* She behaves very decorously and simply. From the begin-
> ning she has tried to display her talents, which are numerous.
> Among these she models in clay *and does it very well.* But Tasya
> [Tchaikovsky's niece, Nataliya] has conceived a most ferocious
> hatred of her, and has suddenly been smitten with a very touching
> love for Miss Eastwood. The latter also received the Frenchwoman
> very grimly, and in her turn is suddenly manifesting a passionate
> partiality for Tasya. Yesterday there was a quite dramatic scene.
> Poor Tasya, who is now miserable, tearful, won't eat, won't smile,
> wanted to go to Trostyanka with her brothers and Miss Eastwood.
> The Englishwoman expressed a willingness to take her, but Sasha
> told Tasya she should ask Mlle Gautier's permission. But Tasya ran
> to complain to Miss Eastwood, and a minute later the latter flew
> into the drawing room looking white and grim, and let forth a
> stream of reproaches at Sasha. 'What's this! I've looked after Tasya
> for five years, I love her, she loves me, yet you won't let her go to
> the woods with me! Look how miserable she is, how awful she
> looks, yet you still won't let her have a break!' – and so on, and so
> on. Sasha calmed her down and explained that the Frenchwoman
> had been engaged for Tasya, and that Tasya had to be under her
> control. *Persephone* [the other governess] is triumphant. For some
> reason she looks upon Mlle Gautier as an ally, and has received her
> with open arms. There now fly from her lips streams of such refined
> French words that it's getting awful. She's even stopped speaking
> Russian with us . . .

And so on, and so on. Yet however much amusement Tchaikovsky
may have derived from observing the lively family politics and
rebellions of Kamenka, it could in no way mitigate that ache that
recurred inexorably every year. As he wrote to his patroness on 25
June, 'On this day exactly twenty-five years ago my mother died. I
remember every moment of that terrible day as though it was yesterday.'

It comes as no surprise that Tchaikovsky would periodically need
to escape from such a turbulent milieu, and Brailov provided the

best guarantee of solitude. In May he visited his patroness's estate while she was away, staying a fortnight, and during this period receiving from his patroness a proposal that would permit both of them next time to be simultaneously living in the same locality, but still without personal contact. 'Near Brailov I have a cottage, Simaki,' she had written:

> This cottage is very pretty, lying in a shady garden with a river at its end. Nightingales sing in the garden. This cottage stands about three miles from Brailov, and there are six rooms. I am sure you would like it. It is such a solitary, poetic spot that if you would agree to come to it for a whole month or even more during the time I am in Brailov, then I should be unspeakably happy. Although, of course, at Brailov I would not be able to walk near your apartment each day, yet each day I would feel you near to me, and from that thought I should likewise be calm and happy.

Tchaikovsky was uneasy, but in August when he returned to Brailov and saw Simaki, he was delighted with it. 'A house as old as the hills,' he reported to Modest:

> A well-stocked garden with ancient oaks and limes, very neglected and thus for some reason delightful, a river at the end of the garden, a wonderful view from the balcony on to the village and a distant wood, absolute quiet, the accommodation arranged with uncommon comfort, consisting of a hall, a large study, dining room, bedroom, and a room for Alyosha – all this could not have corresponded more with my tastes and inclinations.

There could be bathing in the river, there were mushrooms to pick in the woods, books to read (he asked his hostess whether she could also supply any Dickens volumes in French translation), rabbits in the fields, cats in the roof (to scare off bats and mice): all was so much more relaxing than Kamenka.

But, for all his patroness's assurances, he was still uneasy about their proximity, despite her promise that, as in Florence, she would forewarn him of each day's itinerary and its timing. His fears proved well founded. One afternoon he set out on his walk too early, she inadvertently delayed her return home, and suddenly they confronted each other. 'It was *frightfully* embarrassing,' Tchaikovsky informed Anatoly:

Although we were face to face for only an instant, I was still terribly confused. Nevertheless, I raised my hat politely, but she, so it seemed to me, was utterly disconcerted, and did not know what to do. It wasn't enough that she was riding in a barouche, for behind were two more carriages with her family. I wandered for a long time in the wood looking for mushrooms, and when I returned to the picnic table where tea had been prepared, letters and newspapers were lying on it. It seems she had sent a rider to look for me in the wood and to give me the post before tea. Altogether there are no bounds to her attentions. What a wonderful person she is for me!

In the end, nothing had changed. Indeed, it was during his visit to Simaki that he and his patroness had hatched the idea of engineering a match between one of her sons and one of Sasha's daughters that would vicariously consummate their own relationship, a proposal that Sasha proved happy to endorse.

During the summer Tchaikovsky had paid visits to other friends, but on 11 October he was back in Kamenka. For three days he worked on correcting the proofs of his First Suite, but then found himself without occupation. For a couple of days he filled in the time by sharing in such domestic chores as hemming and marking towels, but this in no way provided satisfaction. 'I experienced an over-frequent and almost irresistible desire to sleep,' he wrote to Modest,

a certain emptiness, and finally *boredom*. There were times when I did not know what to do with myself. Finally yesterday it became fully apparent to me what was the matter. I had to get on with something: I find myself absolutely incapable of living long without work. Today I began to create something, and the *boredom* vanished as if by magic.

Tchaikovsky had made a beginning on his Second Piano Concerto.

It did not, in fact, come easily – or so he reported to Anatoly after a week's work. Yet only three days later the first movement was sketched. This done, he suspended work, and it was only in late November that, now in Paris, he returned to it. Again it was his patroness's wish that he should visit the French capital while she also was in residence, and with the splendid piano in the accommodation she had arranged for him, he resumed work on the concerto, shifting his attention to the finale. Again ideas were sluggish in coming, though when they did the movement was quickly sketched, and the second movement was already in his head – so he reported to his patroness. This was completed by mid-December, Tchaikovsky expressing himself especially pleased with it.

Yet it would be five more months before the concerto was scored. There remained the question of the dedication. Tchaikovsky had determined to offer this to Rubinstein, yet memories of the latter's initial reaction to his earlier piano concerto made him pause. In the end his solution was neat: send the concerto to Rubinstein, who was invited to make comments and suggestions on what details needed changing, and then asked to pass it on to Taneyev to make the actual changes – but whatever Rubinstein might think of the concerto's substance, under no circumstances would Tchaikovsky change anything. Thus direct contact with the autocrat himself would be avoided. 'Taneyev has replied that *there's absolutely nothing to change*. That means that's Rubinstein's opinion,' he could in due course report to his patroness. In fact, it was not quite the end of the matter, for in October he revealed how Rubinstein had told him that 'the piano part appears too episodic, and does not stand out sufficiently from the orchestra. If he is right [which he was not] this will be very galling because I took pains precisely on this: to make the solo instrument stand out in as much relief as possible against the orchestral background.' Nevertheless, as far as Tchaikovsky was concerned, the concerto was already in its final form.

However, before proceeding further, I must issue a health warning. Like Leopold Auer with the Violin Concerto, so Alexander Ziloti, a former pupil and then a friend of Tchaikovsky, prepared his own truncated edition of the Second Piano Concerto, presumably daring to do this because Tchaikovsky had himself been prepared to make certain cuts. Ziloti submitted his proposals to Tchaikovsky, but the latter firmly rejected them, mainly because Ziloti had re-ordered some sections. Nevertheless, four years after Tchaikovsky's death Ziloti published his edition which, like Auer's of the Violin Concerto, soon became the universally performed version. Earlier recordings of this perversion may still be currently in the catalogue. Beware!

Piano Concerto no. 2 in G major * * * *(*)

[This is a work that has, at last, come into its own. Its past neglect may have been partly due to its technical difficulty (it has some very challenging passages for the soloist) – and I must still give my prize to the First Concerto. That said, however, I admire the Second greatly: its first movement presents a relationship between soloist and orchestra that makes for a rather unusual experience; the slow movement is gorgeous, and its finale irrepressible. For some readers it could become quite a favourite.]

Tchaikovsky's close friend, Hermann Laroche, remembered that, when they were students together, Tchaikovsky had told him more than once that he would never compose a piece for piano and orchestra because he could not bear the sound of this mixed media. This is interesting. Of course, the mastery with which Tchaikovsky had handled the interaction of these two so different sound sources in his First Piano Concerto could show that this dislike no longer applied, but the Second Piano Concerto suggests otherwise, for perhaps the most striking single feature of its first movement (composed, as in both his earlier concertos, in sonata form) is the degree of segregation of the piano and the orchestra. For listeners trying to orientate their way through the movement this, in fact, makes matters rather easier, for the abrupt changes from one medium to the other are sometimes useful in fixing exactly where you are.

But before scrutinizing the concerto itself, there is a small but fascinating element in the first movement that is better dealt with separately. Ever since Tchaikovsky had written that finest stretch from his finest opera – Tatyana's letter monologue in *Eugene Onegin* – the stepwise-descending six-note scale which she had sung at this, her most critical moment of decision, would become a symbol of Fate that would run through Tchaikovsky's later music, and it occurs in the first movement of this concerto, some two minutes in, after a momentous pause. Its entry is abrupt and intrusive, the tremolando orchestral background dramatic, and the music that very briefly follows these six notes has a certain pathos heard nowhere else in the concerto. The whole incident will recur at the corresponding point in the recapitulation, and between these two appearances it will also provide the nucleus of an orchestral ritornello. Sometimes we can guess why this Fate theme is present (in Tchaikovsky's operas, and works written to a programme, or with a text), but elsewhere, as here, we can, at best, only speculate why it should appear.

There is no kind of preamble to the concerto, no huge introductory section, as in its predecessor; it opens with the first subject itself – a bluff, rather blunt tune, effective enough, but not one of Tchaikovsky's best (evidence of the difficulty he confessed to in getting started?). The piano repeats it, then briefly accompanies a woodwind tune; otherwise, orchestra and piano are virtually segregated, dialoguing with each other until the piano finally takes over, then grinds (I use the word deliberately) to a halt on a thunderously repeated chord, followed by silence. This is the dramatic moment at which the Fate music breaks in – and it is also the point, for me, where the concerto really takes off. The slender theme that follows, introduced by the piano, is the first of the two themes such as normally occur in Tchaikovsky's second subjects, and after a piano flourish, it is succeeded by its partner, an impassioned invention from which Tchaikovsky goes on to build the climactic end to the exposition.

The Fate theme launches, then generates, the powerful ritornello that introduces the central development, whose volume, expansiveness, orchestration and long dying end give this section a particularly portentous tone. From this point there is surprisingly little more that need be said to orientate the listener, for the movement's remaining structure is easy to follow: the piano re-enters and delivers a cadenza that muses briefly on the gentle first theme of the second subject, then builds to a second and larger orchestral ritornello before a second, massive, five-minute cadenza initially gives its attention to the Fate theme. By this time my point about the segregation of piano and orchestra will have become very apparent.

All this has been very extensive, and the recapitulation is easily sorted out; the first subject will be shortened, but the remainder (from the Fate theme) will be run virtually complete as in the exposition. The orchestra will lead off the brilliant coda.

Any listener introduced to the concerto by its second movement could very reasonably believe this to be a triple concerto. Why Tchaikovsky should have decided to give a solo violin and solo cello parity with the piano in this *Andante non troppo* is not known, but it makes for a very sharp contrast with what had gone before: with these two string soloists it will probably, for some listeners, bring to mind the great *pas de deux* for Odette and Siegfried in *Swan Lake*. The slow introduction suffices to tell us we are entering a very different world, confirmed by the tender eloquence of the initial violin solo (which opens with what sounds like a quotation from the once very famous *Ave Maria*, which the French composer Charles Gounod had devised by adding a solo vocal part to the first prelude in Bach's *48 Preludes and Fugues*: could the fact that Tchaikovsky was composing the concerto in Paris have anything to do with this?). The solo seemingly complete, the cello nevertheless forbids closure, itself now retracking through more than half the melody, then extending it as though loath to let it go, the violin all the while freely partnering it. All this is ravishing. It is now the piano's turn with the tune – nor can the orchestra be denied its own brief bite of the cherry before moving us towards the movement's central section.

This is a movement that also needs little further comment. A measure of agitation enters with the new melody, at the climax of which is briefly heard what sounds to be a memory of the fateful brass theme from the Fourth Symphony. Then the two string soloists exult in a succession of short cadenzas before leading us back to the first theme, all three soloists now collaborating. From this point, as I have sometimes written elsewhere, this music is surely its own advocate.

The contrast with the third movement could not be sharper. This *Allegro con fuoco* might almost be a twin of the First Piano Concerto's finale – the same energy, though far more playful. It seems to start as though a rondo were in prospect, but then events occur that challenge this. No matter: this music carries the listener along with its unfaltering exuberance and resourcefulness, and the collaboration of soloist and orchestra is total (no one can say here, as they might of the first movement, that the pianist and orchestra are talking *at* rather than *to* each other). Only once, just before the end, does the movement briefly pause – but not to catch its breath, merely to make the end sound even more brilliant.

Tchaikovsky's Second Piano Concerto was for long neglected. Now, perhaps because Ziloti's mutilation has been ousted and we can gauge its full stature, it is taking its rightful, if slighter lower, place alongside its sibling predecessor.

———

17
The Wandering Recluse:
1812 and Serenade for Strings

Ever since 1877, his crisis year, Tchaikovsky had become increasingly reclusive. With his patroness's generosity giving him the freedom to choose where and how he lived, the years immediately following show him more and more withdrawing from his former professional world and colleagues. If he had a base it was now Kamenka: otherwise he lived where he chose, often pointedly avoiding contacts with persons he would once have readily greeted. Kondratyev was also in Paris, and he saw him daily, but insisted that, if he were introduced to someone new, it should be as 'Mr Petrovsky'. He felt obliged to remain in Paris until his patroness had made her exit, but before 1879 was out she had departed, and the very next day he set out for Rome, where Modest and Kolya were already installed, and where it was planned that they should spend the rest of the winter.

Rome would not have been Tchaikovsky's preferred choice, but when he arrived he found himself more attracted to the Italian capital than he had anticipated. Modest had already explored the city thoroughly, and he proved an excellent guide who fanned his brother's enthusiasm for its cultural riches. Investigating Michelangelo's muscular male figures, Tchaikovsky sensed an affinity between the great Italian sculptor and Beethoven, and he also spent much time contemplating Michelangelo's frescos in the Sistine Chapel, finally deciding that he could truly appreciate them, though his pleasure would always be qualified. Indeed, long and perhaps repeated perusal was the route by which Tchaikovsky now found he could at last engage with a painting. But this could not change his view of which painter gave him the greater pleasure. 'My favourite is still Raphael, that Mozart of painting,' he wrote to his patroness. The comparison is significant; presumably he could detect in Raphael that same sweet lyricism, poise and elegant perfection that had always made Mozart, for him, the greatest of all composers.

It was now that Tchaikovsky made the revision of his Second (*Little Russian*) Symphony, producing the version that, sadly, we invariably encounter in concerts today. One particular pleasure while in Rome was learning of several performances of his own works abroad. His First Suite had already been programmed in New York, the First Piano Concerto had recently been played there, Berlin had heard the latter no fewer than three times, and it had also reached Budapest. All these performances had been enthusiastically received. Indeed, Modest later identified this as the period when his brother's international reputation began to grow in earnest.

This Roman interlude did produce one new work. Tchaikovsky knew well the propensity of Italians to sing everywhere, and he had become familiar with an abundance of their popular tunes; now, exactly as Glinka had, while in Spain in the 1840s, employed native material as the basis of his two Spanish Overtures, so Tchaikovsky used four of these Italian tunes as the basis of his **Italian Capriccio,***** prefacing them with an opening fanfare that (so Modest reported) was a trumpet call they heard each morning from the neighbouring barracks. The result is the product of a highly professional rather than inspired composer, and Tchaikovsky himself made no special claims for the piece. 'It will be effective, thanks to the delightful tunes which I have succeeded in assembling, partly from anthologies, partly from my own ears on the streets,' he explained to his patroness, and his presentation of his borrowed material against effective and contrasting accompaniments, and in a wide variety of orchestrations, makes for undemanding but entertaining listening that requires no further comment.

While Tchaikovsky may have derived satisfaction from having sharpened his appreciation of the visual arts, he found little delight in a new musical encounter. His patroness had just sent him a copy of Brahms's recent Violin Concerto. Though Brahms never wrote an opera, the German composer was in other regards the one contemporary who, both in output and stature, matched Tchaikovsky, and with whom comparisons were obviously likely to be made. (Coincidentally, they shared the same birthday: 7 May.) Some years on the two men would meet and briefly manage a courteous, if never close, personal relationship. There was clearly a guarded respect on both sides, but also deep reservations. For Tchaikovsky it was the inhibition he sensed in Brahms's music, the iron discipline that held the music's full emotional force in check, that troubled him. As he wrote of the new concerto to his donor:

> There are many preparations for something, many hints of something which must emerge imminently and must charm – yet nothing but tedium comes out of this. His music is not warmed by true feelings, there is no poetry in it, though it has great pretension to *depth*. Yet there is nothing in this depth. For instance, let us take the opening of the concerto. As an introduction to something it is very beautiful, it is an excellent pedestal for a column – but the column itself does not exist, and immediately after one pedestal comes another.

This is a fascinating comment and, frankly, tells us more about Tchaikovsky than Brahms. And the final sentence of his verdict is also interesting and, I believe, totally honest. Composers are not usually members of a mutual admiration society; naturally there is rivalry, but often also jealously and antipathy, even hostility fired by rivals' greater public successes. But there is little sign of this in Tchaikovsky, merely an honest statement that Brahms's music did little for him:

> As a musical personality Brahms is simply *antipathetic* to me – I cannot digest him. However hard I try to respond to his music, I remain cold and hostile. It is a purely instinctive feeling.

What did increasingly give Tchaikovsky pleasure were English novelists. On leaving Rome in mid-March, he retreated into *Pendennis* as refuge from a garrulous Belgian count during the train journey to Paris, deciding that Thackeray's novel was as delightful as Dickens's *David Copperfield*. Thence to Berlin, where he saw Wagner's *The Flying Dutchman* and found it 'terribly noisy and boring' (the chimpanzee and dog who shared a cage in the Aquarium's menagerie were far more entertaining). But his arrival in St Petersburg brought him back to hard reality. A price of his growing celebrity was the increasing demands made on his time by others, and this crowded out composition. However, one relationship that began during this visit would prove not only valuable, but also give him much personal pleasure. The Grand Duke Konstantin Nikolayevich, a brother to the Tsar, and already a great admirer of Tchaikovsky's music, wished to meet him. Tchaikovsky could hardly refuse this invitation, but the event itself also introduced him to the Grand Duke's son, the twenty-two-year-old Grand Duke Konstantin Konstantinovich, not only a devotee of music, but also himself a composer and poet. A highly intelligent man of great tact, and fully aware of Tchaikovsky's distaste for formal social occasions, he used his personal friendship with Vera Butakova (she who, as Vera Davïdova, had once caused Tchaikovsky such torment through her love for him) to request her to arrange an intimate evening at her own home where he and Tchaikovsky could meet. The event was an enormous success, the two men talking about music until two in the morning. Seven years later Tchaikovsky would use poems by the Grand Duke for his Six Romances, op. 63, and their friendship would last until Tchaikovsky's death.

Finally able to escape from St Petersburg, Tchaikovsky moved on to Moscow. There he tried to keep his presence a secret, but in vain, and he was quickly engulfed in the social world of his Moscow friends. Desperate to finish the scoring of the Second Piano Concerto, in late April he was at last able to head for Kamenka. For the next seven months this would be his base, except for occasional interludes at Brailov or Simaki.

What now ensued would prove to be Tchaikovsky's longest period of stable existence since the disaster of his marriage. Having no urgent commission to discharge, he decided to allow himself sabbatical leave from major composition. In any case, the various performing materials for *The Maid of Orleans* were in a terrible mess, and he had to devote much time to correcting these. 'I've come to the conclusion that I'm writing too much, and I want for a whole year to compose nothing except trifles,' he warned Jurgenson. But Tchaikovsky was congenitally unable to remain totally idle, and during this summer he composed not only a set of seven songs, but also six duets. Domestic circumstances prompted these. Evidently through the persuasions of his sister Sasha, Tchaikovsky had been drawn into making up a vocal quartet to perform an anthem at one of the Easter week services at the local church. The other singers were his sister Sasha, his eldest niece Tanya, and brother Anatoly. The performance itself was something of a disaster when Tanya lost her place and the ensemble collapsed. The women were desperately embarrassed, but they had the chance to redeem themselves at the Easter Day service. However, it seems that, having heard this family ensemble, Tchaikovsky decided to provide material for further domestic enjoyment, and the result was his **Six Duets, op. 46** **(*)**. Five are for two women's voices (for the Kamenka-resident performers) , the sixth for soprano and baritone (an opportunity for Anatoly or Tchaikovsky to take a part). Mostly Tchaikovsky's vocal sets such as these contain nothing that need detain us, but sometimes something will turn up that immediately commands the attention. Two such pieces are present in this set. One is the final duet, 'Dawn', a quietly blissful aubade that drew from Tchaikovsky a waltz of much melodic distinction. But the more notable is 'Scottish Ballad' for soprano and baritone, a setting of a Russian translation of 'Edward', a traditional Scottish ballad of parricide which seems to have had a curious fascination for non-British composers (Brahms composed a whole piano piece around it), and which begins 'Why dois your brand sae drap wi bluid?' (surely something of a challenge to Alexey Tolstoy even before he came to translate it into Russian). It is a grimly unfolding narrative that progressively exposes an appalling domestic tragedy, and it was set by Tchaikovsky to lean, even curt phrases, with a bleak piano accompaniment, the tension being heightened by some abrupt upward wrenches of key. But most arresting is a sudden move, as the distraught mother demands of her murderer-son what he will leave to her, to new music (but no, it is *not* new: it is a *very* close variant of that climactic Fate phrase which had begun life in Tatyana's Letter Scene in *Onegin*), to which her son replies, 'A curse to the end of your days!' For any listeners who doubt that Tchaikovsky was capable of treating an unremittingly harrowing situation, 'Scottish Ballad' is a powerful corrective.

Back in June, as Tchaikovsky was setting about these songs, news arrived via Jurgenson of a commission for a piece to grace an Exhibition of Industry and the Arts which would take place in Moscow the following year. As we have noted, experience had brought Tchaikovsky to loathe such chores, but it was not politic to refuse the more prestigious, and this was one such. However, his business self-confidence was growing, and he would not begin until the terms were settled. 'For commissioned pieces I need stimulating, encouraging and galvanizing features in the form of precise indications, prescribed dates, and 100 rouble notes (a lot) coming in the more or less distant future,' he informed Jurgenson. 'It is impossible without repugnance to set about music that is destined for the glorification of what, at bottom, delights me not at all.' To his patroness he was even more blistering: 'Think, my dear friend! What can you write *on the occasion of the opening of an exhibition* except banalities and generally rowdy passages!' Such was his distaste that he delayed until October before starting, by which time it had been agreed his contribution would instead be to celebrate the opening of the new Cathedral of Christ the Saviour. Composition was completed in a week. 'The overture will be very loud and noisy,' he informed his patroness when the sketches were completed, 'but I wrote it with no warm feelings of love, and so it will have no artistic merits at all.' Yet what resulted will be, for some readers, the piece by Tchaikovsky they know best: the *1812* Overture.

Festival Overture: *The Year 1812* * * *(*)

[Some brutal things have been written about 1812, and some are not undeserved. First we should note that Tchaikovsky himself took little pride in what he had created – but then let me dare to contradict the composer himself by saying that I think his blanket condemnation of the piece he had created was less than fair – though when I come to the work's ending, I would go along with him; it is shamelessly overblown. But the first two-thirds is a different matter, containing some good music – and there is no reason, of course, why you should not enjoy the whole overture without feeling in the least guilty. After all, Tchaikovsky, for all his own censure of the piece, chose to publish it – so he cannot have felt that bad about it.]

The Cathedral of Christ the Saviour had been built to commemorate the events of 1812, when the Russian army and people (and the Russian winter) had driven the invading French forces of Napoleon out of Russia, and *1812* was designed to reflect this conflict and outcome. The opposing sides are represented by their national anthems, the French by the 'Marseillaise', the Russian by their national hymn 'God save the Tsar', which, at the work's triumphalist end, combines with Tchaikovsky's own jogging cavalry tune (plus bells, a full battery of percussion, and even real cannon) to bring this celebratory piece to the loudest of possible conclusions. In addition to this borrowed material, there is a Russian folksong, an extract from Orthodox chant ('Save us, O Lord'), and an adaptation of part of a duet for two women from Tchaikovsky's own first opera, *The Voyevoda*.

1812 opens impressively with the Orthodox chant played by a sextet of string soloists (two violas and four cellos), later alternating with the woodwind to suggest choral antiphony, a restrained section that

1 The Tchaikovsky family (1848). Left to right at back: Pyotr (composer), Alexandra (his mother), Zinaida (half-sister), Nikolay (brother), Ilya (father) with Ippolit (brother). Foreground: Alexandra (sister).

2 Anton Rubinstein

3 Tchaikovsky (1863)

4 Herman Laroche

5 Nikolay Rubinstein

6 Konstantin Albrecht

7 Tchaikovsky (1869)

8 Mily Balakirev

9 Modest Musorgsky

10 Nikolay Rimsky-Korsakov

11 Alexander Borodin

12 Pytor Jurgenson

13 Hans von Bülow

14 Wilhelm Fitzenhagen

15 Nadezhda von Meck

16 Tchaikovsky and his wife, Antonina (1877)

17 Adolf Brodsky

18 Tchaikovsky and Anatoly Brandukov

19 The Tchaikovsky brothers (1890). Left to right: Anatoly, Nikolay, Ippolit, Pyotr, Modest

20 Sergey Taneyev

21 Tchaikovsky: portrait by Nikolai
Kuznetsov

22 Tchaikovsky with Vladimir ("Bob") Davïdov

23 Tchaikovsky in his Cambridge doctoral robes

24 Tchaikovsky and friends (1890). Left to right: Nikolay Kashkin, Tchaikovsky, Medea Figner and Nikolay Figner (singers)

makes the ensuing irruption of the full orchestra the more striking. What follows is surely a sort of lament, soon followed by intimations of the battle to come. The jogging cavalry (clearly Russian) comes next on woodwind; a pause – and battle commences (in sonata form!). From the quotations from the 'Marseillaise' that soon intervene, we may reliably conclude that the violent first subject represents the incursion and initial supremacy of the French army, the quiet theme of the second subject (the *Voyevoda* borrowing) surely presenting the Russian people. Even more so does the livelier folksong that follows hard on this – providing, incidentally, the second theme that is a normal ingredient of Tchaikovsky's second subjects. The turmoil resurges with the development, which passes straight into the recapitulation. All this is much shortened, as are the recapitulations of both second-subject themes. The French make a final desperate sortie, but five shots from cannon (yes, these are indicated in the score), and they are finally sent packing as the coda is heralded. Here everything will be let loose, even detonate (after a grossly inflated sequence on a motif of four descending notes): the opening chant with bells chiming, the cavalry tune, and then, in counterpoint with it,' God save the Tsar', his Majesty now saluted with cannon.

Tchaikovsky himself cannot have felt all that embarrassed by *1812*, for when the exhibition was delayed a year, he attempted to arrange its premiere ahead of that event, but was advised that this would be improper. However, he would hear with unexpected speed how a second recent work sounded, for on 3 December, less than six weeks after completing his Serenade for Strings, he was entertained to a surprise private performance which had been prepared by Moscow Conservatoire forces for a visit he paid to the institution at which he had once taught. Tchaikovsky's own view of his Serenade was very different from that of *1812*. The two pieces had been written concurrently, Tchaikovsky beginning the Serenade on 21 September, breaking work on it for a week in mid-October to compose *1812*, then resuming and completing everything within a further week. He was well content with the result. 'I composed the Serenade from inner conviction,' he wrote to his patroness. 'It is a heartfelt piece, and so I dare to think it is not lacking in real qualities.' Yet despite the approval gained at the private Conservatoire performance, it was nearly a year before the official premiere was given. This was highly successful, the second movement (a waltz) being encored. But perhaps the most prized reaction for Tchaikovsky was that of Anton Rubinstein, who conducted the Serenade in a concert a year later. As has been noted, Tchaikovsky's former teacher had long deplored the direction Tchaikovsky had taken as a composer, as the latter himself well knew. It was Jurgenson who reported what Anton had now said: 'At the first rehearsal Jupiter [a nickname for Rubinstein] declared to me, "I think this is Tchaikovsky's best piece." He praised it equally unconditionally to others, and at the final rehearsal, said to me, "You can congratulate yourself on publishing this opus."' It would be interesting to know how Tchaikovsky had responded to this unexpected accolade. Sadly we do not.

Serenade for Strings * * * * (*)

[This is one of Tchaikovsky's most perfectly formed pieces of absolutely first-rate quality, which nevertheless presents itself so directly that I will simply offer some comments that may throw light on its character and structure – though I will also point out the truly mischievous joke that Tchaikovsky has at a close friend's expense.]

The term 'serenade' has been given to many different musical styles and forms, but in this instance Tchaikovsky was applying it to a four-movement piece that is essentially a mini-symphony. The difference here lies in the nature of the music from which it is formed, and which does not seek to emulate the grandeur, either in scale or content, of a full-blown symphony; instead it is very direct in its material, and uncomplicated in its workings, aiming not to excite or move deeply, but simply to give delight in the best possible sense of the word. And this is exactly what it achieves. It is dependent above all on Tchaikovsky's supreme melodic gift, but this does not for one moment mean it is a simplistic piece, or that Tchaikovsky will not unobtrusively draw in his more sophisticated skills where appropriate.

We can hear this straight away in the first movement, described as *Pezzo in forma di Sonatina* ('Piece in the form of a Sonatina', that is, 'a little sonata'), a label that perfectly describes Tchaikovsky's unpretentious but captivating movement, for though it is basically in sonata form with a slow introduction, there will be no development. The introduction is built from a dignified theme, which 'is not quite what it seems' (the answer to that paradox will emerge only at the Serenade's end), the quicker first subject, which has a whiff of the waltz about it, duly leads us towards the second subject; there is a moment's silence, and this, a more bubbly theme, enters, runs its rather more capricious course and, in its turn, comes to a halt. There being no development, the first subject, exactly as before, now leads off the recapitulation, its ending adjusted so that the second subject will now enter (again after a tiny pause) in the movement's main key. Otherwise all is essentially as before, and the whole movement's symmetry is completed by a return to the slow introduction's music by way of a coda. All this makes for a delicious movement.

The second movement, headed 'Waltz', requires no comment here, except to confirm that the tunes and their distribution make a movement as satisfying as any. The third movement's title, 'Elegy', might suggest that deeper issues will be in store, but this is no funereal piece – a pensive movement certainly, but without a hint of real melancholy. One interesting point is that, like the preceding waltz, its first melody begins with a rising scale. But this time it does not lead off the main melody; instead it is heard three more times, but each recurrence ends differently. It makes a magical beginning to a beautiful movement, as lovely (I use this word deliberately) as any piece Tchaikovsky ever composed.

To get the full point of the 'Finale (*Tema Russo*)', however, we need to go back to a letter Tchaikovsky had received from Taneyev, his former pupil, now of course his close friend. Taneyev had recently been giving himself a lesson in musical history, and had concluded that 'only that music is lasting which has embedded its roots in the people', adding that all art had once been national. Tchaikovsky profoundly disagreed, and promptly told Taneyev so:

> I value very highly the wealth of material which the slovenly and suffering people [Taneyev's expression] produce. But we who use this material will always elaborate it in forms borrowed from Europe – for, though born Russians, we are at the same time even more Europeans, and we have so resolutely and deeply fostered and assimilated their forms that to tear ourselves away from them we would have to strain and do violence to ourselves.

But, as has already been revealed, Tchaikovsky had an impish sense of humour, and now proposed to give a mischievous demonstration of 'just how right' Taneyev had been (though, in fact, Tchaikovsky's joke proved nothing of the sort, nor was it intended to). The Serenade's finale incorporates not one but two folksongs, the first providing the basis for the slow introduction, the second the first subject of the following *Allegro con spirito*. What follows is, in fact, a full sonata movement with a development, deftly showing how well folksong could be assimilated into as complete a display of Western stylistic and structural methods as Tchaikovsky could devise. But then, towards the movement's end, the dignified theme that had opened the whole Serenade suddenly breaks in, sounding as unlike a folksong as could be imagined – that is, until it is speeded up – and reveals itself to have been the second folksong of the finale. To the best of my knowledge there is no record of Taneyev's reaction to this very pointed but benign joke at his expense.

––––––––

Back in July, while Tchaikovsky was in the Ukraine, Nadezhda von Meck had written from Paris with news that she had engaged a young French pianist who had just completed his conservatoire course; he would teach her children, and partner her in piano duets. Together they had played through Tchaikovsky's Fourth Symphony. 'He is enraptured with your music,' she reported. 'Yesterday I played your Suite with him, and he is utterly delighted with the fugue. He [the pianist] composes very nicely.'

Two months later, now in Florence, she wrote again: 'I am sending a little composition for you to judge, one of many by my pianist. The young man is preparing to be a composer, and he writes very nice pieces, though there are echoes of Massenet, his teacher [which, in fact, Massenet never was]. He is now composing a trio.' This put Tchaikovsky on his guard; could he spot a potential rival? Better to swat him now. 'The *Danse bohémienne* is a very nice little piece, but it is certainly too short,' he replied. 'Not one idea is worked out to its conclusion, the form is shrivelled, and it lacks wholeness.'

Meanwhile the young Frenchman had been delighting his employer by playing various of Tchaikovsky's piano compositions, as well as partnering her in the new duet arrangement of Tchaikovsky's First Symphony. He had also been required to make piano transcriptions of the Spanish, Neapolitan and Russian Dances from *Swan Lake*, and she asked for Tchaikovsky's agreement that they should be published. (Jurgenson held the copyright, and they would appear in 1881, but without the name of the arranger who, for some reason, feared that Massenet would be furious if he came to know about this.)

In early October a young cellist arrived to join Pachulski and replace the pianist who, nevertheless, was asked to stay on a further month so that their employer could be entertained with piano trios. 'Pyotr Ilich, why have you not written a single trio?' she now demanded, little knowing the major creative seed this was sowing. Meanwhile she had a photo taken of her trio, and sent a print to Tchaikovsky. '*Bussy*'s face and hands have a vague resemblance to Anton Rubinstein's,' he observed. 'God grant that his fate may be as fortunate as that of the "Tsar of pianists".' In fact, the young pianist's reputation would finally eclipse totally that of Rubinstein, though as a composer, not a pianist. For '*Bussy*' was the eighteen-year-old Claude Debussy.

18
Family Matters:
Piano Trio

In March 1881 Tchaikovsky had news: his estranged wife had secretly given birth to a child. During the last three years of this present narrative, Antonina Ivanovna has barely been mentioned, yet all this time she had been a constant presence in the background, at times merely a ghost, but at others materializing abruptly and painfully into Tchaikovsky's real-life world. Back in 1878 she had agreed to divorce, and Nadezhda von Meck had been prepared to lodge 10,000 roubles with Jurgenson, to be paid to Antonina as a settlement when the divorce had taken place. But the process entailed agreements and formalities that would be complex and painful, and in the end Antonina settled the matter by disappearing. Again Tchaikovsky's patroness intervened with a proposal that would give Antonina, if she would agree to live away from Moscow, security for the next few years. For a while she observed this condition, but in early 1879 she for a second time asked for divorce, again raising for Tchaikovsky a nightmare vision of the complexities – and revelations – of the court proceedings. Even worse was to come three months later, when she suddenly appeared at Anatoly's apartment in St Petersburg, where Tchaikovsky was staying. This encounter provides the most vivid impression of how Antonina could behave, and of the kind of torment that she was capable of inflicting on Tchaikovsky, even though we must allow that Tchaikovsky's record is one-sided, and no doubt not exact in all particulars:

> Hardly had I appeared than she threw herself on my neck and began repeating endlessly that she loved only me in the whole world, that she could not live without me, that she agreed to any conditions I made as long as I would live with her, and so on. I cannot tell you in detail the whole succession of scenes with which she tormented me for at least two hours. I tried, with as much composure as I could muster, to explain to her that, however blameworthy I might be in

respect of her, and however much I might wish her every happiness – yet under no circumstances would I ever agree to live with her. I confess it cost me an incredible effort of self-control not to tell her of the feelings of loathing she instils in me. Of course during all this she, as always, suddenly digressed, and began to enlarge on the craftiness of my relatives who had such a pernicious influence upon me in the matter, and then spoke of my music for *Onegin*, which she finds superb. Then again tears, protestations of love, and so on. I asked her to cut short her declaration and think over for several days all I had said to her, after which she would receive from me either a letter or else a personal meeting in Moscow. Meanwhile I handed her the extraordinary sum of one hundred roubles for the return journey to Moscow. At this she suddenly became as happy as a child, recounted to me several instances of men who had been in love with her during the winter, and expressed a wish to see my twin brothers, who appeared, and whom she showered with expressions of affection and protestations of love despite the fact that for half an hour she had been calling them her enemies. As she said goodbye she asked me where we would see each other as though she supposed that I was longing for meetings with her. I had to say that I could not see her while here, and I requested her to go off to Moscow today, which she promised to do.

But Antonina did not. One morning Tchaikovsky encountered her near Anatoly's home, only to discover that she had been living in the same block of apartments, with the intention of leaving for Moscow with Tchaikovsky. This was followed by a letter with a long declaration of love. Tchaikovsky decided that the only route open to him was to leave for Moscow earlier than planned, stay there three days, then escape to Kamenka. But it did not work out thus: Modest and Kolya were also in St Petersburg, and the latter fell sick, their departure was delayed, and Tchaikovsky had to endure another painful encounter with Antonina, in which she said she wished, because of the way people were regarding her, to commute his allowance to her into a lump sum of 15,000 roubles; then she would go abroad and devote herself to music. Tchaikovsky promised to give his response in writing, then left Moscow for Kamenka. From there he wrote to Antonina, rejecting her proposal and adding that any letter from her would be returned unopened.

Further such details of Tchaikovsky's marital trauma are unnecessary here. As for the future strategy in dealing with Antonina, Anatoly had undertaken to handle everything. From time to time Antonina seems to have made noises about divorce, but she had also realized there was no point in further harassing her husband, who had in any case added occasional sweeteners to his routine monthly payments. Tchaikovsky had suggested that she should become a schoolteacher and, in the hope that she would seek an appointment in the provinces rather than Moscow, he requested Jurgenson to give her such financial aid as might make this migration possible.

But then, in July 1880, Antonina resurfaced, accusing Tchaikovsky of having rumours about her spread abroad in Moscow through a friend, Amaliya Litke. 'Why didn't you start with yourself, telling her about your own terrible vice?' Antonina wrote furiously. 'Maman has been so kind as to take upon herself negotiations with your lawyer to bring an end to this matter.' Yet Antonina still undertook to leave Moscow and trouble Tchaikovsky no further, provided that she was otherwise guaranteed freedom of movement. This is interesting both for Antonina's ready agreement (and subsequent total silence), and for the transference of any future negotiations concerning herself into the hands of her mother, who also clearly wished closure of the whole matter – though there was an unmistakable threat lurking behind the latter's reassurance: 'You are a man of genius, your good name is dear to you. Believe us, we will not sully it, and we will carry out the honourable undertaking we have given you as befits an honourable, noble family.' From this moment Antonina remained silent – and not surprisingly, for she had now taken a lover, would already have known she was pregnant and that this would enable her husband to divorce her and be freed from further financial responsibility towards her.

As for Tchaikovsky's reaction to this news, his immediate worry was whether the child would be registered in his name, and he asked Jurgenson to take legal advice on the matter. Yet he would never divorce Antonina, for a legal action might drag up matters he now hoped could be considered buried, if not totally forgotten. As it was, Antonina would give him little further trouble. Yet – and this is another revealing and touching insight into the kind of person Tchaikovsky was – for all the misery she had caused him, he still felt a compassionate responsibility for her, and within months he was again seeking Jurgenson's assistance:

If this being [Antonina: Tchaikovsky simply could not bear to write her name] is in need, if she has been deserted by her lover (which is exceedingly likely) and she's nowhere to lay her head, then I must come to her aid. And so I want to ask you to get hold of that gentleman who has already been employed to enquire about her, and again entrust him with seeking her out and discovering whether she needs material help. If so, she must certainly be given money. Forgive me that I am imposing on your friendship.

Then, five years on, in 1886, Antonina would suddenly reappear, claiming she was still passionately in love with Tchaikovsky. Though he knew she no longer had any power over him –

yet all the same, it was incredibly painful to me. But most of all, *despite everything*, I'm sorry for this unfortunate being. She is so deranged that in reply to my first letter, where I said she should abandon any hope of living with me, she sent me an invitation to visit her, to ask the hotel servant whether she had not indeed left her lover (but who is still apparently in love with her, and might appear unexpectedly), and then to make love (according to her, she now knows how to arouse passion in me). Finally I wrote to her an appropriate letter, allotted her an allowance, and I think now she'll finally leave me in peace.

Accordingly, he asked Jurgenson to administer this allowance; then, a year later, when the Tsar granted him an annual pension, he doubled that allowance. There would still be the occasional, but very brief incursion from her into his life, but now at the most these were merely nuisances. Yet her final act would be very public – an ostentatious tribute, but also a calculated act of self-assertion, a very visible reminder to all that she had once had a very special connection with Tchaikovsky. At Tchaikovsky's funeral, beside his coffin was a wreath woven from forget-me-nots and blue ribbon, which stood out for its size. It was Antonina Ivanovna Tchaikovskaya's final caprice.

While the discovery of Antonina's affair had eased one source of torment for Tchaikovsky, a second event far outweighed the relief he felt in that quarter. Nikolay Rubinstein's hectic and disorganized lifestyle had long taken a heavy toll on his health, and his doctor had now ordered him to take a break abroad. Tchaikovsky was by this time in

Italy. Despite the increasing success of a new production of *Eugene Onegin* in St Petersburg, and despite the personal reception he had enjoyed when *The Maid of Orleans* had its premiere on 25 February, his mood was bad. He was now becoming a celebrity with its attendant social pressures. 'I love *fame*, of course, and I strive after it with my whole heart,' he had earlier confessed to Taneyev. 'But it does not follow that I love the manifestations of *fame* which are embodied in those dinners, suppers and musical *soirées* at which I suffer as I always suffer in any company alien to me.' Even Moscow had lost its charms. 'Despite all its shortcomings, my love of this old, dear city has in no way diminished, but it has taken on a certain morbid character,' he had written to his patroness back in December. 'It is as though I am already long dead, as though everything that once was has now sunk into the abyss of oblivion. I have had to drown this mental pain by increased work and by increased libations of Bacchus.' Alexey was now conscripted into the army for a period, and in St Petersburg he had visited him in barracks, and been appalled by his crushed appearance and rigorous existence. Through a cousin who had influence with the regiment's commander he had appealed for an easing of his servant's condition, and this had produced some remission – but at a price: Tchaikovsky now found himself obliged for whole evenings to accompany the singing of the commander's wife. Escape was imperative, and immediately after the premiere of *The Maid*, he set off for Vienna, and by 6 March was in Rome.

Awaiting him there was Kondratyev, who immediately drew him into the social world of their compatriots who were in the city. But without Modest and Kolya, Tchaikovsky was engulfed in a feeling of loneliness, and he acceded readily to Kondratyev's proposal that they should visit Naples, where he climbed to the crater of Vesuvius and visited Sorrento, which he loved. Their next destination was Nice for which, so Anatoly informed them, Rubinstein was heading for rest. But the latter did not arrive. On 22 March, Tchaikovsky heard from Jurgenson that Rubinstein was desperately ill in Paris. The next day he was dead.

It is probably true to say that no death had struck Tchaikovsky so hard since that of his own mother nearly thirty years before. Nikolay Rubinstein had been the cornerstone of his professional life, the man who had given him his first musical appointment, encouraged him to compose, conducted the first performances of so many of his works – above all, perhaps, had been his truest, if sometimes difficult, friend.

Tchaikovsky hastened to Paris for the funeral service in the Russian Church. It was well attended: the composers Massenet and Lalo were there, as well as Turgenev. After the service Tchaikovsky brought himself to view the body. 'He had altered beyond recognition,' he wrote to his patroness the next day. 'My God, my God, how terrible are such moments in life! Forgive me, my dear friend, that I write to you in such detail – but I am terribly weighed down by grief.' What had upset him most was that his own old teacher, Anton Rubinstein, seemed pleased at his brother's death, and Jurgenson, who had come to Paris for the funeral, offered the explanation: jealousy. Again Tchaikovsky felt acute distress as he saw Nikolay's coffin being loaded into a goods van at the Gare du Nord. It was the indignity of this exit that struck him so hard. He would himself have returned to Russia immediately, but delayed several days so that he would not have to witness Anton Rubinstein's indifference at Nikolay's interment.

It seems that, on Nikolay's death, Tchaikovsky had resolved to enshrine his memory in a composition containing a prominent piano part in tribute to his friend's keyboard prowess, but in the immediate aftermath of the event itself he felt unable to compose. In any case, other distractions would intervene. Life at Kamenka had changed much during the ten years since he had conceived for his nieces that embryo which would later grow into the most famous of all ballets, *Swan Lake*. Tanya was now nineteen and wanting to marry a certain Vasily Trubetskoy, an army officer, while the others were in their later teens, and made up a very lively – at times wilful – bunch. But the most serious cause for concern was their mother herself. For years Sasha had been taking morphine for relief from certain discomforts, and now she was drug dependent, and suffering symptoms that necessitated a consultation with a doctor in St Petersburg. On arriving in the city, Tchaikovsky had found Sasha and Tanya already in residence, but the former had now fallen ill, and Lev had been summoned from the Ukraine. Sasha was ordered to Carlsbad (now Kalovy Vary) to take the spa waters, but she was so pining for her family that it was decided that she should remain in St Petersburg with Lev until she could travel thither, and meanwhile Uncle Pyotr would take charge at Kamenka. It proved a very formidable assignment. The children made heavy demands on his time, and since the resident music teacher, a certain Blumenfeld, had remained absent for three months, Tchaikovsky took over his duties. (It was a pity Blumenfeld ever returned, as will appear.) Then Tanya left for Moscow where, it seems, Trubetskoy had been posted, but she had now broken her engagement because he had appeared drunk in her apartment and attempted to rape her. Meanwhile Sasha had returned to Kamenka, and the family realized her improvement could be attributed to her separation from her eldest daughter. All prayed that Tanya would remain in Moscow, but instead she suddenly appeared in Kamenka, sodden by heavy drinking, and also dosing herself with morphine. Sasha had an instant relapse and, in Lev's absence, Tchaikovsky had to cope as best he could, trying to soothe Tanya by talking with her, playing duets with her, encouraging her to read, and attempting to divert her generally. It had little effect, and the return of a gloomy Lev made matters worse.

By now desperate to get away, Tchaikovsky resorted to the stratagem that had extricated him from Moscow when he needed to escape Antonina; he begged Jurgenson to send a telegram informing him that his presence was urgently required in Moscow. Jurgenson obliged, but when it came to the point Tchaikovsky felt he simply could not leave. At Kamenka his habits were known, he could do as he wished and, in any case, 'to leave now would be awkward, as though I were casting them off when bad times had come. How odd is a man's fate!' He continued to Jurgenson:

> Thanks to Nadezhda Filaretovna I am a completely free man, always able to live where I wish. But here is proof that you do not buy freedom by being provided for. Of all places on this earthly sphere I know of none more unattractive (as regards natural beauties) than Kamenka. That which formerly was the single charm of life here, that is, the contemplation of a family of people close to me living happily, has now turned into something quite the opposite. *However*, I'm doomed *to pass a large proportion of my life precisely here*, and I have no right to complain about this, for no one and nothing hinders me from leaving – but I'm staying here, for here I'm *at home*, in a thoroughly familiar spot, no one obstructing me in my habits. It's all very curious!

And so he remained in Kamenka. In early July Sasha at last left for Carlsbad, Lev accompanying her part of the way so that there could be a meeting with two of Nadezhda von Meck's sons, Alexander and Nikolay. Quite apart from the matrimonial scheme that Tchaikovsky and his patroness had hatched for a union between one of her sons and one of Sasha's brood, getting daughters married very young had long been a normal, and pretty universal, parental preoccupation, as readers familiar with the novels of Jane Austen will realize. Indeed, earlier in the year one Hussar officer from a regiment stationed near-by had already made his choice from among the Kamenka girls, and later in July Varvara, though only sixteen, would be married to him. With both parents away Tchaikovsky was once again left for a while in charge of a Kamenka that was now overrun by Hussars. He coped as best he could. Finally, in early September, Sasha returned from Carlsbad, stayed a few days, then left for Yalta to continue her cure for a further month, Lev taking the remaining family to Kiev for their winter migration. At last Tchaikovsky felt himself free to leave. His relief was enormous, though one other item of news had added to his woes: in early September he had heard that his patroness's financial problems had necessitated the sale of Brailov and Simaki, and that these havens, which had come to mean so much to him, were available no more.

Yet for Tchaikovsky the distresses of Kamenka and the loss of Brailov and Simaki would, in the long run, prove beneficial. Despite his current need of Kamenka, over the next two years a longing would grow for a place of his own. It needed to be well removed from the two great cities where residence would endanger his freedom to dispose of his time as he chose, but it also needed to provide ready access to both. And so, in 1885, he would move to Maidanovo, a small town on the railway between Moscow and St Petersburg. Here, and later at nearby Klin, he would make his home for the rest of his life.

In October Tchaikovsky would return to Kamenka, now largely deserted, for some routine work. Meanwhile his niece Vera had become engaged to a naval officer whom she had encountered in Yalta, and he met the young couple when they came so that Vera could receive her grandmother's blessing. The bridegroom's name must have made Tchaikovsky start: Nikolay Rimsky-Korsakov, exactly the same as the composer's. He could see the young man was wildly in love, and this touched him especially. 'Modya,' he exclaimed forlornly to his homosexual brother, 'what unfortunate fellows you and I are! You know, we'll live a whole lifetime without experiencing for a second the fullness of happiness in love!' He attended Vera's wedding in Kiev, then set out for Vienna, ultimately settling in Rome with Modest and Kolya. His urge to compose was returning. Indeed, by mid-December he had already made some preliminary sketches for a new opera, but then his priorities changed. Months before, his patroness had expressed hopes he might compose something for her present resident trio; equally Tchaikovsky himself had expressed his wish to compose a memorial piece for Nikolay Rubinstein containing a prominent piano part. Now he decided to fulfil both requirements in a single creation, and before 1881 was out he had set about his Piano Trio.

It did not at first come easily, yet by 18 January 1882 it was sketched. Tchaikovsky's confidence in its quality grew with the trio itself, but he still had doubts about whether he had handled the medium well, and he insisted to Jurgenson that the players who would give the work its premiere should play it through to 'our whole circle' to gain their views on this. Taneyev, who would be the pianist, was bowled over by the piece: 'I studied it for three and a half weeks, playing it six hours a day. I cannot remember ever having experienced more pleasure when learning a new piece.' The Piano Trio was given its premiere on 23 March, the first anniversary of Rubinstein's death. It achieved great popularity during Tchaikovsky's lifetime, and in 1893 it was chosen, together with the Third String Quartet, to be played in memorial concerts to their creator in both Moscow and St Petersburg.

Piano Trio ****

[With the exception of the First String Quartet, the Piano Trio is, of all Tchaikovsky's chamber works, the one most likely to attract the listener's attention. Taken simply as a piece of music, I do not feel that it is one of Tchaikovsky's most perfect creations, either in the consistency of its themes or, as far as the second movement is concerned, in its consistency of quality. Nevertheless, it is certainly a very imposing piece, and will be relished by listeners who like a good dose of drama in their chamber music.]

The first thing about the Piano Trio that may strike you is its unusual form. As with other chamber music such as sonatas, string quartets and quintets, etc., trios are normally in four movements like symphonies. However, Tchaikovsky's Piano Trio is in two, and an obvious precedent springs to mind: Beethoven's last piano sonata (no. 32 in C minor). Many musicians rate this as the German master's greatest piano sonata (some indeed consider it the greatest piano sonata ever), and like Tchaikovsky's trio, its second movement is a set of variations. Yet there is no obvious reason why Tchaikovsky should have followed this precedent, except that Beethoven's 'op. 111' is, for most listeners, the most 'spiritual', most 'transcendent' of his piano sonatas, and Tchaikovsky perhaps felt it provided the ideal model for his new trio, which was to be a testament to Tchaikovsky's own love and respect for a man who had been, at the deepest level, a wonderful friend and colleague.

If Tchaikovsky had been writing for a piano quartet (piano with three stringed instruments) or, more particularly, for a piano quintet (with four), he would have had a string complement well able to play complete harmony, and which could therefore have been allocated substantial autonomous sections, as could the piano. But with only two stringed instruments this option was not really available except for short stretches. Instead Tchaikovsky treated the violin and cello as two melodic soloists, sometimes, either singly or in dialogue, presenting lines of much individual beauty, the piano both conversing with them and providing harmonic support. The first movement, headed *Pezzo elegiaco* ('Elegy'), is, at least initially, a succession of linked but clearly defined sections, and finding one's way through all this is not very difficult. The trio's opening theme is the business of the violin and cello, and is repeated by the piano before the music moves into what becomes clearly a transition, building to the chunky piano theme that opens the extensive first subject – though the melody introduced forthwith by the violin proves to be the more important. After a powerful climax, the pace is eased and the gently restless second subject is presented by the strings before the music resumes its more turbulent course.

All this has followed the well-trodden route of a first movement's exposition. But what now follows could not possibly have been predicted. The turbulence begins to abate, the piano fastens on a single chord, repeating it ever more quietly and more slowly as the string parts fall away – and then the chord is *very* slightly modified, a signal for the strings to resume and dialogue at length on a new, modest, gently poignant theme in which the piano in due course will share. The trio's memorial purpose has suddenly become apparent in what is perhaps the most beautiful music of the whole trio. It annexes to itself the entire development section, and its influence on the recapitulation will be all powerful, for when that moment arrives and the trio's opening theme returns, it is now presented *Adagio con duolo* ('very slowly and sorrowfully') by the violin, the piano evoking a funeral march, the cello insistently reiterating a tiny four-note figure of restrained grief. And though the recapitulation will at length resume its former manner and ordained course, the memorial music will ultimately slip in, the movement's coda taking us back to the whole trio's opening theme, now played by the piano so slowly as almost to lose its identity, the strings wearily hinting at a funeral march, which finally passes into silence.

The second movement is a theme and variations. In introducing the Rococo Variations for cello and orchestra, I observed that the listener needed to be presented with a theme that, both in phrase structure and harmony, was clear cut and therefore as easy as possible to recall: this would afford him the best chance of sensing something at least of a particular variation's connection to it. In consequence, the Trio's variation theme is every bit as simple (and attractive) as that of the earlier piece. What is again impressive is the way in which Tchaikovsky opens up the expressive range, and sometimes the scale, of the variations themselves to produce a movement that ends in being 'greater than the sum of its parts'. Kashkin remembered that the theme for this second movement was inspired by Tchaikovsky's memories of an enchanting day spent with Rubinstein and others at a beauty spot near Moscow, where peasants had sung and danced for their entertainment. It is cast as a ternary structure (AABA), and there are eleven variations, plus a very substantial *Variazione Finale* and a coda founded on the whole trio's opening theme. In variation 1 Tchaikovsky is content to assign the original tune to the violin (another chance to consolidate the memory of this), the piano providing a much ornamented accompaniment, but in variation 2 he turns it into a waltz for the cello, the violin now obliging with decoration. With variation 3 the tune itself is veiled with more elaborate decoration, though retaining the very clear phrase structure of the original. By this time the listener's memory of the latter has been quietly consolidated, and Tchaikovsky can range more widely in variations 4 and 5, opening and closing the former with a fervent string duet, in the latter making a tinkling piano delightfully imitate a musical box.

By now close affiliation with the original theme has been loosened, and variation 6 is an extensive waltz that opens, unexpectedly, with a portion of the Fate theme born in Tatyana's Letter Scene in the opera *Eugene Onegin*. We may well wonder what this has to do with the theme, and the answer is nothing – until, that is, later, when the piano delivers the *Onegin* opening *fortissimo* and the two stringed instruments in unison simultaneously demonstrate that the opening of the variation's original tune can be fitted against it, reaffirming this point in this variation's coda. The chunky variation 7 brings us back closer to the original theme, but variation 8 is a free fugue, its subject based on the first phrase of the theme (later Tchaikovsky was to sanction the omission of this variation – a not unwise decision). The haunting variation 9, marked *Andante flebile*, is the one that seems to have the most specifically memorial purpose. Variation 10 is a chirpy mazurka. By now we may well have forgotten what the theme was, and variation 11 provides some insistent reminders of its opening in preparation for the breezy *Variazione Finale e Coda*. At this point the piece really ceases to be a set of variations, for what follows is a full-blown sonata movement (the two subjects based on the openings of the A and B sections of the theme), but which Tchaikovsky subsequently (and, again, perhaps wisely) reduced by two-thirds to its recapitulation only. Finally proceedings are brought full circle, Tchaikovsky moving without a break into a *fff* restatement of the whole trio's opening melody, monumentally presented before abruptly subsiding into a brief funeral march which, like the first movement, fades to nothing.

The Piano Trio gained much popularity in Tchaikovsky's lifetime, and it was a work that naturally found its place in memorial events for its creator in both St Petersburg and Moscow. It is a piece that perhaps deserves more attention than it seems to receive today.

The narrative has now reached 1882. It is nearly five years since Tchaikovsky committed the greatest folly of his life in marrying Antonina, and his subsequent existence has been a nomadic one. Unable to settle anywhere for long, he has roamed much throughout Western Europe, rarely lingering more than a few weeks in any one place. If he had a base at all, it was at Kamenka but, as has already emerged, it was no longer the haven where he could find true content-ment, nor would the future bring any respite to the anxieties and strains occasioned by his still precious, but increasingly dysfunctional, family. And thus it would continue for a further two or three years, and there is no point in describing these persistent peregrinations and domestic tensions in any detail; only when something of some signifi-cance occurs will it be noted here.

Yet two matters, both matrimonial, did bring great pleasure to Tchaikovsky at this time, and merit inclusion. The first was Anatoly's impending marriage. Giving periodic moral support to this twin had, for some while, been a very wearing process, and relief was now in sight. But the news also brought back memories of an event of long ago that still haunted him. 'I'm terribly glad you feel you are happy,' Tchaikovsky had written to Anatoly in February, while still in Rome,

and though I have never experienced anything of the sort, yet I think I can understand perfectly everything you are going through. It is a certain kind of need for the care and caresses that only a woman can satisfy. Sometimes there comes over me an intense desire to be fon-dled by a woman's hand. Sometimes I see nice ladies (not, however, young ones) into whose lap I simply want to place my head and kiss their hands.

The image of his mother (that lady with 'hands which, though not small, were unusually beautiful') remained indelibly with him. The other matter was very different. During February, two of his patroness's sons, Nikolay and Alexander, had visited the Davïdovs for four days while in Kiev, and a probing letter to his niece Anna had drawn a highly satisfactory response, which she would consummate with Nikolay two years later.

But now, for a while, we shall focus on the compositions from this phase. The Piano Trio had provided evidence that the vein of richly personal music that, before his marriage, had afforded some of Tchaikovsky's most precious pieces, had begun to reopen, and the opera on which he had already started intermittent work would consolidate this evidence very positively. The subject of *Mazeppa* was drawn from Pushkin's epic poem *Poltava*, an account of the real-life attempt by Mazeppa, an early eighteenth-century Cossack hetman (or commander), to gain his Ukraine independence from the Russia of Tsar Peter the Great; included also was an account of the disastrous love affair of the young Mariya with the elderly Mazeppa. (The tale, told by Byron, of Mazeppa's nightmare ride across the Ukraine tied to a wild horse is pure fantasy.) Tchaikovsky had first shown interest in the subject in May 1881, but it was September before he began intermittent work, basing it on a libretto by Victor Burenin, and composing at least part of the love scene between Mariya and Mazeppa. But then, in early 1882, the Piano Trio claimed his whole attention, and only in May, now in Kamenka, did he set about *Mazeppa* systematically. With Tanya and Sasha still in Kiev, Kamenka was an environment congenial for work, but still the opera grew only sluggishly. Then within ten days came news of the sudden death of Kolya's father, and Modest and Kolya had to leave for the Konradi estate at Grankino. Yet in the end this intervention proved beneficial, for Konradi was separated from his wife, who now disputed the will, of which Modest was a beneficiary. Realizing that his brother might need support, and that Kamenka could lose much of its charm now that Tanya and Sasha had returned, Tchaikovsky set off for Grankino. He had expected to remain a fortnight, but Modest fell ill, and in the end he stayed seven weeks. For *Mazeppa* this enforced residence proved beneficial, for by the time he returned to Kamenka in August, very significant progress had been made, and by late September the opera was sketched. Yet it would be April 1883 before it was scored.

This may seem surprising, for Tchaikovsky had, from the beginning, shown great natural skill and facility in handling the orchestra. But clearly he had increasingly realized that there were orchestral potentials he had never used, and which he now began to search out and exploit – different combinations of instruments, a wider variety of orchestral colour and texture, more possibilities in swift contrasts and refined details. Quietly Tchaikovsky's orchestration was becoming more fastidious and more virtuosic. The process of change was not sudden, but listen to, say, the orchestra in *Swan Lake* (1875–76), then in *Nutcracker* (1891–92), and I think the shift will be felt.

Nothing discloses more clearly the status that Tchaikovsky had now achieved in Russian musical life than the response to his new opera. He suspected, probably rightly, that the Tsar himself was behind the unprecedented decision to produce *Mazeppa* simultaneously in the Imperial Theatres in both Moscow and St Petersburg. Nor was anything stinted in matters of production or design; the miserable parsimony of resources that had so handicapped *The Maid of Orleans* was now to be a thing of the past. The premiere of *Mazeppa* took place in Moscow on 15 February 1884, and the St Petersburg production opened only three days later. Unable to supervise both, Tchaikovsky had concentrated on the Moscow preparations, but the strains of this process were such that, despite the ovations he had received, he fled from Russia the day after the first performance, thus missing the St Petersburg opening, evidently to the displeasure of the Tsar. Yet, despite its initial success and a revival in St Petersburg the following season, *Mazeppa* was not heard again during Tchaikovsky's lifetime. Let it be said here straight away: this should not be taken as a judgement on the opera's quality.

Mazeppa: opera in three acts * * * *

[Mazeppa *contains music and dramatic scenes as fine as any in other operas by Tchaikovsky, yet it is very rarely heard. (Its first performance in the UK appears to have been at ENO in 1984.) The story is, I suppose, the problem for, unlike* Eugene Onegin *(or* The Queen of Spades*), it is not about people like ourselves with whom we can readily identify. This is a pity. Nevertheless, we can connect just with the music of* Mazeppa *in our own homes, and it is a connection worth trying – and obligatory for opera buffs.]*

Like *The Maid of Orleans*, *Mazeppa* is in three acts, divided into six scenes. Its plot is as follows:

Act 1 Scene 1: *The garden of Kochubey's farmstead on a river bank.* An offstage chorus of girls is heard singing as they arrive in boats. They greet Mariya, Kochubey's daughter, then leave. Alone, Mariya reveals she is drawn to the elderly Mazeppa. Andrey, in love with Mariya, appears, and sensing that she is distracted by something, declares his love for her, but she confesses to him her love for Mazeppa. Both leave after an impassioned duet. Mariya's father, Kochubey, his wife Lyubov, Mariya and Mazeppa enter. The last asks to be entertained, and a chorus and gopak are performed. When the others have left, Mazeppa asks Kochubey for Mariya's hand. Kochubey protests that their age difference is an obstacle, but Mazeppa remains adamant and a quarrel begins to develop. Mazeppa now reveals to Kochubey that Mariya has already confessed her love, and wishes to marry him. A furious Kochubey rejects Mazeppa, and demands that he leave. Others have heard the quarrel and now enter. Mariya is torn, but she confirms she is prepared to marry Mazeppa. The latter's patience gives way, and he summons his men. Mariya attempts to intervene and there is a brief calm. But Mazeppa calls in more men, asks Mariya to make a free choice, and she finally runs into his embrace. Mazeppa gives ironic thanks to Kochubey, and leaves with Mariya.

Act 1 Scene 2: *A room in Kochubey's house.* Lyubov's women sing a song of sympathy for their mistress, who voices her grief at the disgrace Mariya has brought on her parents. She dismisses the women, then exhorts Kochubey to direct action against Mazeppa. But Kochubey has a secret plan. All present having sworn secrecy, he tells how Mazeppa had confided to him a plot to join in alliance with Sweden to defeat the Tsar and free the Ukraine; he, Kochubey, will warn the Tsar of this danger. Andrey and Iskra, Kochubey's lieutenant, warmly approve the scheme, and Andrey offers to carry the information to the Tsar, despite the risk, for he wants his revenge on Mazeppa. Iskra and the chorus endorse this. Kochubey thanks Andrey, first broods on the wrong done to him, then longs for revenge. Lyubov and the chorus take up his cry.

Act 2 Scene 1: *A dungeon beneath Belotserkov Castle.* Kochubey is chained to a wall. The Tsar has not believed his accusations, and has delivered him and Iskra into Mazeppa's hands. Tomorrow they will die. Kochubey feels deeply the ignominy of his predicament, his loss of honour, the pain of hearing his blameless supporters' curses, of seeing

Mazeppa gloat as he is executed. Hearing a key in the lock, he thinks it must be a holy hermit come to give him absolution. But it is Orlik, Mazeppa's henchman, who demands to know the whereabouts of Kochubey's treasury, which will be forfeit to the state. Kochubey replies he has only three treasures: his honour, which he has now lost; his daughter, whom Mazeppa stole – and the hope of holy vengeance on Mazeppa. Bitterly he predicts that Mariya will disclose his treasures to Mazeppa after his execution. He begs Orlik to leave him in peace, warning him of the Day of Judgement, which he, too, will have to face. Orlik is unimpressed, and summons the torturer.

Act 2 Scene 2: *A room in Mazeppa's castle, with a door leading on to the terrace. Night.* Mazeppa muses on the beauty and calm of the night, comparing these with his own inner gloom. He broods on the necessity of Kochubey's death, and dreads Mariya's reaction to the news. Orlik enters to report that Kochubey will not yield, and Mazeppa confirms the execution. Left alone, his thoughts return to Mariya, and he extols her, ending with a confession of love. Mariya enters, reproaches him for his recent coldness towards her, and reminds him of what she has sacrificed for him. She does not regret this, for he had sworn to love her – but why has he changed? He reaffirms his love, but she continues to upbraid him for his preoccupation with other matters. Finally she demands to know what these are, and he decides to tell her in confidence; the time is ripe to free the Ukraine, and soon Mazeppa will occupy a throne – as will Mariya. Mariya's doubts are instantly dispelled, but Mazeppa checks her: nothing is certain. But she is prepared to die with him, and during a duet she expresses her excitement and devotion, while Mazeppa's thoughts run on the fate he has prepared for her father. He asks who is dearer to her: him or her father? 'I would sacrifice all for you,' is her reply. 'Then remember your words, Mariya,' is his rejoinder as he leaves.

Mariya now muses on the beauty and calm of the night, contrasting this with the loneliness of her parents without her. But suddenly Lyubov appears and reveals to her the imminent execution of her father. Mariya is uncomprehending, and her mother believes she has changed her allegiance. But gradually the truth dawns as Lyubov tells her what has happened. Mariya faints under the strain. As Lyubov tries to revive her, an offstage military band is heard. The execution is in progress; Mariya recovers, and the two women rush off to try to prevent it.

Act 2 Scene 3: *A field with a scaffold.* A crowd reflects on how men can suddenly fall from grace, and they pray to God to be spared such a calamity. A drunken Cossack is rebuked for unseemly merriment. He defends himself, but all is interrupted by the sound of an approaching procession. Two executioners enter, and then Mazeppa, to whom the crowd makes obeisance. Kochubey and Iskra are led in. The two men join in a prayer of confession, embrace each other and mount the scaffold. The crowd close in, hiding them from view. Drums roll, axes appear above the people's heads. Mariya and Lyubov rush in as the axes fall. Mariya falls into her mother's arms, and the crowd prays for forgiveness for the two men.

Act 3: *As at the opera's opening, though everything is now neglected. Night.* A symphonic tableau depicts the Battle of Poltava. Swedish soldiers are pursued by Russians. Andrey enters searching for Mazeppa, becomes aware of his surroundings, and reflects on what has happened. He calls Mariya's name in vain, and longs for death. Hearing men approaching, he hides. Mazeppa and Orlik enter; they pause for rest, and Orlik leads the horses away. Alone, Mazeppa reflects on what has happened, his agony heightened when he realizes where he is. Recognizing Mazeppa's voice, Andrey re-enters. He denounces Mazeppa, who warns Andrey not to attack him. But Andrey flies at him and Mazeppa, pulling a pistol, shoots him, summons Orlik – but at that moment the moonlight reveals Mariya emerging from the trees. She does not notice Mazeppa, and begins to ramble wildly. Then, seeing her husband, she urges him to silence, in case her parents should hear them. Mazeppa watches helplessly as a mad scene unfolds. With mounting frenzy she asks him to go home with her, but then decides the man before her cannot be her Mazeppa. Orlik enters to warn Mazeppa that their pursuers are approaching. Mazeppa would take Mariya with them, but Orlik opposes this, and the two men leave.

Mariya suddenly spots the wounded Andrey. At first she thinks he is her father, and she bends over him, cradling his head in her lap. She does not recognize who it is: 'It is some child sleeping in the thick grass,' she concludes, and when Andrey whispers her name, she knows the voice is familiar, but still he cannot make her recognize him. She begins a lullaby, Andrey tries again to make her understand, but to no avail. He dies as she resumes her lullaby, rocking him and staring blankly before her.

The overture is clearly concerned with Mazeppa himself, its brusque, powerful opening theme very much his, projecting an implacable force-fulness. The headlong music that follows surely depicts the legendary trans-Ukrainian ride of his youth, the contrasting third theme un-covering his nature's more tender side, which will produce some of the loveliest music of the opera. Act 1 opens with a charming girls' chorus (with five beats to a bar) that instantly places the opera in a Russian world. As for Mariya's following aria, this reveals a young woman who is both passionate and decisive, and the evidence of Andrey's music suggests that theirs could have been an appropriate match. However, the tangle of their voices in the concluding stretch catches the torment and tension within their relationship, as well as providing a powerful contrast to the tone at Mazeppa's and Kochubey's entrance. This is very deliberately relaxed, for the remainder of this scene will be concerned with the ever-mounting tension between the two men, a tension that ends in catastrophe. Mazeppa is entertained with a chorus (based on a Ukrainian folksong) and a gopak that gives us everything we have come to expect from Tchaikovsky when com-posing such a dance.

Now the action begins to move. Left alone, the two men open their critical exchange, at first conversational, but then transformed by Mazeppa's revelation of his love for Mariya, a moment where Tchaikovsky can expose both the tender yet strong nature of the het-man's feelings for Mariya. The tone of the music now becomes increasingly disturbed until the two men's raised voices bring back the other principals and the chorus, to precipitate an ensemble of cor-porate anxiety. But this turns out to be not simply a closed, formal movement; the quarrel itself continues in brief interjections within the ensemble, and the chorus will remain as both commentators and marginal participants as the level of hostility rises. It culminates in the supercharged drama of the scene's ending.

This has been a well-paced spectacle scene. By contrast the follow-ing scene is intimate, though charged with deep-rooted and powerful emotions. Again a women's chorus opens proceedings, this time dis-consolately flanking Lyubov's cry of pain for her daughter. Grief-filled this mother's brief lament may be, but its mounting insistence also suggests inner strength and resolve: Lyubov's later attempt to save her husband should come as no surprise. Now it is to business. Lyubov makes a direct appeal to her husband to act – needlessly, it emerges, for he responds in matching terms. In a scene where so much is continuous dialogue, there is neither room nor need for music that does other than support that dialogue in well-shaped phrases that match its expressive quality and fit its speech structure, with the orchestra giving efficient support, and underlining changes of mood. But there are moments when this free flow consolidates into a corporate, full-throated response, and these moments will be set to fully formed melodies which provide stable landmarks in an otherwise freely unwinding narrative. This compact, dramatically detailed scene is best listened to with the libretto before you so that you can keep up with its dramatic detail.

It has already been noted that Russian opera scenarios, if founded (as *Mazeppa* is) on well-known literary classics, may present consecutive scenes separated by huge time gaps, and which can be comprehensible only through prior knowledge of the plot. Such a gap exists between this conspiracy scene and the one following. The move against Mazeppa has failed, the Tsar has been persuaded that Kochubey and Iskra are traitors, and has condemned them to die. This prison scene is perhaps the grimmest Tchaikovsky ever composed. It is really a soliloquy for Kochubey, with Orlik merely a tool of the plot and, even more than the preceding scene, it requires the listener to be following the libretto, so tied is it to the words and their every nuance. The orchestral introduction is, by turns, both bleak and agitated, Kochubey both tormented yet defiant. Only twice in this harrowing monologue are there moments when the music suddenly loses its pain, the first as Kochubey views the prospect of 'holy vengeance' on Mazeppa and, later, when he warns Orlik of the 'Day of Judgement' that his torturer will not escape. Nevertheless, the scene makes compelling listening. Let it not be said that Tchaikovsky was incapable of providing tough music for the most uncompromisingly pain-filled situations.

Nothing could be in greater contrast to all this than the first sounds of the following castle scene, though we shall also be reminded of the inner turbulence with which Mazeppa views the calm and beauty of a Ukrainian summer night. This is the hetman's moment for private confession, and his tormented feelings are clearly presented in the music that introduces and accompanies him. But his love for Mariya remains absolute, as the formal but deeply moving aria that follows makes abundantly clear. We have not encountered Mariya since the opera's first scene, and her entrance now instantly confirms her positive character; here is no blushing violet. The fragment of an orchestral march that precedes Mazeppa's revelation of his plan for a free Ukraine proves to be ironic, for it is the march to which, in the following scene, Kochubey will be led to execution. During Mazeppa's disclosure of his plans the orchestra quotes two snatches from Glinka's patriotic opera *A Life for the Tsar* (from the mazurka in Act 2, and the concluding 'Slavsya Chorus'), which are unlikely to mean anything to non-Russian listeners but would have had significant resonances for Tchaikovsky's audience. At the prospect of a throne Mariya's mood has changed abruptly, and the splendid, measured span of the brief aria with which she greets the news is confirmation both of her loyalty to Mazeppa and of her decisiveness in embracing her new destiny. Mazeppa urges caution; there is still much to do. But Mariya's happiness (and ambition) will not be tamed, and a brief love scene ensues, culminating in an outwardly calm farewell as a still-troubled Mazeppa leaves. However, Mariya's bliss is short-lived. Lyubov suddenly appears, and quickly there is confirmation of the older woman's character; the strong, broadly arched melody to which she drives home that only Mariya can save her father confirming that, like her daughter, she can be uncompromisingly determined. Twice Lyubov employs this melody before Mariya at last grasps what is happening. The truth having dawned, Lyubov repeats her thematic injunction, Mariya herself instantly picks it up and, to the offstage sound of the execution march, the two women rush out on their hopeless mission.

Like the scene that had preceded this last, the one that now follows is painful, though in a very different way. The execution is imminent, and the crowd is waiting, both fascinated yet terrified by the horror they are about to witness. The introduction of the drunken peasant is a foil to give the horror that will follow more impact. The execution march offstage heralds the approach of the procession, which enters to mounting tumult, and an even more powerful foil to this is provided by the condemned men's prayer, and the crowd's hushed response, which becomes increasingly strong as the two men mount the scaffold. The execution itself is brutally swift, and the orchestra, *ffff*, repeats the final portion of the two men's prayer: '. . . there, where there is no sorrow, lamentation, or the torment of earthly existence.'

Mazeppa's concluding scene is preceded by an orchestral entr'acte, 'The Battle of Poltava', denoting the historical event of 1709 that saw the defeat of Mazeppa's ambitions. It contains material familiar from elsewhere in Russian music: first the folksong already used by Musorgsky in the Coronation scene in his opera *Boris Godunov* (and before that by Beethoven in his second Razumovsky Quartet, op. 59 no. 2), and then the chant Tchaikovsky himself had employed to open *1812*. The first is presumably a symbol of Russian supremacy; the second signifies thanksgiving after battle, while the entr'acte's final section conveys the Russians' joy at victory.

Though in the nineteenth century the supremacy of opera singers in the performing world was being challenged by instrumental virtuosi, the former were still the darlings of their audiences, and each principal singer would still expect (or hope for) some situation in which his or her vocal gifts could be paraded. In *Mazeppa* Burenin had provided a handsome opportunity for each of the four leading singers. Kochubey has had magnificent exposure in the dungeon scene, Mazeppa has had his ample stretch of self-confession, plus an aria, at the opening of the following castle scene, and Mariya's showpiece will be the mad scene that closes the opera. The turn of Andrey, the third principal, is at the beginning of Act 3 – a splendid 'scena' (that is, a highly dramatic section made up of contrasting types of music) followed by a more expressively focused aria. The entry of Mazeppa and Orlik sets the plot moving, a portion of Mazeppa's theme that had opened the overture forewarning of his approach with his henchman. Andrey hides, the newcomers enter, Orlik leads the horses away, and Mazeppa recognizes where he is. Andrey emerges and attacks Mazeppa, who mortally wounds him (there had originally been a duet for the two men here, but Tchaikovsky later deleted it). Mazeppa calls for Orlik, but at that moment Mariya enters and her mad scene begins. Earlier in this act, when Andrey had recognized that he was in Kochubey's garden where the opera had opened, there had been an appropriate quotation of music from the opera's first scene; now there are a number of such recollections – as Mariya appears, a solo violin recalls the final section of her Act 2 love duet with Mazeppa. But now her husband can be only a helpless spectator, and his interjections reflect the pain with which he views his deranged wife. Mariya broods on her father's execution and on Mazeppa as she had known him, and recalls the castle-scene music to which she had hailed him as a future tsar. Orlik now intervenes, and persuades Mazeppa to leave without Mariya. Tchaikovsky has handled all this splendidly and, in its very different way, what follows is as fine.

Mariya spots the dying Andrey, and her maniacal frenzy gives way to tenderness for 'the child' she will now rock to sleep. For a moment, if we are to believe the orchestra, her unspoken thoughts recall the march that had led her father to the scaffold, and also that portion of the Act I love duet which Andrey likewise had remembered. As she cradles Andrey he tries to make her realize who he is, but to no avail, and she begins her tender lullaby. Again, with his dying words, he tries – but, lost to everything in the real world, she resumes her lullaby. It is an ending of unashamed pathos – and absolutely right.

On 8 October 1882, having just completed the sketches of *Mazeppa*, Tchaikovsky journeyed to Kiev to collect the latest instalment of his patroness's allowance. He had often attended Mass at the Brothers' Monastery, but had fled before the service's end, and it was the same this time. Deciding that a letter to the press would be too publicly draconian, he wrote to the Bishop himself. It was both the style of the music and the performance that offended him:

> Last Sunday I listened reluctantly to that strange, mazurka-like, nauseatingly affected *Lord, have mercy*, with rather less patience to the *Unction of grace*. But when they opened the central doors of the iconostasis, and the singers gabbled on one chord *Praise God from the heavens* as though casting aside the heavy burden of praising God in favour of their obligation to entertain the public with concert music, and summoned up their strength to begin performing a long, mindless, shapeless concerto, based in an alien mode, trivial, without talent, overflowing with vocal tricks ill befitting a place of worship, I experienced a surge of indignation which increased, the more they sang. Now a bass bawled out a wild, howling roar, now a solo treble began to squeal, then a snatch of a phrase from some Italian trepak was heard, now an operatic love motif rang out with unnatural sweetness in the most rough, bare, tame harmonization, now the whole choir faded to an exaggeratedly delicate pianissimo, now began to roar, to bellow at the tops of their voices. O God! And where, precisely, did this musical orgy begin? Precisely at that moment when the central act of the whole religious ceremony was being celebrated, when your Grace and your officiants administered the body and blood of Christ.

And so on for many more unsparing lines; Tchaikovsky had not lost his capacity for blistering rhetoric when matters of creative taste and integrity were his subjects. His concern for the state of Orthodox church music had been strengthened by his own endeavour, in his Liturgy of St John Chrysostom, to compose in a style that was consonant with the ethos of the Orthodox Church's rituals, and he would go on to compose further pieces exemplifying styles that he felt were both contemporary yet respectful to the tone and practices of the liturgy. As for the present matter, we know nothing of the Bishop's response, but there can be no doubt that an intervention by a composer with such an established and still-growing reputation can have done no harm.

Concern, though of a very different kind, was about to manifest itself in a far more crucial sector of his own world. After Kiev Tchaikovsky headed for his sister's home, where his eldest niece, Tanya, would precipitate a crisis, the very complex and sensitive consequences of which Uncle Pyotr would find himself having to handle. Stanislav Blumenfeld, the music teacher at Kamenka, had already shocked Tchaikovsky through his persistent intimacies with Tanya, and these resumed when he reappeared soon after Tchaikovsky's arrival. At length these affronts to the latter's sense of propriety became too much, and he announced that he would be leaving for Moscow. Immediately Tanya declared she would go with him. Horrified at the thought of her company, he delayed some days, then concocted a story that he would instead be travelling to Prague to see the Czech production of *The Maid of Orleans*; once he arrived in Kiev, he would report that this production had been delayed, and that he was redirecting himself to Moscow.

On arriving in Moscow Tchaikovsky determined to complete scoring the first act of *Mazeppa*, and this delayed his departure for St Petersburg, where he intended to join Modest. Here he discovered that Tanya was now also in the capital, but was installed with other relatives, and he saw little of her; then, on 9 January 1883, he left for Paris. For a fortnight he revelled in his favourite European city, frequently going to the theatre, and delighting in at least two performances of Mozart's *The Marriage of Figaro*. He reflected on this to Modest (not a Mozart lover), providing yet another insight into what attracted him to that composer's music. He admitted that Mozart possesses neither the depth nor strength of Beethoven, neither the warmth nor passion of Schumann, nor the brilliance of Meyerbeer, Berlioz, Wagner, etc. Mozart neither overwhelms nor stuns me – but he captivates me, makes me happy, warms me, and the longer I live, the more I get to know him, the more I love him.

However, the joy of this Parisian fortnight was brutally disrupted when Modest arrived to join him – for accompanying his brother was Tanya.

The ostensible reason for their niece's presence was the need to consult the distinguished doctor, Jean-Martin Charcot, one of the founders of modern neurology, in the hope of curing her morphine addiction, and Tchaikovsky felt he had to remain to support Modest until their niece's treatment was completed. Meanwhile, Tanya had to be installed in a 'maison de santé' where her own maid and a former governess in the Konradi household shared responsibility for her personal needs and supervision, while Tchaikovsky and Modest shared visiting her on alternating days.

It was also a very sensitive responsibility – for though the reason for their niece's presence in Paris was indeed drug therapy, it was not the main one. Tanya was pregnant by Blumenfeld. Of the family, it was still only Modest and Tchaikovsky who knew the truth; not even her mother or father was aware of her condition, and this secrecy had to be preserved for the sake of Sasha's physical and mental health. However, this had alarming financial consequences for Tchaikovsky. To have solicited from Kamenka money to pay the expenses incurred by the extension of Tanya's stay until after the birth of her child would have revealed her secret to her parents, and in desperation Tchaikovsky applied to his patroness for a two-month advance on his allowance, also obtaining a 2000-rouble loan from Jurgenson. To make matters worse, by mid-April Modest had to return to Russia and Kolya, thus leaving his brother entirely responsible both for decisions regarding Tanya, and for any action that might follow.

How Tchaikovsky took and executed these decisions provides further vivid, and often touching, insight into his character. The baby, a boy baptized Georges-Léon, was born on 8 May, the day after Tchaikovsky's own forty-third birthday. He was surprised at his feelings of tenderness on seeing the new baby. 'I told Tanya that while I had life in me she need have no worry on Georges-Léon's account,' he told Modest. Even for a moment he thought of adopting the child himself. But he was upset by Tanya's equanimity at the prospect of having to live a lie when she returned to her parental home. Meanwhile Tchaikovsky discharged the formalities of registering Georges-Léon's birth and arranging his baptism. As for his future, after a few days the wet nurse took him to her home at Villeneuve to the south of Paris, and for the following three years he would remain in France, Tchaikovsky taking upon himself responsibility for monitoring Georges-Léon's welfare, and visiting him as often as he could in his foster home until, finally, Tchaikovsky's elder brother Nikolay and his wife undertook to adopt the boy.

Meanwhile in March a commission had arrived for two pieces relating to the forthcoming Coronation of the new Tsar, Alexander III, for whom, as Tsarevich, Tchaikovsky had composed his Festival Overture on the Danish National Anthem seventeen years earlier. The first was for a ceremonial march, the second for a more substantial piece – a cantata, *Moscow*, on a text by the poet Apollon Maikov. Both commissions were discharged during this Paris interlude. Tchaikovsky evaluated the pieces very differently:

> The march is noisy but bad, but the cantata is not nearly as poor as might be thought, considering how quickly it was composed. Maikov's text is very beautiful and poetic. There is a bit of patriotic vapouring, but apart from this it is deeply felt. It has freshness and its tone is sincere, which is enabling me to put into my music a measure of the feeling that his beautiful lines have warmed in me.

One curious custom of the Coronation was a ceremonial act where the Tsar dined alone while others watched, and the cantata's premiere took place in the Kremlin as accompaniment to this ritual. Tchaikovsky had charged no fee for the piece, but the Tsar decreed that the composer should receive 1,500 roubles, which would be presented in the form of a ring – just as had happened seventeen years earlier when Tchaikovsky had composed the Danish Festival Overture in celebration of this same future Tsar's marriage. On that occasion Tchaikovsky had lost the ring; this time, being currently insolvent, he pawned it for 375 roubles, promptly lost the redemption ticket, and the only gain he made for his services was, as he put it to his patroness, 'a feeling of having committed some sort of improper act'.

Coronation cantata: *Moscow* * * *

[Though this cantata cannot be numbered among Tchaikovsky's more major compositions, it is a piece of much attractiveness, and for those readers with a particular love of choral–orchestral music, it is well worth investigating. The ending may be rather stiff and formal, but the preceding stretches contain some lovely music.]

Moscow is made up of six movements. For a moment at its opening the listener may wonder whether it is *1812*, but this beautiful section for the cellos, divided into four parts, leads into a choral–orchestral movement of much charm, describing the founding of Moscow, its historical travails and its descent into impenetrable night under assault from Tartar hordes. In the second movement the mezzo-soprano soloist recounts the revival of Moscow, and in the third the chorus rejoices and salutes the emergence of their Tsar. The more sombre baritone solo of the fourth movement is concerned with the Tsar's leadership and his heavy responsibility as the champion of the other Slavonic kingdoms, Serbia, Georgia and Bulgaria; it ends with a triumphant declaration: 'Two Romes have fallen [Rome itself to the Goths in 410, Constantinople to the Ottoman Turks in 1453], the third [Moscow] stands: there shall not be a fourth!' The chorus sonorously echo his words, and the orchestra celebrates. In the fifth movement the mezzo-soprano soloist voices the Tsar's own sober reflections on the responsibilities that now lie upon him; if this music sounds familiar to some readers, it is because Tchaikovsky would rework some of it into Polina's romance, which opens Act 2 of *The Queen of Spades*. The finale is a corporate celebration; the baritone leads off, the chorus responds and is soon joined by both soloists for an appropriately noisy glorification of the Tsar, and an expression of hope for a strong and ideal Russia.

With the matter of Georges-Léon's immediate future settled, Tchaikovsky was free, and on 22 May he left Paris. Anatoly, now contentedly married, had rented a house at Podushkino near Moscow, and it was thither that Tchaikovsky ultimately headed. Anatoly had also recently become a father, and he was no longer the problem brother whom Tchaikovsky had constantly had to counsel and support.

The house's location was very attractive, and Tchaikovsky could delight in wandering in the surrounding woods and picking mushrooms. A second romantic success was to add to his pleasure: his niece Anna was now officially engaged to Nikolay von Meck. Tchaikovsky visited Moscow to see friends, and to act as a diplomat in the affairs of the Conservatoire. Nikolay Hubert had now been driven from his post by a series of internal troubles, and Tchaikovsky interceded in the hope of enabling him to return. This proved unavailing, but he was able to persuade (though with many misgivings) the authorities to offer the vacant appointment to Laroche, his close, very talented, yet unstable friend.

Tchaikovsky remained some three months at Podushkino. But after a month the proofs of *Mazeppa* arrived. One of the chores that every author or composer has to face if his work is being published is to check the accuracy of what it is proposed to issue, and to make the necessary corrections. Proof-reading a book is relatively easy, since the text is a single and continuous chain of words, and all that is necessary is to read it through line by line, and indicate any necessary corrections. But a musical score is very different. There are so many different factors to examine. Not only the pitches of the notes must be checked; so must the length of each note and any expression mark attached to it (any accent, for instance). There are all sorts of other performance indications and phrasing marks to check, and the vertical alignment must be very precise – that is, all the notes that are sounded simultaneously must be placed very exactly – and in one of Tchaikovsky's scores there could be as many as twenty or more such notes at any one time. All this demands an unfaltering and acute attentiveness, and is thus both enormously time-consuming and wearying, especially with a two- or three-hour opera. It is no surprise that the mounting inroads into his own routines made by the numerous other guests and friends who visited Podushkino (and who often issued return invitations) became progressively more intrusive. In addition, his own creative urges were becoming ever stronger, and he had already yielded to these so that when he left Podushkino on 13 September, the sketches for a new orchestral suite existed. Arriving four days later in Kamenka, his priority was to complete this substantial piece.

Tchaikovsky would remain in Kamenka for the next two and a half months, and for the first five weeks would spend some six hours a day working out fully and scoring his Second Orchestral Suite, for he continued studiedly to extend the range and the refinement of his orchestration. Its premiere took place in Moscow the following February, conducted by Max Erdmannsdörfer, who in 1882 had taken over Nikolay Rubinstein's role as conductor of the concerts of the RMS's Moscow branch, and the new work was so successful that it had to be repeated a week later. Tchaikovsky, however, was not present at either performance. So exhausted had he been by the strains of getting *Mazeppa* produced that, as has been noted, after the opera's premiere the day before that of the Suite, he had forthwith fled to the West to recover.

Suite no. 2, for orchestra * * * (*)

[This suite contains some very attractive music superbly presented and, in its fourth movement, one of the most remarkable passages in all Tchaikovsky's works. However, in overall quality it does not quite match up to that of the future Third Suite: hence the bracketed fourth star.]

Despite the title *Jeu de sons* ('Play of sounds') which Tchaikovsky gave to the suite's first movement, his preoccupations with matters of orchestration are not nearly as apparent here as in most of the following movements. It is cast as a sonata structure, with a slow introduction which recurs to round off the piece. Here the *jeu* ('play') is simply between string phrases whose endings are echoed by the woodwind; however, when the fast main movement begins, the constant short-term changes of texture, often with matchingly short-term shifts between string and wind colour, are notable. The exposition has three clear sections, the first energetically busy, the second more straightforwardly melodic, and the third (after a brief pause) marked by the resumption of very swift exchanges of texture between pizzicato and arco strings, and sometimes with wind. The development is a fugue based on the opening of the first subject, but a fugue's nature (that is, a constant and single-themed stream of unbroken sound) does not lend itself to variety of orchestration. It dovetails with the recapitulation, the first subject passing straight into the more melodic second. (Perhaps the super-alert listener may have noted that, at this point, the second subject also re-enters in the bass, Tchaikovsky having designed the two themes to fit together (in a moment this combination is to be repeated, but the other way up).) The entry of the third theme is, as before, easily identified by the preceding pause. As already noted, a portion of the slower music that had opened the movement now recurs to close it.

This has been an intriguing movement, if not one of Tchaikovsky's most ingratiating. But the *Valse* that follows is, like almost all Tchaikovsky's, irresistible. Yet it is a rather new kind of tune. Tchaikovsky's great earlier waltzes had generally been plainer, but this one is more lithe and more wide-ranging (try singing or whistling, say, the waltz theme near the opening of *Swan Lake*, and then the present one, and I think this point will come home), and it includes changes of pace that would create havoc in a ballet performance. And note the repeated 'googling' idea that follows immediately on the first theme: this grabs you because of its intriguing orchestration, not its substance. Tchaikovsky is now introducing, both in matters of texture and colour, much more unobtrusive variety into the accompaniments than would be noticed in a ballet where the attention is divided between stage action and music. Note also the melodic fragments that often so effectively enrich some of the accompaniments. This is a delicious movement.

The third movement, *Scherzo burlesque*, is more ostentatiously brilliant, and it introduces a sound that very few, if any, readers may have heard in a nineteenth-century classical piece. Yes, they *are* piano accordions! Tchaikovsky was always ready to take on board new sounds and instruments. (Some years later, when he encountered in Paris another new instrument, the celeste, he was desperate to keep this a secret in case Rimsky-Korsakov, having heard of it, would manage to use it ahead of him.) This *Scherzo burlesque* is a piece where one almost feels that the orchestration created the music. The prevailing impression is of fragments of melody flying around in all directions, their individuality asserted by their being well spaced out in the texture, and often by their contrasting orchestral colours. Minuscule melodic fragments, even sound dots (one-note jabs from the woodwind, pizzicatos from the strings, for instance) add tiny touches of seasoning. The bold folksong-like tune which the horns introduce as a central section could hardly be in greater (or more effective) contrast. This is truly heady music.

But the most striking sounds – indeed, the most remarkable music in the whole suite – is about to come, and could not be in greater contrast. One might hardly expect to find a radical musical adventure in a piece entitled simply *Rêves d'enfant* ('A Child's Dreams'), and nothing at the movement's opening gives a hint of the strange, even perhaps unnerving sounds that Tchaikovsky will conjure. The scoring of what seems initially to be a reassuring lullaby is as fastidiously judged and resourceful as in any movement in this suite, and though the build to a *fortissimo* will cast some doubts over its sleep-inducing power, what will soon follow confounds this suspicion, for any vestige of reality will dissolve as we are surely drawn into the kingdom of sleep itself. Strange, delicate, fragmented textures, with no recognizable harmonic foundation – fleeting harp arpeggios – an oboe melody spun from a tiny repeated seven-note fragment – a fragment that, now set on high piccolo, will flutter above a low, nagging clarinet–viola phrase, and against a backdrop of ever louder tremolando strings. Even in the music of enchantment that we shall encounter in the ballet *The Sleeping Beauty*, we shall be confronted with nothing quite like this. Perhaps any reader who may have heard Benjamin Britten's opera *The Turn of the Screw* may momentarily wonder whether there will open before him the world of Bly, that other setting for disturbing childhood fears and fantasies. But Tchaikovsky's dream passes into a dying, ever sinking end. A pause – and the lullaby resumes as it had begun, back in a world of safe, secure humanity.

After this extraordinary piece, the suite's concluding number returns us to the more earth-bound society of the preceding movements. *Danse baroque* may seem a curious title for this very un-eighteenth-century caper, but Tchaikovsky is using the adjective here in the sense of 'quaint' or 'grotesque'. Its subtitle, 'Wild dance in imitation of Dargomizhsky' is more helpful, and the actual model is clearly that earlier Russian composer's *Kazachok* 'Cossack Dance', though Tchaikovsky's is vastly superior. It needs no further comment here; suffice it to say that it rounds off the suite excellently.

———

20

Contrasting Relationships:
Third Suite

By now it will be clear that Tchaikovsky was neither gregarious nor a recluse. Within his family and with friends, both professional and social (and among the latter we may presume that some relationships had a homosexual element), he could be a good guest, friend and, where necessary, support. There were moments or phases when outside circumstances and tensions drove him to escape into a more solitary existence, but these were almost always temporary withdrawals. His concern for other people and his readiness to step in with financial support where this could solve, or at least mitigate, a problem has already been exemplified many times, but on other occasions his interventions could be unexpected, sometimes seemingly capricious, even bizarre. Yet, again, there may have been no motivation other than to help an individual whom he saw as deserving. Such a one was Leonty Tkachenko, and this bizarre episode illumines one corner of Tchaikovsky's character as nothing else does. It had all begun back in 1879, and what followed is best told through extracts from Tchaikovsky's letters to Nadezhda von Meck.

The Strange Case of Leonty Tkachenko

It was back in October 1879 that Tchaikovsky received his first letter from Tkachenko, who was living in Voronezh. In it the latter had declared his passionate wish to study music but, not having the means to finance himself, expressed his readiness to become Tchaikovsky's servant in return for tuition:

> Because the letter was written very correctly and was shot through with sincerity, I replied that, although I could not accept his services as my manservant, I could help him if, from his next letter, I saw he was sufficiently gifted and young enough for study to lead to something.

Yesterday I received his reply. He is twenty-two, and his musical knowledge is as weak as his wish to become a professional musician is strong. His letter was so written as to breed in me a great sympathy towards this youth. But what can you do with a person who for twenty-two years has only loved music, and can do nothing except what he has picked up by ear? I had to write in reply my honest opinion was that he *had left it too late*. I am very sorry for him.

A full year passed before Tchaikovsky picked up the tale:

The day before yesterday I received a letter from him. He is returning my letters to me, lest after his death they should fall into someone else's hands. He bids me farewell, and says he has decided on suicide. The letter exuded such sincerity, such a deep despair, that I was very shocked. Judging from his letters he is a strange and wild young man – but intelligent, and very honourable and good.

Tchaikovsky admitted that Tkachenko's letter so affected him that he wept like a child when reading it. Immediately he contacted Anatoly, begging him to request a friend of his who lived in Voronezh to root out the young man. The friend did as asked, discovering Tkachenko in a very sorry state. Immediately Tchaikovsky wrote again:

I certainly must become acquainted with you personally. If I were at this moment a completely free person I would come *to Voronezh*, but for various reasons I cannot, and it would therefore be more convenient if you came to me here. I am sending you fifty roubles for the journey. I have adequate means, and it costs me nothing to show *a friend* (such I consider you to be) not only moral but material support. Look more kindly on life and on the future – and most of all, do not doubt that, although I do not yet know you personally, I am already your sincere and firm friend.

However, Tkachenko's reply, received a fortnight later, dismayed and riled Tchaikovsky:

I had expected him to say thank you to me for the helping hand I had extended to him. Not in the least! He hastens to assure me that it is useless for me *to take upon myself to assure him of the existence of virtue* (though I never thought to speak of anything of the sort), *that I shall not be able to prove to him that it is worth living in this world*, that he did not need the money I had sent him – but he promised, all the same, to come to Moscow on 22nd to hear me out. All this is very strange and incomprehensible.

Indeed! But the odd character arrived punctually:

> In general as a person he is sympathetic [Tchaikovsky's favourite adjective for describing someone he could get on with]. His sufferings have stemmed from the disparity between his aspirations and the blasts of stern reality. He is intelligent, developed – but, nevertheless, for the sake of a morsel of bread he has been forced to serve as a guard on the railways. He is very nervous, timid, and abnormally shy. His views are rather queer – but, I repeat, he is far from stupid, and I am resolved to take him into my care. I have now decided to send him for this half-year to the Conservatoire. Because he inspires in me sincere sympathy I shall not find it difficult to cure him and turn him into a being both useful and reconciled with life.

However, within a fortnight, on the eve of his departure from Moscow, Tchaikovsky learned the consequences of this mind-boggling proposal. His protégé appeared, declared he needed to have a serious talk with Tchaikovsky, who listened with mounting amazement – and anger:

> He is a very strange person. On the eve of my departure he presented himself to me, and forewarned me that he had to have a serious talk with me. This is the essence of his speech. The thought had entered his head that I had rendered him help and assistance *not for his good but for my own, in order to earn the reputation of being a philanthropist.* He compared me to *those ladies* who occupy themselves with philanthropy because it is fashionable, and so that they will be much talked about. He stated that he did not want to be a *victim* of my weakness for making myself popular, that he emphatically refused to consider me his benefactor, and forewarned me I should not count upon gratitude on his part.

This was too much for Tchaikovsky, and he forthwith dismissed Tkachenko:

> I told him I was leaving Moscow, that I would not see him again, and asked him not to think about me any more, but only of his studies.

And that, Tchaikovsky thought, was that. How mistaken he was!

Tchaikovsky would spend the summer of 1881 at Kamenka from where, in late August, he reported a sudden and extraordinary event. His correspondent was now Modest:

This morning I was going to write to you when suddenly Sila [one of the Kamenka peasants] appeared, informing me in confidence that some unknown young man wanted to see me. Because he didn't say who this was, I refused to go. Then Biryukov appeared; he had seen the strange young man, and had been filled with pity for him. He had come from somewhere on foot, and had spent a full day at the station, had had nothing to eat, had stubbornly refused all offers, and declared the police could have him if they wished. From the description I guessed it was Tkachenko, and ran in great agitation to the station. I thought he was waiting for me so that he could forthwith blow his brains out in front of me. I won't describe the desperate condition I found the unhappy man in. He was *inexpressibly* pleased to see me, and could not restrain his hysterical sobbing. He's a strange person! I calmed him as best I could, told Sila to pour him some tea, and let him sit alone in order to calm himself. Then I left, and at evening returned and sent him via Kharkov to Moscow, from which it seems he had walked all the way. His object was to come and decline my allowance in view of his lack of ability, willpower, and his general worthlessness. However, he has promised to send me from Kharkov, where he has a sister, his diary for the whole summer, which contains all he wanted to say, but couldn't *de vive voix*. I'm very exhausted from the upheavals I have suffered today – but Tkachenko has again become sympathetic to me. He has a good but broken nature *à la Dostoyevsky*.

The diary duly arrived, a fat volume covering seven months. It was sometimes disconcertingly frank, but by the end Tchaikovsky believed he had discovered the root of Tkachenko's problems. His youth had been too dominated by sensuality – and Tchaikovsky's reply hints at a recognition of some parallels with his own experience:

As for the moral side of your *excesses*, in the first place I have no right to cast a stone at you, for I myself am not blameless – and, secondly, in my opinion a man in this regard finds himself in a fateful dependence upon his temperament. Very often chastity is no more than the lack of an element of sensuality in the temperament. The whole point is to be able to stand above one's bodily desires, and to be able to control them – and this comes with training. In your case this training was bad. Ah, Leonty Grigoryevich, you are a good, nice person, but morally sick for which, of course, you are not to blame, but circumstances.

By this time Tchaikovsky was forced to conclude that Tkachenko would never make a career in music. But, reading the diary, he decided that his protégé had some literary talent, and this was supported by Modest after he had read something of it. Accordingly, during meetings with Tkachenko towards the year's end, Tchaikovsky persuaded him to leave the Conservatoire, and during 1882 subsidized him. Tkachenko now applied himself doggedly to learning his literary craft. By June this seemed to be yielding results, and Tchaikovsky continued to scrutinize his work closely, both praising and criticizing it. However, the problem was that, though he believed Tkachenko's own diary could have been the basis of a novel and that his craft with words was developing, he could find no signs that Tkachenko understood human nature and behaviour sufficiently to be capable of handling it in fiction. Increasingly, Tchaikovsky tried to edge him towards another goal. Finally, in late November, as tactfully as he could, he set out the position and the new objective to which his pupil should strive:

Since it will still be a long while before, through your own efforts, you make up for the inadequacies in your schooling and become a mature writer, you will need to live for several years, despite having a firmly projected aim, without a definite position and, above all, without those *responsibilities* whose fulfilment completes and adorns our life. What you need is an occupation such as would interest you and make your life useful in the near future before you become a serious writer, while not distracting you from your main aim. And do you know what occupation I find completely suitable for your temperament? *The occupation of a village schoolteacher!* No, in my view, there is no more honourable, more *sacred* service to society than service as a village schoolteacher!

How Tkachenko reacted to this sudden proposal we do not know. Only a brief acknowledgement came, and then total silence, and it seems the relationship was over. As for the final act, this was recorded in a letter to Modest in October 1883 from Verbovka:

> When I arrived here I found awaiting me a parcel from *Tkachenko*, who is in Poltava. It proved to be all my *letters* to him. Because the first time he wanted to kill himself he'd sent me back my two letters, I understood this time that he was, as it were, informing me of his impending suicide. Nevertheless, it was only for the first instant that I was a little worried; afterwards I somehow decided my Tkachenko was almost certainly still alive. And, indeed, today I received a request from him to send money, with no mention of my letters. His letter is, as always, ironical in tone. A pathetic, but rather *un*sympathetic person!

As we have already noted, Tchaikovsky had a natural ability to relate to children and participate fully in their world: it had been within the family world at Kamenka that, for instance, he had conceived the embryo of that most famous of all ballets, *Swan Lake*. But that had been a dozen years earlier; all these children had now grown up, and he had witnessed, and sometimes endured, the wilfulness of his now adolescent nieces (not to mention the extended and very personal distractions caused by Tanya's pregnancy). Yet even as this generation was passing into adulthood, a new one was being born. Brother Anatoly now had a baby daughter, and already Tchaikovsky had a great-nephew and a great-niece, for besides Tanya's Georges-Léon, there was Vera's year-old Irina, whom Tchaikovsky had at first thought unattractive ('she reminds me very much of a widow, and such children are not to my taste'), but whom he soon admitted he came to adore. Meanwhile a third niece, Anna, was about to marry Nikolay von Meck, so there was hope in that quarter. Tchaikovsky had for a while been minded to compile a set of songs for children, and now, only a week after finishing the Second Suite, he composed the first of his **Sixteen Songs for Children,** ** completing the lot within a fortnight. The verses, almost all sentimental, were by a minor poet, Alexey Pleshcheyev, and were about spring, snow, gardens, birds, paupers, orphans and the poor, cosy domesticity, and so on. As a body they need not detain us here, though readers who are drawn to music that relates to the young and their world – those who, say, take pleasure (as I do) in Schumann's set of piano pieces, *Scenes from Childhood* – may find much to enjoy in some at least of these pieces, though they are far less sophisticated than Schumann's. They are a varied bunch, and two particularly stand out for me: 'The Cuckoo', in which the eponymous bird becomes so enraged because other birds are getting all the attention that he determines to command notice by remorseless repetitions of the only two notes in his repertoire (Tchaikovsky's sense of humour here is much engaged). The other piece will already be well known to some readers, though in the four-voice arrangement Tchaikovsky made some years later (usually known under the title, 'The Crown of Roses', with a first line 'When Jesus Christ was yet a child'). It is a sentimental piece, perhaps, but so simple and unaffected that it is both touching and quietly dignified.

Kamenka remained Tchaikovsky's base until the end of November. Meanwhile Tanya continued to be something of a preoccupation. She had arrived in Kamenka with news of having received a marriage proposal from a certain Ferré, a French doctor who had attended her during her confinement; now she intended to return to Paris where the matter might be resolved. Tchaikovsky had counselled her not to rush into any decision, even though he was still supporting her, and marriage would bring an end to such payments. He might reasonably have been expected by now to feel little love for Tanya, but at her departure his own reactions surprised him: 'My heart was wrung when she said goodbye,' he confessed to Anatoly.

> Somehow she has become pitiful and, above all, so distanced from her family that she's like a stranger, and everyone breathed more freely on being released from such a difficult guest. Even her parents, however much they love her, cannot hide that things are better and more carefree when she's away.

Once again humanity had shown itself more powerful than reflex. And though another relationship that was developing brought unadulterated joy, it also stirred a feeling of private regret. Nikolay von Meck was visiting Kamenka, and while Tchaikovsky took pleasure in seeing how he and Anna, who were about to be married, 'sit all day in the corner, and endlessly kiss each other', this also produced an ache. As he wrote to Modest, 'I look at them with envy, and think all the time that this indeed is real happiness, and that I shall never experience it.' He knew this brother would understand. As for the news that soon arrived from Paris, this proved negative. Even before Ferré had entered her life, Tanya had been courted by a rich merchant, Otto Kern, and this earlier suitor was still not completely out of the picture. Now Tanya discovered that, during her absence, Ferré had become engaged to a French girl, and that Kern had faded away. Worse still for her uncle was to discover that news of her child had reached the Kamenka servants, and for some days he was in terror of it coming to her parents' ears. But on penetrating the fringes of the family it was instantly dismissed as too monstrous to be credible, and for the moment the secret remained safe.

What drew Tchaikovsky to Moscow on 1 December was the performance of his First Symphony, which had never been repeated since its premiere in 1868. It was very warmly received. But the following two months were taken up with personal and business matters, and in due course by preparations for the production of *Mazeppa*. As recorded earlier, Tchaikovsky had fled abroad the day after the first performance, not even staying for the premiere of his Second Suite the very next day. On 21 February he arrived in Paris, where loneliness engulfed him, and he even felt gratitude for the presence of Tanya, who had relapsed into her customary idleness, now that all her marital plans had collapsed. He twice visited Georges-Léon, giving no warning of his arrival, and leaving well satisfied that the boy was being properly cared for. He had hoped to proceed to Rome where Anna and Nikolay von Meck were on honeymoon, but lack of funds and a decline in Tanya's health forced him to remain in the French capital. By now he had made many acquaintances in the city, and the pressure to make visits again reawakened dreams of a home of his own: 'Whether this home will be somewhere on the outskirts of Moscow or somewhere a little more isolated I do not yet know. Thousands of plans crowd into my head – but, one way or another, I must finally have a place of my own.' He had intended to return to Kamenka, but Nápravník reported the Tsar's surprise at Tchaikovsky's absence from the opening of *Mazeppa* in St Petersburg, adding that his sovereign wished to see him. Thus there could be no question of further delay, and on 12 March Tchaikovsky left Paris for St Petersburg.

The importance for Tchaikovsky of his meeting with the Tsar a week later can hardly be exaggerated, for what he did not know when he left Paris was that His Majesty was to confer an honour, the Order of St Vladimir (fourth class), upon him. For nearly seven years Tchaikovsky had lived painfully aware of the public knowledge of his marital disaster, and with a consequent gnawing sense of humiliation. Could there be a more visible sign of rehabilitation than this honour conferred by the Tsar himself? The public might never forget what had happened, but at least they would now forgive. His spirits high, on 31 March he moved to Moscow. Here he again acted as amanuensis to Laroche, whose indolence had become such that Tchaikovsky had already in January taken his friend in hand. 'I proposed that I should come each day for a couple of hours so that he could dictate to me an article for the *Russian Messenger*,' he had written to his patroness. 'This so flattered and touched him that half a big article is already prepared and has gone to the printers. He needs a nurse, and I've taken this role upon myself.' Now, with Tchaikovsky again as scribe, the article was resumed and brought to completion. Tchaikovsky also enjoyed some time with Anatoly and his family, and benefited from the numerous, and often splendid, Eastertide services being celebrated in Moscow churches. But all such activity only fortified his determination to have a home of his own, and for the first time he began inspecting possible properties. This proving unsuccessful, he left Anatoly with instructions to inform him of anything suitable that might emerge near Moscow. On 24 April he was in Kamenka for a two-month stay. That same day he began a new diary.

Kamenka Diary

Throughout the greater part of his adult life Tchaikovsky kept diaries, though two years before his death he destroyed a number of these, recognizing that his fame had become such that their contents would be posthumously trawled and would uncover personal matters he would not wish to become public knowledge. The fact that a diary survived suggests, therefore, that Tchaikovsky would have had no objection to later generations knowing its contents. Such a diary is the one he compiled between 24 April and 21 June 1884 when he was based at Kamenka, and it provides the most vivid of all insights into Tchaikovsky within the informal environment of his family, detailing his activities, his views of his companions, and sometimes uncovering his inner world; often they seem like documents of private confession. For the present purpose they are invaluable in recording his day-to-day progress when composing his Third Suite, and also the beginning of the close relationship with his youngest nephew, Vladimir ('Bob'), now twelve years old. Nine years on Tchaikovsky would dedicate his Sixth Symphony (*Pathétique*) to Bob, and his uncle's infatuation with him clearly became increasingly difficult for the lad as he grew to manhood. But Bob himself had problems, and in 1906, thirteen years after his uncle's death, he would commit suicide. One wonders whether, in 1884, he already felt oppressed by his uncle. No matter: it is only Tchaikovsky's attitude that is of interest to us here – and I am convinced of one thing: whatever his feelings for his nephew, Tchaikovsky never acted improperly with him.

Because of the insights this diary affords I have quoted at length from it. Nevertheless, except for a very few entries that are presented almost complete because they provide especially vivid cameos, the following extracts are very much edited down, focusing almost exclusively on the creation of the Third Suite, and on the joint activities of uncle and nephew. Not every day is recorded here. Vint, which is frequently mentioned, is a card game resembling both whist and bridge, and was very popular in Russia.

25 April. Got up late. Still cold. After drinking tea, went to Lev who soon left, and I stayed to strum the piano and think up something new. I hit on an idea for a *Concerto for piano*, but it turned out too wretched, and wasn't new. Walked a bit in the garden. Dinner for two: Sister [Anna Popova, the cousin who had moved in to run the Tchaikovsky household in 1854 on the death of Tchaikovsky's mother] is ill. Played Massenet's *Hérodiade*. Strolled for a bit. Drank tea at home. Read Otto Jahn on Mozart. After supper real vint for two with Flegont [a tutor at Kamenka].

26 April. Again got up late. Visit to Father Alexander [the Kamenka priest] . . . Continue to do nothing, and haven't the slightest inspiration.

28 April. Spent all the time until dinner in the Trostyanka woods, gathering violets and deriving deep enjoyment. Tried to lay the foundations of a new symphony both in the Trostyanka woods and at home after dinner, but I'm dissatisfied with everything. Walked in the garden and conceived *the seed* not of a future symphony, but of a suite. Vint for three: my bad luck was colossal.

29 April. In the morning, despite the cruelly cold wind, I went to the Trostyanka woods. Noted down some ideas.

30 April. Trostyanka woods again and noting down some wretched ideas.

1 May. Woke up off colour. Completed a walk . . . Very dissatisfied with myself because of the banality of everything that comes into my head. Am I played out?

4 May. Went to the station to meet our people. A joyful meeting. Bob. Read for a long time. Collected signatures at home to send to Modya for his birthday. Vint for five. My luck was bad and I got terribly cross. Have just read the *First Book of Kings* [from the Bible].

6 May. Soon I'll be forty-four. How long have I lived and, in truth and without false modesty, how little have I done! Even in my regular occupation – for, putting my hand to my heart, there is nothing *perfect, exemplary*. Still I'm searching, wavering, unsteady. And for the rest? I read nothing significant, I know nothing. Only on vint do I spend an abundance of precious time. But I believe *my health* will *come to no good*. Today I was so cross, so irritated, that I believe another moment, and I would have thrown an ugly scene of anger and hatred. My temper today is generally bad, and my period of calm, quiet life, untroubled by anything, has passed. There's a lot of fuss, a lot of jars, a lot which a madman of my years cannot bear with indifference. No! It is time to live *in my own home and in my own way*.

The whole morning was spent on a pleasant walk. I'd hardly managed to get in my evening walk than I was summoned to supper – this is a new arrangement. I suffered from hunger and from *lack of attention* towards me. Then vint, and endless anger.

8 May. I'm a sort of walking malice! Because Sasha enjoyed getting me into difficulties at cards I was the more enraged since, out of magnanimity in view of her bad luck in the game yesterday, I had only just previously let her have the bid in clubs. How do you like that? Are these the feelings of an artist who enjoys fame? Ugh! Pyotr Ilich, this is shameful, my good fellow! During the morning worked with the maximum effort (the scherzo). Drank tea in my room. Afterwards wrote a bit more. Bob walked about the garden with me. Ah, what a delight this Bob is! After supper (I was out of temper) vint for three. Ugh! What a life!

9 May. After a short walk worked all morning; it was now going better . . . Ah, what a perfect being this Bob is!

10 May. Today has been extremely successful – in the first place, because my work has gone excellently: secondly, because my stomach is in order. In the mornings strolled in the garden with Bob (what a darling he is!). It's very nice when they speak English at dinner. I'm beginning to understand – but Sister always butts in.

11 May. Finished the scherzo.

12 May. Why do I play vint? The only result is upset and bad temper. Spent all day writing the waltz for the suite, but I'm far from certain it's completely satisfactory.

13 May. Continued the waltz. After supper (before which, to his great joy, I played duets with my darling, the incomparable, wonderful, ideal Bob) played vint.

14 May. The waltz came along with enormous difficulty. No, I'm growing old. Laboured on the waltz until nearly 7 o'clock, but got nowhere.

15 May. After strolling in the garden a little, finished the sketch of the waltz.

16 May. Having, with the greatest composure of spirit, sat down to play Mozart's *Magic Flute*, I was, in the middle of the most exquisite pleasure, interrupted by the entrance of *Bob*, with a horrified expression, to tell me of the death of Tusya Bazilevskaya [a young relative of Lev]. Great sorrow . . . At last our vint took place. I am very weary. Darling Tusya! Ah, the poor things, the poor things! And why? But God's will be done.

17 May. After dinner wandered about with Bob. Until 7 o'clock struggled with a spot in the Andante. Sad thoughts and tears about Tusya. Was late for supper. Vint for two.

18 May. Went to Mass. Was very susceptible to religious impressions; stood nearly all the time with tears in my eyes. I'm always touched to the depths of my soul by the manifestation of simple, wholesome religious feeling in the common people. Went to the market with Bob. Worked very successfully. After supper played dances for the children.

19 May. Only managed to work a little. Picked lilies of the valley with Bob.

20 May. Worked all morning – not without effort, but my *Andante* is coming along and I think it will come out very nicely. Tragic details of Tusya's death received – so painful, they make you weep. Worked till 7 o'clock.

21 May. Worked and finished the *Andante*, with which I'm very satisfied.

23 May. Again cold and windy. The first movement of the suite, called *Contrasts*, is so loathsome to me that, having played about with it all day, I decided to discard it and write something completely different. How hard has work become for me! Is it old age at last?

24 May. Played Mozart. After tea was on the point of struggling *again* with the loathsome *Contrasts*, but suddenly a new idea flashed into my head, and the matter sorted itself out. Bob – in the end he will simply drive me out of my mind with his unspeakable fascination.

25 May. Mass finished early. Worked. After dinner sat in my workroom with Bob. After tea composed a bit.

26 May. Worked successfully until dinner. After dinner read Krïlov with Bob.

27 May. Composed the final variation (the polonaise-finale). Worked again after tea.

28 May. Wrote right up to dinner. After tea again worked. Sat for a long time with Bob and Flegont on a bench in the conservatory. Worked at English.

29 May. Sat down to work without taking a walk, and wrote until midday. Played Mozart, and was in ecstasy. Idea for a suite from Mozart.

30 May. I am working too hard, as though I'm being driven. The straining is unhealthy, and it will probably show in the poor suite. I walked. Worked very successfully (the variations before the finale). After this sat with Bob on the roof (I'd only climb up there for this angel!). After this drank tea and then worked furiously so as to be able to begin something new tomorrow.

31 May. In the morning I wrote a variation. With Bob (the darling!) walked to the cliffs, then joined a boating party, and returned home with him. At Vespers. An evening with dances: I was the pianist. Bob was amused beyond words when I played quadrilles on themes that he gave me. At the end, when everyone had dispersed, Nata [a second cousin of Lev, and much liked by Tchaikovsky], who'd been very thoughtful, suddenly said to me, 'Ah, Petichka, life isn't worth living!' Such words on the lips of so healthy and balanced a person as Nata made a very sad impression on me. In the course of the evening Vera Vasilyevna [who had been in love with Tchaikovsky seventeen years earlier] recalled the past – and apparently with regret. But all that she recalls is personally loathsome to me, and I wouldn't want any of it to return.

1 June. At home I managed to write a variation. Vint after supper, at which I lost seven and a half roubles.

2 June. I worked well today, for I wrote a whole four variations. In the morning I only made a tour of the garden, and afterwards worked, finishing at 12.30 in expectation of Bob, who'd promised to come for a singing lesson, but who disappointed my expectations. Walked about vainly searching for Bob.

3 June. Before dinner Bob came, and I played him my children's songs. After tea was sitting down to work, but Bob lured me away. As soon as I'm working or walking I begin to long for Bob, and feel lonely without him. I love him terribly.

4 June. Worked successfully. *Finished the suite!* Wonderful evening. A rehearsal – *Les femmes savantes* [by Molière]?!!?

5 June. Talked a great deal with Vera Vasilyevna. Either I'm mistaken, or she's not completely changed in her old feelings [towards me]. After supper read Gogol with Bob.

6 June. Worked during the morning on arranging the variations for piano duet.

10 June. Worked on the transcription of the variations.

11 June. Worked on the variations. Got Bob ready for his ride on horseback.

12 June. For two hours after dinner was inseparable from my wonderful, incomparable Bob. At first he lounged about on a bench on the balcony, and was enchantingly *relaxed* and chatted about my compositions.

14 June. Wrote the transcription of the finale. After dinner sat in my study with Bob and talked about school matters.

15 June. A strange thing: I'm terribly reluctant to leave here. I think it's because of Bob.

The Diary contains no further reference to Bob during Tchaikovsky's remaining five days at Kamenka.

———

The above narrative has contained the clearest possible record of how Tchaikovsky's Third Suite for orchestra came into the world, though scoring the piece would take longer, and was not completed until 31 July. It was first performed in St Petersburg on 24 January 1885, directed by the great German pianist and conductor, Hans von Bülow, and it enjoyed an extraordinary success. 'I have never had such a triumph,' Tchaikovsky wrote to his patroness. 'I saw the whole audience was moved, and grateful to me. These moments are the finest adornments of an artist's life. Thanks to these it is worth living and labouring.' He might well have added that this unstinted and unanimous approbation was an endorsement by the wider Russian public of what the Tsar's award had signified. The press were unanimously favourable. The premiere of Tchaikovsky's Second Suite had been conducted by Max Erdmannsdörfer, but Tchaikovsky had not been present, having fled to Western Europe that very evening to recover from the personal strains that had attended the premiere of *Mazeppa* the previous day. Erdmannsdörfer, unsurprisingly, had been upset at this absence, and Tchaikovsky now made amends by giving him the dedication of the new Suite, and personalizing the dedication by using characteristically Germanic musical forms (fugue and chorale) among the variations that constitute the Suite's final movement.

Suite no. 3 in G, for orchestra ****(*)

[Unlike its two predecessors, the Third Suite is not simply a collection of contrasting pieces, but more resembles a symphony in four movements, the first being in sonata form. But it does not aspire to the sophistication and seriousness of the symphony; it is music to entertain, but in the highest sense and of the highest quality, and is unlikely to present any particular challenges to the lay listener, except perhaps in its length – some forty minutes. Nevertheless, there are some points worth drawing out that may interest the more searching listener.]

Each of the suite's movements has a title. The first is headed *Elégie,* but the mood is more reflective than melancholy. Though Tchaikovsky cast it in sonata form, its component parts hardly fulfil their usual roles within the broader structure (e.g., the two subjects are not contrasted, nor does the short development present the complexities or challenges normal in such sections); rather, the sonata pattern provides merely a framework on which Tchaikovsky can span out an almost continuous flow of gracious, rather pastoral melody. The first subject is some three minutes long: there is no transition, and the second subject, about the same length, retains much of the mood of the first. The 'development' does bring a change to the music (chattering woodwind and upward flying scales), and builds powerfully to the recapitulation; here the two subjects are heard in reverse order, and an extensive intervention from the cor anglais braces the coda. As for the following *Valse mélancolique,* this is dark-hued rather than melancholy. Its main theme is one of Tchaikovsky's most sophisticated, and in a ballet it would doubtless have foxed some of the dancers (try whistling it, getting not only the pitches right, but also the lengths of the notes). It is designed as a simple rondo and the two melodies that intersect this thrice-heard theme are more regular; throughout, some of the accompaniments that Tchaikovsky provides are unobtrusively striking.

The following *Scherzo* whisks us into a fascinating world in which orchestral colour and texture are the most striking features, the central section being as stunning for the mercurial slenderness of its material as for the dazzling virtuosity of its *pointilliste* colouring (Laroche saw in this a Lilliputian army, tiny elfin soldiers on parade). I can think of no other piece of music quite like this *Scherzo*; it is certainly one of

Tchaikovsky's most brilliant and enchanting confections. It needs no further pointers from me: just listen to it!

The *Tema con Variazioni* finale is an altogether weightier matter, but never ponderous, and full of surprises. The theme, like that of the Rococo Variations for cello and orchestra, is a Mozartian pastiche, a clear ternary structure, simple and clear in outlines and harmony (the one element that is preserved in every variation is a portion of the theme's opening contour). The first four odd-numbered variations are surely tributes to Erdmannsdörfer's nationality, each being contrapuntal throughout, with the original theme retained intact in the first two of these. In the first variation, the pizzicato strings play this theme while two clarinet–flute pairs work a two-strand counterpoint above; in the third, scored only for woodwind (three flutes, two clarinets and two bassoons), the theme is now at the top for the outer sections, at the bottom for the central one, the other six participants providing a complex six-strand network. The fifth and seventh variations are more explicitly Teutonic, the former a 'heavy' fugato (real German fugues are nothing like as ponderous as this: was this treatment intended as a touch of Tchaikovskyan humour?), the latter turning the theme into a solemn German-mannered chorale (that is, hymn tune), which passes seamlessly into a plangent – and very un-Teutonic – cor anglais cantilena. By contrast, the intervening even-numbered variations have a more familiar Russian tone; mark especially the noisy central portion of variation 4, where the theme, now on loud brass, momentarily turns itself into the famous *Dies irae* plainsong. Variation 9 proves to be a gopak. With the exception of the final polonaise, variation 10 is the longest of the set; it is also introduced by a violin cadenza, this new soloist going on to dominate the following variation, which is a kind of halting waltz. Variation 11 returns us to the original theme, though its very different backing gives it a very different flavour, and it leads into the very portentous preparation for the finale, a splendid, enormously expansive polonaise that was bound to prove an audience rouser – but note in the middle of this, if you can, the tiny allusion to that magical central section of the suite's third movement, the *Scherzo*.

21
Celebrity at Last –
and His Own Home

By now Tchaikovsky was very clear about the kind of home he was seeking. As he wrote to his patroness, whose present resident musician, Wladislaw Pachulski, had offered to help in the search:

> Land is quite unnecessary to me – that is, I want only a modest house with a nice, *but established*, garden. A river is certainly desirable. If there is a wood nearby, so much the better – but I mean, of course, a wood belonging to someone else – for, I repeat, I want to own only a modest house and garden. This dacha or cottage must be completely detached, and not in a row of other dachas and, most of all, it must not be far from a railway station so that *Moscow* is always at hand. The most important and vital condition is that the location should be sympathetic and beautiful. If the house is situated somewhere low down so that there is no view from the windows, then it does not answer my requirements. A factory nearby is also very undesirable. That, I think, is everything.

On leaving Kamenka, Tchaikovsky had joined Modest in Kharkov, then headed for the Konradi estate at Grankino. Here there was peace, fresh air and congenial living, and work proceeded apace: the scoring of the Third Suite was soon completed, as was a translation into Russian of the libretto to Mozart's *The Marriage of Figaro*, and some preliminary sketches were made for a third piano concerto – though, on reflection, Tchaikovsky decided it should be a two-movement concert piece instead. Then, on 1 August, he joined Anatoly and his family at Skabeyevo, near Moscow, where his brother was sharing a villa with Laroche, who was now infected with syphilis, to Anatoly's terror and Tchaikovsky's dismay, for the latter realized it was seriously affecting his friend's mental capacity. Nor was Laroche his only problem friend at that moment. In April Tchaikovsky had attended a performance of Mozart's *Magic Flute* at the Moscow Conservatoire, where the opera had been prepared by Taneyev – or so he claimed angrily – but had been conducted by Albrecht. At the time Tchaikovsky had gently reproached this former pupil for begrudging his older and less publicly esteemed colleague a moment of personal glory, but Taneyev had remained unpersuaded. And so, yet again, Tchaikovsky drew on that tact and understanding which he seemed so often to be able to bring to bear on a problem outside himself. Having emphasized Albrecht's integrity, selflessness and conscientiousness, he then confronted Taneyev's cause of offence in a manner both uncompromising yet disarming:

> Even now the circumstance that you did not conduct doesn't particularly trouble me. Let us suppose you had to do all the *menial work*. But with your love of Mozart there cannot be any menial work when it concerns the performance of one of Mozart's best pieces. And most important: if Albrecht were a bad conductor, capable only of spoiling what you had prepared excellently, then I very likely would have been angry. But the point is that he directed the opera *superbly*. Who, therefore, am I to pity? You, because you were deprived of the pleasure of conducting? But I cannot hide that I would have been even more sorry for Albrecht if, in his present position, being capable and worthy of occupying the conductor's rostrum, he had again for the thousandth time hidden in the shadow behind the scenes. Certainly I cannot deplore the fate of Mozart's opera, for though I do not doubt you would have conducted superbly, Karlusha also conducted superbly.

One senses that, in the right situation, Tchaikovsky could have been a very successful diplomat.

After six weeks with Anatoly, Tchaikovsky would have moved back to Kamenka, but his accommodation there was currently occupied by Anna and her new husband. Meanwhile Lev had journeyed to Paris to see Tanya, and had unexpectedly returned with her. Tchaikovsky, ever mindful of Georges-Léon's welfare, hurriedly dispatched 750 roubles through a trusted agent to the child's foster parents (Lev and Sasha still knew nothing of their grandchild's existence). Since Kamenka was not an option, Tchaikovsky asked his patroness whether he could visit her new country residence at Pleshcheyevo – though not before he had detoured through Moscow in order to introduce Taneyev to the now finished sketch of his Concert Fantasia for piano and orchestra, the solo part of which he hoped his friend would play. As for Pleshcheyevo, he found the house over-grand for his taste, but it was well provided with music and musical instruments, books and wine. He stayed a month, encouraging (with his patroness's consent) Laroche to visit him periodically, partly to play through various piano-duet arrangements, but as much to give his friend an activity that might draw him out of his current indolence as to afford Tchaikovsky himself enjoyment; in addition, he hoped to encourage Laroche back into critical writing. Tchaikovsky was reading much not only in Russian, but in French, German and English; for some weeks now he had been working his way through Dickens's *David Copperfield* in English. He also made the acquaintance of some recent operas of which his patroness had obtained scores, including Musorgsky's *Khovanshchina* and Wagner's *Parsifal*. Neither pleased him. He had not, however, been neglecting his own work, and in early October the Concert Fantasia was completed.

Just as hearing the young violinist, Joseph Kotek, had fired Tchaikovsky to compose his Violin Concerto six years earlier, so (as he had told his patroness back in July) what had fired him to compose his Concert Fantasia was encountering 'a certain d'Albert, a young man who arrived in Moscow last winter, and whom I heard a great deal both in concerts there and in a private house. In my opinion he is a pianist *of genius*, and the true successor of the Rubinsteins.' Though Eugen d'Albert was Italian by descent, he had been born in Glasgow and trained in London, later becoming acquainted with Liszt, and pursuing an international career as a pianist; in his own time he also had a reputation as a composer. Although at first Tchaikovsky thought more highly of d'Albert than of Taneyev as pianist, it was the latter who played in the Fantasia's premiere in Moscow in 1885, Tchaikovsky expressing delight at his performance and at the audience's response. The piece enjoyed some popularity during its composer's lifetime, but that has long faded, and it is normally heard today only in a series in which all Tchaikovsky's works for piano and orchestra are being played. It would seem that Tchaikovsky himself had some reservations about the second movement, and he composed an alternative longer ending to the first movement so that this could be performed separately.

Concert Fantasia: for piano and orchestra * * *(*)

[Though certainly not one of Tchaikovsky's more major pieces, his engaging Concert Fantasia is worth the occasional hearing as an interesting experiment in creating something lying somewhere between Tchaikovsky's two three-movement piano concertos and his single-movement Third Piano Concerto.]

The Concert Fantasia is in two movements labelled, respectively, *Quasi rondo* and *Contrastes*, though the title of the second movement signifies that in it music characteristic of a slow movement is partnered (literally at one point) by very lively, typical 'finale' material. Despite the rondo affiliation indicated by Tchaikovsky's own title, the first movement's structure seems more importantly to fulfil a trend already evidenced in the Second Piano Concerto's first movement. In that earlier work, there had been not one but two written-out cadenzas in the development section; in the present piece, the whole central section is replaced by a single massive piano cadenza some eight minutes long. In the flanking sections the main features of Tchaikovsky's three-theme sonata form are present, the piano–orchestral exposition being built from three thematic slabs of cheery music (any reflection of Tchaikovsky's happy condition after his meeting with the Tsar?) ending in the dominant, and these are recapitulated exactly after the cadenza, but adjusted to end in the home key. As for this movement's rather confusing title, *Quasi rondo*, I can only suggest that Tchaikovsky had in mind the typical lightness of mood in regular rondo movements by Mozart and Beethoven, and that it was the corresponding buoyancy of his music here that prompted this title.

At the opening of *Contrastes* a solo cello soon joins the piano, and the rocking horn motif in the gentle *più tranquillo* orchestral extension will no doubt recall *Romeo and Juliet* for some listeners. Even before the powerful climax to this lengthy section is completed the clarinets and bassoons interpolate a lively figure: the 'contrasting' music is giving warning of its approach. For a while the latter music will become rampant, but the earlier music will abruptly return, restoring the mood in which the movement had opened before the piano reintroduces the livelier music, demonstrating that Tchaikovsky had so devised it that the two musics can, literally, simultaneously co-exist. Then, once again, the lively music is given its head. No further comment seems necessary – except to note the touching re-entry of the *più tran-quillo* orchestral theme before the *vivace* coda opens by momentarily recalling the theme that had launched the whole Concert Fantasia.

––––––––––

On 15 October Tchaikovsky prepared to leave Pleshcheyevo, reshelving the scores and books he had used during his time there, and apologizing profusely to his patroness for a mishap to the big clock in his bedroom; it had stopped, and because Tchaikovsky liked to hear its ticking during the night, he had rewound it himself, but over-vigorously, and it would now need major surgery. His first destination was St Petersburg, where a new production of *Eugene Onegin* was being mounted at the express wish of the Tsar, and his presence was required at the final rehearsals. The opening at the end of the month began well and, despite a generally hostile press, the opera drew full houses every night. News of its ever growing success spread throughout Russia; it was taken up by other opera houses, and fifteen years later Modest would identify this as the moment at which his brother's name 'becomes known and appreciated by the masses, and Pyotr Ilich achieves the highest degree of popularity ever attained by a Russian composer within the borders of his native land'. From this moment, too, Tchaikovsky's personal future was secured.

Nevertheless, this evidence of his standing with the Russian public was currently balanced by anxiety: Kotek was seriously ill with tuberculosis at Davos in Switzerland, and at the first opportunity Tchaikovsky set out to visit him. Pausing in Berlin to benefit from a brief but desperately needed period of peace and freedom after the hectic round of the preceding weeks in St Petersburg, he then headed towards Davos. A gruelling eight-hour trek up the mountains in a one-horse carriage brought him to this attractive town. He suspected that Kotek's condition was really more serious than it appeared to be, and he remained with him for six days before setting out for Paris, where he could visit Georges-Léon who, it proved, was thriving. He would remain a fortnight in the French capital, but was far from completely idle. Reflecting that both *Onegin* and *Mazeppa* were running in St Petersburg, and that a revival of *The Maid of Orleans* was in rehearsal, his thoughts turned to his earlier opera, *Vakula the Smith*. His affection for this charming piece, so fantasy-filled yet so human – and sometimes so funny – remained as strong as ever, and he planned a whole series of revisions which he hoped might gain it more popularity, renaming it *Cherevichki*: it is this version which is normally heard these days.

Returning to St Petersburg from Paris, he arrived in time to bolster Modest's nerves, for the latter's play, *Lizaveta Nikolayevna*, was about to be produced. Tchaikovsky had given his brother much help with this drama during their stay at Grankino, and it had a modestly successful premiere. Tchaikovsky's next stop was with Anna and Nikolay in his patroness's own house, where he found bad news of Kotek awaiting him. A week later he learned of his young friend's death, and took upon himself the task of breaking the news to his parents, a mission so distressing that for three days he could not bring himself to discharge it.

This was the moment at which various circumstances conspired to make even more urgent the need to have a home of his own. This realization began during his stay with the newly-weds. Anna had always had an abrasive personality and been given to acid comments on others, and Tchaikovsky had to listen to a stream of malicious accusations from her against various of their relatives. But now Nikolay was taking his cue from his new wife, even describing his mother, Tchaikovsky's patroness, as 'in essence an unbearable and unbalanced old woman', and traducing his brothers Alexander as 'wicked, vindictive and heartless', Vladimir as 'a scoundrel', and Vladimir's wife as 'a dissolute old hag'. As for Nikolay's sisters, Yuliya was 'an evil virago', Alexandra 'a scandalmonger', and Elizaveta 'an arrant fool'. 'Do you remember that good-natured fellow – the Kolya who used to take photos of members of the family?' Tchaikovsky wrote to Modest after bearing this for a fortnight. 'What has Anna made of him?' He also reflected on the backbiting and spiteful gossip that now polluted the atmosphere at Kamenka. There was no longer any question he could live permanently with any of these.

Then there were the remorseless pressures of his professional life. Checking proofs of his compositions required time and undivided concentration, but he was becoming inundated by a deluge of invitations to visit friends and dine out. If he remained in Moscow he could never escape these. And, finally, he was now a celebrity, at risk from all the pressures this status brought. The public acclamations, so gratifying to his self-esteem and confidence, were also a terrible strain. Just such was the rapturous reception of his Third Suite at its premiere.

Tchaikovsky had returned to St Petersburg especially for the event. 'The weariness afterwards was enormous,' he told his patroness. 'The next day I was like some sick person. I suffer rather than take pleasure in my growing success. I have a wish to hide myself; a thirst for freedom, quiet and solitude prevailed over the feeling of a satisfied artistic self-esteem.' On Tchaikovsky's last day in St Petersburg the Tsar attended a performance of *Onegin*. 'The Tsar wanted to see me, chatted with me for a very long while, was in the highest degree sweet and gracious towards me, with the utmost interest and in the greatest detail enquired about my life and my musical affairs. After this he took me to the Empress, who in her turn showed me the most touching attention.' Before leaving Moscow he had inserted an advertisement in a paper: 'Single gentleman seeks a country dacha to rent.' Now the need was even more pressing.

There was no response to this first advertisement, and for a moment Tchaikovsky decided to abandon further searching and go abroad. But on reflection he knew this would be no permanent solution, and by mid-February 1885 he decided he could wait no longer. 'Yesterday I took an heroic decision, and sent Alexey to rent a dacha which I had heard stood in a beautiful location and was provided with furniture, crockery, and everything that was necessary,' he informed his patroness.

> In a week everything will be ready, and I shall move into my own long-term quarters. The house has a lot of rooms, is extremely well furnished, there is a magnificent park alongside the dacha, and the view from the windows is beautiful. I shall have to live there a year, and if it proves that its upkeep is beyond my means, I shall manage to find something more suitable within that year.

The dacha was at Maidanovo, outside Moscow, and on the railway line to St Petersburg. At first Tchaikovsky found the dacha itself disappointing, but his reservations quickly disappeared. 'What a joy to be in my own home!' he exclaimed to his patroness.

> What a bliss to know that no one will come to interfere with my work, my reading, my walks. Now I understand once and for all that my dream of settling for the rest of my days in the Russian countryside was not a passing whim, but a fundamental requirement of my nature. I've begun receiving newpapers and journals, I

read a lot, I'm enjoying getting on with English, my work's going excellently, I eat, walk and sleep when I want and as much as I want. In a word, *I'm living*!

Here, or nearby, he would pass the rest of his life. His nomad years were over.

THE CELEBRITY YEARS

22

Manfred Symphony
and *The Enchantress*

The name of Balakirev, which had once peppered these pages, has scarcely figured in this narrative since he had coaxed and cajoled Tchaikovsky into composing his first masterpiece, *Romeo and Juliet*. That had been some fifteen years before, but now the relationship was about to be restored. In fact, in the meantime Balakirev had gone through a deep personal crisis. By the early 1870s his grip on a substantial sector of St Petersburg's musical life had been lost, he had suffered a serious bout of self-doubt, and in 1871 had fallen under the spell of a soothsayer who had turned him from a free-thinker into a fanatical, superstitious Christian. Abandoning not only his musical activities, but also withdrawing from the society of his friends, in 1872 he had taken a job on the Russian railways, and for some four years had been lost to Russian music. But then, gradually, he had begun to return to his former milieu. In 1881 Tchaikovsky had had occasion to write to him on a business matter, but it was still 1882 before his old mentor at last made contact with him, praising both *The Tempest* and *Francesca da Rimini* – and, besides expressing a wish to see him, adding that he had 'a programme for a symphony to impart to you which you should handle superbly'. Clearly Balakirev was back on form.

Tchaikovsky had expressed instant interest in Balakirev's unnamed programme, and Balakirev had promptly sent it to him. It was for a four-movement symphony based on Byron's dramatic poem, *Manfred*, and had been devised in 1868 by Vladimir Stasov for Balakirev himself. But the latter had felt it unsuited to him, and turned it down. Now it was Tchaikovsky's turn to reject it for the same reason, which he did emphatically, and there the matter rested for two years. Then, in November 1884, on the occasion of the new St Petersburg production of *Eugene Onegin* ordered by the Tsar – the production that, as we have seen, marked the beginning of Tchaikovsky's true celebrity status – Tchaikovsky and Balakirev had met face to face. After their encounter, Balakirev had written to Tchaikovsky:

Dear Pyotr Ilich,

I am sending you the programme sheet copied out for me by Vladimir Stasov, and furnished with my notes. I sincerely wish and hope that *Manfred* will be one of your pearls.

It was so pleasant for me to talk with you today that, if only it is convenient for you tomorrow, don't refuse to come to the Chapel at the same time (11 o'clock).

By then I shall have arrived and, taking you for a walk, will tell you much that is of great importance which I completely omitted today. I shall be disappointed if anything prevents you giving me a couple of hours during the morning. May Christ preserve you!

Ever yours,
M. BALAKIREV

It is clear that their talk had been of religion. It was a phase during which Christian belief had much preoccupied Tchaikovsky. He had recently read Tolstoy's *Confession*, an autobiographical account of the author's search for the meaning of life, and which had led him to conclude that it was the peasantry whose example showed the way: one must serve God, and not live for oneself. Certainly Tchaikovsky had attended the previous Easter services assiduously, and his religious preoccupation was still strong. 'Every hour and every minute I thank God He has given me faith in Him,' he had written to his patroness at that time – though perhaps what he wrote to his cousin, Anna Merkling, a little later was nearer the truth:

What is needed is not to be afraid of death. In this respect I have no grounds for complacency. I am not so imbued with religion as, with certainty, to see in death the beginning of a new life, not enough a philosopher to reconcile myself to the abyss of non-existence into which I shall have to plunge.

Whatever the real truth about Tchaikovsky's creed, his mood was still such as to make him engage willingly in discourse with a believer like Balakirev. Certainly he had listened attentively, and the following day he replied:

Dear, kind friend,

I was deeply moved by our conversation of yesterday. How good you are! What a *true* friend you are to me! How I wish that that *enlightenment* that has come to your soul would also descend upon mine. I can say in all truth that more than ever I *thirst* for solace and support *in Christ*. I shall pray that faith in Him may be confirmed in me.

It would seem that, within the closeness that the two men had achieved through this very personal encounter, Balakirev had reintroduced the *Manfred* project, and Tchaikovsky had accepted it. But circumstances rendered a further meeting between them impossible, and it seems they had no further discussions. Nevertheless, Tchaikovsky had given a promise, and he would hold to it.

Byron's eponymous hero is a solitary man who has wandered through the Alps, overwhelmed by grief and guilt for what he has done to his former beloved, Astarte. The poem is peopled by supernatural beings, an Abbot who represents the other side of the spiritual equation, and a Chamois Hunter as representative of common humanity. Byron himself had been notorious as a romantic womanizer, and among those to whom he was attracted was his half-sister, Augusta. It was this illicit affair that had prompted *Manfred*, and the wrong his hero had done Astarte ('the only thing he seem'd to love – as he, indeed, by blood was bound to do') was incestuous seduction, as Byron intimated in his verse:

> Thou lovedst me
> Too much, as I loved thee: we were not made
> To torture thus each other, though it were
> The deadliest sin to love as we have loved.

Since then Manfred had roamed the Alps, haunted by guilt – solitary, gloomy, longing in vain to forget his sin. As for Tchaikovsky, he was all too aware of the inner tensions and torments that had arisen from society's views of his own sexuality, and from the sense of isolation, even rejection, that this can bring. Certainly the figure of Manfred gripped him; here was another outsider in a kind of predicament he himself had known and could understand only too well.

Tchaikovsky could not begin work immediately, for his visit to the dying Kotek in Switzerland was still to come, and it was only in April

1885, after he had settled into Maidanovo, that he could at last start composition. While in Switzerland he had read Byron's *Manfred*, and he now had before him not only Stasov's 1868 programme, but also some specifications from Balakirev and a list of 'helpful materials' that Balakirev thought would prime Tchaikovsky's inspiration in each of the symphony's four movements.

If we are to take literally some of the remarks Tchaikovsky jotted down on his sketches for the *Manfred Symphony*, it proved hard going. '25 May – but before the end a very great deal still needs to be done . . . Today is 18 July, but I still haven't got very far . . . And today's 12 August – and, oh, how far it is to the end.' In fact, despite these gloomy asides, his overall confidence in the piece had been quietly rising and, even before its completion, he was extracting a promise from his friend, the soprano Emiliya Pavlovskaya, who had created the part of Mariya in *The Oprichnik*, that she would attend its premiere: 'I'm very proud of this work, and I want those persons whose sympathy I value most in the world (and you are in the first rank of these) to experience, when they hear it, an echo from the joy with which I wrote it.' Inevitably, when he informed Balakirev of the work's completion, his old self-appointed guru had asked to see the piano-duet transcription so that he could suggest improvements. Tchaikovsky had flatly refused to send it.

The *Manfred Symphony* was first heard in Moscow in March 1886. It had been very well rehearsed and the performance was excellent. 'The first movement proved undoubtedly the best,' Tchaikovsky wrote to Balakirev:

> The scherzo was taken very quickly, and when I heard it I did not experience disenchantment as I frequently have [with such movements because of their technical difficulties]. The *Andante* doesn't sound bad. The finale gains *very much* in performance, and proved to be the most effective movement *with the audience*. I think it's my best symphonic work, though because of its difficulty, impracticability and complexity it is doomed *to failure, and to be ignored.*

The *Manfred Symphony* was, in fact, the most extended and challenging orchestral piece he had ever written, demanding the largest complement of players. Recognizing that it would not be frequently performed, Tchaikovsky offered it to Jurgenson free of charge. Yet before the year was out it had been played three times in St Petersburg – and had even reached New York.

Manfred Symphony: (after Byron) * * * * *

[*This is a truly major piece, and a demanding one. The music is often very tough, the first movement completely original in its form, the second containing music at the opposite extreme: diaphanous, seemingly insubstantial, but brilliantly original and absolutely right. Only the finale raises questions about its coherence – but each listener can form an independent opinion about this.*]

Stasov's programme for the *Manfred Symphony* had been suggestive of mood and manner, with only minimal prescriptions on musical matters:

First movement: Manfred wandering in the Alps. His life is broken, his obsessive, fateful questions remain unanswered; in life nothing remains for him except memories. From time to time *memories of his ideal, Astarte*, creep in upon him. Memories, thoughts burn, gnaw at him. He seeks and begs for oblivion, but no one can give him this.

Second movement: The way of life of the Alpine hunters, full of simplicity, good nature, and of a naive, patriarchal character, with which Manfred clashes, affording a sharp contrast. This is a quiet idyllic *Adagio* incorporating Manfred's theme which, like an *idée fixe*, must infiltrate the whole symphony.

Third movement: The Alpine Fairy appearing to Manfred in a rainbow from the waterfall's spray.

Fourth movement: A wild, unbridled *Allegro*, full of savage audacity. Scene in the subterranean halls of the infernal Arimanes. Further on there follows the arrival of Manfred, arousing a general outburst from the subterranean spirits – and finally the *summons and appearance of Astarte* will present a lovely contrast to this unbridled orgy: *this must be music light, limpid* as the air, and ideal. Further on the diablerie comes again, finishing *Largo* – Manfred's death.

To this Balakirev appended his own list of 'helpful materials':

For the first and last movements: *Francesca da Rimini* by Tchaikovsky; *Hamlet* by Liszt; finale from *Harold in Italy* by

Berlioz; preludes in E minor, E flat minor, and C sharp minor (no. 25: separate from the others) by Chopin. For the *Larghetto*: *Adagio* from the *Symphonie fantastique* by Berlioz. For the scherzo: *Queen Mab* from *Romeo and Juliet* by Berlioz; scherzo (B minor) from the Third Symphony by Tchaikovsky.

Those already familiar with Berlioz's four-movement symphonies, the *Symphonie fantastique* and *Harold in Italy*, will recognize how influential had been their existence on the programme Stasov had prepared from Byron's *Manfred*, and all readers will see how crucial, in its turn, was Stasov's programme for Tchaikovsky when he came to compose his *Manfred Symphony*; his truly major change was to reverse the order of the second and third movements. Tchaikovsky's preface to his own first movement is explicit in what it represents: 'Manfred wanders in the Alps, tormented by fateful pangs of doubt, rent by remorse and despair, his soul the victim of nameless suffering.' Its embodiment is presented in five extensive musical slabs, spaced out by four silences. The brooding first theme, briefly unharmonized, then partnered by a succession of gruff detached chords from the lower strings as it descends to darker regions, projects Manfred himself, and its opening two bars will resurge almost unchanged in all the symphony's later movements as the surrogate of this fated, tormented man. This is music both spacious and monolithic, and a second Manfred theme for strings promptly consolidates this portrait, the tiny, nagging figure in the hushed passage that follows suggestive, perhaps, of Manfred's guilt-ridden obsession. A powerful *crescendo*, an abrupt and brief silence – and this whole section is repeated at a different level to provide the second musical slab, but this time pushing forward to the loudest climax Tchaikovsky had ever composed: this past, the whole section is rounded off by the opening theme's earlier descent into darker regions, fading finally into a second and clearly inconclusive silence.

My prose here has been heightened, but what I have just described is the most powerful and uncompromising musical span Tchaikovsky had yet created – a magnificent projection of a truly formidable, tough figure, now enduring an anguish that even he can scarcely bear. But the Manfred of the third musical slab seems calmer, though still strong: there may be a persistent restlessness in the accompaniment, but the second Manfred theme develops a new breadth, and the climax to which it builds has power in plenty, but none of the frenzy that had marked some of the earlier music, though the loud, repetitious ending sounds stunned – and rightly so, for the third silence marks the appearance of Astarte's ghost.

If what we have heard so far has contained some of Tchaikovsky's toughest music, what we now hear is some of his loveliest and most deeply felt. As with Tatyana, Joan and Mariya in his three last operas, for Tchaikovsky Astarte was a young woman who had become the victim of Fate, and as with these predecessors, she drew from Tchaikovsky music of a special quality and, in her case, tenderness. At first seemingly frail and hesitant, her utterance gains a breadth and intensity that is proportionate but which, even at its peak, never compromises the vulnerability that Manfred has abused. Even more gently does Astarte's music finally fade into the fourth silence.

Confronted with such eloquence, Manfred's emotional defences are breached. No longer able to contain his pain and grief, his opening music returns; violins, violas and cellos now deliver his main theme in unison and *ffff* against powerful but irregular throbbing from the rest of the orchestra, and all culminates in a climax every bit as frenetic as anything heard earlier. This time there is no dying end; as in *Romeo and Juliet*, a series of savagely abrupt chords will finally impel this movement to the most unmitigated of conclusions.

Some two years later Tchaikovsky, now able to review the *Manfred Symphony* with detachment, came to a disconcerting conclusion; he condemned the middle two movements as poor, the finale as loathsome, and declared that, if Jurgenson agreed, he would destroy them. Yet, he wrote, he would retain this first movement, 'making a symphonic poem out of a symphony that is impossibly long-winded. Then I am sure my *Manfred* will be capable of pleasing. Indeed, it must be so: I wrote the first movement with enjoyment – the remaining ones are the result of straining from which, I remember, I felt myself for some time very unwell.' Certainly this verdict confirms his pride in this first movement. Fortunately Tchaikovsky never carried out this threat – for which, I think, our thanks can never be too numerous.

For very different reasons the scherzo is equally remarkable. Its content is simple: 'The Alpine Fairy appears before Manfred in a rainbow,' as Tchaikovsky headed it. His concern in recent years to explore fresh possibilities in orchestration had enabled him to present his music with new colours and more refined contrasts, but though the music may have been adjusted especially to make the exploitation of these possible, it had still been made from tunes and harmonies as before. In the *Manfred* scherzo, however, the priorities are almost reversed, for it is no longer the orchestration that conditions the music; it is the orchestration that creates the music as though Tchaikovsky has thought directly in terms of colours and textures, and made these the priorities when spinning the web of sound. Put in the simplest terms: there is no tune, little definition of any harmonic base – at most, the tiniests of melodic fragments and the lightest film of harmony, and where such things do slip in, they quickly melt away. Like magic, it moves us into a world that is alluring, fragile and elusive, and it makes for magical listening. The point is brought home when a 'real' tune enters to fill out the movement's central section – surely the Alpine Fairy's musical incarnation. The contrast is perfectly judged, and this new melody will in due course be partnered by Manfred's surrogate, which now takes its character from its graceful companion (note also, if you can, the tiny slivers of scherzo music that slip in). And if a little later, when the movement's rainbow music is about to return, Manfred's theme returns far less graciously, it will sound almost wistful when it slips in at the movement's end while the Alpine Fairy is flickering upwards, only to disappear.

The slow movement brings us gently but firmly back into the human world: 'A pastoral. The simple, free and peaceful life of the mountain people' was Tchaikovsky's label. Balakirev had prescribed Berlioz's *Adagio* (the *Scène aux champs* from the *Symphonie fantastique*) to be Tchaikovsky's model here, but it is more the *Sérénade* from *Harold in Italy* that Tchaikovsky chose. It opens with a siciliana, a gentle, tripping dance which had long been composers' choice when portraying a pastoral world. Further on a hunter is heard, his three-note horn call set against a single, sustained woodwind chord (when this is heard for the third and last time towards the movement's end, note the very simple, but very beautiful progression of string chords that now supports it). The opening theme returns – and then we hear a snatch of (presumably) a lively peasant dance, and an agitated outburst (a heavy shower?) before the opening melody is again resumed. A rapidly oscillating (and accelerating) three-note figure from the flutes, joined by a high trill from the first violins (bird calls?) introduces the movement's second main theme, its more restless mood increasing in preparation for Manfred's intrusion. But the latter's impact on this bucolic world is brief and minimal: the earlier mood is recovered, the hunter is heard a second time, and the opening pastoral theme returns more spaciously and in a fuller, more decorated scoring. Manfred's intrusion has left no mark, normality has returned, Manfred is forgotten. The hunter, now distant, sounds his horn, the little peasant dance recurs, and a tiny scampering, muted-string interlude precedes the final fading chord that supports echoes of the movement's opening tune. It makes a charming ending to a charming movement.

If only . . . *if only* Tchaikovsky's finale had consistently matched the achievement of the preceding three magnificent movements, then the *Manfred Symphony* would have been an unchallenged equal of any of Tchaikovsky's other great symphonic pieces. The problem is not really the music itself; it is the programme. 'Arimanes' underground palace,' so Tchaikovsky's note reads. 'Manfred appears in the middle of a bacchanale. Evocation of Astarte's ghost. She predicts an end to his earthly sufferings. Death of Manfred.' So far Tchaikovsky has very successfully reconciled the extramusical specifications for each movement with the basic requirement that a musical structure shall be satisfactory in itself. Now, however, the programme takes over, and the result is a fragmented movement with musical disruption and non sequiturs that culminate in what, I suppose, Tchaikovsky felt was an obligatory ending: an apotheosis of Manfred himself (with organ), achieved by a grandiose Germanic-style chorale tune (how much better did Tchaikovsky manage such an episode towards the end of *Romeo and Juliet*!). In fact, the final dying end does improve matters, but it cannot totally redeem the situation.

Yet the problem had begun much earlier, and much more seriously. The movement had opened so promisingly. The bacchanal is vividly conjured at length, the impact of Manfred's abrupt intrusion is well caught in music that conveys the dislocation it causes and the bated breath with which the horde views this strange intruder. Manfred identifies himself with his second theme – all this is very well handled. But heaven only knows why Tchaikovsky should have chosen a fugue to convey the horde's response to Manfred, once they had recovered from their initial surprise (but perhaps a fugue's 'learned' character would suggest that the horde were holding a debate on the matter. I doubt it!). A fugue is, by its very nature, totally undramatic, implacably inward-searching in its fixation on one thematic idea (its subject), and remorselessly measured in its progress: in this context, it cannot sound other than stodgy – which it does. It is *the* fatal flaw of the symphony, from which it can never subsequently recover completely, for all the resumption of the orgy, followed by Astarte's entrance (to her first-movement music, but now with harp washes and the incorporation of new material), Manfred's response, then a return of his music which had closed the first movement. But there follows an overblown apotheosis: too much gesture, too little true substance. However, some listeners may feel I have been too harsh. I leave it to them to decide.

If the first three movements had not been so marvellous, I suppose I would not have felt so harshly about aspects of the finale; my words were written in sorrow, not anger. But setting my reservations aside, I would agree that the *Manfred Symphony* is an achievement as fine as anything Tchaikovsky had composed before the intervention of Antonina. He was fully himself again, truly back on form.

There is a rather sad tailpiece to the *Manfred* episode. Tchaikovsky retained an immense respect and affection for Balakirev. 'He's a strange man – between ourselves, be it said, a *madman* – but all the same, essentially a wonderful person,' as he put it to Jurgenson. And this was, after all, the man who had prompted and then, to a degree, shepherded the *Manfred* project. But Balakirev had already prescribed what Tchaikovsky's next work should be ('a piano concerto in F sharp minor or C sharp minor'), and Tchaikovsky saw the danger that could lie ahead if he was not careful. He did meet Balakirev in 1886, but though the latter pressed him to visit whenever he might find himself in St Petersburg, Tchaikovsky seems to have avoided a meeting. In 1891 they exchanged their last very brief and very businesslike notes. Their relationship proved to be over.

The move to Maidanovo transformed fundamentally Tchaikovsky's personal life. Modest's detailed account of his brother's new environment gives us many insights into aspects of his daily life, telling us a good deal more about his more mundane attitudes and his day-to-day activities than we have been able to glean from the evidence of his letters or the memories of others who knew him, corroborating things we have noted from his earlier words, but filling these out with some fascinating detail. Tchaikovsky hated change. 'From this time traditions were established for a particular arrangement of his things, an arrangement that was preserved as far as possible through every change of residence so that, wherever Pyotr Ilich was living, the appearance of his rooms remained almost the same,' Modest remembered. He had no interest in luxuries, in style, or in appearances, did not complain that a table rocked, that a cupboard did not close properly, or that a curtain was made of inferior material – though he was very proud of having 'his own cook, his own laundress, his own silver, his own tablecloth, his own dog'. Alexey had been with him so long that he knew 'what the master would like', and he not only organized Tchaikovsky's day-to-day existence, but was even left the responsibility for such things as choosing the furniture. The only things that Tchaikovsky really cherished were his books and musical scores, having them re-bound where necessary, and chasing up books friends had borrowed but not returned promptly.

Modest described a typical Tchaikovsky day at Maidanovo, both confirming and amplifying what we have learned from his earlier record. His brother would get up between seven and eight, drink tea between eight and nine, and – perhaps surprisingly – would read the Bible, then occupy himself with English. He also read books in German – for instance, Otto Jahn's *Mozart*, and philosophical works by such as Spinoza and Schopenhauer. During this he would consult the dictionary and write out the words he did not know. If he had a guest there would be a morning walk together, and he would spend the rest of the day in routine matters such as writing letters, proof-reading, or orchestrating a piece. But if he was composing, he demanded absolute privacy. The only person he would tolerate near him during such a phase was Alexey, whom he could simply 'shut out', even if he was in the room. But there must be no conversation; on the one occasion when his servant had ventured a comment (highly favourable) on a chorus from *Onegin*, Tchaikovsky was not only surprised but distressed. As Modest put it:

> He was enormously gratified that this was the first and only moment of illumination in the impenetrable night of his servant's musicality. It seems that the most important luxury of Pyotr Ilich's new situation was precisely the solitude it provided during this compositional phase – and if not the sole, was certainly the chief adornment of his stay at Maidanovo.

Modest added that, whereas in his brother's early years he would show a piece he was composing to others, inviting their opinions, 'from 1885 he ceased almost completely revealing his new works to anyone, the first person to get to know them being Jurgenson's engraver'.

If the morning was free of other pressures, from 9.30 to midday was devoted to composition.

At twelve precisely Pyotr Ilich would have lunch at which, thanks to his splendid appetite, he found whatever was given to him to have been excellently prepared, being profuse in his praises of the chef or cook, and requiring Alexey to convey to them his gratitude with a request to have it as well prepared more often. But because, in regard of his cuisine, the master of the house was very undemanding, it happened that guests would often have preferred to convey not compliments to the kitchen, but the contrary. Pyotr Ilich always ate with pleasure, but very abstemiously, especially when he was alone. After lunch he went for a walk, whatever the weather. For the most part his walk was a time of composition. During it the embryos of the principal ideas were formed, consideration was given to the skeleton of the work, and the noting down of the principal ideas took place. The next morning he would place these sketches before him and would put the finishing touches to them at the piano. As far as I know, except for two scenes in *Onegin* and some of his piano pieces and romances, he always developed his sketches at the piano, during which time, because he could not trust his appalling memory, he wrote down everything, even in places indicating the instrumentation. For the most part a composition was fully worked out in these sketches.

Modest remembered that if, during his walks, music was not Tchaikovsky's preoccupation, then he might improvise (in French) pieces from plays. Tchaikovsky was fascinated by insects, especially ants, and observed them carefully. He would give generous tips to children he encountered, but this would produce a problem, for the numbers of these youngsters soon began swelling. To evade them he tried walking in the more secluded woods, but now increasing numbers of children began emerging from among the trees. Next their parents got the message. In fact, the situation became so bad that for a while Tchaikovsky had to confine his two-hour walk to the private park at Maidanovo.

'Towards four o'clock Pyotr Ilich returned home for tea,' Modest continued:

If he was alone he read the papers, historical journals, and if anyone was staying with him he very much liked to chat. From five until seven he again went off by himself to work. Before supper (which was served at eight) Pyotr Ilich would, if it was summer, take yet another walk to admire the sunset: this time he would very readily take it in company. In autumn or winter he would play the piano by himself for his own pleasure or, if Laroche or Kashkin (his favourite guests) was staying with him, music for four hands. After supper he would sit with his guests until eleven. When partners were available he loved three or four rubbers of vint, and when they were not, he greatly loved being read to aloud. His favourite reader was Laroche, not because he possessed some particular skill but because, when he read, his delight in what he was experiencing was expressed in every phrase, especially when the book was by Gogol or Flaubert. If there were no guests Pyotr Ilich for the most part read historical works about the late eighteenth and early nineteenth centuries, played patience, but always found himself a little restless. At eleven he went off to his room, wrote his diary, and again read for a long time before going to sleep. Since the summer of 1866 [when he had brought himself close to complete nervous collapse through over-work on his First Symphony] he had never composed a single note in the evening.

Tchaikovsky's first task on settling into Maidanovo had been to make the revision that would turn *Vakula the Smith* into *Cherevichki*, the form of that opera which is normally performed today. This completed, he had devoted the middle months of 1885 to the *Manfred Symphony*. Yet these were far from the only significant matters to absorb his attention during this time. Tchaikovsky had now been appointed a Director of the Moscow branch of the RMS, and this required him to share in the annual examinations at the Conservatoire in late May. Nor was this the only chore he felt bound to undertake during his three weeks in Moscow. His new celebrity status had brought with it an added authority which was no doubt valuable when he intervened in the chaos into which the Moscow Conservatoire had descended since Rubinstein's death four years earlier. The successive directorships of Hubert and Albrecht had been disastrous, and back in April Tchaikovsky had made an appeal to Rimsky-Korsakov, an outsider and therefore impartial, to accept the position.

But Rimsky had declined, and the young Taneyev, though not yet thirty, had seemed to Tchaikovsky the obvious choice. Accordingly, he applied all his diplomatic skills to placating the two former directors, persuading them to remain on the staff, while at the same time urging Taneyev's nomination, which was finally agreed. Nor, on a very personal level, was he inactive, for his friend Kondratyev and his wife had agreed on a separation, but this had proved quite unmanageable, the result being that Tchaikovsky devoted four whole days to bringing a resolution to this sad, very human problem. As for the Conservatoire, he would still have to remain active, for Taneyev was detained abroad, and in the new Director's absence Tchaikovsky set himself to recruit new staff, including the young pianist and conductor, Vasily Safonov, who would become one of the institution's finest teachers, succeeding Taneyev as Director in 1889, and doing much to increase its prestige both through his growing personal reputation as a teacher, and through his energetic leadership.

All this had been unfolding while Tchaikovsky had been engaged on the *Manfred Symphony*, and these distractions were no doubt a major reason why progress on this piece had proved so laborious. But by late August a very wearied Tchaikovsky had been able to settle back into Maidanovo, and visits from his closer friends had begun to revitalize him. Then, during a five-day trip he had made to Moscow in late September, Alexey had supervised their removal to a more pleasant and secluded dacha at Maidanovo, a move that delighted Tchaikovsky. His guests were now becoming confined to weekend visits, his life was growing less hectic, and the *Manfred Symphony* was brought to a swift conclusion. Five days later he could start work on his eighth opera, *The Enchantress*.

Tchaikovsky had first encountered Ippolit Shpazhinsky's drama *The Enchantress* in the preceding January, had been immediately drawn to it, and had written to its author suggesting he might convert it into an opera libretto. But Shpazhinsky, despite giving ready assent to Tchaikovsky's proposal, had proved a very sluggish collaborator, for his day-to-day life was distracted by divorce proceedings. As a result it was six months before Tchaikovsky received a first portion of the libretto, and because Shpazhinsky remained appallingly dilatory, the opera could not be fully sketched until August 1886, by which time Tchaikovsky had realized that its length had to be radically reduced (even in its final form it remains the longest of his compositions). Nor was this all, for in the meantime the Empress had requested him to compose and dedicate a set of songs to her, and he had to divert his attention to composing his Twelve Romances, op. 60, as well as supervising the production of *Cherevichki*, which he had agreed to conduct. This in itself would have been a formidable challenge, for his first sorties into conducting while still a student had proved traumatic; feeling his head might roll off his shoulders, he had habitually clutched his chin with his left hand while conducting with his right, and since then he had never repeated the experience. However, at the opera's premiere in January 1887, he kept a grip on himself, and subsequently conducting would play a more and more important part in his musical life, especially because he realized that this would ensure that his own compositions would receive more performances.

This deluge of distractions had impinged drastically on the fortunes of *The Enchantress*, and the opera was not finished until May 1887. Its premiere was given on 1 November (Tchaikovsky again conducting), and though he was generally well satisfied with the performance, and the final applause suggested that the opera was a success, audiences soon began to fall off, and after the twelfth performance it was withdrawn from the repertoire.

Briefly, the plot of *The Enchantress*, a tragic love story, runs as follows. Nastasya (nickamed Kuma, and the 'enchantress' of the tale) has an inn on the banks of the River Oka. Prince Nikita visits the inn, falls for Kuma, but she rejects him. When his wife, Princess Evpraksiya, hears of this, she is violently jealous, and when their son, Prince Yury, learns of the situation, he swears to kill Kuma. But meeting her, Yury is overwhelmed by her beauty and seeming innocence, falls passionately in love with her, she with him, and they plan to elope. Learning of this, the Princess decides to poison Kuma, proceeds to meet a Wizard who will supply the necessary potion, then encounters Kuma as the latter arrives to flee with Yury. The Princess tricks Kuma into drinking the poison, Yury enters as Kuma dies, and he denounces his mother. His father appears, Yury denounces him too, and is stabbed to death. The Princess throws herself on her son's body, is borne away and, to the sound of a gathering storm and the Wizard's maniacal laughter, Prince Nikita goes mad.

It must seem incredible that Tchaikovsky could ever have been attracted to such a contrived and, by its end, ridiculous plot. But that his perceived view of it was very different is uncovered in his letters to Emiliya Pavlovskaya, whom he hoped would create the part of Kuma, but who had herself expressed doubts about the wisdom of Tchaikovsky's choice of subject, and about the implausibility of his heroine managing to turn the young prince into a passionate and devoted lover. Tchaikovsky responded by claiming that, though Kuma's most obvious charms were the mundane ones that ensured success for her hostelry, she also possessed other far higher qualities:

> The point is that in the depths of the soul of this loose country woman is a *moral force and beauty* that had merely had no place in which it could declare itself. *That force is love.* Her nature is strongly feminine, capable of falling in love only once and for ever, and of giving up *everything* for the sake of that love. While *love* was no more than an embryo, Nastasya had disposed of her *power* lightly – that is, she had amused herself with what made one and all who came across her fall in love with her. In this she is simply an engaging, attractive, though also depraved, country woman. She knows she is *captivating*, she is content with this knowledge, and having been enlightened neither by religious belief nor education while she was an orphan, she has made her sole mission in life to live gaily. But the man appears who is destined to touch her *instincts'* better strings which till then had remained silent, and she is transformed. Life becomes *nothing* for her unless she attains her goal; *the power of her attractiveness*, which before had functioned instinctively, now becomes an invincincible weapon which in an instant demolishes the alien power – that is, the *hatred* of the young prince. After this both surrender to the ungovernable torrent of their love which leads to inevitable catastrophe, to her *death*, and this death leaves in the spectator a sense of reconciliation and tenderness.
>
> Since being tempted by *The Enchantress* I have remained completely faithful to my soul's fundamental need to illustrate in music what Goethe [in his *Faust*] said: 'Das Ewig-Weibliche zieht uns hinan.' ['The Eternal in woman leads us on.']

But Tchaikovsky's attempt to equate Kuma with the ideal of Marguerite, who had saved Faust's soul in Goethe's great epic, was ludicrous. Kuma was Kuma – and that was that. Clearly what led to the opera's ultimate failure was the realization by Tchaikovsky's audiences that the opera had no true dramatic heart, and that the characters of the participants were as hollow and generally as uninteresting as the events into which they were caught in Shpazhinsky's libretto. Yet Tchaikovsky's music is often a very different matter. Most of it is at least very good, and the best excellent. In fact, Act 1 is quite splendid – well planned and paced, and of a very consistent quality. Yet more impressive still is the love scene in Act 3, which is not a conventional operatic celebration of a confessed love, but traces in detail the stages of the process in which Kuma converts Prince Yury, who has come to kill her, into her passionate and committed lover. It is so sad that *The Enchantress* should have become the inevitable casualty of its creator's misjudgement of his chosen subject, and though the opera has received a very occasional revival in more recent years, it will never become a repertoire piece. Nevertheless, for those who remain interested in getting to know the opera, especially the finer parts, I have provided the following guide.

The Enchantress: opera in four acts * * *(*)

[This is perhaps the saddest case among all Tchaikovsky's major works: an abundance of excellent music saddled with an unworthy subject. Classifying it has been very difficult. I did originally give it a three-star grading, but having returned to it after a long period, I find its general musical quality so high that I have upgraded it and allocated it more generous space. Those readers who are utterly committed to Tchaikovsky's music and can tolerate the more ludicrous aspects of the drama should listen to it in its entirety; others should pass on. Because of the opera's length I have, in this instance, conflated the musical commentary with the outline of the plot.]

Overture: This is in two sections, the first based on Kuma's touching aria in the middle of Act 1, the second on a Russian folksong.

Act 1: This is by far the most consistent of the four acts, and is particularly interesting because Tchaikovsky goes back to the self-consciously Russian idiom he had employed in the earlier 1870s (notably in his Second Symphony and *Vakula the Smith*), but rarely returned to subsequently. The first scene is set on the banks of the Volga where Kuma has her hostelry. The musical idiom is festive and folky, though we learn that Kuma is alleged to be a witch and that this will be bad for her with Prince Nikita. The revellers pause for a moment as the sound of women's voices marks the approach of a group of girls with Kuma, who soon establishes herself as the centre of attention, but is warned that a dry, elderly deacon, Mamïrov, is planning to bring Prince Nikita to see for himself the iniquities of Kuma and her companions. A second group, male guests this time, arrive in boats, soon church bells from the city across the river are briefly heard, and after some further exchanges, Kuma sings a very contrasting song in praise of 'our benefactress, mother Volga', based on the two themes of the overture. Prince Yury appears on the river with a hunting party, but cannot spare the time to land (but his appearance has served to introduce him to us, and for Kuma's agitation to reveal that she is already attracted to him). Suddenly Prince Nikita is seen approaching. There is consternation: some revellers flee, but Kuma takes control, and orders that a table be set for him. This has brought a total change of mood, and the stern string theme that introduces Nikita instantly defines him as a very formidable figure. Mamïrov lists the evils of the place, but Kuma parries by saying that Nikita can judge about these for himself. Faced with the accusation of sorcery, Kuma denies this with quiet dignity, and invites Nikita to be her guest. He assents, praises her for her wine, and throws a ring into his cup.

All this has been excellently paced. But now a decimet intervenes – a corporate and static movement for all ten solo singers, each voicing his or her private reaction to what has now transpired, the chorus also providing some backing. Obviously only fragments from any of the ten texts will ever be heard, but that scarcely matters: rather, the movement serves as a breathing space in the drama before the act's last phase, the bating of Mamïrov, is played out. The Prince is now enamoured of Kuma, and she offers the hapless deacon wine. Then Kuma suggests a vigorous tumblers' dance in which, at Kuma's prompting, the Prince finally orders the deacon to join. Mamïrov's humiliation is complete.

The tone changes sharply with Act 2. The setting is now the garden of Prince Nikita's house, and the main concerns of the act are the individual members of the royal family and their problems. The Princess comes first, the orchestral introduction presenting the opening snatch of her main theme which then recurs obsessively in a variety of guises and within an increasingly tempestuous context before declaring itself in full: this woman is clearly tormented and furious, tough and resolute,

another in Tchaikovsky's line of matronly women whose natural vulnerability is matched by resolve and a seemingly prodigious power of
endurance (think of the Boyarina in *The Oprichnik*, or Kochubey's
wife, Lyubov, in *Mazeppa*: note that the latter, too, had a chorus of
attendant women). Mamïrov enters to tell of the Princess's husband's
visits to Kuma, and she enjoins him to be her eyes and ears. She will
have no truck with her maid's attempt to calm and comfort her: Kuma
must die. Yury now enters, and the music that accompanies him –
leisurely in tempo, calm in mood – reflects his own relaxed mood. His
mother tries to hide her troubled state, but then discloses that she and
his father have chosen a bride for him. He brushes that aside: he is
more troubled by his father's irascibility and his mother seeming so
preoccupied. In her turn she tries to brush this aside and, their conversation ending inconclusively, before she leaves they join in an
extended duet of mutual devotion. Outwardly it is untroubled: 'God
grant that we shall live in happiness!' – but it is also a powerful foil for
the turbulence to come.

Paisy, a drunken vagabond monk, and a frequenter of Kuma's
hostelry, enters, tries to ingratiate himself with Yury (note how many
chains of repeated notes there are in his part – a legacy from the
trails of repeated notes so characteristic of religious chants?), but is
interrupted by Mamïrov's entry. Yury leaves, and Mamïrov orders
Paisy to be his spy at Kuma's hostelry. Paisy leaves (to fidgety music)
and, alone, Mamïrov vents his anger at Nikita for having made a
fool of him at Kuma's. Nikita enters (again to strings playing in
octaves, though now his music is restless and troubled). Ordering
Mamïrov to summon the Princess, he gives voice to his own torn
feelings and the distress he has caused his wife because of his continuing inability to forget Kuma. A piece of her own music marks the
Princess's re-entry. The confrontation that follows is the most
formidable of the act. Nikita tries to talk about other matters, but
his wife gets straight to the point, accusing and reproaching him,
revealing at length the full force and sheer strength of her personality.
It is a most impressive performance. Nikita tries to browbeat her, but
without success, and finally threatens to confine her to a religious cell.
There can be no reconciliation here, and they end by rushing out in
opposite directions.

An orchestral interlude prefaces the forced intervention of a
group of peasants to complain that Prince Nikita's servants have

been robbing them. This is the first really weak moment in the plot (but not in the music), clearly a contrived incursion as much to introduce some variety into a relatively unpeopled act as to demonstrate the authority and respect that Yury commands with the peasantry. The instant he appears the intruders fall respectfully silent, he tells them to go back home, and they leave. The Princess emerges and reproves Yury for having intruded into a matter that was his father's business, asks where her husband is, and Paisy reveals that he is at Kuma's. At last Yury hears the truth and, once he has fully digested it, his music assumes a more martial tone. Perhaps, after all the furious agitation of the Princess's music in her earlier exchanges with her husband, we may feel some surprise at the stability and absence of manifest agitation in some of her final utterances, but by this stage what I can only call 'the ecstasy of transcendental hatred' has possessed her. She has a champion, and her rival's death is certain.

Kuma has not appeared in the second act, but in the third she is the dominant player. The location is her modest cottage, and the scene's opening has a corresponding sense of intimacy. The introductory music is hers, as is confirmed when it provides the basis for her first words. With her is Prince Nikita, deeply depressed by her lack of response; he is now the supplicant – and how different is his tone at this scene's opening from that of the authoritarian figure of Act 1! He pleads his case, but in vain, and she confesses she loves another. He demands who his rival is, but she will not say. There is little need of comment from me on what immediately follows. Kuma plays on her vulnerability in the face of his power, but when finally Prince Nikita attempts to take her by force, she draws a knife, threatening to kill herself. In a rage he leaves and a brief orchestral interlude changes the mood drastically. Alone, Kuma reflects on what the reaction would be if her love for Yury becomes known, but her reverie is interrupted by the agitated entry of her friend, Polya, and her uncle, Foka, with news that Yury believes her to be a witch and has sworn to kill her. Having told her to secure her cottage, they leave. It is a moonlit night, and Kuma spies two men outside. In terror she retreats to her bed, and closes its curtain. Yury enters with Zhuran, a huntsman, draws his knife, and pulls back the curtain.

And so begins what Tchaikovsky himself described as the '*most important* scene of the opera' – and which makes a truly splendid ending to Act 3. It is a love scene, and it traces an evolving situation.

Shpazhinsky had paid particular attention to its construction. 'I am offering you the possibility, through your lovely music, of conveying our heroes' feelings through nine motifs,' he explained to Tchaikovsky. And the latter responded magnificently. Because a full appreciation of this scene's effect requires a fairly detailed awareness of each of these successive stages, I have presented it through a table, indicating where each 'motif' (as Shpazhinsky put it) begins by a snippet of translation. It is probable that these snippets will not, in your libretto, use the exact language of mine, but I hope that where they come can be identified. As heard in the opera, the scene seems to me more readily to encompass ten stages, but perhaps Shpazhinsky viewed the final celebration of committed love as being beyond the system.

Orchestra: Violent *tutti* – Yury sees Kuma for the first time

1 Kuma: Disingenuous innocence – 'Where are you going, Prince . . . ?'
  Yury: Embarrased accusation

2 Kuma: Gentle mockery – 'That's not all: I gave the Prince a potion . . .'
  Yury: Warning
  Kuma: Desire to explain

3 Kuma: Self-justification 1 (defiant tone: the peasant girl) – 'Woe to you! In this matter you believed a vague slander . . .'

4 Kuma: Self-justification 2 (imploring tone: 'the enchantress') – 'In tears, Prince, I bow before you . . .'
  Yury: Weakening (embarrassed)

5 Kuma: Confession of love 1 (preparation) – 'But the blame was mine . . .'
  Yury: Confusion

6 Kuma: Confession of love 2 (appealing) – 'Everywhere, my falcon, have I stealthily shadowed you . . .'

7 Kuma: Confession of love 3 (assertive) – 'Let me finish, Prince! You swore to tear out my heart'
  Yury: Confused – finally promises Kuma protection

8 Kuma: Confession of love 4 (pleading) – 'But you depress my spirits with a terrible anguish . . .'

Yury: Confused – tries to leave, but is powerless to do so

9 Kuma: Confession of love 5 (self-sacrificing: bids him farewell) –
'I have opened my heart to you . . .'
Yury: Final stage of capitulation

10 Yury–Kuma: Mutual love – 'When you calmed the anger in my
heart . . .'

The challenge this extended love scene presented to Tchaikovsky was
daunting, and what he achieved is therefore all the more remarkable.
Here he shows himself not only as the creator of splendid music in
itself, but also as a genius for creating whatever kind of music was
required for each character at each stage. It makes for a magnificent
ending to the act.

If only (again!) . . . If only the plot of the final act had maintained
the level of the preceding three! Nevertheless, there are some very
good things in it. The entr'acte's opening theme is a folksong, a sibling
of the one in the opera's introductory entr'acte, thus providing a modest frame for the opera so far; by contrast, the horn calls that follow
forewarn of what is to come. The scene is a forest on the banks of the
Oka, and after the Wizard, Kudma, disgruntled by the noise, has
retreated into his cave, Zhuran and other hunters appear. Zhuran is to
await Yury, and has made arrangements for his master and Kuma to
elope. Yury arrives, resists Zhuran's persuasions to abandon his plan,
and launches into a rapturous song of praise to his beloved – one of
the musical peaks of the act. That done, and a bear having been spot-
ted, all leave in pursuit. Paisy and the Princess, the latter disguised as
a pilgrim, enter. The Wizard reappears, Paisy flees in terror, the former
greets the Princess ungraciously, and she instantly and angrily silences
him. Seeing a money-filled pouch, he decides not to turn her into a she-
wolf. Has he the most deadly and agonizing of poisons? Yes, he has –
and both revel at the prospect of its dire effect, then disappear into his
cave where he will prepare it.

This whole incident could have been rather ridiculous, but it is
redeemed by the resurgence of that venomous ferocity which the
Princess had brought to her encounter with her husband in Act 2. The
arrival, backed by the folksong from the preceding entr'acte, of a boat
bearing Kuma with some friends from her hostelry is well handled;
their mutual farewells are affectionate and deeply felt, and the party

retire to their boat where they will intercept any pursuers. Alone, Kuma in her turn sings of her longing for Yury, a declaration that matches Yury's earlier soliloquy, both in expressive depth and quality. But this is virtually the last substantial moment in *The Enchantress* where the human drama (that is, not the atmospheric *melo*drama) enables Tchaikovsky to compose something that moves the listener *within* rather than excites through its masterly, sometimes brilliantly graphic substantiation of a trail of highly charged (and sometimes over-the-top) incidents. True, all this is, in its way, very exciting, but only Kuma's death, Yury's desperately sad lament over Kuma's body, and the men's requiem as they bear her away are likely truly to touch something deeper.

But – to complete the summary of the act's last, and very complicated, stages – the Princess emerges from the cave, spies Kuma, and approaches her, describing herself as a pilgrim who has outpaced her companions, and will now wait for them. Once again it is the Princess who raises the general dramatic level, here through the ingratiating ruthlessness with which she insinuates herself into the confidence of her unsuspecting victim. Claiming the local spring has restorative powers, she offers Kuma a cup of water from it, slips the poison into the cup, Kuma drinks – and the Wizard's laughter is heard from offstage. The Princess withdraws, Kuma waits, and Yury rushes in, embraces her, and they sing of their blissful future, while the Princess and Wizard gloat from behind.

Suddenly Kuma feels strange. Yury is alarmed (the Princess and Wizard in the background are gleeful). Kuma tells how she has been given water, the Princess comes forward triumphantly, reveals the truth, exclaims 'I have purged the shame of my family' – and the Wizard withdraws into his cave. Yury denounces his mother, hunting horns are heard, Kuma dies, the Princess tries self-justification, Yury denounces her again, and is led aside. The Princess orders the huntsmen to throw Kuma's body into the river. They carry it off. Recovering himself, Yury asks where Kuma's body is, and his mother tells him. Yury is in despair. It grows dark. Boats with Prince Nikita and servants appear. Nikita demands to know where Kuma is (he now knows of the lovers' plan to escape). Yury charges him with causing Kuma's death, and Nikita stabs him. The Princess cries out in horror as her son dies, throwing herself on his body. Distant thunder. Yury's corpse is carried away, to a men's chorus of mourning. The storm breaks, the Prince's reason begins to give way, the Wizard approaches him, the Prince sees him and recoils in horror, the Wizard laughs demonically, and the Prince goes mad.

As already noted, much of the music in the later stages of this final act has been concerned simply to heighten, or at least substantiate, the veritable torrent of incident that concludes *The Enchantress*. (If Tchaikovsky had lived two generations on, he would certainly have matched Prokofiev as a composer for films.) But we have finally been moved out of a situation to which we can give any credence; all has become overblown, breathless melodrama, and despite Tchaikovsky's genius for conjuring and sustaining atmosphere, the tale being told has left behind the world of credible human emotions and relationships. It is such a pity – for there is so much that is splendid, sometimes truly great, elsewhere in *The Enchantress*.

23
Widening Horizons:
Pleasures – and Pains

The transformation in Tchaikovsky's personal life brought about by the move to his own home at Maidanovo, and the sudden awareness that his music was becoming not merely respected but popular, was to be reflected also in his own attitude to the world around him. Suddenly he seemed to gain a new self-confidence. But what is so striking is that this did not manifest itself in an access of arrogance, but in a greater ease in his contacts with others – in a greater warmth in his existing relationships and in his increased willingness to make new ones and collaborate in matters of common interest. And that thoughtfulness which he had so often shown towards family members and sometimes complete strangers, and his readiness to intervene with advice and practical help where he could, seemed to grow even greater. Emiliya Pavlovskaya, who had created the part of Kuma in *The Enchantress*, knew she was now nearing the end of her singing career: how could she cope with the ultimate void of retirement? Tchaikovsky had suggestions both recreational and practical:

Can you not *walk* – that is, not in the sense of movement, or simply mooching around, but in the sense of lively intercourse with the infinite and inexpressible beauty of nature? Can't you busy yourself with translations from Russian into Italian, of which, it seems, you have an excellent command? Surely Russian literature is now a strong interest in the West? Forgive me that I allow myself to give advice but, you see, I'm not interested only in *Pavlovskaya* – that is, in my best advocate on the stage – but also in Emiliya Karlovna, whom I shall love in twenty-five years times as much as I do now.

Then there was Yuliya Shpazhinskaya, the former wife of *The Enchantress*'s librettist, and now a single parent with a family to rear. As he had with Leonty Tkachenko before her, Tchaikovsky thought she could perhaps become a writer, and over the next six to eight years, he wrote to her over eighty letters, some very lengthy, offering advice, criticism and encouragement in her halting efforts to learn her trade, and then negotiating, though unsuccessfully, with the Imperial Theatres to get her work performed.

Such interventions absorbed time, but others involved financial support. Family members facing some difficulty which money could ease would be helped, and all this time there was still Georges-Léon to support. Then there were the outside beneficiaries. On arriving in Maidanovo, Tchaikovsky had ordered that all royalties earned during that year from performances of his works should be given to the Musicians' Benevolent Fund. Conservatoire students also benefited; in the same season one received a hundred roubles to fund her through an untimely pregnancy, while another, a piano student who had been surcharged for being admitted as a supernumerary, had her extra fee paid, Tchaikovsky doing this secretly and the student never knowing who her benefactor had been.

Finally there were benefactions to the community around him. Only months after his arrival two-thirds of Maidanovo had been ravaged by fire, and Tchaikovsky had not only helped in tackling the flames but had contributed handsomely to the relief fund. Yet his biggest single community service was educational. The more he got to know his impoverished neighbours, the more his admiration for them grew. 'Their cottages are of the most pitiful, tiny, dark sort,' he wrote to Nadezhda von Meck:

> They must be terribly stuffy, and when you remember that they have to live in this dark and crowded state for eight months of the year, your heart bleeds. I do not know why, but the people here are especially poor. Yet – and this is the most noticeable thing – the adults, old and young, and the children have a thoroughly happy and contented appearance: in no way do they complain of their ill-starred fate – and the less they express their dissatisfaction with their life, the more I pity them and am touched by the Russian race's humility and long-suffering. The children have surprisingly sympathetic faces. There is no school and the nearest is four miles away. I should like to do something.

Which he did. The village priest confirmed that, if he would finance the project, then permission would be granted. Tchaikovsky wasted no time, and in February 1886 the Maidanovo school was opened.

Three days later Tchaikovsky conducted an inspection, deciding that at this stage the teaching was marked more by good intentions than expertise. All the same, twenty-eight boys and girls were now receiving the basics of an education: it was money well spent, and he continued to support the school for the rest of his life.

In the preceding chapter the narrative had jumped ahead in its account of how *The Enchantress* came to be composed, and now this biographical gap requires filling. If in the months after February 1885, when Tchaikovsky had settled into Maidanovo, he had thought he would find permanent relief from the outside pressures which had become more and more intolerable in his professional life, his new celebrity status would soon disabuse him. The winter of 1885–86 was to be increasingly filled with meetings in Moscow, official events, committees, receptions and social occasions, as well as individual consultations, not to mention visits to Maidanovo by family, friends and acquaintances. There were also some minor compositional demands, including a substantial piano piece, *Dumka (Scène rustique)*, which he composed for the French publisher, Félix Mackar, with whom he had established a business relationship to foster his music in France, and also a little 'melodrama' (that is, a piece where an actor declaims against a musical background) for a revival of Ostrovsky's play, *The Voyevoda*, which had been the subject of Tchaikovsky's first opera. It was to support a monologue from the Domovoy (or house-spirit), and the music was required to express 'the noises of the night'. Tchaikovsky was given only six days' notice for this, and had been warned that the orchestra would be 'so vile that you can't entrust any serious piece to it'. But Ostrovsky was a friend who, years before, had helped him to the first big public exposure of his music, and in the event Tchaikovsky's offering for five woodwind instruments, harp and strings proved to be a little gem. However, all these and other commitments made him all the more determined to accept without further delay the standing invitation from brother Anatoly, who had now moved to Tiflis in the Caucasus, to visit him in his new home. Thus, having attended the premiere of the *Manfred Symphony*, then spent five days catching up on business affairs, on 4 April 1886 he could leave Moscow, briefly visit brother Ippolit and his family at Taganrog, then head south.

Tchaikovsky had never journeyed so far within Russia itself, and he found the Caucasus scenery, and especially the last stage to Tiflis, overwhelming. His delight in it all comes across vividly in his account to Modest:

At first you approach the mountains rather slowly, then the valley of the Terek becomes even narrower, then you come out into the Daryalskoye Gorge – terrifying, gloomy, wild – then, little by little, you enter the region of snow. Finally we climbed up between two high walls of snow. At six in the evening we descended into the valley of the Aragvi and spent the night at Mleti. I dined, took a walk along the gallery in the moonlight, and went to bed at nine. We left early next morning, constantly coming across picturesque villages and every different kind of dwelling. The descent was made at a speed which was sometimes truly frightening, particularly on the bends. Not far from the station at Dushet there suddenly opens up a distant view so amazingly wonderful that you want to weep for joy. The farther you go, the more the south makes itself felt. Finally we passed through Mtskheta, and at about 4.30 we were already in Tiflis.

The town's delightfully picturesque. Not all the trees are yet in leaf – but then, in the gardens all the fruit trees are in blossom, the masses of flowers stand out vividly, it's as warm as June and, in a word, it's the most true of springs, exactly as it was in Naples when we left it four years ago. The main streets are very lively, the shops are luxurious, and it smells totally of Europe. But today, when I went into the native quarter (Maidan), I found myself in an environment completely new to me. The streets are unusually narrow, as in Venice. Downstairs on both sides is an endless row of small shops and craft establishments of all sorts where the locals sit cross-legged, working in full view of the passers-by. There are bakers and special kinds of food shops where they bake and fry various things. It's very interesting and novel.

It was more than just a family visit that had drawn Tchaikovsky to Tiflis. The conductor at the local opera house was the twenty-six-year-old Mikhail Ippolitov-Ivanov, who four years earlier had arrived in Tiflis, where he was now in charge of the local academy of music and of the regional branch of the RMS. More important from Tchaikovsky's point of view: he was conductor of the local opera house, and had recently had the enterprise to mount Tchaikovsky's still-new *Mazeppa*. Excited to have this now famous Russian composer

present, Ippolitov-Ivanov ensured that Tchaikovsky would gain pleasure from his stay, arranging a performance of *Mazeppa* for his forty-
seventh birthday on 7 May, and a week later an all-Tchaikovsky gala
concert, in which was included *Romeo and Juliet*, the Serenade for
Strings, and Tatyana's Letter Scene from *Eugene Onegin*, sung by his
wife, Varvara Zarudnaya. As Tchaikovsky entered the directors' box
he was greeted with an ovation, an address of welcome from the RMS,
and was presented with a wreath made from wrought silver. The occasion was rounded off by a grand supper with speeches. Tchaikovsky
had anticipated this evening with dread, but when he wrote of it to his
patroness five days later, it was the sincerity and genuine warmth of
his reception that he recalled: 'It all exhausted me terribly, but the
memory of this triumph, with the like of which I have never been
favoured anywhere, will for my whole life remain pleasant for me.'
Modest later set it in a larger context: 'It was the first public acknowledgement of his service to the Russian peoples.' His brother was now
becoming recognized as Russia's greatest composer.

Tchaikovsky remained in Tiflis for a month, and when he left a
crowd saw him off at the station, and threw flowers into the train. His
ultimate destination was Paris, but his intention was first to proceed
by sea to Marseilles, and thence to the French capital. The twelve-day
voyage from Batum started along the north Turkish coast with numerous dockings which allowed time for ventures ashore, including at
Trebizon: 'Very picturesque, very interesting – especially the bazaar.
Drank coffee in a coffee shop, and smoked a hookah. Went up a
mountain on horseback to a monastery – only two Greek monks.
Amazing view.' Arriving in Constantinople [now Istanbul], he spent a
night ashore, attended half a concert, slept in a bug-infested room, and
took a guided tour of the city: 'Saint Sofiya amazed and delighted me
– but in general Constantinople is unsympathetic'. Passing close to
Greece, the vessel then headed for Sicily where Etna was in eruption,
and Tchaikovsky was awakened at 2 a.m. to see the spectacle: 'The
sea proved to be rough, and it is impossible to convey the beauty of the
combination of moonlight with the fire of Etna and the stormy sea.'
They passed through the Strait of Bonifacio between Sardinia and
Corsica: 'Sardinia reminded me of a lunar landscape as seen in a book
by Flamarion [a popularizer of astronomy]. Corsica is grand and picturesque.' On 23 May they berthed in Marseilles.

The previous six weeks had been one of the pleasantest interludes in his life. But Paris meant business matters, though not before he had settled Georges-Léon's long-term future, the arrangement now being that brother Nikolay and his wife, Olga, who were childless, would adopt the boy, and that Olga would journey to Paris, then return to Russia with the lad and Tchaikovsky. There were legal formalities to complete, and Tchaikovsky also saw as much as he could of the boy to help accustom him to a new family environment. He discussed business matters with his French publisher Mackar, and discovered that many of the leading French composers wished to see him, including Delibes, who showed a gratifying deference ('which I value especially because I consider him the most talented of French musicians after Bizet'), Ambroise Thomas ('a very nice and gentle old man'), Lalo, and Fauré ('whom I liked extremely, both as a man and musician'). At a specially arranged soirée one of Tchaikovsky's string quartets and several of his songs were performed. But after four weeks the longing for Russia became irresistible. With masterly innocence Georges-Léon, not quite four years old, himself capped the completion of the formalities that would allow him to leave France: 'Suddenly he broke the silence by beginning to sing the *Marseillaise* at the top of his voice. Even the *chef de bureau*, a stern old man upon whom everything depended, started to roar with laughter.' Yet the preoccupations of a hectic three-day journey could not drive out the memory of an event of thirty-two years earlier. Writing up his diary on the second day, he ended: 'anniversary of mother's death'.

Nor was this the only cause for sorrow. It would seem that from time to time on his travels Tchaikovsky would strike up a fleeting relationship, clearly homosexual, with another man. Such, it would appear, was the case with Ivan Verinovsky, an artillery officer whose name turns up almost daily during the last three weeks of the diary Tchaikovsky kept while in Tiflis, and who, for some unknown reason, committed suicide only three days after Tchaikovsky's departure. Usually it is only Verinovsky's name that the diaries mention, but occasionally there are cryptic additions ('sympathetic' or 'attractive Verinovsky'); there is mention of a 'rendez-vous', but also a hint that it was not primarily Tchaikovsky who was taking the initiative ('again, exaggerated expressions of love from Verinovsky'). There are two curious mentions of Tchaikovsky finding Verinovsky 'being dressed in my clothes'. But it is also clear that Tchaikovsky was personally very concerned about him ('news of a night at cards, and of

Verinovsky's losses'), and it is also clear that Anatoly's wife, Praskovya (nicknamed 'Panya'), who had already shown herself to be a flirt, had turned her attentions to Verinovsky ('At Panya's. Her outrageous behaviour a propos Verinovsky', 'at lunch a quarrel with Panya over Verinovsky', 'infinitely sorry for Verinovsky, and am furious at that wretched woman'). It was while he was in Paris that Tchaikovsky learned accidentally of Verinovsky's suicide. Back in Russia, he at last received 'details of Verinovsky's death, and wept so violently that I was almost hysterical, and was unable to eat anything'. In October, still tormented by the thought that he might have been the cause of Verinovsky's death, he sought details from both Anatoly and Ippoli-tov-Ivanov and, on receiving them, and despite learning that he could have done nothing to help, 'wept endlessly on account of Vanya Veri-novsky'.

July saw Tchaikovsky home in Maidanovo. His three-month trip had been his longest and most wide ranging so far and, with evidence of his reception in Paris to confirm his growing international reputa-tion, it would prove to be only the harbinger of many such profes-sional expeditions, including visits to England and, most ambitious of all, a tour in the United States. But all this public exposure was in the future; by contrast, currently he found himself appreciating more and more the growing richness of his inner life made possible by the rela-tive seclusion of his country home. He started a special diary to record his own responses to whatever was at the time engrossing him. For a while he was much occupied with Tolstoy: 'More than ever I'm con-vinced that Lev Tolstoy is the greatest of all writers who have ever existed. He alone is enough for the Russian man not to have to bow his head in shame when everything that Europe has given humanity is reckoned up.' At the other end of his quality scale came Brahms. He had been playing one of the German composer's symphonies during a piano-duet session with Laroche. 'What an untalented S–! It angers me that this presumptuous mediocrity is recognized *as a genius*!' Very soon, on meeting Brahms, his view would soften. He found increasing pleasures in simple things – the flowers in his garden, in feeding chick-ens and, less innocently, in using his binoculars to spy on his neigh-bours when they were eating. One matter on which he profoundly disagreed with Tolstoy was alcohol. Tchaikovsky recognized the dan-ger in over-indulgence; nevertheless, 'I – that is, a sick man filled with neuroses – emphatically couldn't manage without the *poison*. Each evening I'm drunk. In the first phase of inebriation I feel the most complete happiness, and in that condition I *understand* infinitely more than I understand when making do without the poison. Nor have I noticed that my health has particularly suffered in consequence of it. But then: *quod licet Jovi, non licet bovi* ["What is allowed to Jove is not allowed to the ox"],' he added contentedly.

With the arrival of autumn his greatest professional irritation – the noise of pianos from the surrounding dachas – departed with their summer occupants. However, by the end of October over-assiduous work on scoring *The Enchantress* had taken its toll, and he headed for St Petersburg for a three-week break with Modest, enjoying the company of his family, reassuring himself that Georges-Léon had settled into his new environment, and meeting Bob, now fifteen, as tall as his uncle – and more handsome than ever. As noted earlier, Tchaikovsky's new celebrity status put him at far greater ease with his fellow composers, both on a personal level and in regard of his own judgements on their works. But it was not simply the respect he enjoyed with his fellow professionals that delighted him: it was also the love of his music by the wider public, and which was reflected in their attitude to him personally. 'From everywhere, at every step in St Petersburg, I encountered so many expressions of sympathy and love that frequently I was moved to tears,' he recalled to Nadezhda von Meck. He had just been elected an honorary member of the St Petersburg Chamber Music Society (CMS), and the event had been marked by a concert of his music, including the Second String Quartet and the Piano Trio. 'The enthusiasm was genuine, and I left overwhelmed by emotion and gratitude. Two days later I was still thoroughly out of sorts from the emotions I had experienced.'

If the end of 1886 found Tchaikovsky's professional morale, on a public level, higher than it had ever been, the next year would bring two very painful events. The year 1887 had begun well with his triumph as conductor at the premiere of *Cherevichki*, his major revision of *Vakula the Smith*. Tchaikovsky never became a virtuoso at this trade. Some years later a violinist who played under him in a concert in Kharkov recalled his manner of directing, and the problems it posed:

> He did not hold the baton in his fingers, as most conductors do, but clasped it firmly in his fist. He then raised it above his head, on the

first beat brought it down sharply, on the second raised it to his left shoulder, on the third to his right shoulder, and on the fourth again raised it. The players were not accustomed to such a way of conducting. Everyone glanced around, but the sense that the composer himself was conducting the piece made us quickly forget this initial awkwardness, and we tried our best – and by the end of the rehearsal we were already accustomed to Pyotr Ilich's idiosyncratic way of conducting.

Clearly, as with Sir Edward Elgar and the London Symphony Orchestra some fifty years later, it was the respect with which the players held Tchaikovsky that made them co-operate in a way they would not have done with a lesser composer. As for the audiences, his success stemmed from the increasing affection he had earned from them for the many rich and varied experiences they had now gained from his music.

Yet it was only hours after conducting the premiere of *Cherevichki* that a telegram arrived informing him that his eldest niece, Tanya, Georges-Léon's mother, whom he had supported so assiduously, and for whose son's welfare he had taken such care and prolonged responsibility, and who had at last seemed to be bringing more order into her life, had collapsed and died at a masked ball in St Petersburg. It struck Tchaikovsky very hard: as he wrote next day to his sister-in-law, Parasha: 'Poor Tanya! Now that all's over, you involuntarily forget all her dark sides, and remember only what a marvellous girl she was twelve years ago.' He conducted the second performance of *Cherevichki* but – 'It's time to go home! O, how it's time!' he wrote to Modest, having survived that nerve-racking experience. Tanya's sister, Anna, was in Moscow, and he broke the news to her, but her preoccupation with her newly born daughter fortunately provided some distraction. With Moscow-based relatives he attended a special Requiem for Tanya – then, as soon as his term conducting *Cherevichki* was over, he returned to Maidanovo and scoring *The Enchantress*.

This time he would spend three and a half months at his rural home, but with constant visits to Moscow or St Petersburg to deal with all the various matters, some professional, others personal, which seemed increasingly numerous, but which his conscience told him he could not ignore. There were talks and negotiations about Conservatoire affairs and the politics of the Imperial Theatre (he played a significant role in getting rid of a dictatorial and incompetent head of the latter), and he

devoted much private time to the young Anton Arensky, now a professor at the Conservatoire, but whose latest composition, an orchestral fantasia, *Marguerite Gautier*, dedicated to Tchaikovsky himself,
he nevertheless felt was badly flawed. Having penned a very long and
detailed criticism of the piece, Tchaikovsky then privately negotiated
with Rimsky-Korsakov in St Petersburg, who was about to conduct a
concert including *Romeo and Juliet*, to replace this with a piece by
Arensky, simply to hearten the latter. One item of news particularly
pleased him: Mackar reported from Paris that an all-Tchaikovsky
concert had drawn an audience of a thousand, of whom two hundred
had had to stand. So, too, was he gratified by an invitation from St
Petersburg to conduct a concert devoted entirely to his own works. It
was the first time he had appeared as conductor at a public concert,
and the event was a sensation, several pieces being encored, and the
press (even his old tormenter, Cui) enthusiastic. There was, however, a
sad side to this visit: his friend Kondratyev was seriously ill with
syphilis, and in due course Tchaikovsky would return for a week simply to visit him.

All this finally brought total exhaustion, and at the beginning of
June Tchaikovsky left Moscow for Tiflis, this time heading east to
Nizhni-Novgorod so that he could travel down Russia's greatest river,
the Volga, to its mouth. Quickly his mood improved. During the trip
he accompanied, in one of his own songs, a young conservatoire student who did not know his identity, and who found his understanding
of the music defective, her authority being her own teacher who had
studied the song with Tchaikovsky himself! Tchaikovsky never let on.
Along the Volga they made a number of stops, including at Kazan
('very beautiful from a distance') and Saratov, where he saw that *Onegin*
had been performed the previous evening. After crossing the Caspian
Sea, they docked at Baku, already a significant source of oil. From
Baku he took a train to Tiflis. He would pass nearly a month in the
Caucasus, but only twelve days in Tiflis, for the town's musical season
was over, and the Ippolitov-Ivanovs were away. A touring theatre
company was presenting Shpazhinsky's play, *The Enchantress*, and a
reluctant Tchaikovsky was persuaded to see it. He hated it, but had
compensation in the knowledge that Ippolitov-Ivanov proposed to
mount Tchaikovsky's opera – and, indeed, at the end of December
The Enchantress was given, Tchaikovsky having agreed to conduct (in
the event he had to withdraw). On this present visit he was able to

repay the town for the warmth and generosity of their reception of him the previous year. A new opera house being under construction, but there being insufficient funds to complete it, Tchaikovsky promptly wrote to the Tsar, and His Majesty equally promptly allotted the nearly a quarter of a million roubles needed to complete the building.

After twelve days in Tiflis, Tchaikovsky passed what he intended should be a six-week stay at Borzhom, a small spa town where there was an ample choice of walks, beautiful vegetation and, above all, relative privacy. He took the waters after a local doctor had decided, curiously, that pressure from his stomach had exiled his liver to some place where it had no business to be. Not having composed anything for a month, he now set about a Fourth Suite, compiled this time not from newly composed music of his own, but from orchestral arrangements of four pieces by Mozart, to which he gave the collective title *Mozartiana*.*** The year 1887 was the centenary of Mozart's *Don Giovanni*, and this would be his homage to, as he heard it, the greatest piece ever written by the greatest composer ever. As for the four items themselves, it would be a case of 'the old given a contemporary treatment'. His choice fell on three piano pieces: the Gigue in G, к. 574, the Minuet in D, к. 355, the Variations on 'Unser dummer Pöbel meint', к. 455, and one of Mozart's most exquisite shorter pieces, his *Ave, verum corpus* for voices, strings and organ, к. 618, though working from Liszt's piano transcription, to which the Hungarian composer had added an introduction and a coda.

Tchaikovsky's treatment of the three piano pieces was both deferential and affectionate: deferential in the sense that he took Mozart's pieces as they stood, affectionate in that he availed himself of late nineteenth-century orchestral resources, but only to make his beloved Mozart that little bit more winning for an audience of Tchaikovsky's own day. The remaining piece is a different matter. In using Liszt's piano transcription Tchaikovsky's musical text was already 'corrupt', and his use of celestial strings and twangling harp abetted Liszt's benign vandalism, converting what in Mozart was ethereal tenderness into glutinous sentimentality. Does this matter? Not really – as long as we recognize that Mozart knew his own business, and in no way does Tchaikovsky's act of homage (for that is how Tchaikovsky would have seen it) invalidate Mozart's original.

Tchaikovsky had hoped that a remission in Kondratyev's illness, which had permitted his friend's removal to Aachen in the hope that the mineral waters of this spa town would further prolong his life, would mean that he could complete his summer break as planned. But then a telegram had arrived: 'Supplie venir: votre arrivée peut me ressusciter.' Abandoning all his further plans, Tchaikovsky journeyed by sea to Odessa, then by train to Aachen. On 27 July he was with Kondratyev.

He found his friend supported neither by family nor friends; not even his wife was there, and for a fortnight Tchaikovsky filled the gap. The patient's condition was clearly dreadful and his moods fitful, optimism quickly giving way to despair, with frequent outbursts of anger and ingratitude at those looking after him. Tchaikovsky's diary records something of his own torment and self-questioning during this time; what follows here are only snippets from this record:

29 July: Still more and more I see that I was very necessary to him . . .

3 August: Now I'm remorseful. Take now, for instance. I sit here, and all the while I take pride in my *sacrifice*. But there is no sacrifice . . . I can enjoy myself in peace, gorge myself at the *table d'hôte* . . . Am I not, quintessentially, a *self-centred individual*? . . .

5 August: I found him talking with Sasha [his servant] about the fact that in reality there is no improvement. He wept a lot. Ah! How painful this was! I can no longer remember what I said to him, only that little by little he became quieter . . .

12 August: Talked with Sasha in his room. We are coming to the conclusion that things are bad . . .

After a fortnight Tchaikovsky realized that a break was imperative, and he left for Paris where various of his friends were, where there were diversions, and he could meet Mackar. But his break was no more than a week:

19 August: . . . After my dinner and walk I found him still weaker. I sat with him. Sudden anger at me. Although I could not get angry, I was terribly cold . . . Then it passed, but with difficulty. Pity took over. He was suffering terribly . . .

23 August: He roused painful thoughts in me. His self-centredness and lack of true goodness declare themselves so sharply and in so unattractive a manner that by now, except for pity, I nourish no feeling for him. Shall I soon tear myself from this hell? . . .

At last one of Kondratyev's nephews, Dmitri Zasyadko, had agreed to come to Aachen, and an end was in sight for Tchaikovsky's vigil:

27 August: Ten more days to live in this hell!!! . . .

Sunday, 28 August: He is much worse since morning. He's in utter despair. I cannot describe the scenes that took place: I shall never forget them . . . Hours of torment. A strange thing – I was thoroughly weighed down by *horror* and *anguish*, but not by PITY!!! . . . And yet, God, how he suffers! No! I know I'm not wicked and heartless . . .

30 August: From this morning the *ray* of freedom has shone on me, for *in a week* I shall not be here . . .

31 August: He was quiet and meek. In such a state he especially arouses my pity . . . Lying in bed, I began to think of him, of his endless depression and suffering, and for a long time I sobbed like a child . . .

2 September: He is very weak . . . from time to time he complains and weeps. Wearying, terrible hours!

The nephew arrived on 4 September:

All today I lived in a nightmare. His rampant selfishness tears me to shreds. One thought: to leave!!!! My patience can no longer be confined . . . Lord, is it possible a time will come when I shall no longer suffer thus! Poor Nikolay Dmitriyevich! Poor Mitya Zasyadko! What lies before him!

On 6 September Tchaikovsky set out for Maidanovo, so drained that he had to rest in Berlin. In St Petersburg he met Kondratyev's wife, and on 11 September he was home. Having observed so closely death confronting another, he drew up a new will of his own.

This diary is an extraordinary record of one incident in the life of an extraordinary human being. Tchaikovsky was fast becoming the most famous commoner in all Russia after Tolstoy, but to the end of his life he never lost his human touch or his capacity for active compassion, nor ever became grand. It is no surprise that, when he died only six years later, silent crowds swarmed on to the St Petersburg streets to pay their respects, holding up his funeral procession for four hours.

The first requirement for Tchaikovsky on his return to Russia was to attend the final rehearsals and then conduct the premiere of *The Enchantress*. A week later he conducted in Moscow a concert of his own works, including *Francesca da Rimini* and *1812*, as well as the first performance of *Mozartiana*. The concert was such a success that it had to be repeated the following day. Then it was back to Maidanovo for three weeks, as much to rest as to tidy up some of his musical affairs. He had composed very little during 1887, and nothing of much significance. In Paris, during the break in his Kondratyev vigil, he had encountered Brandukov, and had managed to compose his *Pezzo capriccioso*,**(*) for cello and orchestra, as a distraction when not at his dying friend's bedside, but the result is an unremarkable piece. This, plus a set of six songs on verses by the Grand Duke Konstantin, and a handful of other vocal pieces (and, of course, *Mozartiana*), is the sum total of his compositions for the year.

The news that Tchaikovsky would begin conductiong his own works beyond the boundaries of Russia spread with phenomenal speed. Instantly invitations began to pour in. In July the Hamburg Philharmonic Society had invited him to conduct a concert of his own works; in September an agent had secured for him an engagement in Prague, to be swiftly followed by an invitation from the Berlin Philharmonic Orchestra. Tchaikovsky recognized that accepting these invitations would be the best way to promote his music outside Russia, and he readily agreed, in the end taking in Leipzig, Berlin, Hamburg, Prague, Paris – and London. Before leaving Russia he still had to conduct the first St Petersburg performance of *Mozartiana*. Having fulfilled this promise on 24 December, he was within three days on his way to Berlin to begin his first international tour.

24

First Foreign Tour; A Relationship Renewed;
Fifth Symphony and *Hamlet*

Tchaikovsky's first engagement was in Leipzig, where he would conduct his First Suite. But far more significant was what happened ahead
of the concert. The violinist Adolf Brodsky, who had given the premiere of Tchaikovsky's Violin Concerto in 1881 and become its dedicatee, had invited Tchaikovsky to lunch, and when the latter arrived
he found his host rehearsing Brahms's C minor Piano Trio, with the
composer himself at the piano. Then, before the rehearsal was over,
another figure appeared, 'a very short man, middle-aged, of frail build,
with a head of prominent wavy fair hair, a very thin, almost youthful
beard, and unusually attractive, blue eyes of an inexpressibly captivating nature, recalling the look of a charming innocent child'. It was
Grieg, together with his wife, also very short (when later they sat with
Tchaikovsky at a concert of his own works, one member of the audience declared it was 'Tchaikovsky with his children'). He took to
these two immediately; as for Brahms, this first encounter at least
broke the ice, and Tchaikovsky wrote to Jurgenson that he had found
him 'a very nice person, and not at all proud as I had imagined'
(though to Modest he described him as 'rubicund, pot-bellied, and a
dreadful toper'). In order to consolidate these new relationships, the
Brodskys mounted a quiet and exclusive dinner party for the three
composers, which ended, we are told, convivially with Brodsky performing conjuring tricks from one of his children's Christmas presents, Brahms demanding to know how each was done. Tchaikovsky
would spend six days in Leipzig, encountering Brahms several more
times, finding the latter did everything he could to be agreeable, but
was easier as a drinking companion than as conversationalist.

Tchaikovsky's first rehearsal with the magnificent Gewandhaus
Orchestra went very well. Brahms was present, and it was reported
that he had expressed approval of the Suite's first movement (the
introduction and fugue), but had been silent about the rest except for

the tiny march, about which he was scathing. As for the concert itself, it was judged very successful. An all-Tchaikovsky chamber recital was given the following day (very clear evidence of how his international stature had grown); this included the First String Quartet and the Piano Trio. Tchaikovsky's next commitment was in Hamburg, and on 9 January he travelled thither with Brodsky, who had an engagement in the city. Since Tchaikovsky's own appearance was ten days away, and he feared that, if he remained in Hamburg, he might be drawn into social engagements, he moved on to Lübeck, which he found an attractive town, with a good cultural life. While there he learned that the Tsar had awarded him an annual pension of 3000 roubles. Tchaikovsky, with typical generosity, decided that Antonina should enjoy a share. On the debit side was a bad attack of homesickness. Back in Hamburg on 16 January to prepare for his part of the concert (the Serenade for Strings, First Piano Concerto, and variation finale of his Third Suite), he was resignedly drawn into a social whirl, with many introductions. Most of these were eminently forgettable, but one, the most improbable of all, would by chance have an extraordinary and profound impact on his own creative life. It was with a certain Theodor Avé-Lallement, a teacher of advanced years, who nevertheless struggled to all Tchaikovsky's rehearsals, then told him frankly he disliked his noisy scoring and especially his excessive use of percussion, adding that he could improve his music if he settled in Germany and followed their classical traditions, but who nevertheless respected Tchaikovsky sufficiently to have his photo taken as a memento of his visit, and who had in general shown him such warmth that, as Tchaikovsky put it, they 'parted great friends'. As for the wider reaction to his music, he was at least satisfied: 'It's not that I roused never-ending rapture, but I did awaken *great interest*,' as he put it to Yuliya Shpazhinskaya.

His next concert was in Berlin, but that was still a fortnight away. Nevertheless, he headed for the city for a day to finalize the concert's programme, then visited Magdeburg for two days, but spent the rest of this break in Leipzig, where he met the young Gustav Mahler, one of the four resident conductors at the local opera. News of Tchaikovsky's successes had already brought in offers of further engagements in Weimar and Dresden, as well as in Paris. The Berlin concert was an all-Tchaikovsky programme including the First Piano Concerto, *1812* (Tchaikovsky was surprised the Berliners had chosen this rather than *Francesca da Rimini*, which Tchaikovsky rated far more highly, and thought would have been more to their taste), and *Romeo and Juliet*. Both Grieg and the Brodskys travelled from Leipzig for the final rehearsal and concert, which drew a generally more favourable press than had those in either Leipzig or Hamburg. This was Tchaikovsky's final appearance in Germany, and his self-confidence had risen hugely. 'Would you now recognize in this Russian musician travelling across Europe that man who, only a few years ago, had absconded from life in society and lived in seclusion abroad or in the country!!!' he wrote to his patroness.

Next stop was Prague. On the way there Tchaikovsky passed a night in Leipzig, and next morning was awakened by a military band serenading him from under his window (this had been organized by the bandmaster, who was already a Tchaikovsky devotee). It was highly flattering, but it came at a price, Tchaikovsky being forced to stand at an open window for an hour on what was a bitterly cold morning. But even this spontaneous compliment could not have prepared him for his reception in Prague.

There was forewarning of this when his train reached the frontier. As he reported to Modest:

> The senior guard enquired whether I was Tchaikovsky, and he looked after me all the way. At Kralupy, the station before Prague, a veritable crowd and a deputation awaited us, and accompanied us to Prague. At the terminus there was a mass of people, deputations, children with bouquets, and finally two speeches, one in Russian, the other in Czech. I went to my carriage between two walls of people and cries of 'Slava!' ['Hurrah!']

He was forthwith installed in a splendid hotel room, and a carriage was put at his disposal. At a performance that evening of Verdi's brand-new *Otello* he was greeted by František Rieger, a leading nationalist politician (Tchaikovsky realized early on that this visit to fellow Slavs had a political anti-German element to it). He was given tours of the city, met Dvořák, who was very hospitable, was introduced to other Czech celebrities, was installed in the place of honour at a ball and afforded a torchlight serenade from the street, to which he had to listen from his hotel balcony, was taken on a visit to the Rathaus where the assembled members rose to greet him, then received a welcome from the Students' Society, an ovation from the

Civic Society, while the Artistic Society, an association of leading figures in the arts, arranged a grand musical evening for him, with his portrait displayed and garlanded in flowers. At the Conservatoire there was a special concert, which included Dvořák's D minor Symphony, the autograph score of which Dvořák presented to Tchaikovsky as a memento of his visit.

Tchaikovsky himself was to conduct two concerts in Prague. At his first of three rehearsals he was greeted with a fanfare, Dvořák attended all three, and the concert (which included the First Piano Concerto, Violin Concerto, *Romeo and Juliet* and *1812*) was a triumph. At the following banquet he managed a speech in Czech (written out in phonetics). Later that evening he would write in his diary that 'there is no doubt this has been one of the most notable days in my life. I love these kind Czechs very much. With good reason, too!!! God! How much enthusiasm, and all this not for me at all, but for dear Russia!' He had not previously realized how much the Czechs hated the Germans. His second concert was two days later, but this time he conducted only half the programme (which included the Serenade for Strings), for the second part consisted of a performance of Act 2 of *Swan Lake*. '*A moment of complete happiness*,' he noted in his diary.

Tchaikovsky's exit from Prague was as much an occasion as his arrival, and he was sad to leave. But now he had to be in Paris for his first rehearsal. Modest believed that, whereas his brother's reception in Prague had a deep and genuine root, his popularity in France was merely because things Russian happened to be in fashion, and that his current success arose simply because the moment was opportune. His first concert was at the grand home of an expatriate Russian, Nikolay Bernardaky, who had already done what he could to promote Tchaikovsky's cause in France. The French programmes were all far more fragmentary than the German and Czech ones, and Tchaikovsky had to conduct only two movements from the Serenade for Strings, and the *Andante cantabile* from his First String Quartet, arranged for string orchestra, though he also provided the piano accompaniment for the two solo singers, the de Reszke brothers, Jean and Édouard, two of the now legendary stars of the late nineteenth century. The audience of three hundred was drawn from the cream of Parisian society, and Tchaikovsky did not arrive home until 4.30 a.m., it having proved 'a famous evening', as he noted in his diary. His other conducting commitments were for two half-concerts with Edouard

Colonne. The players had greeted him with enthusiasm, but the press was cool, perhaps because the Concert Fantasia (with Louis Diémer as soloist) and *Francesca da Rimini* were not much to French taste. But in the wider Parisian world he was lionized, the *Figaro* mounting a special soirée in his honour. He met Gounod ('very aimiable') and Delibes ('most sympathetic'), and the young pianist, Jan Paderewski – who would also become both prime minister and foreign secretary of his native Poland, and his country's signatory in 1919 to the Versailles Treaty after the First World War. Tchaikovsky was particularly delighted to hear that his very early song, 'None but the lonely heart', had achieved sufficient fame to feature in a novel, *Le Froc*, by Émile Goudeau. He also attended an *audition* by Louis Diémer and his pupils, all playing pieces by Tchaikovsky – in all, some forty ('touched, but weary', as he noted in his diary).

By now Tchaikovsky was, indeed, very weary. He had received no fees for his French engagements, and the only thing that now persuaded him to press on to London was the remuneration he would receive. The first stage of his journey was not pleasant; the Channel crossing was rough (at least, he discovered, he was not liable to seasickness), while Kent was blanketed in snow, and the train was five hours late in London. But the French-run Hôtel Dieudonné in Ryder Street proved an excellent base for his five days in the capital. His hope had been that Grieg could have been tempted to London to share as conductor in his single concert, but in this he had been disappointed, and instead the pianist, composer and conductor Frederic Cowen conducted part of the concert as well as acting as interpreter between Tchaikovsky and the orchestra. Tchaikovsky was struck by that sight-reading facility for which British orchestras have always been noted, and at the concert the applause for both the Serenade for Strings and the variation finale of the Third Suite was highly satisfactory, coming as it did from a public that Tchaikovsky had been warned was not noted for being demonstrative. Indeed, so pleased were the concert's promoters that they increased his fee from £20 to £25, and though he had conducted in only one concert, he would find that his popularity would become greater in Britain than in any other foreign country except the United States.

In London he had been spared the social round that had been forced on him in France, but instead had found himself often bored, and London itself cheerless. He had relinquished the lease on his Maidanovo

331

house, and since Alexey had not yet found a new one, he decided Tiflis would be his first destination. Leaving London on 24 March, he would have preferred to retrace in reverse the land-and-sea-route that had brought him from Tiflis to Paris the previous year. But he feared Mediterranean and Black Sea storms, and instead chose a more direct overland route, journeying through Aachen, where memories of Kondratyev resurged distressingly, and thence to Vienna, where he paused to write various letters of thanks to those who had contributed so much to making his tour both successful and pleasurable. He addressed Dvořák with special warmth:

> I shall never forget how well and in how friendly a fashion you received me in Prague. Dear friend, convey my heartfelt greetings to your dear wife, and allow me to say again that I am very happy and fortunate to have gained your most precious friendship.

In Vienna he saw an English opera – but one act of *The Mikado* was as much as he could take. In Taganrog he paused for three days with Ippolit and his wife. For all the travails of his conducting marathon, he had gained a taste for the kind of success, both personal and musical, that he had enjoyed on this tour. 'I shall try to get an invitation to conduct in America next year or in two years' time,' he confided to his patroness. 'Is it not strange that after more than three months of exhausting travel abroad, I am already again dreaming of a journey?' On 7 April he was with Anatoly and Parasha in Tiflis.

All these concerts had been splendid occasions that had greatly enhanced Tchaikovsky's international standing. But, at the other end of the scale, when Tchaikovsky had arrived in Berlin on the first stage of this tour, he had had a surprise reunion that both touched him very deeply and would have a major consequence for his creative activity. It was now some twenty years since he had last encountered Désirée Artôt, the woman who in 1868 had briefly seemed poised to become his wife. Now they met again, and their reunion seems to have touched them both. Then in early February 1888, when Tchaikovsky returned to Berlin to conduct his concert for the Berlin Philharmonic Society, they met again and, at a reception that Artôt had arranged, she asked Tchaikovsky to compose a song for her. He assured her that he would, though he pleaded that current commitments precluded a swift discharge of this undertaking. Artôt was untroubled: 'I am in no hurry. One day when you are composing songs and you think I could perform one or another of them well, then just think of dedicating one to me. That's all I wish.'

Five months passed – but the delay had fruitful consequences. As he wrote the following October:

I have just delivered to Jurgenson, my publisher, six *Mélodies* which I have composed for you, and I ask you to consent to accept the dedication. I would very much hope these *Mélodies* can please you, but I must confess that latterly I have been working too much, and it is more than probable that my new compositions are more the product of *good intentions* than true inspiration. But then, one is a little intimidated when one is composing for a singer one considers the greatest among the great.

For her part, Artôt also seemed a little intimidated by the size of her former suitor's gift:

I asked for but one song – and so generously you have composed six for me. They say 'generous like a king': they have forgotten to add 'or like an artist'. Naturally I am very curious to make this new acquaintance, but I do not wish to cause you additional work. I will wait until Jurgenson has published them – but then ask him to send them to me immediately.

However, Jurgenson was slow to act, and in the meantime, in February 1889, during his second European concert tour, Tchaikovsky was trapped in Berlin for eight hectic days, and was unboundedly grateful for her presence. 'My sole comfort is *Artôt*, who is invited everywhere with me, and whom I like enormously,' he reported to Modest. As for the songs, they were published in May, but Jurgenson failed for three months to send Artôt her copy. When this finally arrived, she hastened to acknowledge receipt:

At last, at last, dear friend, your songs are in my hands, waiting to be transferred to my voice. Yes, indeed, four, five and six are superb, but the first, 'Sérénade', is adorable and has charming freshness. 'La déception' also pleases me enormously. In a word, I am *in love* with your new offspring, and proud that you have created them while thinking of me.

But Artôt would soon present problems. Early in 1890, when she was in Paris, a minor French writer, Joseph Capoul, had devised a libretto on a Russian subject and shown it to Artôt, who had promptly decided that only Tchaikovsky could provide the music, and had forthwith written to him in Florence, where he was immersed in composing *The Queen of Spades*:

> He [Capoul] is ready to come and meet you, and submit it [his libretto] to you personally. Send me a word in reply, and if you wish to be even nicer, send a telegram saying, 'I await Capoul': that will suffice. Two hours later he will be *on his way.*

This, however, was too much for Tchaikovsky, especially with his current commitment. Desperate to forestall Capoul's appearance, he telegraphed Artôt that he was leaving Florence imminently, and followed this up with a letter claiming that he already had a trail of commissions which would keep him occupied for the next few years. All this was, of course, totally fictitious. Yet Tchaikovsky simply could not bear to damage permanently his friendship with Artôt: in any case, she might discover the truth. 'I end by confessing to you *an untruth*,' he wrote.

> I am not leaving for Russia this evening. I told this untruth so that M. Capoul would be quite certain he would not find me. I feared that, encouraged by your friendship towards me (which I enormously value), he would have come to find me here. Thank you, thank you a thousand times for singing my songs. I do not know when I shall be coming to Paris; I know only that, if I should come, I shall be enormously happy to see you.

Artôt did not reply, and they never met again.

Tchaikovsky would spend three weeks with Anatoly and Parasha recovering from the strains of his conducting tour. While at Tiflis he pondered what his next composition should be, and decided emphatically on a symphony. He was delighted by the new house Alexey had found for him at Frolovskoye, even though it was a little further from Klin than Maidanovo. It had a superb view, 'but what's most precious of all is that you can go straight from the garden into a wood and stroll there all day. There's not a trace of the inhabitants of the dachas' – nor, he might have added, of their pianos. Alexey had now succeeded in marrying. An earlier attempt had failed when his first bride had taken fright and run away on the day of the wedding, but his second had worked, and Tchaikovsky approved of his choice: 'extremely nice and sympathetic' – though he found her best feature was her teeth. In fact, Tchaikovsky became very fond of Feklusha, and her death from tuberculosis in 1890 saddened him deeply. The one current reason for distress was Kamenka, which he visited for ten days. Sasha's morphine addiction had become worse and she had aged, Bob was growing unhealthily fat, and Tasya's good looks had faded. Back in Frolovskoye Tchaikovsky reviewed his various compositional options, but within ten days had returned to the decision he had made at Tiflis. On 21 May he set about his Fifth Symphony.

However, there was now a clash of interests. Twelve years earlier Modest had offered his brother a programme for a symphonic poem on *Hamlet*, but instead Tchaikovsky had settled to composing *Francesca da Rimini*. Nevertheless, *Hamlet* had continued to haunt him, and during his recent concert tour his actor friend, Lucien Guitry, had asked him to provide some incidental music for a charity performance of Shakespeare's play. The event was cancelled, but the subject had now firmly embedded itself in Tchaikovsky's creative mind, and when he arrived back in Russia he had already jotted down some ideas for a symphonic poem. However, he had now decided that sketching the symphony should take precedence, but having finished this by the end of June, he proceeded straight to *Hamlet*, and within five days that, too, was drafted. Other commitments now intervened, and it was late October before both pieces were complete. Their premieres took place in November within a week of each other. Both were triumphs with their audiences, but less successful with the press, including Cui, who described the symphony as 'routine'.

In fact, superficially, Cui's judgement can be understood – which brings us back to the previous January in Hamburg, and the elderly music teacher, Theodor Avé-Lallement. To get to the fundamental point (but also to generalize very widely): the nineteenth-century symphonic tradition was an Austro-German one growing out of the work of, primarily, Haydn and Mozart in the later eighteenth century, and this had established a line of symphonic works extended by composers such as Beethoven and Brahms in the nineteenth, and characterized by 'thoughtful' practices, often with a strong intellectual element that came naturally to peoples famed for the strength of their powers of reasoning (many commentators on a classical symphonic work will still talk about its 'argument'). But Slav composers created much more impulsively. Tchaikovsky's description of his own creative processes reveals this vividly and, for such composers, entering this mainstream symphonic tradition meant adopting some practices and attitudes that did not come naturally to them. Put it this way: whereas a symphonic creation of an Austrian or German composer was (to use an analogy from chemistry) a *compound*, that of a composer from outside was more a *mixture* – or take Musorgsky's succinct, but far more precise, dictum: 'A German, when he thinks, first analyses, then creates. A Russian first creates, then amuses himself with analysis.' That the greatest of nineteenth-century Russian composers, such as Tchaikovsky, so often modified traditional symphonic forms, even in some instances seeming virtually to abandon them, was often a cheering sign of their recognition that, if they were to be truly themselves, they had to be prepared to go out on a limb. The great first movement of Tchaikovsky's Fourth Symphony is a classic example of this. It is recognizably in sonata form, but this has been drastically modified and reshaped so that Tchaikovsky's most natural creative gifts can exercise themselves to the full. However, what Tchaikovsky has done in the Fifth Symphony's first movement is even, in a way, bolder than that radical adventure; he has fearlessly presumed to enter the German–Austrian symphonic citadel and occupied it on his own terms. The relative lengths and characters of its four movements reflect the German–Austrian model; the structural proportions within the individual movements correspond to those typical of a classical symphony, and only in the slow movement are there intimidating irruptions of the kind observed in the first and last movements of the Fourth, but not typical of the West European tradition. Yet – and this is the crucial point – the music of the Fifth Symphony could be by none other than Tchaikovsky. Let us not underestimate the achievement this represents.

And if we have any doubts about who was responsible for this shift in Tchaikovsky's style, the answer lies, surely, in the symphony's dedication: 'To Theodor Avé-Lallement'. The piece was, in fact, a deliberate and delicious refutation of Avé-Lallement's prescription. Tchaikovsky had no need to leave Russia, and settle permanently in Germany, so that classical traditions and conditions of the highest culture would rectify his shortcomings. He could do that perfectly well in Russia – but in his own way and without sacrificing his own style.

There was, however, to be a rather sad ending to this episode. The following year Tchaikovsky would once again tour Europe, and include Hamburg in his itinerary. On his programme was, perhaps pointedly, the Fifth Symphony. Sadly, however, his dedicatee was unable to be present, and could not give his verdict on the work on which he had so unwittingly had such an influence.

Symphony no. 5 in E minor * * * * *

[As already noted, the Fifth Symphony is a more regular (I do not use the word 'conventional', which might suggest mundane) work than its predecessor, and the closer examination of it will be less extensive than was that of the Fourth Symphony. Do not assume that this reflects on the importance of the piece.]

Among the sketches of the Symphony there is evidence of a programme to the first movement:

> Introduction. Total submission before Fate – or, what is the same thing, the inscrutable design of Providence.
> Allegro. 1 Murmers, doubts, laments. Reproaches against . . . *xxx*;
> 2 Shall I cast myself into the embrace of faith?
> A wonderful programme, if only it can be fulfilled.

Whether the object of reproach signified by the triple *x* was Tchaikovsky's homosexuality we cannot say, but the mention of faith suggests that, this time, there is a possibility of escape from some catastrophic outcome through the divine, implying a confidence in clemency. That there is an optimism behind this symphony would also seem to be contained in the work's opening phrase, which appears to be a quotation from Glinka's opera *A Life for the Tsar*, where it sets the exhortation 'Do not turn to sorrow', and which seems to become, in this symphony, the hope theme – and note that it is immediately succeeded by a six-note stepwise-descending phrase that seems to echo the six-pitch Fate theme that I first identified in Tatyana's Letter Scene in the opera *Eugene Onegin*. Indeed, there are strong hints of a loose programme encompassing the whole symphony.

The Symphony has a muted and lengthy slow introduction, opening (as has been observed) with the Glinka-derived Hope theme, followed by the six-pitch Fate theme. The exposition enters quietly with pizzicato

337

chords that will support a theme which, though faster, seems almost an extension of the introduction's, but which builds to a very strong climax: clearly there is some powerful rhetoric in store. As is customary, Tchaikovsky's exposition contains three themes, the second easily identified as the strongly rising tune that enters abruptly on the strings, and which will go on to alternate with a repeated two-note chordal motif in the woodwind; from this close dialogue the third theme, which might fairly be described as a gentle waltz, emerges. Or – and this is a teasing point for those readers familiar with key usage – did the third subject *begin* with the repeated two-note idea, with the second subject's rising theme overlapping briefly into it? In fact, it would seem that this is so, since the third subject's key, D major, is reached here.

The exposition moves smoothly into the development, which begins quietly (there should be no problem in identifying this moment). Material from all three themes is worked intensively, and the recapitulation opens as quietly as had the development, and (led off by a solo bassoon) becomes largely a rerun of the exposition, allowing for adjustments of key. The coda returns to the music that had opened the development, though subsequently directing itself in business-like fashion to an ending as quiet as that in which the movement had opened.

The second movement, *Andante cantabile, con alcuna licenza* ('melodiously, at a walking pace, with some licence'), quickly confirms just how different this symphony will be from its predecessor. The supercharged first movement of the Fourth Symphony had been followed, very necessarily, by a relaxed slow movement *in modo di canzone* ('like a song', as Tchaikovsky expressly indicated); here the quietly majestic series of chords, which conducts us into the slow movement itself, forewarns that something of very weighty substance is in store. Very interestingly, it is said that the movement's second melody (for oboe) was paired with the words '*O que je t'aime! O mon amie!*' ('O how I love you! O my friend'), which readily confirms the impression that this movement could be a deeply personal outpouring of love (though it should be noted that the final 'e' of 'amie' indicates that the object of love is a woman, not a man). Whatever the case, here is the expressive heart of the whole symphony, and it is among Tchaikovsky's greatest slow movements, opening with one of music's most famous horn solos, soon joined in quiet dialogue by a solo clarinet.

The oboe intervenes with the movement's second main theme (the Love theme?), the clarinet falling silent as the horn now becomes the shadowing partner before the massed cellos return to the horn's theme, with countermelodies provided by the three former soloists. Again the second theme recurs expansively, now on the strings, to lead this rich flow of melody to its dynamic climax before fading and rounding off the first of the three main sections that will make up this movement.

The second main section, introduced by a new third theme on the clarinet, seems more relaxed. But it, too, will build, this time to an even more dramatic climax, for it will be the Glinka-derived Hope theme that had launched the whole symphony so unobtrusively, and has not been heard since, that will break in defiantly on trumpets *ff*, substantiating the indication provided by Tchaikovsky's brief programme that this symphony has been more than simply a moving, but otherwise purely musical, creation, and that personal drama has a part to play in it. This is a slow movement so eloquent that the third main section needs little further comment from me, for it retracks its way, though with modifications, through the first section, embracing the Love theme, but this time ending with a second defiant intervention of the Hope theme. All will now move towards a kind of resolution, the Love theme (calmly, and now on the violins) directing the movement to an ending even quieter than that in which it had all begun. Indeed, is this at first hesitant, then serenely assured, peaceful conclusion the 'embrace of faith' in Tchaikovsky's fragmentary programme?

The quiet assurance in the conclusion of this great slow movement seems substantiated by the first sounds of the following *Valse*. True, it is Tatyana's six-note Fate theme from *Onegin* that opens this third movement, but instantly it sounds untroubled, setting the tone for a relaxed, cheerful intermezzo – a ternary structure, the central section filled with lively decoration which spills over into the return of the first section. And at the movement's end, having intruded so importunately in the slow movement, the Hope theme slips in benignly to join the dance. The symphony's prevailing mood has shifted fundamentally.

The slow introduction to the finale confirms this shift, returning to the Hope theme that had opened the first movement, though it is now in the major key, *mf* and *maestoso* (majestic, stately), sounds confident, its self-assurance celebrated with abandon in the *Allegro vivace* that provides the body of the movement. This is a sonata structure into which the Hope theme is twice exultantly incorporated, the first time between the exposition and development; the recapitulation explodes after the long diminuendo which ends the development very quietly. Only one thing I will add: I do find the coda with its grandiose trumpeting of the Hope theme over the top. The tune itself is, frankly, not a particularly good one, which did not matter in the contexts within which it has earlier been heard. Indeed, the brashness of its irruptions in the slow movement is almost a virtue if, indeed, they represent blows against a malign and implacable obstacle to happiness, where only matching force, and not well-mannered requests to be reasonable and go away, can achieve victory. There *is* a place in music for the commonplace, even for ugliness, even for what many would consider vulgarity. Listen to how brilliantly Mahler, for instance, could use the otherwise banal – but its justification depends on its context. However, such ostentatious celebration, as here, can savour of triumphalism, and I find it a touch distasteful. There, my fellow listener, you have a challenge – but I believe that if you have followed me through the greater number of case studies I have presented in this book, then you are probably sufficiently versed (and some, I know, may already have been well versed before picking up this book) in getting to grips with music to be able to begin coping with critical challenges, and making considered judgements (though you may not *always* be right: nor, indeed, am I). One more point to note that is not in dispute: the symphony ends by trumpeting, *ffff*, the first subject of the first movement, thereby providing a frame for the whole conception.

––––––

Fantasy overture: *Hamlet* * * *(*)

[This relatively concise piece has never gained the popularity of either Romeo and Juliet *or* Francesca da Rimini, *and it is not, to my ears, as perfectly formed a piece as either of these predecessors. Nevertheless, it contains some very powerful music. Perhaps one reason for its neglect is that Hamlet's beloved, Ophelia, though a young and tragic figure, is neither as fully formed nor as central as were Juliet and Francesca in the earlier works, and Tchaikovsky's personal engagement was not as strong. No matter: for those who revel in these earlier pieces (not forgetting* The Tempest*), Hamlet will afford much pleasure.]*

Of all the subjects Tchaikovsky chose for his six symphonic poems, *Hamlet* was certainly the most formidable. *Romeo and Juliet* and *Francesca da Rimini* had both been tragic love stories, and at the heart of *The Tempest* had been a third such, though this time a happy one, and much simpler because this entailed no trail of conflict or misery to take account of, thus leaving Tchaikovsky at liberty to track Stasov's programme and incorporate also Ariel and Caliban in distinctive cameos. Then add to this a couple of touches of magic from Prospero, throw in a storm, and frame the whole with a representation of the sea to seal it all into a tidy package and – as I have heard said – 'Bob's your uncle!' This had worked well enough when the actual plot of the play itself was really a fantasy, and relatively loose. But it would not do for *Hamlet*, a real-life story of a young prince whose father has been murdered by his own brother, who now occupies the throne. The ghost of the murdered king appears, calling on Hamlet to avenge him, but the tale that follows is of Hamlet's constant indecision, which can only generate a sprawling succession of catastrophes involving a clutch of characters with powerful and diverse motivations. It presented a very daunting challenge to the composer, a possible solution being the draconian one of focusing single-mindedly on the central character himself (as Liszt did in his remarkable symphonic poem *Hamlet*); the other was to compose a whole three- or four-hour opera on it. What I am really suggesting is that there will always be a sense of something lacking in a concise symphonic poem that attempts to embrace such a complex tale as Tchaikovsky had chosen – though otherwise *Hamlet* probably suited him. In fact, what clearly drew him to the subject was (yet again) his perception of Hamlet as another victim of Fate, whose agent is represented so plausibly in the play by the Ghost of his murdered father; the only other character whose presence Tchaikovsky decided he required was the tragic Ophelia, Hamlet's beloved – though also necessary, if only in our imaginations, is Laertes, Ophelia's brother and formerly Hamlet's friend, but who accuses Hamlet of causing his sister's death and who dies with him in their final duel; also necessary is Fortinbras, the Norwegian Prince, who appears only in transit in the main body of the play, but who is needed to preside over its catastrophic end .

It is the Ghost (and Fate) theme with which we are straight away confronted at the fantasy overture's opening (above this moment in his score Tchaikovsky wrote 'To be or not to be', the words from the second of Hamlet's great soliloquies, and perhaps the most famous of all Shakespearean quotations). It makes for a portentous beginning, its first five notes later becoming a grim sign of its spectral presence. There are two flurried interjections of louder music: subsequent events may suggest these are harbingers of Hamlet's death. Horns toll midnight, then a mighty gong stroke heralds the appearance of the Ghost itself, with his tale of regicide, followed by his daunting injunction that Hamlet avenge him, delivered *fff*, and reinforced by a pounding *ffff* section before the spectre withdraws. While the stressed music that instantly follows is manifestly Hamlet's response (but note the two brief breaks in this: are these already reflections of his fateful Achilles heel, his indecisiveness?), equally there can be no doubt that the gentle, slightly nervous oboe cantilena represents Ophelia, and the broad string theme is Hamlet's confession of love. Though not really one of Tchaikovsky's best love themes (Balakirev, who never liked the piece, wrote here in his own score: 'Hamlet pays compliments to Ophelia, handing her an ice-cream'!), we must remember that Hamlet's behaviour towards Ophelia becomes cruelly ambivalent, his devotion lacking the integrity and depth of Romeo's for his Juliet. The following march surely marks Fortinbras's first appearance before Hamlet's stressed music resumes. Ophelia reappears, a residue of Hamlet's music persisting uneasily beneath hers; this time she is clearly apprehensive. Again Hamlet's love music – but it would seem that he also is less at ease than before. The Ghost/Fate theme recurs insistently as, presumably, the final duel between Hamlet and Laertes begins. Fortinbras is heard approaching from a distance, the last fateful stage of the duel is fought, Laertes is now dead and Hamlet mortally wounded. It is here that those two flurried interjections in the opening music recur, and the long-descending scale in the cellos is perhaps another final token of Fate's over-arching presence. A brief death march presided over by the Ghost's theme closes this rarely played piece, which, whatever its shortcomings, should be heard more often than it seems to be at the present.

———

25
Second Foreign Tour:
The Sleeping Beauty

The summer of 1888 would be largely uneventful. In such quiet conditions company became a necessity, and Laroche was resident at Frolovskoye for a month. A more unusual guest was the wife of
Kondratyev's manservant, Alexander Legoshin, who had so devotedly
tended Tchaikovsky's old friend during the latter's last weeks.
Tchaikovsky had clearly developed an affection for the whole
Legoshin family, and he bought a perambulator for their two-year-old
daughter, who suffered from rickets. For his own name-day he
arranged a party with Jurgenson, Albrecht and Ziloti among the
guests, the two-day event allowing liberal opportunities for
Tchaikovsky's favourite card game, vint. There were, of course, the
regular trips to Moscow and St Petersburg. At the end of the summer
he paid a visit to Kamenka, his first for over two years. His feelings
about it remained mixed, and his week there was overshadowed by
grim news from Paris. It was little more than a year since the sudden
death of his eldest niece, Tanya, and now a second, Vera, was dying of
tuberculosis in the French capital.

The manifest success of his first foreign tour as conductor was
already bringing in proposals for further forays abroad. By August he
had committed himself to concerts in Dresden and Berlin, to which
Frankfurt, Cologne and London were soon added. Ahead of this he
had two in St Petersburg, after which he would have to redeem his
promise to conduct *Onegin* in Prague. The first of the Russian concerts was that at which the Fifth Symphony received its premiere, and
also on the programme was Laroche's overture, *Karmozina*, which
Tchaikovsky had orchestrated for his friend. At the rehearsal the piece
had been heavily criticized for its brashness, but Tchaikovsky, determined that the work should not be a failure, fabricated (without
Laroche's knowledge) a programme that was circulated ahead of the
concert, claiming that the overture was intended as the prelude to an

opera that opened with a Venetian Carnival orgy. Meanwhile he had, by his sustained encouragements, extracted a play from Shpazhin-skaya, but had failed to manipulate the Imperial Theatres into mounting it. Hearing now of its rejection, he personally broke the news to the authoress, softening the blow as best he could. In addition, his friend and former colleague, Nikolay Hubert, had recently died, and Tchaikovsky had been giving financial support to his widow. Kashkin, too, was in financial difficulties, and Tchaikovsky organized a secret loan to help his friend. Then on 26 November, all these various commitments and interventions having been discharged, he headed for Prague.

This time his Czech sortie was comparatively low key. On his previous visit he had foregone all fees, but now he was to receive half the takings. As it turned out, the concert he was to conduct had been badly timed and organized, the audience was small, and the receipts low. But the press having expressed outrage at this, Tchaikovsky's reception at the opening of *Onegin* was a personal triumph, with endless ovations. During this visit he invited Dvořák to conduct in Moscow, and on his return to Russia he personally supervised the arrangements, including fee, for this visit – though Dvořák insisted that it should be no earlier than March 1890 for fear of Russian frosts. As Tchaikovsky passed through Vienna on his way home, he read in a newspaper of Vera's death and, assuming that her body would be brought back to St Petersburg for burial, directed himself to the capital. After conducting two concerts in Moscow, he returned to St Petersburg for a third, this time promoted by the publisher, Mitrofan Belyayev, and which included *The Tempest*, the rest of the programme being made up of works by 'The New Russian School' – that is, the *kuchka*. Tchaikovsky had long had good personal relations with most of its members, and by now he knew he need have absolutely no fear of comparisons with them, and that any problems or tensions with its members had been finally put to rest. These and other matters having been delivered or completed, on 6 January 1889, the Russian Christmas Day, he was back in Frolovskoye with four free weeks ahead of him. At last he could set in earnest about composing his new ballet, *The Sleeping Beauty*.

For a while we will pass over the month devoted to sketching this masterpiece, and follow Tchaikovsky on his second European tour as conductor. He left Russia on 5 February, delaying in Berlin to consult with his impresario, Hermann Wolf, and to enjoy some time with Artôt. His first concert was in Cologne, where he conducted his Third Suite and was received very warmly, with a triple fanfare at the concert's end. Frankfurt was next. *1812* was to have been part of the programme, but now the promoters had become nervous about its very noisy ending (despite the Berliners having coped with this unflinchingly), and it was quietly dropped. But the Third Suite received an ovation, and Tchaikovsky was pressed to return before the year's end.

Two days later he was in Dresden – a more demanding commitment this time (Fourth Symphony and First Piano Concerto), made more difficult by an inferior orchestra and an indiosyncratic soloist, Emil Sauer. Inevitably the concert went less well, though the audience warmed to the symphony as it proceeded, and there was a single fanfare at the end. Meanwhile, his longing to be home grew. As he wrote to the Grand Duke Konstantin Konstantinovich:

> I cannot express to you how much *Heimweh* [homesickness], as the Germans call it, fills me with misery, yearning, pining and pain. Last year also I felt this terribly grievous longing for my homeland, but to an infinitely lesser degree. It is not the rehearsals for the concerts, nor the concerts themselves that are particularly burdensome, but the constant gyrating among strange people, even though they are sometimes extremely interesting. But worst of all is that I am scarcely ever alone.

Nevertheless, he had to confess himself well pleased with his self-evident personal success, and before proceeding to Geneva for his next engagement, he was able to relax for two days with his friends, the Brodskys, in Leipzig.

The Geneva orchestra proved both small and inferior, but the players were pleasant and keen, the daily rehearsals brought much improvement, and Tchaikovsky's contribution to the concert (the Serenade for Strings and the First Suite), given to a packed house, brought an ovation, and a gilded wreath from the local Russian colony. In early 1876 he had spent some weeks there with Sasha and her children, and now, writing to Bob, he recalled especially his two nieces who had so recently died:

> Yesterday I went to the Boulevard Plainpalais where you stayed. I remembered Tanya and Vera so vividly, their arms red from running

345

to school in the cold, and you with your tiny nose and not that trunk you now have instead of a nose, and myself not as grey when I was a whole thirteen years younger. I became terribly sad:

> *Nessun dolor maggiore*
> *Che ricordarsi del tempo felice*
> *Nella miseria!*

Tchaikovsky's arrival at his next stop, Hamburg, brought a surprise, for installed in the neighbouring hotel room was Brahms, who had delayed his departure for a day so that he could attend a rehearsal of Tchaikovsky's new Fifth Symphony. Having heard the piece, Brahms told Tchaikovsky he approved strongly of the first three movements, but did not like the finale. Honest criticism such as this rarely riled Tchaikovsky. 'Brahms is very amiable,' he wrote to Modest. 'After the rehearsal we had lunch together and drank well. He is a very sympathetic person, and I like his integrity and simplicity.' Forthwith he tried, though unsuccessfully, to persuade Brahms to conduct in Moscow during the next season. As for the Fifth Symphony's reception by the wider Hamburg audience, this was a triumph. But there were now four weeks to fill before his next engagement, which was in London, where he was hoping especially to further the fortunes of the twenty-year-old pianist Vasily Sapelnikov, who was to be the soloist in the First Piano Concerto. Paris was an easy choice to fill the time gap. Tchaikovsky now had many musical acquaintances there, the city offered an abundance of theatrical and musical events, and there was the new Eiffel Tower to inspect, then ascend. Learning of his presence in the city, Colonne included the *Theme and Variations* from the Third Suite in one of his concerts, which was followed by a reception at which some of Tchaikovsky's songs were sung.

On 9 April Tchaikovsky was in London at the Hôtel Dieudonné, waking the next morning to find the capital blanketed in a 'peasouper' (a particularly dense fog caused by pollution: some older readers may still remember these). His single concert included the First Suite as well as the concerto, and Sapelnikov scored a special success; he would return to London repeatedly in subsequent years. Early next morning Tchaikovsky slipped into Sapelnikov's room, kissed the sleeping lad, then left the hotel on his way to Anatoly and Parasha. Passing through Paris en route for Marseilles, he embarked on another Mediterranean crossing.

From time to time Tchaikovsky would strike up a brief relationship with some individual whom he would never meet again, but who had so attracted him that, maybe years later, he would become the dedicatee of one of Tchaikovsky's compositions. Such a one was Vladimir Sklifosovsky, the son of an eminent Moscow surgeon. On this crossing they traversed together the Strait of Bonifacio, observed a spectacular volcanic eruption on the Lipari Islands, endured a gale off Messina, and together visited the Greek island of Siros. The following port of call was Smyrna (now Izmir), where they again toured the sights – and bought fezzes. On reaching Constantinople, however, Sklifosovsky disembarked. Tchaikovsky wept on parting, and the following year he learned that the youth had died. Yet four years on he would still remember their encounter, dedicating *Chant élégiaque*, no. 14 of his Eighteen Piano Pieces, op. 72, to Sklifosovsky's memory.

Tchaikovsky found the voyage along the northern Turkish coast wearying, and it was with relief that he reached Tiflis, though he would find little relaxation in his sister-in-law's endless socializing. It was gratifying that, in his honour, the Artistic Society mounted a concert of his music which included the Piano Trio, but it was still a very tired Tchaikovsky who, on 14 May, set off for Moscow, following in reverse the route that had brought him to the Caucasus for the first time. There was, however, no respite to be found in Moscow. The Conservatoire was in crisis. Taneyev had resigned as director, and Safonov would agree to replace him only if Albrecht was dismissed. Tchaikovsky knew that there had been tension between these last two, but loyalty to Albrecht fortified his determination that his old friend should not leave under a cloud, and he at length persuaded Albrecht to resign (Tchaikovsky himself drafting his letter of resignation for him), while persuading Taneyev to remain as professor of counterpoint. But even with all this and the Conservatoire's annual examinations to cope with, he still found time to arrange that Hubert's widow should fill Albrecht's now vacant position.

Next stop was St Petersburg to visit Modest and Kolya, consult with Ivan Vsevolozhsky, the Intendant of the Imperial Theatres, about the mounting of *The Sleeping Beauty*, and to participate in the arrangements to celebrate Anton Rubinstein's golden jubilee as a pianist. Rubinstein himself being unable to be present at the first concert, Tchaikovsky persuaded Rimsky to replace him as conductor, Tchaikovsky himself making his debut as a castanet-player in Rimsky's

347

Capriccio espagnole because the professional percussionist proved incompetent. On 31 May he was back in Frolovskoye to complete *The Sleeping Beauty*, which the theatre required by the middle of September.

Whereas we know very little about the background and composition of *Swan Lake*, there is ample data about the birth process of *The Sleeping Beauty*. The idea for a ballet to be based on a folktale as told by the seventeenth-century French writer, Charles Perrault, had come from Vsevolozhsky in May 1888, and the scenario would be basically his. Tchaikovsky was quickly captivated by it, in September conferring with both Vsevolozhsky and Marius Petipa (today remembered as one of ballet's legendary choreographers), during which everything was worked out down to the finest detail. Tchaikovsky's excitement was such that in October he could not resist making a start on the music, though it was only in January 1889 that he could begin composition in earnest. Yet in little more than a fortnight a very substantial part of the ballet was sketched. Tchaikovsky's second European tour brought another interruption, but within a week of his return to Frolovskoye, the sketches of *The Sleeping Beauty* were complete. 'I finished on 7 June 1889 at 8 p.m. Praise be to God!' he wrote at their end. 'In all I worked ten days in October, three weeks in January, and now a week – so, in all, about forty days.' The scoring, however, took much longer than that of *Swan Lake*, for Tchaikovsky now wanted his music to be presented with much more variety of colour and texture than in the earlier ballet, and it was August before this operation was finished. He was disappointed by the ballet's rather muted reception at its premiere, but this reaction was probably occasioned by the music's extra sophistication. Though *The Sleeping Beauty* has never been able to match the popularity of *Swan Lake*, it is arguably (dare I say it?) the finer piece.

The Sleeping Beauty: ballet in four acts * * * * *

[This is the sort of piece about which I am tempted to say so much here that I would anticipate a good deal of the following commentary. The Sleeping Beauty lacks, of course, the pathos of Swan Lake, which reaches to the heart (ballets seem especially in danger of losing out if they have happy endings), but there is a magical inventiveness and sophistication (and a far greater consistency of quality) in

Tchaikovsky's music for his second ballet that compensates for its 'softer' drama. No matter: I am sure that if you like one of the ballets, you will like the other (individual opinions are likely to be less divided here than they may be about Tchaikovsky's symphonies, for instance).]

The following summary of the ballet's plot omits much action detail:

Prologue. The Christening of Princess Aurora: a banquet in the King's palace. March (no. 1): Courtiers assemble and await the arrival of the King and Queen while Catalabutte, the master of ceremonies, checks the guest list. Trumpets announce the entrance of the King and Queen with their newborn daughter, Aurora. *Scène dansante* (no. 2): Aurora's godmothers, the good Fairies, enter, then the Lilac Fairy, Aurora's chief godmother. Royal gifts are presented to the Fairies. *Pas de six* (no. 3): The Fairies in turn present gifts to their god-daughter. *Finale* (no. 4): The Lilac Fairy prepares to present her gift, but a noise offstage warns of the approach of a furious Carabosse, the evil Fairy, whose invitation to the christening had been overlooked. A terrified Catalabutte admits this was his mistake. All are alarmed. Carabosse, accompanied by ugly pages, appears in a wheelbarrow drawn by six rats. The King and Queen promise to punish Catalabutte for his mistake, the latter begs forgiveness, but Carabosse torments him. She declares that she wants to present a gift to Aurora. Despite the good Fairies' intervention, Carabosse cannot be mollified, and she delivers her 'gift': Aurora will grow to be beautiful, but will fall into eternal sleep the first time she pricks her finger. All are dumbfounded and Carabosse exults. But the Lilac Fairy has not yet presented her gift, and she can still mitigate the curse: a handsome Prince will one day come, his kiss will break the spell, and he and Aurora will marry. A furious Carabosse leaves, and the good Fairies surround the cradle protectively.

Act 1. *The park of the King's palace. Scène* (no. 5): Aurora is twenty, and the King is happy that Carabosse's curse has not been fulfilled. A law now prohibits all needles and pins, and Catalabutte reproves a group of peasants who are carrying some; they beg forgiveness, but are sent to prison. The King and Queen, accompanied by four Princes, enter. When told by Catalabutte why the peasants are going to prison, the King and Queen condemn them, but the Princes intercede, urging that no tears be shed at Aurora's coming of age. The King agrees, and frees the peasants. General rejoicing. *Valse* (no. 6): Peasants dance.

Scène (no. 7): Having only seen her portrait, the Princes wish to see Aurora herself, who has been given free choice as to which of them shall be her husband. Aurora rushes in, and the Princes are astonished at her beauty. *Pas d'action* (no. 8): Aurora dances with the Princes in turn – and rejects all of them. Her parents urge her to marry, but she wishes to preserve her freedom – and dances off. Noticing an old woman beating time with a spindle, she snatches it from her, and teases the Princes by dancing with it as though with a sceptre. *Finale* (no. 9): Suddenly Aurora feels her finger being pricked, dances wildly, then falls lifeless. The old woman reveals herself to be Carabosse and disappears, as do the Princes. However, the Lilac Fairy materializes, mitigates the curse, reassuring the King and Queen, and prophesying that Aurora will fall asleep for a hundred years, to be awakened by the kiss of a handsome Prince, whom she will then marry. They leave with their daughter, and the Lilac Fairy casts a spell over all who remain onstage, the other Fairies appearing so as to protect the peace of the sleepers.

Act 2 Scene 1. *Prince Désiré's hunt. A wooded place beside a river, with a cliff. Entracte et scène* (no. 10): Huntsmen and women appear, then settle down to eat. Désiré enters with his tutor, Galifron, and courtiers. *Colin-Maillard* (Blind man's buff) (no. 11): A diversion is organized. *Scène* (nos. 12–13): Various dances. *Scène* (no. 14): The Prince decides not to join the next hunt, and is left alone. The Lilac Fairy appears from along the river. She tells the Prince she will show him his future bride, and the cliffside opens, revealing a sleeping Aurora and her retinue. *Pas d'action* (no. 15): Aurora rises and dances for the Prince, who is increasingly captivated. Aurora disappears into a cleft in the rocks. *Scène* (no. 16): An enamoured Prince begs the Lilac Fairy to take him to where Aurora is. The Lilac Fairy leads him to the boat, which moves off, the scenery becoming wilder. *Panorama* (no. 17): Night falls. A distant castle, the goal of their journey, is seen. They disembark, the Lilac Fairy opens the castle gates with her wand, and the pages and guards are seen asleep. All is then enveloped in dense clouds, and quiet music is heard.

Entr'acte (no. 18): (Never used in performance).

Act 2 Scene 2. *The Sleeping Beauty's castle. Symphonic entr'acte* (no. 19): The clouds disperse. Aurora is asleep on a canopied bed. The King, Queen and courtiers are also asleep: dust and cobwebs everywhere. The Lilac Fairy and the Prince enter. The Prince runs to the bed, but cannot awaken Aurora; he is in despair. Finally he kisses her. *Finale* (no. 20): The spell is broken, Aurora and all awaken, and the dust and cobwebs disappear. The Prince asks for Aurora's hand in marriage, and the King assents.

Act 3. *The Wedding of Prince Désiré and Princess Aurora. The esplanade of the King's palace. March* (no. 21): The courtiers assemble for festivities. Catalabutte allocates the guests their places. The King and Queen enter, together with the newly-weds and four Fairies. *Polonaise* (no. 22): Procession of participants in the divertissement. *Pas de quatre* (no. 23): The four Fairies. *Pas de caractère* (no. 24): Puss in Boots and the White Cat. *Pas de quatre* (no. 25): Cinderella and Prince Fortuné. The Bluebird and Princess Florine. *Pas de caractère* (no. 26): Little Red Riding Hood and the Wolf. The Bluebird and Prince Fortuné. *Pas berichon* (no. 27): Tom Thumb, his brothers, and the Ogre. *Pas de deux* (no. 28): Aurora and Désiré. Entrance of the corps de ballet: *Sarabande* (no. 29). Finale (no. 30): Apotheosis.

Some fifteen years separate *The Sleeping Beauty* from its predecessor, *Swan Lake*, and there is a correspondingly wide gap between the two ballets' dramatic natures. In its own time *Swan Lake* represented a remarkable achievement in that – and, above all, in its final act – its music had addressed the listener with an unsparing power and precision which many a ballet audience of the time must have found disconcerting. Nowadays *Swan Lake* poses no such problems for ballet-goers drawn, as they are, from a far wider social range and a very different musical environment; indeed, it is probably *Swan Lake*'s high dramatic tensions and deep emotional issues – and Tchaikovsky's magnificent responses to these – that are the prime reasons why it has retained a popularity that *The Sleeping Beauty* has never been able to match. In this later ballet there is no pathos-filled tragedy, no incident loaded with true pain or distress, and its outcome we know is one for which every spectator has wished, and which is lavishly celebrated in the final act (which, in the past, it was not uncommon practice to perform separately in an evening of ballet excerpts under the title *Aurora's Wedding*). Yet – and I love *Swan Lake*, and never miss an opportunity of seeing it – *The Sleeping Beauty* is the finer piece, dramatically as focused as can be, with a far smaller proportion of purely decorative dancing such as dilutes *Swan Lake*, with a scenario that is consistently as 'dramatic' as possible, and with a composer who now had all the insight and skill demanded by such a challenge.

As in *Swan Lake*, the orchestral prelude introduces the musical representatives of the two forces that will struggle for supremacy over the destiny of the two lovers, Aurora and Désiré. Carabosse comes first, her musical badge violent, vicious, a tight patchwork of menacing fragments, while that of her rival, the Lilac Fairy, is serene, benign and 'safe', a lovely, open-hearted melody, its harmonies as stable as its contours are smooth. It slips straight into the Prologue, which opens with a royal entry. This is an event of great pomp and ceremony, and fully justifies Catalabutte's fussy interventions, which also serve to delay the crucial moment of the royal couple's appearance, thus making it all the more momentous when it arrives, and meanwhile excusing a generous spread of supporting music. Five godmother Fairies now float in to delicate, airy sounds, and then the sixth, the Lilac Fairy, appears (more fully scored music): these supernaturals, too, are guests and must be formally – and unhurriedly – greeted and seated. This gives way to a more explicit, but equally delicate, waltz as pages and young girls present these dainty visitors with gifts. Royal matters simply must not be hurried, and Tchaikovsky's music has supported this very substantial span with unfaltering flair and aptness.

It is now the Fairies' turn to offer their gifts to the baby Aurora, but the individual presentations are preceded by a *pas de six*, a substantial movement for all of them, opening with a gentle clarinet melody to a harp-washed accompaniment, followed by six tiny solo dances, none more than a minute, two barely half a minute, during which they in turn present their gifts. Each of the first five is a very individual piece, exquisitely wrought, but the more substantial sixth (a waltz) is allotted to the Lilac Fairy. Finally this mixture of formality and individuality is rounded off by a vigorous corporate coda.

Until now all has been relaxed and joyful – and studiedly so, for this is about to change abruptly and hideously. As the Lilac Fairy steps forward to present her gift, a commotion from outside is heard – a furious Carabosse approaches, then bursts in to the music that had opened the ballet. Nothing could be further removed from the secure formality and tone of all we have so far seen and heard; now all will be action-packed, and it is the torrent of successive events that determines the musical course. Fortunately there are some very tiny silences that punctuate the action, and which make marking out these events easier. The first of these mini-silences signals Carabosse's moment of entry in her rat-drawn wheelbarrow, with grubby pages in attendance, her music from the orchestral prelude confirming that it is she – and note how often, when her music returns in the ballet, it is given some sort of new presentation, for Carabosse is devious, a manipulator: there is no telling quite what she is, or what she will do. Her cackles, and those of her followers, can be heard in the music that immediately follows. A desperate Catalabutte begs for mercy, but receives none (Carabosse's theme again, with more cackling), the good Fairies entreat Carabosse to forgive the King and Queen for their oversight (the calmer string melody), but Carabosse only laughs maliciously, then delivers her curse (the widely striding bass theme with chugging accompaniment). A tiny silence – and the King and Queen cry out in anguish as Carabosse waves her wand in all directions, and her rats and pages dance and laugh gloatingly. Another tiny silence – and all seems suddenly to freeze as the Lilac Fairy, who has remained hidden, comes forward, her music as calm as ever. Yet the crisis is still to come, for Carabosse attempts frantically to intervene (her music struggling to assert itself) and, for an instant, she succeeds. Again a silence. But the good Fairies quickly crowd protectively round the cradle, and the Lilac Fairy's music resumes. Carabosse's attempt to restore her complete curse has failed.

The opening of Act 1 is as relaxed as the opening of the Prologue, though this time it is the peasantry whom we see, and there is a kind of playful innocence about their music. When Catalabutte spies peasants with knitting needles, the musical chatter momentarily falters, and the rushing string passages substantiate his anger and his drastic decision to send them to prison. The sudden pause and slower music mark the arrival of the King and Queen with Aurora's suitors, the four Princes. The King's anger at the peasants raises the musical temperature, and the Princes' very contrasting pleading on their behalf is easily identified: what is less obvious is that tiny elements of Carabosse's music now stealthily appropriate the quieter passage during which the King's anger abates – though because she is disguised we cannot yet see that she is actually present. This passage leads into the *Valse*, the first of the ballet's great set-piece dances. Yet because it does not have the scale of the waltz that had intervened in the first act of *Swan Lake*, this one does not feel like an intrusion, instead serving simply to divide the simple rural matters that have preceded it from the portentous royal ritual to come. It also clears the dramatic field for Aurora to make her entrance, and after it she skips in merrily, a carefree young woman whose affections will be instantly challenged by four suitors.

The *Rose Adagio* (so called because each suitor presents a rose, each of which Aurora discards as a sign of rejection) is the second of the four great set-piece dances in *The Sleeping Beauty*. The dignified wind-and-harp introduction signals that something of real moment is imminent, and what follows certainly does not disappoint. The drastic reduction in the proportion of decorative formal dancing in *The Sleeping Beauty*, as compared with *Swan Lake*, makes a movement as substantial as this stand out the more clearly. In any case, the action has not been frozen, for by the *Adagio*'s end we will have seen Aurora turn down each of four highly eligible suitors, and when she goes on to provide, as her *variation* (a solo dance), the last of the three supplementary dances that follow (the one with solo violin obbligato), she will confirm, at some length, that she remains the same carefree girl we had glimpsed before the *Rose Adagio*. The two brief dances ahead of Aurora's (the dance of the maids of honour and the pages, and then the pages' own brief dance) take the places of what would have been the customary individual *variations* for the four Princes. As for the coda that follows Aurora's own *variation*, this leads into her ever more reckless dance with the snatched spindle, an exhibition with which she hopes to dazzle her rejected suitors, but which drives straight into the act's *Finale* at the moment she pricks her finger, and something of Carabosse's music at last emerges explicitly.

This is a moment where it is worth pausing to note a splendid example of how Tchaikovsky could use a musical idea to project, in its own way, an active moment in the drama. Carabosse's theme had provided the very first sounds of the ballet's prelude, and it had a very distinctive 'dum-dum-diddle-diddle-dum-pom-pom-pom-pom-pom-pom' rhythm, the 'diddle-diddle-dum' bit being a nervous little five-note figure. In a moment that figure will emerge and, as the rest of the orchestra falls away, be repeated with intervening silences to mark out Aurora's faltering steps. But then, as she begins her 'vertiginous dance', the little rhythmic figure resumes and literally 'spins' the melody that 'entangles' her before she suddenly drops unconscious. I can think of no better example of music being, as it were, the *activist* that *creates* the action.

The parents' grief is heart-rending, and a gloating Carabosse now throws off her disguise, celebrating the triumph of her curse in a full, brazen statement of her melodic badge. The Princes draw their swords, but in an instant she has disappeared and, now terrified, they flee. Once again the Lilac Fairy appears, and she and her theme will preside over the remainder of the scene as she orders the arrangements for Aurora's century-long sleep, only her spell music (after a great tam-tam stroke) briefly intersecting her own theme as she mitigates the curse. All finally fades into silence; all are now bound by the spell of sleep.

The first stages of Act 2 Scene 1 are the most relaxed of the whole ballet. But Prince Désiré must be introduced and a situation devised where he can be left alone to be processed for the role of Aurora's saviour and spouse. Hunting horns forewarn us of the scene's dramatic setting, and the floor show which is offered for the Prince's lunch-time entertainment, though superfluous to dramatic requirements, affords the space in which we can at least observe Désiré, as well as providing an excuse for a modest spot of more formal dancing. It also releases the tension after the traumas of the preceding act. There is a slight whiff of the baroque in the music to which the hunting party enters, and even more so in the staid music that immediately follows, once the racy game of blind man's buff has been played out (in fact, the first dance is an explicit and decorous sarabande). But with the departure of the hunt without the Prince, the real business of the scene can begin. A harp-wash signals the arrival of the Lilac Fairy in her mother-of-pearl boat. She waves her wand, and the cliff face opens to reveal a vision of the sleeping Aurora. Another wave, and Aurora wakens. At first she is sprightly, then begins her dance of seduction.

Here is the third of the ballet's great set-piece dances, this one as intimate as the *Rose Adagio* had been grand. It is mostly a vast, almost unbroken, cello solo, at first almost ingenuously appealing, but then, with tiny, upward-flashing woodwind scales and a more active cello line, growing in allure. Constantly Aurora evades Désiré's attempts to touch her. Repetitions of a tiny pathos-filled woodwind phrase increase the emotional pressure on the Prince. The music suddenly grows in volume, and the opening melody returns, now on the full battery of cellos. Confident that she has captivated him, Aurora can reinforce her hold through a brief exhibition of her very extrovert, sprightly self; two further short appendages seal her conquest, and she disappears whence she came, while Désiré, now totally her slave, excitedly begs the Lilac Fairy to take him where he may find the embodiment of this vision. Together they embark on that mission.

The journey is truly an enchanted one. The *panorama* to which they leave is so tranquil, so unruffled, its harmony so simple, each chord so long sustained, and the shifts between chords so smooth, that there is only the gentlest sense of movement: even the two flute-coloured passages that alternate with this in no way threaten the pervasive calm. Even more timeless is the *entr'acte symphonique (Le Sommeil* (Sleep)*)* that follows,¹ taking us yet deeper into a spellbound world. Listen out for the top of the music – a *very* quiet high C for the violins, unbroken for some four minutes (managed by making the first and second violins alternate in overlapping four-bar shifts); this indicates the 'binding' presence of magic. And beneath this the other emblems of the supernatural continue to whisper: the Lilac Fairy's spell of sleep, Carabosse's theme and the Lilac Fairy's own melody. The stage has become shrouded in mist, and during this the scene will have been changed so that, when a crescendo at length signals that the clouds are breaking, we shall find ourselves back in the scene that had ended Act 1. Nevertheless, a fundamental stillness remains, and only with the entry of the Lilac Fairy and Désiré does Carabosse herself begin to stir, her music ever more desperate as the Prince approaches Aurora's bed and, with his kiss, awakens her. A mighty stroke on the tam-tam marks the breaking of the spell; the King and Queen, and all the courtiers wake, and universal joy returns.

The great feature that makes the dramatic pacing of *The Sleeping Beauty* so much more satisfactory than that of *Swan Lake* is the drastic reduction in the number of conventional and formal dances that had so obtrusively punctuated the narrative in the earlier ballet. Instead, following the precedent of Delibes's *Coppélia*, Tchaikovsky compensated for this loss by appending an extra act that could be filled with decorative dancing in celebration of the lovers' union. It also gave him total freedom to make these dances whatever he chose, and what is so striking is the dazzling variety of

---

1 When Tchaikovsky first composed this section he included an *entr'acte* for solo violin and orchestra (as noted with *Swan Lake*, this would have been designed to enable the court violinist, often a leading virtuoso of the time, to perform an obbligato solo). However, this *entr'acte* was dropped before the premiere for, though it is a worthwhile piece in itself, it would have catastrophically broken the spell of this section as well as extending it intolerably. Nevertheless, in modern recordings it is normally included, so the best thing is to be ready to jump across this track.

their characters. The act opens with two large movements that confirm the grandeur of the occasion, the *march* supporting the entry of the King, Queen and courtiers, together with the newlyweds and the four jewel fairies, and the *polonaise* accompanying the procession of those who will provide the royal entertainment, plus other participants from the preceding acts (including Carabosse: clearly there has been a royal amnesty), the Lilac Fairy bringing up the rear. And so the entertainment begins. It is set out as a series of mostly concise movements, in each of which the varied and colourful orchestration is often a striking feature. First a *pas de quatre* for the jewel fairies, then a solo *variation* for each (is it coincidence that the very unusual five-beats-in-a-bar rhythm (divided by Tchaikovsky as two-plus-three beats) given to the Sapphire Fairy corresponds to the numerals in the jewel's chemical formula, Al_2O_3?), followed by a corporate coda. Then comes (for me) the real treasure of the act: the *pas de caractère* for Puss in Boots and the White Cat, who miaow, paw, claw and spit at each other. This is followed by a second *pas de quatre*, this time for Cinderella and Prince Fortuné, the Blue Bird and Princess Florine, in which the two couples each have a *variation* before the coda. A second *pas de caractère* comes next, this time for a nervous Red Riding Hood and a roaring Wolf. Cinderella and Prince Fortuné have a second and larger *pas de caractère* which begins very animatedly, but then changes to an elegant waltz, and the cabaret ends with a *pas berrichon* (Berry being a region of France) for Tom Thumb, his brothers, and an Ogre, in which the last strides monstrously, and the others scuttle about the stage. And to conclude the entertainment, the two lovers themselves step forward for a *pas de deux*.

This is the fourth and last of the great set-piece dances of *The Sleeping Beauty*. First a leisurely passage in which the dancers may take their places: then the dance proper begins with the *adagio*. Here is a splendid love dance within which the ritual of courtship, then confession, then commitment, is enacted. A restrained tenderness marks the beginning of the *Adagio*, the glissando on the piano (not normally an orchestral participant, but one heard in several places in this act) and the following pause signalling hesitancy. The *adagio* begins again, taking a different course, yet ending, as before, with a glissando. But already a suppressed excitement is to be felt in the two brief phrases that follow, for their spans are far shorter – yet each time there is the same hesitancy. Then suddenly, as with all true love, constraint vanishes, the declaration is frank and rapturous, the midway break merely a breathless pause before the lovers may revel in it all over again. As is usual in classical ballet, the dancers each have a *variation*, Désiré's masculine and athletic, Aurora's delicate and playful, before their joint coda.

This grand celebration – and the ballet itself – must now be wound up. Decorum is firmly reinstated in the dignified *sarabande*, and this choice of dance, with its archaic style, reminds us that the action of *The Sleeping Beauty* has been envisaged as taking place during the reign of the 'Sun King', Louis XIV of France, a reign of especially ostentatious splendour. And though formality is thrown to the winds in the corporate *mazurka* of the following finale, this will be stopped dead in its tracks so that the *apotheosis*, based on the French tune, 'Vive Henri IV', may be a proclamation of the dignity as well as the splendour of kingship.

The Sleeping Beauty is a masterpiece. Taken just as we see it in the theatre, as a bevy of costumed figures creating the various roles and driving the action, it makes an impression that is vastly impressive, and also, perhaps, rather moving. But what makes this ballet additionally remarkable, for me at least, are the extra resonances I detect within it, and which elevate it to the plane of myth in a way that might have been denied it, had it been presented as an opera. Because an opera libretto uses language, it defines events and actions, feelings and meanings very precisely; by contrast, ballet, because it lacks the definition and exactitude that words impose, leaves the listener more freedom to respond at will, and to imagine. We may take the tale as a several-sided metaphor of life: childhood, youth, love, marriage – or of the seasons: autumn (sowing), winter (sleeping), spring (waking), summer (reaping) – or it may even stir a metaphysical awareness: birth, death, regeneration, salvation. Such resonances may be stirred especially when Désiré's journey begins. The magical, unbroken drift of the *panorama* begins to suspend time, while the 'Sleep' *entr'acte* takes us yet deeper into the kingdom of magic itself, where everything floats, rational order barely survives, and the only slender thread of control and coherence is the violins' unbroken high C which binds all to itself. Only then do we slip back into the dynamic of the ballet's narrative.

Some readers will question all this, and – fair enough! But there is something very special, very mysterious here that affects me quite differently from almost any other passage in Tchaikovsky's music.

––––––

I wrote earlier in this book that there are three works by Tchaikovsky which I would wish to preserve if – perish the thought! – I had to sacrifice all the rest. It is only a personal choice, and readers may very well choose differently. One is the opera *Eugene Onegin*, and the second is this ballet, *The Sleeping Beauty*. There is still one to come.

26
Two Further Relationships:
The Queen of Spades

For all his pleasure in Frolovskoye, Tchaikovsky was aware of its shortcomings. Despite his numerous visitors, he could still feel lonely there, and from July 1889 he also rented a flat in Moscow, especially since he was becoming increasingly involved in the musical life of that city. It seems sometimes that Tchaikovsky, once he had seen close to him a problem where he could help, found it almost impossible not to intervene. The problem might involve an individual, or else some cause for which he had special sympathy. This was very much the case with the RMS in Moscow. The Society was ailing, and during the later months of 1889 Tchaikovsky would be much occupied with organizing its next concert season, a task he seems to have discharged almost single-handedly, often himself acting as the impresario. He personally conducted the negotiations with Brodsky not only so that the latter should perform the Violin Concerto dedicated to him in one of the concerts Tchaikovsky himself would conduct, but also so that Brodsky should bring his string quartet to Moscow for four recitals. In Tiflis Tchaikovsky had been much impressed with Ippolitov-Ivanov and his singer wife, Varvara Zarudnaya, and he took personal charge of the arrangements that would enable the couple to be heard in Moscow during the season. Determined to engage more celebrity musicians, he coaxed Nápravník, the conducting star of St Petersburg, to appear in Moscow for a much reduced fee.

Meanwhile Tchaikovsky's own conducting career had been expanding rapidly. In late September a splendid new production of *Eugene Onegin* had been mounted in Moscow, and Tchaikovsky had presided over some of the rehearsals, then conducted the opening night. But it was not only in Moscow that he was required, for only two days later he was in St Petersburg for a ten-day stint, not only to supervise rehearsals for the premiere of *The Sleeping Beauty*, but also to participate in organizing the celebrations of the fiftieth anniversary of Anton

Rubinstein's debut as a pianist. This would be inaugurated on 30 November, and in the meantime Tchaikovsky would conduct two concerts in Moscow. As for the Rubinstein anniversary, Tchaikovsky would compose a chorus of greeting for its inauguration, and also an *Impromptu* for a presentation album of piano pieces; then he had to conduct, on successive days, the two initial concerts of Rubinstein's own works, one concert involving eight hundred performers. Five days later he was back in Moscow in charge of a charity concert, the programme including Beethoven's Ninth Symphony – then back to St Petersburg for rehearsals of *The Sleeping Beauty*, and to conduct the first half of yet another concert. It was a prodigious schedule, and inevitably he emerged from it totally exhausted. Yet he judged it had been worth the hassle, for apart from the increasing personal prestige he gained from his public appearances, there was also the satisfaction of observing the manifest improvements in the RMS's fortunes, mainly, it seems, as a consequence of his personal efforts to attract star performers to Moscow.

Relationships among Russians can often appear very volatile, and sometimes irrational, when compared with the more solid (though not necessarily superior) ways in which we conduct ours (mostly). The relationship between Anton Rubinstein and Tchaikovsky, his former pupil, was curious and ambivalent on both sides. Privately Tchaikovsky could be blistering about the quality of some of his former teacher's works – yet, Modest remembered, he was personally overawed by him:

> In Anton Grigorevich's presence he [Tchaikovsky] was always ill at ease, flustered as befits one who adores. He regarded Rubinstein as a being standing so far above him as to exclude any possibility of equality in their relations.

We can see this – and also how tactless, even cruel, Rubinstein could be – in an incident at the meal after the second St Petersburg concert Tchaikovsky had conducted in his former teacher's honour:

> When someone tactlessly expressed a wish that Anton Grigorevich should drink a toast 'as brothers' with Pyotr Ilich, the latter was not only confused but became indignant about it, and in reply protested sincerely and with passion that 'his tongue could never bring itself to address Anton Grigorevich as *ti* [equivalent of the more intimate

French form of address, *tu*], that this would impair the essence of their relationship, that he would be happy if Anton Grigorevich addressed him as *tï*, but that he would refuse for ever to change his own use of *vï* [equivalent of French *vous*], which expressed the sense of veneration which he nourished towards Rubinstein, that distance which separated the pupil from the master, the man from the embodiment of his ideal.

It might have been hoped that Rubinstein would have responded with something to mitigate Tchaikovsky's evident distress. But he did not: in fact, he made the situation even worse – and in so doing, uncovered the gnawing jealousy he had felt at Tchaikovsky's close relationship with his brother, Nikolay. Alexandra Panayeva, who had sung in the first part of the concert, was sitting between Rubinstein and Tchaikovsky, and recalled what happened next:

> Suddenly Anton Grigorevich, bending over me towards Pyotr Ilich, interrupted him with a laugh. 'Now let us assume, Pyotr Ilich, you do not love me but love my brother – then I thank you for that.' A confused Pyotr Ilich was about to protest, but Rubinstein repeated, 'You love my brother – and for that, thank you!' Humiliated, Tchaikovsky crumpled in his chair, and silence followed until Vasily Safonov jumped to his feet to make an indignant defence of Tchaikovsky.

Tchaikovsky himself had long been aware of Anton's jealousy of Nikolay, having in Paris eight years earlier observed Anton's barely concealed satisfaction at Nikolay's death as the latter's remains were being loaded on to a train for their return to Russia. Patently what was so galling to Anton was that he, having been responsible for turning Tchaikovsky into a professional composer, had seen the latter become the star of his brother's empire in Moscow, with Nikolay himself gaining prestige through his association with the premieres of so many of Tchaikovsky's works. Perhaps Tchaikovsky's recognition of this did much to soften his reciprocal resentment. Certainly bitterness remained. Writing to the German critic, Eugen Zabel, in 1892, Tchaikovsky revealed how ambivalent his feelings were: 'I have the pain of confessing to you that Anton Rubinstein did nothing, *but nothing at all*, to further my plans and projects. This has always distressed me.' Yet, he continued, 'I see him from time to time, and always with pleasure, for this extraordinary man has only to hold out his hand to you, and direct a smile at you, for you to be on your knees before him.' For Tchaikovsky, despite everything, Anton Rubinstein always remained the most revered personality among living musicians.

Nor, on Rubinstein's side, did this distressing incident reveal more than a part of his view of Tchaikovsky. Nikolay's death in 1881 had clearly done much to ease his jealousy. Indeed, two years before this distressing post-concert incident, Anton had approached Tchaikovsky to see whether the latter would assign his new opera, *The Enchantress*, to a company Rubinstein was anxious to form, and which would perform only operas by Russian composers. And if this was not possible, Anton continued, would Tchaikovsky compose an opera especially for them? 'It will all be prepared carefully – you have nothing whatsoever to worry about. May I hope? Scribble a couple of words in reply.' Then for the 1892 concert season of the St Petersburg branch of the RMS, Rubinstein would propose that Tchaikovsky should be given the prime role as conductor of 'ten concerts on "indispensable" [the most important?] days, with an augmented fee, and agreement that there should be no constraints on his rehearsal time'. The following year, writing to his sister, Sofiya, who was in Odessa, Anton would list the musical pleasures in prospect for her in that city – 'the Russian opera, and Tchaikovsky with Sapelnikov. You are lucky. I'm becoming envious!' And, finally, there is the pain-filled note Rubinstein would send her seven months later when the pupil, whose talent he had done so much to foster, was no more. Here was the final verdict of the man who had so distressed Tchaikovsky at the post-concert dinner:

> What do you say about Tchaikovsky's death? Is it possible that this was the will of God? What a loss to Russian music! Yet, you know, he was in the prime of life, he was only fifty [in fact, fifty-three] – and all this because of a glass of water! What a nonsense are all such tricks – and this life – and everything, and everything.

Tchaikovsky's relationship with Anton Rubinstein would span his whole adult life: that with the young story-teller and playwright, Anton Chekhov, would be only brief. Yet it is a touching incident, and one worth narrating, partly because it was between two of Russia's greatest creative artists, but also because it affords us yet another glimpse of the human Tchaikovsky, always ready to support young talent. Modest already knew of the twenty-eight-year-old doctor who, as a sideline, had begun publishing short stories eight years earlier, and in December 1888, at Modest's home, Tchaikovsky and Chekhov met. The former was already familiar with Chekhov's work, and the two men discovered that their admiration was mutual. Then, a year on, at the time when Tchaikovsky was already heavily involved in organizing the Moscow RMS's concert season, Chekhov wrote to him:

Dear Pyotr Ilich,

This month I am going to begin printing a little collection of my own stories. These stories are as tedious and boring as autumn, their tone is monotonous, and artistic elements in them are closely entwined with medical ones. Nevertheless, this hasn't prevented me from daring to turn to you with a very humble request: permit me to dedicate this little collection to you. The idea of dedicating this anthology to you was sown in my head as far back as that very day when, dining with you at Modest Ilich's, I heard you had read my stories. If, together with your assent, you would also send me your photograph, then I shall receive more than I'm worth, and I'll be happy to all eternity. Forgive me for so troubling you.

Tchaikovsky was delighted by the dedication, visited Chekhov to convey his thanks, then followed this up with a letter:

Dear Anton Pavlovich,

I enclose my photograph, and earnestly beg you to entrust yours to the messenger. Did I adequately express my gratitude for the dedication? I think I did not, and so I will tell you again that I am *deeply touched* by your kindness. I press your hand warmly.

Chekhov was quick to respond:

I am very, very touched, dear Pyotr Ilich, and I give you boundless thanks. I am sending you both the photograph and the book, and I would send you the sun, too, if it belonged to me. You left behind your cigarette case. I am returning it to you. Three cigarettes are missing: these were smoked by the cellist, the flautist, and the teacher. I thank you again, and allow me to remain your heartfelt, devoted Anton Chekhov.

The informality of tone in the last sentence reveals the ease that

Chekhov now felt in this new relationship, and that it had already become mutually a very relaxed one is substantiated by his inscription in his book: 'To Pyotr Ilich Tchaikovsky, from his future librettist'.

Nothing could demonstrate more clearly not only the warmth in this new relationship, but also the confidence Tchaikovsky felt in this still-little-known author's ability to be the librettist of his next opera. It was to be based on *Bela*, a tragic love story concerning a cynical young Russian officer and a beautiful Caucasian girl, and was drawn from *A Hero of Our Time*, a classic Russian novel by Mikhail Lermontov, a younger contemporary of Pushkin. However, there being no hope he could undertake anything for the moment, Tchaikovsky responded with a personal gesture in compensation:

> I am sending you a season ticket for the symphony concert series of the RMS. I am terribly glad that I can be of some little service to you. I cannot deliver it myself, for all this week is being swallowed up in preparing for the first concert, and in looking after our guest, Rimsky-Korsakov. God grant that next week I shall be able to talk with you as I would like.
>
> P.S. I would point out that the ticket can be used by anyone, if you so wish.

In the following spring Chekhov's book, *Gloomy People*, an anthology of ten stories dedicated to Tchaikovsky, was published, but as Tchaikovsky was based in Italy at the time, Modest took delivery of his copy. Chekhov's covering letter to Modest was further confirmation of his view of Tchaikovsky:

> I am prepared day and night to mount a guard of honour at the porch of Pyotr Ilich's house – I revere him so much. If we're talking of ranks, then he occupies in Russian creativity the second place after Lev Tolstoy, who has long occupied the first (I allot the third place to the painter, Ilya Repin, and award myself the ninety-eighth). The dedication would, I thought, be a partial, minimal expression of that great critical opinion that I, as a writer, have formed about his magnificent talent. Unfortunately I have had to fulfil my dream through a book which I do not consider my best. It is made up of especially gloomy psychological studies, and bears a gloomy title, such that my dedication must be little to the taste of Pyotr Ilich himself and his admirers.

In fact, the ten tales in the collection were some of Chekhov's best, and on hearing of the writer's kind words about himself, Tchaikovsky was deeply touched. 'You can't imagine how pleasant I find Chekhov's words about me,' he wrote to Modest. 'I'll write to him when I've returned a little to normal.'

But no such letter exists, and by the time of Tchaikovsky's return to Russia, Chekhov was some thousands of miles away on a sociological expedition to Sakhalin Island, off the eastern coast of Siberia. Their next, and final, contact came nearly two years later. It was Chekhov who wrote, but his letter had little to do with his own affairs, being concerned with Chekhov's ambitious cellist friend, a certain Marian Semashko, though the letter did give Tchaikovsky notice of the new collection of Chekhov's stories which would be published imminently. Chekhov's hope was that Tchaikovsky might be able to help Semashko in securing a good professional appointment. In fact, Tchaikovsky had already met Semashko (he was the cellist who had smoked one of Tchaikovsky's cigarettes), and had been rather less than impressed by him. Accordingly, in his reply he told Chekhov that he thought Semashko was aspiring to a position for which he was not really suited, and that he should seek an orchestral appointment. But now Tchaikovsky felt obliged to make his own excuses for not having written earlier to Chekhov:

> How glad I am, dear Anton Pavlovich, to see from your letter that you are in no way angry with me, for I did not really thank you for the dedication of *Gloomy People*, in which I take immense pride. I remember that during your expedition I was always going to write a long letter to you, even attempting to explain which qualities in your talent so captivated and bewitched me. But there wasn't time for it – and, above all, I had not got it in me, for it is very difficult for a musician to express in words what and how he feels in regard of this or that artistic phenomenon.
>
> And so – my thanks for not complaining about me. I warmly thank you in advance for the book. God grant that we shall be able to see each other, and have a talk. I press your hand warmly.
>
> Sincerely devoted to you,
> P. TCHAIKOVSKY

But it seems the hoped-for meeting never took place. No further letters passed between the two men, but the mutual respect clearly remained. Like Anton Rubinstein, Chekhov was genuinely distressed by Tchaikovsky's sudden passing. Two days after his death, Chekhov telegraphed Modest: 'The news staggered me. It is a terrible anguish. I loved and revered Pyotr Ilich very deeply, and I am indebted to him for much. You have my heartfelt sympathy.'

With the premiere of *The Sleeping Beauty* in St Petersburg on 15 January 1890, and one more concert to conduct in Moscow three days later, Tchaikovsky had at last completed his current stint as composer–consultant and conductor. He was exhausted, but longed to return to composition, and his plans were already laid. Three years earlier the minor composer, Nikolay Klenovsky, had commissioned Modest to devise a libretto on Pushkin's short story, *The Queen of Spades*, and three scenes had been written before Klenovsky lost interest in the project. Tchaikovsky, it seems, knew nothing of this until the autumn of 1889, when Vsevolozhsky suggested he should compose an opera on the orphaned libretto. His interest was immediately aroused, meetings were held with those who would be responsible for mounting the production, and on 26 January Tchaikovsky headed for Berlin. He needed to settle somewhere where he could compose undisturbed, and his choice fell on Florence. He arrived in the Italian city on 30 January. The following day he set about the opera.

Pushkin's short story, *The Queen of Spades*, could hardly be more different from *Eugene Onegin*, a novel in verse. Where the latter had been a heart-rending love story, the former was an ironic ghost story, a tale of obsession, tersely told. Hermann, an officer in the engineers, is obsessed by gambling, watching others play, but never participating himself. By chance he hears of an old Countess's secret of three winning cards. To discover this, he targets Liza, the Countess's young ward, who is her mistress's drudge. Working on Liza's affections, Hermann gains access to the Countess, but in trying to extract her secret, he frightens her to death. He attends her funeral: she winks at him from her coffin. Her ghost appears to him in his room and reveals the three-card secret: three, seven, ace. Hermann visits the gambling house, plays on three and seven, and wins spectacularly. But playing a third time, it is the queen of spades that turns up – and the card winks at him. Hermann goes mad – and Liza marries a 'very pleasant young man somewhere in the civil service, and with a good income'. Indeed,

Pushkin's tone throughout his whole narrative had been ironic. Tchaikovsky's would be very different.

Tchaikovsky had arrived in Florence with the libretto of the first two scenes only, and Modest was hard pressed to keep ahead of his brother. When Modest's work arrived, Tchaikovsky found much of it needed pruning, for he recognized that, as in Pushkin's text, there must be no padding, especially in those scenes where the crucial events of the drama are played out. His engagement with his subject became such that he found working on the bedroom confrontation between Hermann and the Countess 'so terrible that a feeling of horror still remains with me', as he admitted after being preoccupied with it a couple of days. Just as he had totally identified with Tatyana and her misfortunes while composing *Onegin*, so he empathized wholeheartedly with Hermann, and on composing Hermann's death scene, he found his reaction was as violent as it was unexpected. As he wrote to Modest:

> I pitied Hermann so much that I suddenly began weeping copiously. Afterwards I began to ponder why, for there has never been a similar occasion when I have wept at my hero's fate. It seems to me that Hermann was not just a pretext for writing this or that music, but all the while a real, living human being, at the same time very 'sympathetic' to me. Because Nikolay Figner [who was to create the part of Hermann] is also very 'sympathetic' to me, and because all the while I imagined Hermann in the shape of Figner, I likewise felt the most lively concern for his misfortunes. Now I think that this warm and lively relationship with the opera's hero has probably expressed itself beneficially in my music.

It appears that, when Figner himself at last became acquainted with the role, he found it one with which he could identify completely. 'He is in raptures about his part. He speaks of it with tears in his eyes,' Tchaikovsky could report to Modest.

The whole of *The Queen of Spades* was scored by early June, and its premiere took place on 19 December in St Petersburg, where it was a sensational success. No expense had been spared in mounting it, the performance was splendid, and audience reaction ecstatic. The press was less kind. Some very fundamental modifications had been introduced into Pushkin's story – and this sacrilege had been perpetrated on one of the best-known and best-loved of Russian literary classics. The opera was produced in Kiev only twelve days after the St Petersburg premiere, but it did not reach Moscow for nearly another year. By this time, however, criticism was dying away, and *The Queen of Spades* was on the way to establishing itself as second only to *Onegin* in popularity among all Tchaikovsky's operas.

The Queen of Spades: opera in three acts * * * * *

This is the most overtly dramatic of all Tchaikovsky's mature operas, containing some of his most radical music. While, perhaps, it does not have quite the consistency of Eugene Onegin, *its expressive range is broader and, with* Onegin, *it must be ranked as one of the greatest of nineteenth-century operas.*

The Queen of Spades is in seven scenes set in St Petersburg in the time of Catherine the Great (empress: 1762–96), and not, as in Pushkin, in the writer's own adult lifetime (*c.* 1820–37).

Act 1 Scene 1. *A recreation area in the Summer Gardens.* It is spring. Nursemaids and others are sitting, strolling and chatting, while children play at being soldiers, finally marching off. Cheklinsky, a gambler, and Surin, an officer, discuss the preoccupation of Hermann (an engineering officer of German extraction) with gambling; he is always watching others play, yet never participates himself. To Tomsky, another officer, Hermann confesses he is in love, though he still does not know his beloved's name. Tomsky expresses amazement that Hermann is capable of such a passion, but the latter declares that he will die if his beloved cannot be his. Meanwhile a crowd of promenaders has swarmed in, and now exults in the wonderful weather. Prince Yeletsky appears, and Chekalinsky and Surin congratulate him on his engagement. Asked who his intended is, he indicates Liza (in the opera the Countess's granddaughter), who has just entered with the Countess, and who recognizes Hermann as the man who has repeatedly appeared beneath her window. Hermann in despair, together with Liza, the Countess, Tomsky and Yeletsky, joins in a quintet, each voicing his or her thoughts, Liza seeming especially agitated on seeing Hermann. The Countess then asks Tomsky who Hermann is, Yeletsky greets Liza, and Hermann sits himself gloomily on a bench.

Tomsky now reveals how the Countess had, as a youthful beauty in Paris, restored her gambling fortunes through the secret of three winning cards which the Comte de St Germain had confided to her 'at the price of a rendezvous'. Later she had twice told her secret, but a ghost had predicted that she would be killed by a third man who would come, as a lover, to extract it from her. Overhearing this, Hermann nevertheless rejects the temptation the three-card secret offers – and, as a storm breaks, vows Yeletsky shall never have Liza.

Act 1 Scene 2. *Liza's room. A door to the balcony leads into the garden.* It is the day of Liza's betrothal to Yeletsky. She and her friend, Polina, sing a duet to a group of approving girls. Polina, at the suggestion of a much preoccupied Liza, sings Liza's favourite song, a sad one that brings on a sad mood – and so she launches into a clapping song to which the girls, but not Liza, dance. The governess appears, chides them for their unbecoming behaviour, the noise of which displeases the Countess, and the girls leave with her. Polina teases Liza, then also leaves. Liza dismisses her maid, Masha; alone, she reflects tearfully on her impending marriage to Yeletsky, then confesses her secret obsession for the stranger who haunts her home.

Suddenly Hermann himself enters from the balcony. Liza threatens to cry out if he does not leave, but he launches into a confession of love. Liza weeps – but is clearly responding. Suddenly the Countess is heard approaching. Signalling Hermann to hide, Liza admits the Countess and her maids. The old woman questions Liza, then leaves with her maids. Hermann emerges, recoiling in horror as he remembers the ghost's words – but then resumes his pleading. Seeing Liza is weakening, he pretends he will leave. In desperation she cries: 'I am yours!'

Act 2 Scene 1. *A great hall.* A masked ball is in progress. The master of ceremonies invites the guests to a fireworks display outside. Chekalinsky, Surin and Tomsky linger to discuss Hermann's obsession, then leave. Only Yeletsky and Liza remain, and the former sings her an aria of love: then they also leave. Hermann enters the now empty hall: he has a letter from Liza, and is to meet her after the interlude – but again the three cards torment him. The interlude, *The Faithful Shepherdess*, a pastoral entertainment involving three singers, dancers and chorus, begins. A quadrille and sarabande are danced. Prilepa is sad; her beloved, Milozvor (played by Polina), has not joined the dance, but he now enters and declares his love. They duet happily.

Zlatogor (played by Tomsky) enters, bearing costly presents. He asks Prilepa to choose between him and Milozvor. While Zlatogor tempts with riches, Milozvor can only offer love. Prilepa chooses Milozvor, and they duet. Amor and Hymen enter with the nuptial crown. Again the quadrille.

The guests talk while Hermann reflects on the fateful prediction – and suddenly encounters the Countess, while covertly Surin mocks him as before: 'Look, there's your beloved!' Liza slips Hermann the key to the garden door, and gives instructions for finding her room the next day – but Hermann insists on tonight. The master of ceremonies announces the arrival of the Empress. There is great excitement as all prepare to received her.

Act 2 Scene 2. *The Countess's bedroom.* Hermann enters, surveys the room, would leave if he could but, hearing footsteps, he hides. Maids lead the Countess to her dressing room. Liza and Masha enter, then leave, Liza to her own room. The Countess returns, chooses to sleep in an armchair, muses at length on her past in Paris, dismisses her maids, again muses, then dozes. Hermann emerges. The Countess is terrified. He attempts to reassure her: all he wants is the secret of the cards. But his pleadings and cajolings having failed, he draws a pistol. In terror the Countess falls back dead – and Hermann realizes that her secret has died with her. Disturbed by the noise, Liza enters, now discovering how she has been used. She turns on Hermann, dismissing him. Weeping, she throws herself on the Countess's body.

Act 3 Scene 1. *Hermann's room in the barracks.* It is late evening. Offstage sounds of drums and trumpet calls. Distressed, Hermann is reading a letter from Liza, who now believes he did not wish the Countess's death, and begs him to meet her on the banks of the Winter Canal at midnight. Sounds of a distant choir startle Hermann, and he recalls how, in the church, the Countess had winked at him from her open coffin. The wind howls, someone appears at the window, then vanishes. Again knocking, the wind blows open the window, the candle is blown out – and Hermann opens the door, to be confronted by the Countess's ghost. 'Save Liza, marry her. Three cards will win in turn. Remember: three . . . seven . . . ace . . . three . . . seven . . . ace . . . three . . .' Hermann repeats these words as she vanishes.

Act 3 Scene 2. *Beside the Winter Canal.* Liza, having convinced herself of Hermann's innocence, awaits him, and sings of her love. Midnight strikes, at first she is in despair, but then Hermann enters. They embrace and sing of their mutual love. He says he must fly, she asks whither, and is stunned by his reply: 'To the gambling house!' – and he tells her of the ghost's instructions. Now she realizes that her worst suspicions have been confirmed, yet still she tries to persuade him to go with her. But Hermann is demented, no longer recognizes her, and Liza throws herself into the canal.

Act 3 Scene 3. *A gambling house*. Guests, including Chekalinsky, Surin and Tomsky, are playing or dining in a relaxed atmosphere. Yeletsky has come for the first time – a consequence of the collapse of his disastrous love affair. Tomsky supplies a humorous love song: the others join in and dance. Play resumes, and Hermann appears. Yeletsky foresees a duel in prospect, asks Tomsky to be his second – but Hermann only wants to gamble and, to the amazement of all, wagers forty thousand! He stakes on the number three – and wins. Stunned amazement. He stakes on seven – and wins again. He calls for wine. 'What is our life?' he sings. 'A game . . . Who is lucky here, my friends? Today it's you, tomorrow 'tis I!' Despite the urging of the others to take his winnings, Hermann calls for a challenger. Yeletsky steps forward. Hermann stakes on ace – but turns up the queen of spades. The Countess's ghost appears, smiling at him. Hermann curses her, stabs himself, begs Yeletsky's forgiveness, then thinks he sees Liza before him. 'O how I loved you, my angel!' he whispers as he dies. The chorus prays for the peace of his soul.

Like *Eugene Onegin*, *The Queen of Spades* opens with the briefest of orchestral introductions, but this one is yet more crucial, for it introduces not one, but three themes relating to the forces that will drive the drama. The opening briefly presages Tomsky's ballad in Scene 1, in which he tells the tale that will sow in Hermann's mind the obsession that will bring about his destruction, and the third is the love music with which Hermann will seduce Liza in Scene 2. But heed especially the second, central one – not really a theme, but a tiny three-note motif representing the three fateful cards – the *tri karti* (three cards) – and which will itself often be heard three times (that is, 3x3: the heightened obsessiveness of this double symbolism is unmissable). This tiny morsel will infiltrate so many moments in the opera that it may haunt the listener, even when it has ceased to haunt Hermann.

An opera has three fundamental elements: its characters, its action and its context. *Onegin* had concerned itself straight away with its characters, albeit only two marginal ones chatting, then joined by Tatyana and Olga. But *The Queen of Spades* focuses our attention initially only on the setting. Nurses and governesses, with their charges, are enjoying a spring day in St Petersburg's Summer Gardens. This choral tableau is extended by a group of children playing at soldiers and giving a demonstration of their competence at parade-ground manoeuvres (no doubt a direct debt to the crowd of urchins who mimic the real-life soldiers in the first scene of Tchaikovsky's second favourite opera, Bizet's *Carmen*). But all this has been simply a preliminary: what follows is a model of how a first scene can progressively introduce the main characters, and through their exchanges simultaneously provide the information necessary for us to understand what is to come. First we meet Chekalinsky and Surin, who comment on Hermann and his current mood ('gloomy, like a demon from hell', as Chekalinsky puts it), then stroll off, to be followed by Hermann himself with Tomsky, to whom (and us) Hermann confesses the reason for his misery: he is in love, even though he still does not know his beloved's name (note the solo cello tune to which Hermann had entered: its first phrase will become his love theme). They, too, pass on, and a punctuation mark in the main action is provided by a new crowd of promenaders, who comment joyfully on the marvellous weather.

The marshalling of the opera's central characters is then resumed and completed. Hermann and Tomsky re-enter, still in conversation (Hermann elaborating on his distressed state), Prince Yeletsky appears, then Chekalinsky and Surin, who congratulate the Prince on his engagement (again more information for us): Yeletsky and Hermann simultaneously, though independently, extol their beloveds, and finally we meet the two characters who, with Hermann, will be central to the whole opera: the Countess (her entry is readily recognized, for the three-card motif is briefly heard in the orchestra) and Liza, whom the Prince identifies as his bride-to-be.

This has been a most skilfully planned beginning. Now, as he had done in *Onegin* in the quartet that had followed hard upon Onegin's entry, so Tchaikovsky provides a quintet in which the five principal players – the two women, the two lovers and Tomsky – will be singled out for our attention. Of course we cannot possibly hear their every word or phrase, but we shall catch enough to realize that all are, for a variety of reasons, disturbed (as each sings at the end: 'I am afraid!').

And note how, during the exchanges that follow the quintet, the three-card motif is again heard in the orchestra.

All the main participants being now assembled, it is time to set the opera's fateful plot in motion – which Tomsky does through his ballad, the largest set-piece movement of this scene, and an extended narration that brings a passage of relative stability to the action itself. Tomsky, first using recitative, recounts how the Countess in her youth had come by the secret of the three cards, then concludes with a four-stanza song. The first sets the three-section pattern of each stanza (though the music of the third stanza will be mostly new). It begins by echoing something of the introduction's opening melody, then breaks away and briefly introduces other, very atmospheric music, and finally it rounds off each stanza with a sort of parody of the first musical phrase from Hermann's earlier confession of love (what I have labelled his love theme), now set – very significantly – to the mantra that recurs throughout the opera: '*Tri karti, tri karti, tri karti!*' Thus Tchaikovsky deftly embodies in a single phrase the opera's conflicting forces: love (in the music), and obsession (in the words).

The remainder of this scene requires little further comment. It takes place against a gathering storm, a meteorological metaphor of Hermann's inner turmoil. Chekalinsky and Surin tease Hermann with the ghost's words, and all take cover except Hermann, who himself reflects on these same words – yet, despite the temptation, he still opts to possess Liza rather than riches.

As in *Onegin*, the second Scene of *The Queen of Spades* is intimate, and culminates in a love scene, though whereas in the earlier opera this had been a personal and ecstatic celebration of a first experience of love, in the latter it is a calculated seduction. The duet and song that entertain the girls in Liza's room are sentimental romances, Polina's a skilful reworking of an arioso from *Moscow*, Tchaikovsky's Coronation Cantata of 1883. (Why waste a good piece composed for a larger 'occasional' composition that might never be performed again?) Polina is a cameo role of a kind that Tchaikovsky included elsewhere in his operas, the character entering only once, yet making an impact greater than might have been expected from so brief an appearance. (Gremin, Tatyana's elderly and adoring husband in *Onegin*, is perhaps the most notable instance in Tchaikovsky's operas.) An even briefer appearance is that of the French governess who interrupts the girls' Russian dance, reproving them for behaviour ill becoming young ladies: she is a delicious, twittery being, neatly conjured. All this makes an excellent foil for the very serious matter to come: Hermann's intervention, and the ensuing love scene. This is beautifully prepared. First comes Polina's teasing of Liza, and then, as the maid prepares Liza's bed, the cor anglais's quiet introduction of the music to which Liza will herself, when alone, tearfully reflect on the prospect of a good but loveless marriage – and then Liza's shift of mood as her thoughts turn with mounting excitement to her mysterious lover (note how the orchestral tone shifts towards the end of all this, and a measure of ecstasy enters). As for the love scene itself, this impresses above all for the way it unfolds. First there is a stunned silence when Hermann appears and he and Liza stare at each other; then comes Liza's panic, Hermann's almost tearful initial entreaties (substantiated by the orchestra, which now, for the first time within the opera itself, gently picks up the love music that had ended the opera's introduction), and Liza's pity as she, now quietly, begs him to leave. Hermann makes a second appeal, this time pleading rather than urgent, and at the end takes her hand, which she does not withdraw, a sign of hope that prompts a sudden outburst from him, abruptly terminated by the approach and entry of the Countess. The latter's intrusion also brings sudden, quiet irruptions of the three-card motif, and for a moment these continue to haunt Hermann, even after the Countess has left. But quickly recovering his self-possession, he returns to his calculated pleading until, clearly sensing that he is winning despite Liza's desperate pleas that he should leave, he threatens to do just that. The stratagem works: Liza yields.

This has been a highly personal and very crucial scene: Act 2 Scene 2 is the very opposite. It is set in a Great Hall and is hardly relevant to the main dramatic thread, though it does provide a context in which we can learn that Liza wishes to meet Hermann again, and where she manages to pass to him the key to her room. Yet there is another intimate encounter that should not be passed over here, and for which room is provided, once everyone else has been tempted away to the firework display. It is a very troubled Yeletsky who now hymns Liza in a bid to gain the affection, if not the love, of his young affianced bride, and in the Prince's declaration, as sensitive as it is dignified, Tchaikovsky skilfully suggests a man who is both strong and caring. As for the broader purpose of this whole scene, it is to provide a brilliant foil to the three very intimate scenes that will follow, and to allow the chorus and dancers to have a role in the opera as providers of a formal entertainment for the aristocratic guests, with the *Faithful Shepherdess* interlude offering opportunities for some solo dancing.

And, having mentioned the *Faithful Shepherdess* interlude, I have touched on what is perhaps the most intriguing single feature of this scene. Mozart was Tchaikovsky's idol – and nowhere in his work is his adoration of that composer more manifest than here. From this scene's very beginning, both in the orchestral introduction and in the chorus that follows, Tchaikovsky gave himself up to the spell of Mozart where he could. Take this substantial orchestral prelude and opening chorus, incorporate the voice parts of the latter into the instrumental parts of the former, and you have an abbreviated sonata-form movement such as a late eighteenth-century composer might have produced, and this pastiche treatment is extended into the exchanges between some of Hermann's colleagues ahead of the entry of Liza. As for the later *Faithful Shepherdess* interlude, it is again back to Mozart, evidently with some direct quotations from, or at least allusions to, pieces by him or his contemporaries. It has been suggested that this Milozvor–Prilepa–Zlatogor tale has ironic resonances with the Hermann–Liza–Yeletsky drama, but personally I find this difficult to accept. I also – again personally – question whether it was wise to interpolate into this otherwise taut opera such a protracted interlude of very charming, but also very slight music, though it certainly reinforces the contrasting background to the events of the following scene in the Countess's bedroom. As for this ballroom scene's own conclusion, Tchaikovsky returns to the music to which Hermann's colleagues had talked ahead of Yeletsky's declaration of love, and again they covertly torment him, with the result that Hermann wonders whether he is indeed going mad. Liza passes him the key, tells him to come the following night, but Hermann refuses to delay: he will come tonight. Finally the master of ceremonies announces the approach of the Empress herself (Catherine the Great), and all line up to receive her – though the curtain had to come down before her actual appearance, since in 1890 it was still unlawful to impersonate a Russian Emperor or Empress on the stage.

And so to the heart of *The Queen of Spades*. This fourth scene, set in the Countess's room, contains some of the most radical music Tchaikovsky ever composed, and it is as atmospheric and tense as any scene in opera. Even before the curtain has risen we can feel an

irrepressible unease in the muted-strings introduction, with its obsessive, naggingly nervous six-note figure in the violas, played 210 times
without a break (as with the high sustained C in the *Sleeping Beauty*'s
Sleep Entr'acte, Tchaikovsky organized this in a shift pattern (two
bars on, two bars off) to make it tolerable for the players – and who
might otherwise have lost count!). Note also the four-note pizzicato
figure that haunts the bass. As for the restless tune above, this is a child
of Hermann's quietly pleading theme just ahead of the Countess's
intervention in the bedroom scene: after all, love is still a part of the
motivation that has brought him here. No opera contains an air of
suspense stronger than that which is conjured here by Tchaikovsky's
brilliantly conceived music. Hermann steals in and surveys the room
until he hears the Countess and her maids approaching, then hides.
The maids' song is a gay one – no doubt they are well practised in trying to counteract their mistress's persistent dour and grumpy moods
and ill temper. Having dressed her for the night and installed her in her
chair, they remain as their mistress begins to muse on her distant past.
Note the orchestra's descending six-note scale that will now haunt the
old woman's musings (an echo of Tchaikovsky's Fate theme?) – and
note, in due course, the melody heard quietly in the orchestra: this is a
French tune, 'Vive Henri IV', a song the Countess herself had sung in
her youth, to the admiration of noble admirers. Even more – note the
lengthy, French-texted song she next sings: this is, in fact, an aria from
the 1784 opera *Richard, Coeur de Lion* by the French composer,
André Grétry, another memory from the days of the Countess's social
glory. Suddenly she realizes that her maids are still in attendance,
angrily dismisses them, begins repeating Grétry's aria, but finally drifts
into sleep as the six-note orchestral figure falls ever lower until it, too,
fades.

The critical point on which the whole opera will turn has now
come. The dramatic pace has slowed to stasis; when it quietly resumes,
it is the thrice-heard three-card motif that steals in, Hermann's emergence signalled by an agitated resurgence of his love theme, the
Countess's mute terror by quiet bursts of intensely nervous music. I
believe that, with such gripping music, little further comment is
necessary here. Hermann makes his appeal to the old woman, his tone
at first controlled, finally peremptory. He pulls his pistol, the Countess's terror music briefly recurs, then she collapses. Hermann takes her
hand, makes a last appeal, then realizes the truth: she is dead – and the

muted string theme, a derivative from Hermann's love music, which had opened the scene, rises powerfully in the orchestra. Roused by the noise, Liza bursts in and the terrible truth of what has happened dawns on her. In tearful anger she peremptorily dismisses Hermann as the orchestra blares out what had once been his love theme. Both Liza's and Hermann's hopes have been shattered.

The fraught, if less tempestuous, mood is maintained in the sixth scene, which shifts to Hermann's barracks. The orchestral preamble is the longest in the opera, the offstage simulation of distant chanting by a choir punctuated by bugle calls and extended side-drum rolls. When the curtain at length rises, Hermann is discovered reading Liza's letter (initially spoken), finishing against the background of the offstage choir as he recalls with horror the wink the dead Countess had given him from her coffin at the funeral service. But a sudden and sustained orchestral outburst is preface to the scene's spectral end. Hermann rises, terrified, allusions to his love theme alternating with tiny eruptions of the three-card motif, and an even more powerful orchestral outburst marks his opening of the door, and his confrontation with the ghost. Then on a monotone, quietly and implacably, the spectre gives her instructions and discloses the three-card secret itself. The stillness of this is chilling. Her mission fulfilled, she turns and disappears, leaving a mesmerized Hermann to pick up and mechanically repeat her last words: three . . . seven . . . ace . . . three . . . seven . . .

The scene by the Winter Canal has no place in Pushkin, but was invented by Tchaikovsky himself because, so he reasoned, the audience would want to know what had happened to Liza. Her aria is one of grief, but of a different kind from Hermann's – not an expression of anger and distress at a scheme thwarted, but of the pain of a vulnerable woman who has been betrayed in love, but who now hopes to retrieve the once promised happiness. It is perhaps the most direct, most open-hearted piece of the opera; it is also the most overtly Russian. Yet midnight strikes, despair replaces hope – but then Hermann rushes in. Clearly concerned to give the scene some amplitude, Tchaikovsky allows Hermann to appear first as an honest lover, and thus provide an excuse for an amorous exchange before his true motivation emerges. Frankly, this is not really Tchaikovsky at his best, and it is, wisely, relatively short. When Hermann reveals his true objective, the ghost's command music from the previous scene is recalled, and Liza's frenzy on discovering, for a second time, Hermann's duplicity brings a return to her earlier despair music. As Hermann's excitement grows, the three-card motif is heard, and the scene ends with Hermann rushing out and Liza throwing herself into the canal.

If this last scene has been the opera's weakest, the final scene amply restores the situation. The liveliness of its opening seems all the greater for following on the grim, dark events of the preceding three scenes, Tchaikovsky breaking the substantial stretch of conviviality only briefly to note the entry of Yeletsky, a surprise presence, but a necessary one so that he can play his ironic role as the instrument of Hermann's destruction. Otherwise, the pervasive mood is festive, with Tomsky's mischievous love song spurring his audience to a vigorous dance accompanied by whistling and shouting. No sooner has the company sat down to supper than Hermann appears and the action suddenly becomes significant – as the intrusion of the thrice-heard three-card motif signifies. Hermann's first two throws are quickly dealt with, a threefold statement of the card motif signifying the moment when each of his huge bets is laid, the moment of play prompting a taut rhythmic outburst from the orchestra, Hermann's success greeted with corporate incredulity the first time, by a stunned mutter the second, thus affording space for Hermann's defiant song where, at last, he reveals his true self. 'What is our life? A game! Who's happy? Today it's you, tomorrow 'tis I!' he sings, a combination of defiance and fatalism driving him on to the final throw. This time only once is the three-card motif heard – and this time its final note is a wrong one. Hermann has lost all, the ghost of the Countess appears and smiles at him, he stabs himself, begs Yeletsky's forgiveness, and reaffirms his love for Liza, the orchestra quietly recalling his love music as he dies. The chorus joins in an unaccompanied prayer for the dead Hermann, and the opera ends with the orchestra again recalling his love music.

———

27
A Relationship Ends:
American Tour

For his Italian expedition, during which he would compose *The Queen of Spades*, Tchaikovsky had been deprived of the company of Alexey, for the latter had remained at Frolovskoye to tend Fekla, his wife, who was dying of consumption. In consequence, he had been replaced in Florence by Modest's valet, Nazar. Tchaikovsky found the Florence hotel to be an ideal choice – inexpensive, and with few other guests. His routine was a typical Tchaikovsky one: rise before eight, read the papers, work till twelve-thirty, dine, go for a walk till three, spend an hour with Nazar watching the world go by, then work till dinner at seven. All this while, Nazar was keeping a personal diary of his temporary master's daily activities. It was an on-the-spot record made by a very dispassionate observer, as such probably giving a more genuinely objective account – and certainly a more engagingly detailed one – than any other source. If we are to judge from Nazar's narrative tone, his relationship with his temporary master was very relaxed. A sample will do:

> P[yotr] I[lich] is in a good mood today. He has already begun the second scene and I can see it's going well. Every time before he finishes work I go into his room and say that it's time for lunch or supper. I don't know – perhaps I disturb him by this, but he doesn't seem to show any displeasure. If I'd noticed this, of course I wouldn't have gone in. I went in at seven. P.I. hadn't yet finished. I said: 'It's time to stop.' He answered: 'Yes' – and then goes on writing notes. I say: 'It'll soon be seven o'clock.' 'Coming,' he says, and writes yet another note, striking a piano key. I continue standing. He pulls out his watch, opens it. 'There's twenty minutes to go. I can work another ten.' I said something, but he replied: 'Let me have just ten minutes.' I left. Ten minutes later he came to me. 'Well, I've finished,' and he began asking what I was doing (I had been writing;

as he came in I had closed my diary), and went into his room. P.I. began walking up and down the room, but I stood by the table. He talked about Feklusha, Alexey and suchlike. For the first time I heard from Pyotr Ilich that his new composition would get a flattering reception. 'If God grants, the opera will go so well that you will pay off [my] debts, Nazar.' 'God grant that it does go well,' I said – and thought to myself, 'And may God grant you good health.'

Matters other than the opera occupied Tchaikovsky while in Florence, and two would be solved very satisfactorily. The first concerned Antonina who, Tchaikovsky heard, had written to Rubinstein, asking to be appointed to a senior post in the Moscow Conservatoire. This extraordinary request posed no direct threat to Tchaikovsky himself, but it was a sign of how unbalanced Antonina continued to be, and he recognized she could still make trouble for him. Too upset to work, for a day he agonized, then decided to take a stand, writing very bluntly to her that her request was preposterous, that since she behaved like a child, she would be punished like one, and that for a year he would reduce her allowance by two-thirds. Jurgenson implemented the decision – and Antonina crumbled. At last Tchaikovsky had found the strategy that would subdue this troublesome woman, and she would disappear for ever from his personal life. The second matter had to do with the Moscow RMS. Tchaikovsky's efforts on its behalf during the previous season had cost him dear. He had already undertaken to conduct six concerts in the following season, but the pressures on him to conduct elsewhere in Russia and abroad were growing. There were also problems caused by the RMS's internal politics, and he could see far worse conflicts involving him ahead, and these might become public. The result was that he resigned his position as a Director of the Moscow branch, and also withdrew from the six concerts he had undertaken to conduct, urging that Ziloti should be assigned three of them.

Having completed the vocal score of *The Queen of Spades* in Florence, in early April Tchaikovsky moved on to Rome to score the opera. For a week he managed happily to alternate work on this with enjoyment of Rome's civic and cultural riches, but then news of his presence leaked, and unwanted demands on his time began to mount. At the beginning of May he was back in St Petersburg in time to celebrate his fiftieth birthday. Another week, and he was home in Frolovskoye.

Here he found little to cheer him. One of the location's great charms, the surrounding woods, had been felled. 'Only the grove behind the church remains. *There's nowhere to walk!*' he lamented to Modest. He visited Feklusha's grave, and approved the memorial Alexey had mounted over it. Nor were matters in Moscow any better, for he felt the way in which the RMS was evolving was a betrayal of those things that mattered to him. As for St Petersburg, that too was now a place where his appearance could immediately be the signal for very varied demands to be made on his time. (He had already rejected a request from a former pupil to be godfather to her child: he would be prepared to accept by proxy, but his excuse given for not attending was that he feared he might drop the baby.) Yet with the opera scored and his time more free, within five days he had set about redeeming a promise given in 1886 to compose a piece for the St Petersburg Chamber Music Society who, as noted earlier, had made him an honorary member. He had jotted down the main theme of what would be the slow movement while engaged on *The Queen of Spades* in Florence (thus prompting the new work's title, *Souvenir de Florence*), and the more he progressed, the more he felt satisfied, though he admitted that the medium he had chosen – a sextet made up of two violins, two violas, and two cellos – had initially proved a challenge. A private performance, followed by its premiere in December, left Tchaikovsky not entirely happy with the piece, and a year later he heavily revised the third and fourth movements.

String Sextet in D, *Souvenir de Florence* * * *(*)

[This large, but mostly relaxed piece, has much charm, and the first two movements are particularly fine. In general it makes easier listening than Tchaikovsky's earlier chamber works, and more experienced listeners may find further help from me through the first three movements unnecessary; for others I provide below a brief guide. However, the finale is more complicated, as my commentary on this movement reveals. This sextet is frequently heard played by a chamber orchestra, but unless it has been very judiciously rehearsed, the heavier sound can become wearing.]

None of Tchaikovsky's chamber works has a more positive opening, and the first movement has an impressively broad but rather gentle second subject, the exposition finally winding down and fading almost completely. The large development overlaps with the recapitulation, and on first hearing you may easily miss the actual point of transfer, but if you do, you will almost certainly soon realize that it has, in fact, already arrived. The recapitulation of the second subject and the (relatively) short coda follow.

The slow movement is in ternary form. Following on the sonorous richness of its introduction, the simplicity of its main section is perhaps even more striking, especially when one notes the great span that Tchaikovsky spins out of melody that is very simple and very touching, whether heard as a single violin line or with that line in eloquent dialogue with a cello before they are joined by a viola in preparation for the whole section's strong climax; Tchaikovsky never wrote anything more engaging that this section. The music of the central section, directed to be played at the tip of the bow, sounds almost furtive, and provides little more than a breathing space before the first section returns, the violin and cello now exchanging roles.

After this very affecting music, the third movement moves us, at least initially, into a fresh, folky world. Also in ternary form, its opening might suggest a gentle dance in prospect, though the relative complexities in some of what soon follows undermines this assumption (note the neat, gently witty coda that rounds off this main section). The movement's flighty centre is more plausibly a dance – assuming, that is, that the dancers can keep up with it. It is very brief, and the opening section then returns seamlessly – though loudly – out of it.

Even more folky is the lively opening of the finale, though this movement will also go stylistically to the opposite extreme by incorporating a fugue. In fact, a taste of the fuguing to come is provided early on during the transition to the second subject, the latter turning out to be a sturdy and broad tune that will lead straight into the very brief development (try, perhaps, to spot the moment when the slow chordal introduction to the slow movement is slipped in (though here it is played much faster): this is the point at which the exposition ends). The recapitulation begins with the folky first subject presented very loudly, and then comes the full-scale fugue, its subject based on the movement's opening folky tune, but later also drawing in the quite different subject of the little fugato near the movement's beginning.

No doubt this studied example of high academic expertise was there to impress the significant German membership of the St Petersburg Chamber Music Society – and I have no doubt it did.

––––––––

Tchaikovsky's three-and-a-half months in Italy had been succeeded by three in Frolovskoye, with only rare trips to Moscow or St Petersburg, and relatively few visitors. But by the later summer he was longing for the company of more relatives and friends, and being now free of winter commitments to the Moscow RMS, he passed the last week of August with Modest and Kolya Konradi, the latter now twenty-two years old, at Grankino; then, with Kolya as companion, he headed for Kamenka.

His sister's home had now become a calmer, but much sadder place. Two nieces, Tanya and Vera, were dead, and a third, Natalya, had already wedded Vera's widower and departed, while Sasha, their mother, was a cause for major concern. Worn down emotionally by domestic stress, she was grossly overweight, and liable to fits from her long dependence on drugs, to which she had now added alcohol. After a rather melancholy fortnight Tchaikovsky and Kolya moved on for two days to Kopïlova where Nikolay von Meck, Tchaikovsky's niece Anna, and their two children had an estate; thence they directed themselves to Tiflis, arriving on 19 September and installing themselves in a flat, which afforded Tchaikovsky some protection from the very active social life of brother Anatoly's wife, Parasha. For a fortnight their living was relaxed, and Tchaikovsky could set about a new composition – a symphonic ballad, *The Voyevoda*. This was based not on Ostrovsky's play, which had been the basis of his first opera, but on a ballad by Pushkin, in which a provincial governor (the voyevoda) returns home to find his wife in the garden with her lover. He orders his servant to shoot the man but the servant shoots the *voyevoda* instead. Tchaikovsky worked on it for about a week; then on 4 October he received a letter from Nadezhda von Meck. Little did he know that this was the harbinger of one of the most distressing events in all his life.

The letter itself was very cordial, though sad. There had been a myriad of problems in his patroness's own family, but as far as Tchaikovsky himself was concerned, its tone contained nothing to alarm him, and its ending was characteristically warm:

Forgive me, my dear, that I am plaguing you with my complainings; hearing them is no joy for anyone. Keep well, my dear, matchless friend, have a good rest, and do not forget one whose love for you is boundless.

NADEZHDA VON MECK

P.S. Please address your next letter to Moscow.

Though she did write once more, that letter has been lost, and this present one proved to be her last surviving written communication with Tchaikovsky. However, we may readily guess some of the missing letter's contents from Tchaikovsky's reply. His patroness too had been involved in the disasters she had described, and she could no longer afford to pay his allowance. And with this she now wished their correspondence to cease.

For Tchaikovsky it was an appalling shock. 'My dear, dear friend,' he wrote:

The news contained in your letter deeply saddened me, *though not for myself, but for you*. That is not at all an empty phrase. Of course I should be lying if I said that such a radical reduction in my budget will have no effect upon my material welfare. But it will affect it to a much smaller degree than you perhaps think. The point is that in recent years my income has greatly increased, and there is no reason to think that it will not continually and rapidly grow. Thus if, from the endless number of circumstances you have to worry about, you are sparing some small thought for me also – then for God's sake, I beg you, rest assured that I have not experienced even the slightest passing regret at the thought of the material deprivation that has befallen me . . .

As for her conclusion about how he must have reacted to her news –

The last words of your letter hurt me a little. Do you really believe me capable of remembering you only while I was using your money? Could I really even for one moment forget what you have done for me, and how much I am indebted to you? I can say without any exaggeration that you saved me, and that I should probably have gone out of my mind and perished if you had not come to my aid. No, my dear friend, be assured that I shall remember this to my dying breath, and will bless you. I am glad that it is now, when you can no longer share your resources with me, that I can with my whole heart express my boundless, fervent gratitude, which is simply incapable of being expressed in words.

But this was only one side of Tchaikovsky's feelings at the turn of events, and the letter he wrote to Jurgenson some days later has a very different tone:

I have borne this blow philosophically, but all the same I was disagreeably struck and surprised. She had written so many times that I was guaranteed this subsidy to my dying breath. Now I have had to disabuse myself; now I shall have to live differently, and on a different scale, and shall probably have to seek some employment in St Petersburg with a good salary. I'm very, very, very *hurt*, just *hurt*. My relationship with her was such that her lavish giving was never burdensome to me. Now, retrospectively, it is; my pride is wounded, my confidence in her unbounded readiness to support me materially and bear every kind of sacrifice for me has been deceived. Now I wish that she was completely ruined so that she would need my help. But then, you see, I know perfectly well that, as *we* would see it, she's still terribly rich; in a word, a sort of sick, silly joke has occurred which I find shameful and sickening.

While the narrative I have recorded of the kindly, positive and generous side to Tchaikovsky's nature in his relationships with other people is well founded on fact, this letter now shows there could also be another side to him. Of course Tchaikovsky was right: she still was 'terribly rich', but for him it would mean the abandonment of his hopes of purchasing an apartment in St Petersburg and a house at or near Frolovskoye. Nor was it long before he heard that her financial position had indeed been restored. But she had forbidden him to write to her, and he continued for some months to correspond with Wladislaw Pachulski, a young Pole who had suceeded Kotek as her resident violinist, and who had also been an aspiring (but untalented) composer whom Tchaikovsky had reluctantly coached at his patroness's request, and who in the meantime had become one of her sons-in-law. Pachulski was now in a very powerful strategic position, and though he would transmit cordial but formal messages from his mother-in-law, yet the embargo on direct communication remained absolute.

After eight months of this Tchaikovsky could contain himself no longer, and wrote the bitterest of letters to Pachulski:

I believe entirely that Nadezhda Filaretovna is ill, weak, and her nerves disordered, and that she cannot write to me as before. What distresses, troubles and, speaking frankly, does hurt me deeply is not that she does not write to me, but that she has lost all interest in me. Not once has she entrusted you to ask me how I am living, and what is happening to me. I have tried through you to establish a regular relationship with N.F. through correspondence, but every one of your letters has been merely a courteous reply. In the country during the autumn I read through her earlier letters. Neither her illness nor her misfortunes nor her material difficulties, it would seem, could have altered those feelings which are expressed in those letters. Yet they have altered. Perhaps it was just because I never *personally* knew N.F. that I imagined her as an ideal being. I could not imagine fickleness in such a demigoddess – it seemed to me that the earth's globe would crumble to little pieces rather than that N.F. would become another person in relation to me. But the latter has happened, and this has turned topsy-turvy my attitudes towards people, my trust in the best of them. It has disrupted my calm, poisoned that very portion of happiness given to me by Fate. Of course, though not wanting this, N.F. has behaved very cruelly towards me. Never have I felt myself so humbled, has my pride been so wounded as now. And what is most painful of all: in view of N.F.'s health I cannot, because I fear to distress and upset her, tell her all that torments me. I cannot express myself – and that alone could relieve me. Of course, not a word of this to N.F.

Pachulski's reply was very matter of fact, and he returned Tchaikovsky's letter to him. Nadezhda Filaretovna's illness, he wrote, had brought a great change in his patroness that had affected all around her, himself included – though if Tchaikovsky would only write to her direct, Pachulski was sure she would respond wholeheartedly. But *she* had forbidden Tchaikovsky to do this. Their correspondence was over.

Nevertheless, there may have been another, and more sensitive reason for her own refusal to write. While at Kopïlovo only days before receiving her final surviving letter, Tchaikovsky had been told by her son, Nikolay, of the increasing difficulty his mother was experiencing in letter-writing, and this was supported to me personally by Nikolay's daughter, Galina von Meck, whom I met in 1984 in Richmond, Surrey, shortly before her death. She confirmed that her grandmother did indeed have an atrophied arm which made writing virtually impossible in her later years, adding that the reason she would not dictate a letter to Tchaikovsky was that what she had to write to him was for his eyes alone, and should remain a secret from all others. But Galina also believed that there had been a final reconciliation between her grandmother and Tchaikovsky. For some three years Galina's mother, Anna, had tried to persuade her composer-uncle to talk about the rupture, but he would say nothing. Then in August 1893, only weeks before his sudden death, Tchaikovsky had approached Anna, who was about to leave for Nice to take her turn in nursing her dying mother-in-law, asking her to tell Nadezhda that he regretted his silence (which she neverthless had prescribed) over the past three years, and begged to be forgiven. The apology was wholeheartedly accepted, and the news was passed to Tchaikovsky.

I cannot say that the lines of evidence I have used here are all totally reliable, though I have no reason to doubt that there is a core of truth in all this. What I most vividly remember is Galina herself telling me the story, and the last words we exchanged. She was in her nineties, lying on a chaise-longue, and as I bent over to take her hand in farewell, she put her other hand on my arm, looked me in the eye, and said, 'And you will write that they were reconciled?' I said I would report what she had told me. I cannot, of course, guarantee that it is the truth, though I find it plausible.

It was a week before his patroness's first letter arrived that Tchaikovsky had settled to the composition of his symphonic ballad, *The Voyevoda*, and despite the anxiety prompted by her letter, he completed the sketches within a further fortnight, though it would be another year before the piece was scored. By that time Tchaikovsky was having serious doubts about it. Some of his friends, including Taneyev, also expressed reservations, and though the piece was successful with the audience when Tchaikovsky conducted its premiere, he himself turned violently against it and, on returning to the artists' room, he began ripping the score to pieces, then turned to the attendant and ordered him to collect the orchestral parts. Ziloti, who was the promoter of the concert, recorded what followed:

Seeing his excitement and knowing that the score's fate now also threatened the parts, I decided on a desperate remedy, and said, 'Pardon me, Pyotr Ilich, here in this concert I am the master and not you, and only I can give the orders' – and I immediately instructed the attendant to collect all the orchestral parts and take them to my apartment. I spoke all this so sternly, so brazenly, that Pyotr Ilich was, as they say, flabbergasted. He only muttered quietly, 'How dare you talk to me like that!' and I replied, 'We'll discuss this another time.' At that moment visitors entered the room and with this our confrontation ended.

Tchaikovsky did indeed destroy the score the next day, but the parts belonged to Ziloti, who retained them, using them to reconstruct the piece after Tchaikovsky's death. It appears that Taneyev, having heard *The Voyevoda*, had radically changed his evaluation of it, voicing regret that he had so misjudged it as to have threatened its survival.

What must still seem puzzling to us now is Tchaikovsky's own fierce rejection of *The Voyevoda*, for nine days after the concert he could still write to Jurgenson that he was

profoundly convinced it is a work that compromises me. If I were an inexperienced youth it would be a different matter, but a hoary old man ought to go forward, or else should remain on the heights he has already reached. If such a thing recurs in the future, I shall again tear it to pieces – and then give up composing altogether.

Tchaikovsky was, surely, far too harsh on himself. It would be very tempting to suggest that the trauma of Nadezhda von Meck's action had something to do with the work's tone, but it was sketched when that incident had scarcely begun. In many ways *The Voyevoda* is a work in which Tchaikovsky took a leap forward, and there is one point in which he did exactly that, for the final bars anticipate very closely that last, most violent eruption in the first movement of the Sixth Symphony – his greatest orchestral work, and also, as Fate would decree, his last completed composition.

Symphonic Ballad: *The Voyevoda* * * * (*)

[This is a maverick piece. It is rarely heard in concerts, yet it contains some of Tchaikovsky's most radical music. Barely half the length of Romeo and Juliet, The Tempest, let alone Francesca da Rimini, it does not fit comfortably into conventional concert programmes; nor, perhaps, is it, as a totality, as instantly appealing. Yet it makes for a fascinating experience quite unlike that offered by any other piece by Tchaikovsky. For the adventurous listener?]

If the story of Pushkin's *The Queen of Spades* had been ironic, even more so (as we have noted) is that of Tchaikovsky's ballad *The Voyevoda*. Tchaikovsky's very concise piece (it lasts little more than ten minutes) is cast as a ternary structure; its flanks are the province of the wronged husband, its centre the love scene. The music concerned with the *voyevoda* himself is some of Tchaikovsky's most radical, its desperate urgency compacting its fierceness; by contrast, the love music is some of Tchaikovsky's most opulent, its colouring enriched by his incorporation of a celesta, a very new keyboard percussion instrument at the time.

The very eloquence and directness of *The Voyevoda* renders more detailed commentary hardly necessary, but a few additional points may be helpful. The piece opens with what is clearly the intimidating approach of the returning *voyevoda*, the urgent rhythmic figure that underpins this also resurging, but furtively, in the quiet section that follows; no doubt the muffled mutterings here on bass clarinet mimic the *voyevoda*'s words as he spies the lovers. The central love scene is its own advocate, but the ending (the urgent rhythmic figure again suggesting the *voyevoda*'s nervous rage, with bass clarinet mutterings mimicking his words), is as brutal as it is concise. *The Voyevoda* is rarely played in concerts, which is a great pity, but I imagine it could produce some challenges in rehearsal if the performance is to be faithful to the story's spirit.

––––––––––

Fame comes at a price, and by now no one knew this better than Tchaikovsky. The pressures on his personal time increased, and it is unnecessary to detail such things here. In a slight but nevertheless significant way he had cause to notice the price of his heightened prestige when, on returning from Tiflis at the beginning of November, he was met at the station in Moscow by a whole group of his friends, who promptly bore him off to a restaurant to honour his return. Already Jurgenson could see reason to expand his publications of Tchaikovsky's music. The former had earlier begun issuing a collected edition of the piano music, and now he was turning his attention to the songs. However, if the songs were to be published also in transposed editions (i.e., moved to higher or lower keys to suit the requirements of different voices – that is, from soprano down to bass), then Tchaikovsky insisted he would have to check these himself, and this would absorb much time. The premiere of *The Queen of Spades* in mid-December was followed by a trip to Kiev to conduct the premiere of a second production being mounted in that city. On arrival Tchaikovsky excused himself from this undertaking, offering instead to conduct an orchestral concert four days ahead of the opera's opening. As for the first night of the latter, the enthusiasm of the Kiev audience eclipsed that of St Petersburg. After the first scene there was an ovation, and there would be more to follow, but the cumulative excitement of this was also exhausting. As Tchaikovsky himself recalled:

> It would be ludicrous even to compare the enthusiasm of the reception in St Petersburg with that in Kiev. It was something incredible, but I'm unimaginably tired and, at bottom, am constantly aching and suffering. Uncertainty about the immediate future also torments me. Should I turn down a concert tour abroad? My head's empty and I haven't the slightest wish to work.

Kamenka was the short-term answer, and was the more cheering because Sasha seemed much improved in health. But Tchaikovsky had already agreed to compose a double-bill – a one-act opera, *Iolanta*, and a ballet, *The Nutcracker* – for the 1891–92 season of the Imperial Theatres in St Petersburg, and meanwhile he had to honour his promise, given in 1888 to his actor friend, Lucien Guitry, to provide the incidental music for a production of *Hamlet*, to be mounted only weeks ahead in Paris. By mid-January he was home in Frolovskoye and, unenthusiastic as he was, he as usual discharged this undertaking as promised. And while all this was happening, requests to appear abroad were proliferating, among which was one to conduct in the concerts celebrating the inauguration in April of the new Carnegie Hall in New York. The fee would be $2,500, and was irresistible.

Reckoning that a concert in Paris would be timely, Tchaikovsky requested his Paris publisher Mackar to make arrangements. From Paris he would proceed to Le Havre for the Atlantic crossing. On 22 March he was in the French capital.

Tchaikovsky had already managed a little work on *The Nutcracker*, but his fortnight in the French capital was swamped by visits and invitations to dine out, his only personal pleasures coming from the presence also of Modest, Sapelnikov and the pianist Sophie Menter, whom Tchaikovsky had known and come to like during the 1880s in St Petersburg. His concert at the Châtelet, which included the Second Piano Concerto and Third Suite, was a tremendous success resulting in yet more demands on his time. There being little chance of composing in Paris, on 10 April he moved on to Rouen, where he intended to remain eight days before embarking at Le Havre. However, his mood was gloomy, there were bursts of longing for Russia, and working proved very difficult. Realizing that he could never have the double-bill ready for the coming season, he wrote to Vsevolozhsky, explaining that it would have to be postponed until the following one. The pressure being now relieved, and with three days left before embarkation, he decided to return to Paris. Finding a *cabinet de lecture*, he entered to glance at the Russian papers. Picking up a copy of *New Time*, he turned to the back page – and what he read caused him to rush out into the street. Sasha was dead.

For some hours, it seems, a dazed Tchaikovsky wandered the Paris streets, only much later heading for Menter's and Sapelnikov's lodgings. They provided him with a bed for the night, and the following morning he decided to continue with the American tour, for he had already bought his ticket and been given a handsome advance on which he had drawn heavily. The voyage began sadly, for a young man threw himself overboard and Tchaikovsky, as one of the few passengers who knew German, was called on to translate the suicide note. But soon his spirits rallied, and among his fellow passengers he found much to fascinate, and sometimes amuse him. There were alarming occurrences – a full-scale storm in mid-Atlantic, which proved he was not immune to seasickness, and fog off Newfoundland, with the ship crawling and the ominous blare of the hooter sounding every half-minute. His purse was stolen from his cabin – and then his celebrity identity was discovered, bringing with it a deluge of demands on his time. Finally the ship was struck by a hurricane.

On docking in New York, a delegation of five led by Morris Reno, who was in charge of Carnegie Hall, met him, piloted him through Customs, and took him to his hotel, where he gave way to a flood of tears, then took a walk up Broadway, was surprised by the number of Negroes and the height of some of the buildings ('*Nine* [*sic*!] storeys'), returned to his hotel, again gave way to tears – but then wrote to Anatoly and Parasha, admitting that when the tour was all over, he would recall it with pleasure.

Three things were to strike him about America. First was the hotel accommodation, with its private bath, water-closet, hot and cold running water, speaking tubes, and lifts. Second was that his reputation had preceded him. On the day he arrived, the *New York Herald* carried a banner headline, 'Tchaikovsky is here!', followed by an article about him. 'It seems that in America I am better known than in Europe. There are pieces of mine which Moscow does not yet know that are played here several times a season.' And third was the openness of Americans:

Compared with the impression made by Paris, where in every advance, every kindness from a stranger one senses an attempt to exploit, the plain dealing which you find here – the sincerity, generosity, cordiality without ulterior motive, the readiness to oblige and be nice – is striking and, at the same time, touching. This and American ways in general, their manners and customs, I find very sympathetic.

He met Walter Damrosch, the conductor whose advocacy had been primarily responsible for his invitation to America, and Andrew Carnegie, the émigré Scot who had made a fortune, much of which he had devoted to public and philanthropic causes, but who had remained very much his own modest, friendly self. American hospitality, Tchaikovsky found, could be prodigious. He was impressed by the formality of dinner parties, the dress codes, the importance of flowers, the courtesy and the food – except, it seems, when it was 'native American'. ('Unusually revolting,' he wrote in the diary he kept during this American tour.) Guests might even be provided with personal carriages when both coming to and leaving a formal social event. 'One must be fair to American hospitality: only amongst us could you meet something similar,' he noted.

His role at the official opening of the Carnegie Hall was only a nominal one: to conduct his Coronation March. ('Went excellently: a great success,' he noted in his diary.) The press were mightily impressed by his conducting: 'One of the few first-class composers who have also been great conductors,' wrote one critic; 'He conducts with the authoritative strength of a master, and the band obeys his lead as one man,' enthused another. Tchaikovsky's first full concert was on his birthday, 7 May:

> Never, I think, have I been so afraid. Is it that they direct their atten-
> tion to my exterior? However that may be, having endured several
> painful hours, I finally went out, again had an excellent reception,
> and produced, as they say in today's papers, a sensation. After the
> Suite I sat in Reno's office and gave an interview to some reporters
> (O these reporters!).

By now he desperately needed to be alone –

> and so, squeezing my way through the crowd of ladies who were
> surrounding me in the corridor and staring at me with eyes in which
> I could not but with pleasure read enthusiastic interest, and declin-
> ing the Reno family's invitation, I rushed home.

His Third Suite, Tchaikovsky discovered, had enjoyed a special success: 'A marvellous production. Russian music certainly threatens that
of Germany,' wrote one critic; 'The sensation of the afternoon was Mr
Tchaikovsky's Third Suite – original, unique, and full of local colour,'
wrote another; 'Heard yesterday as it was interpreted under the mag-
netic and magnificent conducting of the composer, it produced an
overwhelmingly great effect,' wrote a third. It was much the same at
his next appearance, this time conducting some of his religious choral
music. But his greatest triumph was his final concert, in which he conducted his First Piano Concerto with, as soloist, Adele aus der Ohe, a
Liszt pupil who had now built up a formidable reputation in America:

> The enthusiasm was such as I have never succeeded in arousing even
> in Russia. There were endless recalls, they cried 'Upwards!' [sic!],
> waved their handkerchiefs – in a word, it was clear that I am indeed
> loved by the Americans. I especially valued the orchestra's delight in
> me.

His New York concerts were now over, and he was exhausted – yet
still his waking hours were taken up by people wanting interviews,

people who just wanted to meet him or wanted his autograph. One, an old man, brought along a libretto he had written in the hope that Tchaikovsky might use it. All seem to have been American, or at least living in America – that is, except one, a Russian lady journalist, with whom he could talk in Russian as to a Russian. A surge of longing for his homeland overwhelmed him. 'Suddenly tears welled up, my voice began to tremble, and I could not hold back my sobs,' he wrote in his diary. 'I ran into the next room and didn't emerge for a long while.'

The following day Carnegie gave a dinner in Tchaikovsky's honour, at which his host displayed charmingly his reverence for his special guest. 'During the whole evening he showed his affection for me in his own unusual way,' Tchaikovsky wrote in his diary.

> He seized my hands, crying that I was the uncrowned, though very real, king of music. He embraced me (not kissing me: here men never kiss each other), in expressing my greatness he stood on tiptoe and lifted his hands high in the air, and finally threw the whole company into raptures by showing how I conducted. He did this so seriously, so faithfully, so accurately, that I myself was delighted.

At eleven o'clock Reno, who had been his main guide through all these events, walked him back to his hotel.

There was now a break in Tchaikovsky's conducting commitments, and pastoral care shifted to Ferdinand Mayer, a German who worked for the piano-making firm of Knabe, and who, with his associate, Wilhelm Reinhard, acted as one of Tchaikovsky's minders. Tchaikovsky's hosts had decided that he should make a journey to the Niagara Falls, and Mayer had made all the arrangements ahead for ensuring he was looked after and, where necessary, shepherded. It made the most welcome, interesting and relaxing of interludes; Tchaikovsky 'did the Falls' very thoroughly, emerging fortified for the days ahead when again he would be subjected to the so generous but so overwhelming hospitality of his New York hosts ahead of his other American engagements. The first of these was in Baltimore, where the orchestra would be the travelling Boston Festival Orchestra. Again Adele aus der Ohe played the First Piano Concerto, Tchaikovsky's other contribution being the Serenade for Strings. The hall was not full, but the press reaction was as enthusiastic as in New York. Washington came next with a soirée at the Russian Embassy, in which Tchaikovsky's Piano Trio was paired with a Piano Quartet by Brahms. It was the easiest engagement of the tour, for there was no language problem, and at three o'clock the next morning a very relaxed Tchaikovsky was returned to his hotel. A free day enabled him to visit the Washington Monument and the Capitol. His final appearance as conductor was in Philadelphia, again with the Boston Touring Orchestra and Adele aus der Ohe playing to a well-filled hall and to great enthusiasm. We do not know whether Tchaikovsky was gratified by press reviewers' attempts to characterize his appearance (one noting that 'he looks like a broker or clubman rather than an artist, seems to be rising sixty, but is well preserved', another that he was 'more like a prosperous merchant, or a United States Senator'), for he took the train straight back to New York.

Tchaikovsky's conducting commitments were now all discharged, and there remained only a concert of his works at the Composers' Club, the programme comprising the Piano Trio, Third String Quartet, and some of his songs. There were to be abundant farewells (sadly, he had to tell the elderly librettist that he would not be using his work), presents were heaped on him, and in the middle of the concert there was a speech addressed to him, to which he replied in French, receiving an ovation. Afterwards there were people to talk with, and autographs to sign. Then, with Reno, Mayer and Reinhard, Tchaikovsky returned to his hotel, packed, then shared two bottles of champagne with his companions. His final farewells were to the hotel staff.

Despite all the longings for home that had periodically punctuated his tour, the three-and-a-half weeks in America had been a personal triumph for Tchaikovsky – exciting, heartwarming, and the strongest evidence yet of just how universal and enthusiastic was the love of his music. He returned to Europe in a frame of mind very different from that in which he had set out – but then, as he had predicted on first arriving in New York, when it was all over he would recall it with pleasure. Disembarking at Cuxhaven, his journey home was completed by train from Hamburg, via Berlin. On 1 June he was back in St Petersburg.

Even while Tchaikovsky was in mid-Atlantic, the *New York Herald* took stock of his visit:

If we are to count up all the men and women of genius now adorning the world, how long would that list be? Should we be able to name the twelve or ten or six such people? Men whose claim to the high honor would not be disputed by even the most skeptical and cold? Let us try.

To head the list we should, of course, have Bismarck. Then might come Edison and Tolstoy, Sarah Bernhardt and perhaps Ibsen, with Herbert Spencer and two great composers – Dvořák and Tchaikovsky. The right of Tchaikovsky to a place on the roll will hardly, we think, be denied.

28
Double-Bill:
A Relationship Renewed

Tchaikovsky's mood on returning from America was ambivalent. The status his name had already gained in this distant land and the ecstatic ovations that he and his music had roused were the strongest evidence to date of his growing global reputation. Back in St Petersburg it was good to see again his family and friends, and enjoy the enhancement of his personal standing that his American triumph now brought. But his American hosts' overestimate of his age continued to nag. 'No! the old man is obviously in decline,' he wrote to his nephew Bob a month after his return:

> Not only is his hair thinning and white as snow, not only are his teeth falling out and declining to chew his food, not only are his eyes weakening and wearying easily, not only are his legs shuffling rather than walking – but even the one and only ability he has for any sort of occupation is failing and evaporating.

Even before his American tour the deforestation at Frolovskoye had so depressed him that he had instructed Alexey to move everything back to their former house in Maidanovo. Nor would there be any more trips to Tiflis which he had so come to love, for Anatoly had been promoted to a post in Estonia, and his only hope was that Ippolitov-Ivanov might invite him to conduct there. But such invitations elsewhere would proliferate. The Americans wanted him back, but the fee offered was paltry. Tchaikovsky countered with a demand three times higher – and that was that! But engagements nearer home were both practicable and profitable, as well as beneficial to his reputation – but they also absorbed time and energy. The directions taken by the Moscow Conservatoire and the local RMS had fostered an antipathy to both, and this had affected his personal relations with some former close associates: there would be no more house parties with them in Moscow. Business matters with Jurgenson, including revised and corrected editions of some of Tchaikovsky's earlier works, would increasingly demand his attention; moreover, he discovered that some of Jurgenson's proof-readers had been very careless, and he had to take more and more of this laborious time-consuming chore on himself. Yet despite all this, his characteristic financial generosity, and his willingness to give of his own time to try to help others continued. Among these interventions was an instruction to Jurgenson to buy twenty tickets against Tchaikovsky's account for a young pianist's debut concert in Moscow, then distribute them among friends because Tchaikovsky feared the audience would be small. There was support, too, for Shpazhinskaya, who was near breaking point over her family situation, and even more time was devoted to healing a breach between Modest and Kolya Konradi. The latter had felt that Modest had treated his mother insultingly during the disputes of Kolya's troubled childhood, nor did Kolya consider that he should still be paying Modest a salary. Tension had for a while been eased, but now it had resurged, and Tchaikovsky suggested Modest should break his more formal relationship with Kolya, and that the salary payment should end. It did, but at no financial loss to Modest, for the latter later admitted that he had ever since then been receiving 2000 roubles a year from brother Pyotr – significantly, exactly the the sum Kolya had been paying him. And acting in a completely different sphere, Tchaikovsky approached the head of the Moscow theatres on behalf of a singer who had created the title role in the Moscow premieres of *Onegin* and of Eletsky in the recent *The Queen of Spades*. Tchaikovsky's letter tells us as much about its writer as about the grounds that prompted it:

Dear Pavel Mikhailovich,

The day before yesterday, when I was with you, I forgot to approach you with a further *very important* request. I had promised dear, sympathetic *Khokhlov* to petition you on his behalf: that when he performs the role of the Demon in Rubinstein's opera for the hundredth time, you would permit this to be advertised on the posters. I totally understand this fervent wish of his, and I consider that he fully, fully merits those enthusiastic ovations which should be anticipated if the public are made aware of this jubilee, unprecedented on our stages. Please, I beg you most earnestly, respect *Khokhlov*'s petition. He is a favourite with his colleagues, the public, the composers of operas, the Moscow ladies – in a word, he is a universal favourite, and you will afford great pleasure to all if you accede to this request.

Yours very truly,

P. TCHAIKOVSKY

Eleven days later Khokhlov received his deserved public tribute.

Inevitably composition became a victim of these inroads into Tchaikovsky's time, and in his remaining two years only one work – though a stunning one – would come from him that could truly match the greatest of its predecessors. Meanwhile, his first priority on returning to Russia was to complete the double-bill of *Iolanta* and *The Nutcracker*. Tchaikovsky had read Henrik Hertz's one-act play, *King René's Daughter*, nine years earlier, been captivated by it, and promised himself he would one day set it to music. Modest had devised a libretto, but as yet Tchaikovsky had composed nothing, and Frolovskoye would become his base until the middle of September, when the sketches for the opera would be completed. By the year's end the scoring was done and, with *The Nutcracker*, *Iolanta* received its premiere in December 1892. On this occasion it scored a success, but the press were generally very unfavourable ('In it Tchaikovsky repeats himself . . .'; 'This time unfortunately the composer's melodic inspiration was far below its usual level . . .'; 'Tiresomely long, the musical images of the characters are tediously sketched, and there are no new, fresh creative ideas in it' – and so on). That *Iolanta* was paired with the perennially popular ballet, *The Nutcracker*, did not help its longer-term fortunes, for the double-bill involved two very different and star-studded casts, each of which in normal circumstances would have had its own orchestra, while the opera by itself would make a very short evening. Opportunities of seeing *Iolanta* are thus very rare.

Iolanta: opera in one act * * *

[*Iolanta is an opera of much charm, but of uneven musical quality. The earlier stretches are attractive, and the love scene that follows contains some touching, sometimes very beautiful music. However, the later stages are less interesting musically.*]

The story of *Iolanta* is set in fifteenth-century Provence. Iolanta, King René's daughter, has been blind from birth, and is therefore unaware she is different from other people. Her attendants are never to mention light, and an outsider enters the garden on pain of death. Iolanta is betrothed to Robert, Duke of Burgundy, and René has kept her isolated, hoping to conceal her disability from him until she is cured. Ebn-Hakir, a great Moorish physician, examines Iolanta, but tells her father that she can be cured only if she longs to see the light: thus she must be told of her blindness. Robert and Vaudement, a Burgundian knight, arrive. In fact, Robert loves another, but Vaudement is captivated by Iolanta. When she is unable to tell red roses from white, he perceives the truth, and Iolanta becomes aware that she is not as others are. 'What is light?' she asks. 'The Creator's first gift,' Vaudement replies. On returning, René is appalled, but Ebn-Hakir realizes that the condition for cure now exists – and René also sees how he can rouse Iolanta's will to see, for Vaudement has entered the garden without permission, and so he must die, the King decrees – that is, if Iolanta is not cured. Iolanta readily goes off with Ebn-Hakir, and when she returns she can see. Robert has now admitted his affections lie elsewhere, and Vaudement is established as a suitable match for Iolanta. All rejoice.

Iolanta is a slight and uneven piece, though the love scene between Vaudemont and Iolanta contains music equal to Tchaikovsky's best. The orchestral introduction, being scored only for wind instruments, provides a well-judged foil to the lovely music that opens the opera itself, muted strings and harp substantiating the gentle world in which Iolanta exists. (Older readers who know the 'Minuet from *Berenice*' by Handel, once second only to that composer's 'Largo' in popularity, may reasonably suspect that this was haunting Tchaikovsky when he composed the opera's opening.) Iolanta's arioso is a very touching piece, the women's choruses have much charm, as does the lullaby to which they finally lull their charge to sleep. But musical interest dips in the acre of accompanied recitative that follows on the fanfares that signal a stretch of explanations and proceedings before the King and Ebn-Hakir enter, and the former sings a pain-filled, yet dignified aria. Even more impressive in its way is Ebn-Hakir's response after he has seen Iolanta, for his aria circles round and round the same constricted phrase, as though unsparingly driving home to the King that Iolan-

401

ta must be told of her blindness if she is to be cured. The entry and reactions of Robert and Vaudement are efficiently treated; the former's revelation of his passion for Matilda is appropriately lusty, Vaudement's that of a man who is still longingly awaiting the first true experience of love. 'O come, bright vision,' he sings, then opens the door leading from the terrace – and his wished-for vision lies sleeping before him.

This is the heart of the opera, and the quality of Tchaikovsky's music in what follows is no surprise, for Iolanta is yet another of those young, vulnerable heroines who had so profitably preoccupied him in some of his earlier operas. Here Tchaikovsky became truly engaged with his subject, and the hesitant first exchanges between the lovers are sensitively presented, Vaudement's declarations both passionate and tender, Iolanta's responses engagingly ingenuous. But bewilderment is coupled with mounting curiosity at her unseen lover's words and at his amorous tone that is so new to her: this, and her suitor's impassioned outburst of pity as he discovers Iolanta's blindness, then perceives what this costs her, are beautifully handled. If only *Iolanta* had maintained this level, it could have been a minor jewel in Tchaikovsky's operatic treasury. But when the metaphysics intervene, a stiff tune rather like the motto theme of the Fifth Symphony signals a formal duet conclusion in prospect, and formula replaces vibrant creativity.

Sadly nothing in what follows matches the best of what has gone before. All is efficiently delivered, but mostly it is concerned with an expeditious despatch of the abundant unfinished business of the plot, culminating in a noisy finale on what is certainly not one of Tchaikovsky's best tunes.

The Nutcracker: ballet in two acts * * * * *

[The Nutcracker is perhaps, of all Tchaikovsky's larger pieces, the one that requires least comment from me. Assuming that the listener has well-banded CDs, there is no need for me to do more than help my reader to connect the stage action with the music and sharpen a little his/her awareness of interesting details. It is easy to criticize, even ridicule, aspects of the story, but Tchaikovsky's music is so inventive,

varied, and superbly orchestrated that I still find simply listening to the whole piece at home an experience both relaxing and enriching.]

Though *The Nutcracker* is in only two acts, its macro-structure reflects that of *The Sleeping Beauty* in that it narrates a story, then appends a floor show. The difference is one of proportion, for whereas in the four-act *Sleeping Beauty* the story had occupied the first three acts, the divertimento being confined to the fourth, in the two-act *Nutcracker* the story is the business of Act 1 and only a morsel of Act 2, the divertissement annexing the remainder of that act. The plot is based on a short story by the early nineteenth-century German writer E. T. A. Hoffmann, adapted into two acts by the choreographer, Marius Petipa, in collaboration with Tchaikovsky

Act 1: *A hall in the Silberhaus's house.* The Christmas tree is being decorated, to the excitement of the Silberhaus's children, Clara and Fritz, and their friends. Drosselmeyer, Clara's godfather, enters and presents the children with four mechanical dolls which dance when wound up. For Clara and Fritz his special present is an odd-looking doll, a Nutcracker, which Fritz plays with, and breaks. Clara rescues it, rocks it, then lays it in her favourite doll's bed. The guests dance the old *Grossvatertanz* (a traditional seventeenth-century German dance for concluding balls) to round off the party. Clara wants to take the doll to bed, but this is not allowed. The guests gradually disperse, and the hall becomes empty.

As soon as it is quiet, an anxious Clara returns to discover how the Nutcracker is, but is alarmed by what she sees and hears: twinkling lights from chinks, Drosselmeyer's image on the clock face, and mice everywhere. She seeks refuge in the Nutcracker's bed. In the moonlight the Christmas tree grows to intimidating proportions, and the toys come to life. Gingerbread soldiers appear, as does an army of mice. Battle is joined, and the mice win. Suddenly the Nutcracker jumps out of bed and orders the alarm to be sounded. Tin soldiers, armed with cannon, leap out of boxes, and the Mouse King orders his army to attack. Finally he challenges the Nutcracker to single combat. But Clara, seeing the increasing danger threatening the Nutcracker, hurls her shoe at the Mouse King's back, and the Mouse King flees with his army. The Nutcracker turns into a handsome Prince, falls on his knees before Clara, and begs her to follow him. They disappear among the Christmas tree's branches as the setting is transformed into a pine wood. The snow begins to fall and the corps de ballet performs a big snowflakes' dance as the storm subsides and a winter landscape is illuminated by the moon.

Act 2: *Confiturenburg: the Palace of Sweets*. The Sugar Plum Fairy and Prince Coqueluche, who are awaiting Clara and the Nutcracker Prince, are standing in a sugar kiosk decorated with dolphins, from whose mouths gush sweet and refreshing drinks. Various fantastic fairies representing flowers and sweets appear and bow before them. The major-domo announces the approach of their two expected guests, who float in, sitting in a gilded nutshell. Little Moors in hummingbird-feather costumes help Clara disembark. She and the Nutcracker Prince are greeted by the Sugar Plum Fairy, Prince Coqueluche, and the sisters of the Nutcracker Prince, who explains how Clara had saved him. The Sugar Plum Fairy orders the festivities to begin. These consist of: Spanish dance (chocolate); Arabian dance (coffee); Chinese dance (tea); Russian dance (Trépak); *Danse des mirlitons* (sugar candies); Mother Gigogne and clowns; *Valse des fleurs*; *Pas de deux* (Sugar Plum Fairy and Prince Coqueluche). Clara is in raptures, and a delighted Nutcracker Prince tells her of the fairy-tale wonders of the Kingdom of Sweets. Final waltz and Apotheosis.

In the neat compact overture (in sonata form, but without development) Tchaikovsky excludes both the lower strings and all the brass except two horns: this is to be no high-drama event, and the touch will be light. What is soon striking about the ballet itself is how swift and incident-packed it is when compared with *Swan Lake* and *The Sleeping Beauty*. Preparing the Christmas tree is Silberhaus's and his wife's business in the first number (note the strange music that comes as the tree is illumined – a harbinger of the magic world that will open up later in the act): the noisy music is the excited children bursting in – but when they see the tree, even they are spellbound. Silberhaus orders a march to be played, after which the children dance around and, to more formal-sounding music, the children's parents enter, and then guests dressed as eighteenth-century dandies – until everyone is drawn up sharp by the sudden entrance of Drosselmeyer, his bizarre character and appearance very deftly caught in his quirky tune. Some of the children are at first frightened by him, but he takes charge and produces the first two presents, a big doll and a soldier: a momentary silence, and both dance. The children plead to stay up late (the string tune), and then Drosselmeyer's other two dolls are produced and perform a furious Russian dance.

During the following waltz Silberhaus refuses to let the children play with their new toys and, to console them, Drosselmeyer produces from his pocket an odd-looking Nutcracker, and makes it dance (the graceful string tune) before Fritz breaks it. Clara takes it, puts it to bed, and soothes it with a lullaby. Fritz and his friends twice try to awaken it with a trumpet fanfare and, to counter this noise, Silberhaus invites his guests to dance the *Grossvatertanz* (what exactly the lively outburst that intersects this dignified music is I do not know: more noise from Fritz and Co.?). Clara's lullaby resumes and fades as the guests leave, the children are sent to bed, and the stage empties.

The music that follows could not be more different from that of the party. Here all Tchaikovsky's prodigious skill as an orchestrator is enlisted; in none of his works is the scoring more important to the effect the music produces than here. Especially striking is the use of wind instruments and harp. All becomes dark, spooky, unstable and unsafe; against a gently quivering muted string background are heard snatches of melody, harp washes, sometimes little chains of rapidly repeated notes, sudden brief eruptions. Midnight strikes as Clara enters this ever more unnerving world – then suddenly the Christmas tree begins to grow, and grow, and GROW – one of the most awesome passages Tchaikovsky ever wrote. It is basically so simple: a little stepwise phrase, in three stages ever more powerfully rising and ever more powerfully supported as, onstage, we see the majestic burgeoning of the Christmas tree. Then the lilliputian battle – a prodigious turmoil of drum rolls, bugle calls, fanfares, strident woodwind outbursts, galloping strings, rampant rabbits, hares, mice devouring gingerbread soldiers, the Nutcracker rallying the troops, and finally Clara hurling her slipper at the unsuspecting Mouse King, then 'collapsing in a faint'. Finally the emergence of the humble Nutcracker as the Nutcracker Prince, and his developing relationship with Clara – beautifully handled with music that is kindred with that of the Christmas tree, and likewise spacious. The snowflakes' waltz, complete with girls' voices, provides a formal end to the act.

Some critics are dismissive of the music of *Nutcracker* as mere confectionery. But as we enter Act 2's kingdom of sweets is that not exactly what it should be? The musical substance of the opening is almost simplistic; it is Tchaikovsky's virtuoso skill in decoration and orchestration that provides the allure (note the upward-running scalic music that accompanies the repeat of the opening theme; does this not add immensely to its seductive charm, could what is needed here be bettered?). Clara and the Nutcracker Prince enter (presumably to the grandly repeated descending scale on the brass), Clara meets her escort's sisters, and the Prince recounts how Clara had saved him (here a quotation from the battle music of Act 1). Flora is praised for her service, and all settle down to enjoy the entertainment in store.

First comes the Spanish Dance with its prominent role for the trumpet, its locale soon confirmed by the castanets. Then we are moved to the east, first for the hauntingly sultry Arabian Dance (founded on a Georgian cradle song provided by Ippolitov-Ivanov) scored for muted strings over a hypnotically rocking ostinato accompaniment (note the oboe, then bassoon countermelodies in its second half), then further eastwards still for the quaint Chinese Dance, its one-minute duration as tiny as the initial gap between shrill piccolo and popping bassoons is huge. Next on to Russia for an athletic Trépak, followed by the famed *Danse des mirlitons* (for older readers, the TV 'fruit-and-nutcase' commercial), with its prominent three-flute tune. Last among these shorter dances that for Mother Gigogne, whose children are supposed to jump out from under her skirt to the tunes of two French songs, 'Giroflé-girofla' and 'Cadet Rouselle', before the more substantial, corporate – and famous – *Valse des Fleurs*. Finally comes the great *Pas de deux* for the Sugar Plum Fairy and Prince Coqueluche, its main idea springing from that powerful downward scale heard in the act's preliminaries. It is a splendid decorative piece, and the second of the two solo variations is the most famous piece in the whole ballet, the *Dance of the Sugar-Plum Fairy* (here it is longer than the familiar version heard in the Nutcracker Suite), with the most famous of solos for what, at the time, was the very newly invented celesta. The *Pas de deux* has a short brilliant coda, after which the *Valse finale* provides the backdrop for what remains of the plot, the final Apotheosis representing (to quote the official scenario) 'a huge beehive with bees flying round it, vigilantly guarding their riches'. I have never seen a production that incorporated this.

Tchaikovsky's remaining two years would be a record of public celebrity, concert tours and all the social pressures that are the inevitable consequence of fame: indeed, as noted earlier, when Tchaikovsky died, he was second only to Tolstoy in the esteem of the Russian people. But what remains so striking is that, to the end, his modesty and humanity remained unchanged. Never was he spoiled by his celebrity. His own record of two brief visits give us touching insights into his view of what really mattered to him: his continuing relationship with his family, and with those who had played some critical role in his life. What had once drawn him to Kamenka had now largely disappeared. Sasha was dead, Lev was absent, and the nephews and nieces were either dead or dispersed. Yet he could still return to their old home and gain pleasure from the residue of relatives remaining, many older than himself. On the Russian Christmas Eve (5 January 1892), as he was about to embark on a conducting tour that was intended to take in Warsaw, Hamburg, Amsterdam and The Hague, he arrived at Kamenka with a travelling companion, Boris, the son of the estate manager. 'It was not without a painful feeling that I entered the courtyard, in the middle of which the empty, locked house produces a doleful impression,' he wrote to Bob.

> *Sister* [Tchaikovsky's cousin, now eighty-four years old] met me and invited me to drink tea with her. During tea she said such strange and nonsensical things that Boris spluttered with laughter three times. It seems she has declined greatly and become much more confused than before. After changing I directed myself to the big house. Lev's mother and elder sisters are, by contrast, much better, and more cheerful than they were in the summer. I visited Nikolay Vasilyevich [Lev's elder brother], who again told me how in the summer he had stumbled over a basket when his daughter was sowing seed on the left and had pushed him into the bucket, as well as several other familiar tales to which I listened with great pleasure, for I love Nikolay terribly, and am happy when I see he is still the same. Then I hurried off to *Sister*, who simply cannot understand that in no way have I come here only to drink tea with her all day, and is endlessly surprised that I don't confine myself to my own room and hers. Then there was dinner at the big house (lean and very tasty). The *Yashvils* [relatives of Lev], brother and sister,

arrived, and after them, unexpectedly, my nephew, *Mitya*, very cheerful and much improved in appearance. Lev's mother, the aunts and Nikolay Vasilyevich were *literally in tears* of pleasure at his unexpected arrival. At eleven-thirty I returned home with Mitya and went to bed. At six a creaking door awoke me, and from behind the wardrobe I heard *Sister*'s sepulchral voice: '*Darling, do you want tea?*' I didn't reply. She went off, muttering some nonsense. After that I went to sleep again. Today, after tea at *Sister*'s, I walked, attended an endless Mass, sat at home and chatted with Mitya, who told me how cheerless and boring it was living where he did. I was dreadfully sorry for him. Then there was a sumptuous lunch at the big house, preceded by a little service. Today it's the Christmas tree. *Kolya Sandberg* [Nikolay Vasilyevich's grandson] is very busy with it. Tomorrow I leave.

But his frame of mind was very different when, four days later, he wrote to Bob from Warsaw:

You ask what my mood's like. Bad! Again, as during last year's tour, I am counting the days, hours and minutes to the end of my wanderings. It's not that I am physically tired from the journey – in no way! But what wearies me is that with strange people I cannot be myself. As soon as I am not alone, but with new and strange people, then without perceiving it myself, I take on the part of a person who is amiable, mild, polite, and also apparently absolutely delighted in a new acquaintance, instinctively trying to charm them by all this, which for the most part I do successfully, but at the price of extreme strain, joined with an aversion to my own dissimulation and insincerity. I want to say to them: 'Go to the devil, the lot of you!', but I utter compliments, and sometimes am so carried away, even become so much the part, that it's difficult to tell where the real 'me' is speaking and where the false one, the one that only 'seems'. So, in a word, all this is a mask which, with incredible relief, I shed when I remain alone.

But then, abruptly, the tone changes:

You are constantly in my thoughts, for at every feeling of sadness, melancholy, at every clouding of the mental horizon – like a ray of light the thought occurs that you exist, and that I shall see you in the not so distant future. On my word of honour, I do not exaggerate.

Incessantly, of its own accord, this ray of comfort breaks through: 'Yes, it's bad, but it's nothing – Bob is still in this world!'

These, surely, sound less like the words of an uncle to his nephew than of a husband to his wife or mistress.

The second visit occurred a year later. The preceding March Tchaikovsky had received a letter from Fanny Dürbach, the beloved governess of his very early years, and whom he had not seen for nearly half a century. Fanny had finally returned to France to settle in Montbéliard, and a further European tour now made it possible for Tchaikovsky to visit her briefly. 'Dear Pierre,' her letter had begun:

Permit me to call you thus; otherwise, if I were not to address you as when you were my dear little pupil, it would seem to me as though I was not writing to you. This morning my sister came up to my room with your letter in her hand, saying, 'Here's something that will give you great joy!' I confess I had given up hope of the pleasure of seeing your handwriting again. When my present pupils had insisted that I should write to you, I had said to them, 'We shall see each other in heaven.'

Because you are in France nearly every year, come the more quickly so that I may yet see you and talk with you about all those things which you and I have loved. How much there is about which only you can tell me! I know life well enough to foresee that there will be much that is sad. We will unite our memories and regrets. You know how good your dear parents were to me, and how I loved you all, and I hope you will find it pleasant to chat about them with an old friend who has lived her life with such sweet memories.

How much I would like to know how life has unfolded for all of you! I have thought a lot about Nikolay, that tall, handsome boy, about your dear sister, Zina, about Ippolit and Lidiya. Do they, like you, still have memories of their old friend?

Come, we have so much to talk about. You will not find yourself unknown in our town. But if it is quiet you want, then we have here a hotel with a garden run by honest people. You will find it very good. In Russia it is possible to offer hospitality: everything is conducive to it. Here it is not so. We live very modestly in our own small house; we also have a garden and all that is necessary. All the same, I thank you heartily for the thought that it might be otherwise: again I thank you for your good letter and the photograph.

The more I look at it, the more I recognize you.

Your last letter, which I hold as something very precious and which I have re-read many times, was written in 1856. You were then sixteen. You were telling me of your mother's death.

But your father: was he also able to take pleasure in your successes? And your dear Sashenka: was she happy in her marriage? Tell me about your younger brothers – but, most of all, about yourself. Allow me to hope for a quick reply from you in expectation of our meeting.

I have written to you without constraint. When you come, your presence will remind me that I must no longer talk with you as with my dear boy of long time past. I shall address you with all those titles that fame has conferred on you. God bless you and give you happiness.

Your old governess and friend,
FANNY DÜRBACH

Their meeting was an instant success, Tchaikovsky being astonished at how little Fanny had changed. 'I had been very afraid there would be tears, scenes – but there was none of this,' he wrote to Nikolay, who had also known Fanny well:

She received me with joy, tenderness and great simplicity, as though we hadn't seen each other for a whole year. Immediately I understood why both our parents and all of us had loved her very much. Soon there began endless recollections of the past and a whole stream of all sorts of most interesting details about our childhood, about mother and all of us. Then she showed me *our exercise books*, and your and my letters – but what was most interesting of all, several wonderfully sweet letters from Mama. I cannot describe the delectable, magical feeling I experienced as I listened to these tales and read these letters and exercise books. The past in all its detail arose so clearly in my memory that it seemed I was breathing the air of our Votkinsk home, I was listening to the voice of Mama, Venichka, Khamit, Akulina, and so on. At times I was so carried back into that distant past that it became somehow awesome, but at the same time sweet – and all the while both of us were holding back the tears.

I sat with her from 3 to 8, and failed totally to notice how the time passed. I spent all the following day with her, except that she sent me off to the hotel to dine, saying frankly that her and her sister's table was too wretched, and that it would embarrass her to feed me. I had to pay two visits with her to close friends and a relative who had long been interested in me. In the evening I exchanged kisses with Fanny and left, having promised to return sometime.

For Tchaikovsky this was one of the most moving encounters of his last years, for the world-famous composer and the unknown provincial governess had each been able joyfully to relive memories of four wonderful years so long gone. Yet for her there was one disappointment. 'There is no one more convinced of your talent than I. I saw its emergence as the gift of a poet (which I would still have wished to see you become). But nevertheless I still bless God for your successes, and it seems to me He has sent down to you your reward. How many renowned people are not recognized in their lifetimes!' They continued to exchange letters right to the end, and she tried to tempt him back to Montbéliard, where he could relax and they could again talk. But, sadly, her hoped-for meeting never materialized.

29
The Final Celebrity Years:
Sixth Symphony

The two highly personal, intimate encounters recorded in the last chapter had neatly flanked a further event of highly personal significance to Tchaikovsky: the acquisition of the ideal home which would become the base for what remained of his life. None of his previous abodes had proved entirely satisfactory, but in May 1892 he bought and settled into a large comfortable house at nearby Klin. It seems he had for some time known and admired it, and it had the bonus of a more than adequate garden. Tchaikovsky would bequeath it not to Modest, but to Alexey – a clear sign of the personal relationship that had consolidated between these two so very different men over the years, and, together with Modest, this former servant would convert the house into a museum to Tchaikovsky's memory, leaving it nevertheless as it was in its late master's time.

The house at Klin became even more than its predecessors a haven to which Tchaikovsky could escape from professional pressures and the ever growing adoration (and that is not too strong a word) of his compatriots. The conducting tours at home and abroad proliferated, and the ovations grew ever more ecstatic and prolonged. To take just one instance: nothing could have been further removed from the gentleness and intimacy of his reunion with Fanny than the adulation he endured only three weeks later during his fortnight-long visit to Odessa, where he was to supervise rehearsals and be present at the opening performance of *The Queen of Spades*; there were also five concerts in which he had to conduct, and attendance at a trail of receptions and social events mounted in his honour. The furore began with a delegation of friends and representatives of the local branch of the RMS meeting him at Odessa's railway station, continued at his first opera rehearsal, where he was greeted with ceremony and boundless applause, then found this topped by his reception at the end of his first concert, in which the audience demanded that several pieces should be encored not once, but *three* times. As one Odessa newspaper reported:

> At the concert's end the whole audience rose from its seats, cries of gratitude rang out from different directions, the ladies waved their handkerchiefs, the gentlemen their hats, while from the platform the orchestra kept up a constant flourish. But this had seemed insufficient for the bemused members of the orchestra; recognizing what a great talent was among them, in the interval they had, one after the other, kissed his hands. This was not done on enthusiastic impulse, but deliberately and reverentially. Pyotr Ilich grasped the total sincerity of their greeting, and thanked the players.

On such visits Tchaikovsky had become prepared for much soliciting of his attention from individuals. Such demands could be very wearing, but on this visit there was one that would give him great pleasure: the Ukrainian artist, Nikolay Kuznetsov, begged to be allowed to paint his portrait. Tchaikovsky agreed, and before he left Odessa the canvas was completed. Kuznetsov's proved to be the only from-life portrait of Tchaikovsky ever painted, and Tchaikovsky himself was delighted with it, Modest confirming that it had caught the 'tragic side' of his brother remarkably well. It now hangs in the Tretyakov Gallery in Moscow.

Tchaikovsky was, of course, deeply moved by such genuine and spontaneous tributes paid to him by the inhabitants of Odessa, but there was a downside to all this – and a touch of bitterness, as he confessed to Modest:

> Never have I been forced to weary myself with conducting as in Odessa – but then, never at any time or anywhere have I been so exalted or fêted as there. If only sometime I might receive in our capitals just a tenth of what has happened in Odessa. But that's impossible – or, rather, it's unnecessary. What I need is to believe in myself again – for my faith has been undermined; it seems to me my role is over.

Yet, extraordinarily, within twelve days of writing this, he would complete the sketches of one of his greatest first movements.

However, Tchaikovsky had, perhaps, some real cause for self-doubt when he surveyed his most recent compositions, above all a grand symphony in E flat that he had projected in 1889, but which he had begun to sketch only in 1891 during the voyage back home from his American tour. A little later he roughed out a programme for the piece:

> The ultimate essence of the symphony is *Life*. First movement – all impulsive passion, confidence, thirst for activity. Must be short (the finale *Death* – result of collapse). Second movement love: third disappointments: fourth ends dying away (also short).

Nevertheless, it was May 1892 before he began serious composition, and the symphony was completed in November. Yet returning to the piece after a break, he judged it to have been 'composed simply for the sake of composing something', and discarded it.[1] But then, in July 1893, he returned to the piece, converting the first movement into a single-movement concert piece for piano and orchestra, and in October, only weeks before his death, redrafting the symphony's second and fourth movements to provide the basis for a full three-movement concerto. Unlike the first movement, however, these remained in sketch form after Tchaikovsky's death, and Taneyev would complete and score them. This full version is now never performed, but the completed first movement is given the occasional airing.

Piano Concerto No. 3 in E flat (one movement) * * *

[Though certainly not one of Tchaikovsky's finest, this lonely movement makes agreeable listening for those with a penchant for concertos.]

That this movement was not conceived as a concerto is betrayed by the piano writing, which is lacking in Tchaikovsky's characteristic boldness; it is sometimes pretty skeletal, sounding all too clearly as though it has been incorporated into the music rather than having participated in its creation. The movement's structure is readily grasped. As in Tchaikovsky's previous two piano concertos, there are three subjects, the first lively, the second more lyrical, and the third like a vigorous folk dance. The development opens with piano and orchestra

---

1 In the 1950s the Soviet scholar, Semyon Bogatïrev, recomposed and scored a hypothetical version of the E flat Symphony ('No. 7', as he described it), drawing on and scoring various of Tchaikovsky's materials.

collaborating, but then the forces are segregated, the orchestra having a lengthy stretch to itself (the second part of this is particularly appealing), the piano completing the development with a cadenza. The recapitulation's structure is regular, and there is the expected vigorous coda.

————

On 9 February when, after his triumph in Odessa, Tchaikovsky had written so gloomily to Modest about his creative self-doubts, he had set out for a five-day visit to Kamenka, and then returned to Klin. In fact, his inner creativity had already been active, even seething, and it is clear that he had been revisiting the programme he had mapped out for the now rejected E flat symphony. So strongly were his creative powers working that he had already gestated a great deal of the new symphony in his head, and on the day after his return to Klin, he began setting it down on paper. Writing to Bob only a week later, he could report remarkable progress:

> The work went so fast and furious that I had the first movement completely ready in less than four days, and the remaining movements are already clearly outlined in my head. Half the third movement is already done. There will be much formal innovation in this symphony – and, incidentally, the finale will not be a noisy *Allegro* but, on the contrary, a most long-drawn-out *Adagio*. You cannot imagine what bliss I feel, being convinced that my time is not yet passed, and that I can still work. Perhaps, of course, I'm mistaken – but I don't think so.

Tchaikovsky frankly admitted that he was composing to a programme, but one 'that would remain a mystery to all. It is completely subjective, and not infrequently during my journey, as I was composing it in my head, I wept copiously.' For the moment he wished no one to know that he was working on the symphony.

Composition was now interrupted by a visit to Moscow to conduct at an RMS concert. It was the first time in three years that he had directed one of the Society's concerts, for there had been serious disagreements with Safonov, the Conservatoire's Director (no doubt one of the main causes for the bitterness he had alluded to in his letter to Modest). But now Safonov had sought a reconciliation, and Tchaikovsky's concert was the predictable success: a welcoming flourish from the orchestra, rapturous applause from the audience, and encores galore. Back in Klin in early March, Tchaikovsky completed the new symphony's third movement in a few days, but progress was further interrrupted by family visits and yet more concert engagements. This time Tchaikovsky's first destination was St Petersburg, where he learned that Lev, Sasha's widower, had married a woman thirty years younger than himself. The news had divided the family, and Tchaikovsky's cousin, Anna Merkling, had been especially upset. Once again, even in the middle of such compositional preoccupations and exhausting professional engagements, Tchaikovsky could find time to set out what he saw as the positive consequence of Lev's action, and so soothe Anna's feelings:

> Ah, Anna, with our years we ought not to be so emphatic in saying yes and no. Remember how we were all angry when my father married Lizaveta Mikhailovna. And so what? Nothing except unqualified happiness came from this late and, it seemed to us, unsuitable match. For a moment I found it distasteful to learn that Lev was marrying but, reflecting on his situation, not for one moment did I nourish any anger towards him, or wish to cast a stone.

If Tchaikovsky's own feelings remained ambivalent at this stage, he would find reassurance in the way the marriage would evolve in the coming months.

After two further concerts in Moscow, Tchaikovsky moved on to Kiev. Yet again his overwhelming popularity in the Russian provinces was confirmed – a delegation to meet him, a musical greeting and applause from the orchestra at the rehearsal, furious clapping from the audience, and another orchestral fanfare (threefold this time) and audience ovation when he attended a performance of Verdi's *Rigoletto* at the opera house, a choral–orchestral greeting before his own concert, an address of welcome, an abundance of wreaths and flowers, deafening applause, countless recalls at the concert's end, and finally a triumphal exit from the hall in a chair borne aloft by local youths, all followed by a banquet with countless toasts. The next day, 28 March, there was a musical matinee in his honour. But on 31 March he was back in Klin: five more days, and on the final page of his new symphony he could inscribe: 'O Lord, I thank thee! Today I have completed the sketches in their entirety.' This task accomplished, he set the symphony aside, returning to it in August to score it. As with some of his other more recent works, this took longer than expected. But, as he observed to Anatoly, 'It's not the consequence of failing strength or old age, but that I've become infinitely stricter with myself, and I no longer have my former self-assurance. *I'm very proud* of the symphony, and I think it's the best of my works.' He knew it could prove a challenge to even his strongest supporters, 'but I definitely consider it the best and, in particular, *the most sincere* of all my works. I love it as I have never loved any other of my musical offspring'.

On 21 October there was a private trial of the symphony, using staff and students from the Moscow Conservatoire. Clearly some of the players remained puzzled by it, and at the premiere the audience response was merely polite, while the press in general rated the symphony lower than its predecessors. Yet Tchaikovsky was sanguine about this. 'It's not that it displeased, but it produced some bewilderment,' he wrote to Jurgenson two days later. 'As far as I myself am concerned, I take more pride in it than in any other of my works.' It had been billed simply as 'Sixth Symphony: B minor', and Modest claimed credit for its final title. After the performance the brothers had discussed, but without success, what this should be. 'I left the room with Pyotr Ilich still undecided,' Modest recalled. 'Then suddenly the title *Pathétique* came into my head. I returned, and I remember as though it was yesterday pronouncing the word while standing in the doorway. "Capital, Modest, bravo, *Pathétique!*" – and in my presence he inscribed on the score the name that has remained ever since.'

Symphony No. 6 in B minor: *Pathétique* * * * * *

[Earlier in this book I observed that, for me, Tchaikovsky composed three supreme masterpieces. Two I have identified: the opera Eugene Onegin *and the ballet* The Sleeping Beauty. *The third is this B minor Symphony, his Sixth, the Pathétique. The originality and power of the piece are prodigious; it is also one of Tchaikovsky's most consistent and perfectly composed. But it is no wonder that some in its first audience were evidently bewildered by it, for the total experience it presents is unique, and some passages may still provide something of a challenge. But its totality is overwhelming.]*

It must seem strange that when a human being is enjoying public adulation as overwhelming and sincere as that which Tchaikovsky was now customarily receiving, he should produce his most tragic and, in the end, most pessimistic work. But Tchaikovsky would have found nothing strange in this; as he himself had, years before, frankly observed to his secret patroness: 'In a happy situation I can produce a piece that is imbued with the most gloomy and hopeless feelings.' Nor should we forget that the seed of what would become the *Pathétique* had been sown during his voyage home from his American tour some two years earlier, though clearly at that time his creativity was not yet ready to conceive and deliver that particular piece. What is perhaps significant is the sense of apparent creative decline ahead of the event, audible in the E flat Symphony, part of which became the unfinished Third Piano Concerto. Was something far greater germinating all the while within his creative faculty, a concept so novel that it could not be rushed but which, once it was fully formed, could scarcely be contained? Certainly the speed and the assurance with which the Sixth Symphony, as near a perfect masterpiece as music can offer, came into the world is itself prodigious, and the result is surely not only Tchaikovsky's ultimate masterpiece, but one of the half-dozen greatest symphonies composed since the death of Beethoven.

Yet no symphony opens more unobtrusively. It begins inaudibly in Stygian gloom (this very slow introduction was, in fact, added by Tchaikovsky after the rest of the movement had been composed). But with the entry into the *Allegro con moto* exposition, the bassoon's weary four-note figure is transformed by the strings to launch the first subject, the music gathers strength, and we enter a bright, even vivacious world; probably, indeed, in no earlier symphony had such a radical transformation of mood occurred as swiftly as here. The music seems confidently to gain more power, reaches a climax, then starts to fade, finally reducing to a single violin line which rises slowly aloft, fades yet further, and finally expires. There is a silence, and then the string line resumes, but retracing its steps downwards. Will Tchaikovsky now move on towards the second subject? No – because this is it – this *is* the second subject itself which unfolds as a slow elegiac theme that twice, it seems, seeks to lift itself out of its pervasive weariness, but which is fated (I use the word deliberately) to sink back ineffectually both times.

Already this movement has revealed just how different it will be from Tchaikovsky's earlier symphonic first movements. However, as in most of his preceding sonata expositions, there are to be three themes here, and the third (that is, the second part of the second sub-ject) opens as a dialogue between flute and bassoon on a livelier phrase, spreading itself at some length before yielding to a return of the preceding elegiac theme. This is now louder and stronger, yet still seems unable to shed its sombre mood, and it is followed by a long-dying coda leading to a yet slower and quieter restatement by the clar-inet of this same melody. The first subject had ended by fading to nothing; so now will the second subject, but drawing out even more its ever quieter descent, fading to *pppppp*, the most extreme dynamic instruction Tchaikovsky ever prescribed, the last note marked to be long held. The exposition – even, it might seem, the movement itself – has petered out, has drained away. This, of course, is not so, though Tchaikovsky has, in terms of real time, already reached the move-ment's halfway point – yet the development, recapitulation and coda are all still to come.

This prolongation of the second subject and of the exposition's long-dying end has been very deliberately schemed, for the contrast between what we have just heard and what will follow is to be the most savage in all Tchaikovsky's music, and the urgency such that the development, recapitulation and coda will be compacted, but without loss of weight, to balance in length what we have already heard. Clearly to achieve this compression, the strategy must change, and nothing alerts (I use the word deliberately) us more clearly to this almost brutal transformation than the chord that opens the development (I have seen unprepared audience members almost jump out of their skins at this). The shift of mood is as violent and sustained as could be; 'scorching' is perhaps an appropriate adjective to describe what immediately follows. The first subject, now not shy as at the exposition's opening, but fierce and self-assertive, sets the new mood. Earlier in this movement the proportion of downward scales had surely hinted at the presence of Fate: now a strident descending scale on trumpets indicates unequivocally both the presence and the power of this implacable force. Tchaikovsky's imme-diate answer is personal and explicit: the turmoil abates, and trom-bones and tuba enunciate the Orthodox Requiem's traditional chant setting the words 'With thy saints, O Christ, give peace to the soul of thy servant': if there ever was any doubt that this symphony 'is about something', this surely disposes of that. Nevertheless, the respite is brief; once again the music grows in dynamic power, but this time less drastically, then subsides in preparation for the recapitulation.

Tchaikovsky is now about to build his most powerful climax ever, and to enhance its impact he first introduces a moment of relative calm, then moves towards a fierce recapitulation of the first subject. But this is merely the first stage in a far grander scheme. Dwelling at some length on this subject, Tchaikovsky proceeds to heighten even more the sense of high drama until the subject is unceremoniously swept aside by the descending Fate scale on trumpets and lower brass. The cataclysmic climax of the movement is at hand: from this low-pitched beginning, the music heaves itself almost wearily aloft to permit a gigantic, slow scalic descent through two octaves with majestic interpolations from the brass. Finally a further crescendo to a *ffff* chord from all the lower wind and brass, then a *ff* chord that quickly dies to *pp* – finally to nothing. I doubt there is, in all music, a silence more eloquent than this.

The distinguished early twentieth-century writer on music, Sir Donald Tovey, described this passage as 'undoubtedly the climax of Tchaikovsky's artistic career, as well as of his work'. I would not dispute this; it is truly awesome. The recapitulation of the first subject having already taken place, it is the elegiac second subject that enters after the pause. As for the third theme, there is simply no place here for its relatively relaxed persona, and it is in a mood of resignation that the symphony's opening idea is converted into a solemn, measured theme beneath which Fate stalks on pizzicato strings.

We cannot, of course, know what went on in Tchaikovsky's mind after completing this stupendous movement, but even he must have been aware of the challenge it posed to produce something very contrasted, yet not inappropriately lightweight. In the Fifth Symphony the great slow movement had been one of his weightiest, laden with human emotion, yet it was not tragic, and the explicit and elegant *Valse* that had followed had worked perfectly. But something as relaxed as that was unthinkable here. Yet, in its way, Tchaikovsky's solution is also a 'Valse', but this time different. Try to dance to this one, and you are in trouble because it is not, in fact, a waltz. Instead of three beats to a bar, it has five, which feels like 2+3. Perhaps it could be described as a 'limping waltz'; whatever the case, this change of metre is sufficient to give it a less fluent flow. Yet this 'impairment' in itself would not have been enough. The form of Tchaikovsky's second movement is essentially that of the classical minuet and trio as composed by Tchaikovsky's idol, Mozart, in his own symphonies – that is, identical flanks with a central trio, both components being cast in binary form. But whereas Mozart's trios were habitually more laid back than the identical flanking sections, Tchaikovsky's brings with it a pathos generated by the persistent dissonance in every third-beat chord, as well as the nagging drum/double-bass throbbing that underlies the whole section. Yet the movement does have one un-Mozartian feature – a coda that follows seamlessly, incorporating echoes from the central trio section, alternating in its final bars with the first bar of the movement's first theme.

Even more is the third movement a surprise. We might have expected a slow movement, but this one is the very opposite – a consistently bustling *Allegro molto vivace* that is a *tour de force* of musical inventiveness and sustained energy, yet which ends in being something far more portentous, even critical, than might ever have been expected after such an unclouded beginning. Because of its unbroken consistency of style and absence of easily recognizable 'punctuation points', there is no way in which I can identify for my reader the separate sections that make up the form, but I am not sure that doing this would really be helpful in this instance. What is important here is not the structural coherence (though it is as carefully schemed as any movement by Tchaikovsky), but the fact that the piece begins as a kind of lively *moto perpetuo* that seeks to project a state of untroubled being, but which, through its very length and, towards its end, its very vehemence, only confirms that the search is futile. It is a truth devastatingly declared in the very first sounds of the following movement, which is not a conventional vigorous finale, but a most pain-filled, tragic utterance – a disconcerting return to the mood of the first movement, but this time with an ending that suggests not resignation, but only oblivion.

Let's look more closely at this extraordinary finale. But a moment of caution before we begin. This is the last piece which I shall be examining not only here but anywhere, for this will certainly be my last book. Writing about music presents many challenges, and poses many questions. Some would say that you simply cannot define the substance of music in words, that any description of what a piece of music 'is about' is simply a fiction, a subjective indulgence that may tell the reader much about the author, but little about the music itself: at best it is allowed to be misguided, though well intentioned. As someone who has spent the last fifty-plus years in trying to attune my listeners/readers to a musical experience by the use of metaphor (for that is really what I am doing, with all my adjectives and descriptive phrases), at least I can plead good intentions, and if by so doing I have, at least from time to time, said or written something that has helped at least some readers to apprehend a little more clearly something of the profound and precious experience that another human being of true genius has embodied in a complex of sounds, then I am unapologetic.

So let me take my own 'ego trip' (as some would say) through this great, and stunningly original, finale. It has two principal thematic elements, the first opening unsparingly with a brief, then repeated, pain-filled phrase as the point of departure to an increasingly sustained and ever louder, dissonance-filled paragraph, which finally sinks into silence. The movement's opening is repeated, but this time there is no crescendo, for the whole passage is underpinned by the bassoons who, starting on a high note, and at first very slowly, but then with increasing pace, trace a stepwise descending line which finally monopolizes the section, drawing the music ever downwards until, again, it fades into the depths. All this, I would suggest, is the active side of grief, the shock and despair. Again a silence (how important in musical experience can be those moments when *nothing* is heard) – but now it is the movement's second theme that enters, this time a sustained one of great breadth. If the first music had embodied a more outward reaction to adversity, this surely reflects the inner (and deeper?) apprehension of it. This music is seemingly poised and controlled, no longer manifesting the pang of an initial shock but, instead, the ache that lingers and lingers, caught into music which (like the second (string) theme of the first movement) ruminates on the same phrase, then rises as inner tension grows, only to fall back – but then rises again, this time to resume more powerfully at a higher level; then, as though the self-control has finally broken, it collapses almost convulsively into an abrupt silence, to be followed by a series of terse, separated phrases, which lead back to the shock and despair music with which the movement had opened (a sentence that, I think, is about as broad as the passage on which it is a commentary). This is how the first half of this movement *sounds* to me. And if my reader accepts that my extrapolation thus far is plausible, I think he or she should be left to extrapolate further for him- or herself. And does it matter if we should differ? No, of course not. It is the experience, as each of us individually hears it, that matters. And do we need the programme (even Tchaikovsky's programme?) to enjoy this musically? I think not. Only functional music dutifully written to a set scenario (most film music, for instance) requires such knowledge. Tchaikovsky was no doubt conditioned by his own programme in composing the *Pathétique*, but the symphony that resulted can still have a tremendous impact on the innocent listener simply because, whatever the extramusical prompt of the moment, Tchaikovsky was still devising it above all as a devastating but coherent *listening* experience.

Let me finally draw attention to one tiny detail near the symphony's end. The final bars are founded on what I have called the music of inner apprehension, though now there is no element of agitation, merely a measured descent and a final fading into utter silence (though, I suppose a philosopher might query whether this symphony is still going on even now – except that we cannot hear it). But just before this section begins there are four very quiet and separate chords that lead into the chord from which the fast-fading end begins. The structure these chords create is one of the clichés of Western classical music, used millions upon millions of times, especially by eighteenth- and nineteenth-century composers, to establish the end not only of a whole piece but perhaps also of subsections and even single phrases within that piece. When we hear them in such contexts, we barely notice them (if at all), and certainly hear no particular significance in them. But here, after the tensions and turmoil of this great finale, the promise of imminent finality they bring can be almost chilling. The tragedy happened, the grief remains, but the tale itself is done, and all ends in oblivion.

And how shall I round off this, the last of my investigations of Tchaikovsky's music? I hope I may be excused for repeating my own words at this same juncture in my four-volume life-and-works of Tchaikovsky:

> Thus ends the greatest of Tchaikovsky's instrumental works, and surely the most truly original symphony to have been composed since Beethoven's Ninth. In the Fifth Symphony Tchaikovsky had sought to prove he could submit to the Western view of the symphony, yet remain wholly himself. But in the Sixth there had been no compromise; the method, the form, the ethos were as personal as the musical invention and the expressive experience that shaped its

structure. Had he lived, it is impossible to imagine any direction he could have taken beyond this. But the matter never arose. Within nine days of conducting its premiere he was dead.

30

Cambridge Honour:
The Final Mystery

During Tchaikovsky's last months the general pattern of his life continued as before. But one event stands out supremely – and one that is of particular interest to British readers. Tchaikovsky had already received high honours from learned societies in other European cities and countries – from Prague, France and Holland: now in June he was to receive an honorary degree from Cambridge University. It was the fiftieth anniversary of the Cambridge University Musical Society ('CUMS', as it is colloquially called), and there was a proposal that honorary degrees should be conferred upon certain eminent composers. Brahms and Verdi were the two initial choices, but neither was prepared to attend the ceremony, and a remarkable group of alternative graduands was quickly mustered: not only Tchaikovsky, but also Grieg, Saint-Saëns, Bruch and Boito (also a composer, though best known for his libretti for Verdi's final two operas, *Otello* and *Falstaff*).

Tchaikovsky promptly decided this could be the moment to conduct another concert for the Philharmonic Society in London, and one was arranged for 1 June. He arrived in London two days earlier, having till the last moment contemplated withdrawal, but finally installing himself once again in the Hôtel Dieudonné in Ryder Street. He was still in a bad mood, berating London, and lamenting, among other things, its lack of *pissoirs*. He was to share the concert with Saint-Saëns, and it was not an easy pairing for Tchaikovsky. Saint-Saëns was already very popular in England, and he would also appear as soloist in his own Second Piano Concerto, while Tchaikovsky's Fourth Symphony was unknown in London, and its success by no means guaranteed. Before the first rehearsal Tchaikovsky was introduced to the Scottish composer, Alexander Mackenzie, who was to conduct the other items in the programme, and who seems to have shepherded him through the rehearsals, taking him off to his own home to rest after the second. Both rehearsals were rather nervous occasions, though (according to the young Henry Wood, who was present) Tchaikovsky finally drew the required spirit from his players by exclaiming, 'Vodka – more vodka!'

He need not have worried. 'The concert went brilliantly,' he could write to Bob, 'that is, I enjoyed a real triumph, so that Saint-Saëns, who appeared after me, suffered somewhat.' Indeed, the capacity audience had applauded all four movements of the symphony, and at the end had given him an ovation. Among the audience was the young Bernard Shaw, at this time still working as a music critic, and who remarked on the high standard of the playing under both composers.

The Cambridge event being still eleven days ahead, a string of social engagements filled the gap. The following day the two composers were entertained to dinner at the St Stephen's Club in Westminster, the event ending at 11.30 p.m., after which Mackenzie and Tchaikovsky wandered the London streets until one o'clock in the morning, discussing music. Over the next days there would be a host of appointments. What Tchaikovsky himself may have thought of this continuous limelight we may easily guess, but there is no doubt that he endured it successfully, endearing himself to the many who had contact with him. Francesco Berger, Secretary of the Philharmonic Society, and the man who had been largely responsible for Tchaikovsky's first professional visit to England five years earlier, was one who entertained him. Tchaikovsky had insisted that the event should be informal ('no party and no evening dress') and intimate. 'Accordingly there were only four of us,' Berger recorded. 'His conversation, carried on in French and German, was easy without being brilliant, and in all he said there was apparent the modest, gentle spirit which was so characteristic of the man.' But George Henschel, the singer, composer and conductor, who had first encountered Tchaikovsky eighteen years earlier in Russia, saw the other side of him – that he was –

> even more inclined to intervals of melancholy than when I had last met him. Indeed, one afternoon, during a talk about the olden days in Petrograd [St Petersburg] and Moscow, and the many friends there who were no more, he suddenly got very depressed and, wondering what this world with all its life and strife was made for, expressed his own readiness at any moment to quit it.

Nevertheless, Henschel's nine-year-old daughter, Helen,[1] uncovered a rather different aspect of him:

The melancholy was naturally not evident to me as a small child, but the gentleness and kindness were. One of my life's minor tragedies is that he wrote me a long letter when he left London, that the wind blew it off the table into the waste-paper basket, and that the housemaid lit my fire with it.

As for Mackenzie, despite having met Tchaikovsky only on this visit, he seems to have summarized well what so many others would come to feel about him: 'His unaffected modesty, kindly manner, and real gratitude for any trifling service rendered, all contributed to the favourable impression made by a lovable man.'

In Cambridge there would be a concert in which the honorary graduands would each conduct one of his own works. Tchaikovsky had selected *Francesca da Rimini*, and a first rehearsal was arranged at the Royal College of Music in London on 9 June. That evening, Charles Villiers Stanford, Professor of Music at Cambridge, and who was about to retire as conductor of CUMS after twenty-one years' service, gave a soirée that included performances of English madrigals and part-songs by an amateur choir, the Magpie Minstrels.

Two days before leaving London, Tchaikovsky summarized for Modest his feelings about the past week and what would face him in Cambridge:

It's the devil of a life! There's not one pleasant minute – only eternal anxiety, melancholy, fear, fatigue, aversion, and so on. But now the end's already close. On the other hand, in all fairness I must say there are a lot of nice people, and I've been shown much kindness of all sorts. All the future doctors have arrived except Grieg, who is ill. Among them, besides Saint-Saëns, I find Boito a sympathetic individual. But to make up for it Bruch's a loathesome, haughty figure. The morning of the day after tomorrow I travel to Cambridge, and I shan't be staying in a hotel but in a flat assigned to me at a Doctor Maitland's [Downey Professor of Law, and a great enthusiast for music] from whom I have had a most kind letter of invitation. In all

---

1 Some older readers may remember that during the 1940s, when *Children's Hour* at 5 o'clock was a daily weekday BBC radio programme, Helen Henschel had a regular spot 'talking about music' each Monday.

I shall spend one night there. On the day of my arrival there's a concert and a banquet, and the ceremony on the following day. In four hours it'll all be over.

At the concert in Cambridge's Guildhall Tchaikovsky's conducting of *Francesca da Rimini* scored a great audience success. Later Saint-Saëns would write generously of the piece, and of Tchaikovsky himself:

> Bristling with difficulties, Tchaikovsky's *Francesca da Rimini*, which lacks neither pungent flavours nor fireworks, shrinks from no violence. In it the gentlest and most kindly of men has unleashed a fearful tempest, and has had no more pity for his performers and listeners than Satan for the damned. But such was the composer's talent and supreme skill that one takes pleasure in this damnation and torture.

A short visit to Trinity College followed, then the CUMS dinner at King's College, at which Tchaikovsky found himself sitting beside Walter Damrosch, who was on holiday in England from the USA. Next came a *conversazione* at the Fitzwilliam Museum, at which a presentation was made to Stanford on his retirement from CUMS. The degree congregation would be at noon the next day.

Tchaikovsky summarized this occasion for Nápravník's son, Vladimir:

> At 11.30 we gathered at the appointed place and put on our doctoral robes, which consist of a white gown (silk) faced with crimson velvet, and a black velvet beret. Four doctors of law were admitted to their degrees along with us, one of whom was an Indian ruler (a raja) who wore a turban adorned with precious stones with a value of several million roubles, and one a field marshal. All the professors and doctors of the university in robes like ours, but of a different colour, collected in the same hall. At noon the procession set out on foot. I walked beside Boito and behind Saint-Saëns. Watched by a lot of people, we crossed a big courtyard to the university's Senate House, which was filled to overflowing. Each of us sat in an allotted place on a high platform, the public orator (that's what they call the gentleman whose special job is to make the speeches at these ceremonies) entered, and delivered a speech in Latin about each of us in turn, which was a eulogy of our services

to science and art. During the speech the one in whose honour it was being delivered stood motionless at the front. While this was going on, according to medieval tradition the students who filled the rows whistled, hooted, sang, cried, and to all this you must pay no attention. After the speech the orator leads the doctor by the hand and describes a semicircle with him towards the chancellor, who is sitting in his special place. He takes the doctor by the hand and says in Latin: 'In the name of the Father, Son, and Holy Spirit I declare you to be a doctor.' There's a firm handshake, after which you are led off to your place. When this was over the procession returned to the first hall in the same order, and a half-hour later everyone, in his own clothes, set off for an official lunch, at the end of which an ancient loving-cup was passed round among the guests. Afterwards there's a reception at the Chancellor's wife's, and with this it's all over.

Tchaikovsky admitted that the new doctors of music were overshadowed by the other graduands. The 'field marshal' was Lord (later Earl) Roberts of Kandahar, currently commander-in-chief in India, who was rapturously received and treated to a rendering of 'For he's a jolly good fellow!' At the Raja's installation the Christian references were discreetly omitted. Commenting on the occasion, the *Pall Mall Gazette* noted that the students' performance exhibited 'more vigour than musical ability', and observed of the composers' reactions that Saint-Saëns twisted his fingers, while Tchaikovsky 'sank into ineffable meditations'. During the latter's presentation, one wit provoked roars of laughter by shouting 'Good old Shakemoffski!'

After the Chancellor's luncheon and his wife's garden party, Tchaikovsky set off for London, where he was to return the hospitality of various of his London friends with a meal at the Dieudonné. Next day he was in Paris. For all his earlier laments about the trials of his English sortie, he found much he could recall with pleasure. The Cambridge interlude he had truly enjoyed. His stay at the Maitlands' 'would have been terribly uncomfortable if he, and especially his wife, had not turned out to be the most charmingly sympathetic of people I've ever met – and moreover, Russophiles, which is a great rarity in England,' he wrote to Kolya Konradi. 'Now it's all over I find it pleasant to recall my success in England and the unusual cordiality with which I was received everywhere.' Being in no special hurry to be home, it was the end of June before he was, at last, back in Russia.

We may pass over specific events of the next three months. There were the usual business matters to attend to, concerts to conduct, concerts to arrange for the next season, trips to visit members of his now more widely dispersed family (and sometimes to give help in easing domestic problems and tensions), and visits to (and by) friends. Sadly several of the latter had recently died, and others were in a terminal condition. The Shilovsky brothers departed this life within a month of each other – Konstantin, who had contributed to the libretto of *Onegin*, dying while Tchaikovsky was still in Cambridge, and Vladimir, who had once been very close to Tchaikovsky, within days of the latter's return to Russia – though, hearing back in February that his friend was mortally ill, Tchaikovsky had made a point of visiting and spending more time with him. Still more distressing was the passing of his former Conservatoire colleague, Konstantin Albrecht, who, over the years, had become a close friend: typically, Tchaikovsky was quick to instruct Jurgenson to provide, out of Tchaikovsky's own funds, anything his old friend's widow might need. Then at the beginning of September, on the eve of his departure for Hamburg to attend a revival of *Iolanta* and consult about the intended production of *The Queen of Spades*, he would learn of the death of his former schoolfriend, Alexey Apukhtin. 'At this moment, as I write this, *they're reading the burial service* over Apukhtin!!!' he would write to Bob. 'Though his death was not unexpected, it's still terrible and painful. He was once my closest friend.'

Tchaikovsky's reaction to his new home at Klin was a different matter. During his June absence Alexey had done much to improve it, installing a new water-closet, repairing the fences and gates, and ordering and tending the garden. Tchaikovsky was equally delighted with Alexey's son who, now fifteen months old, he confessed to spoiling shamelessly. Another joy was discovering fully a third English novelist, George Eliot, and revelling in *The Mill on the Floss*, *Silas Marner*, *Adam Bede*, *Middlemarch*, and *Scenes of Clerical Life*, even seriously considering 'The Sad fortunes of the Reverend Amos Barton' from this last one as a possible opera subject. However, there were more pressing creative demands, and in July he converted the first movement of the E flat Symphony into the Third Piano Concerto, and also read the proofs of a set each of piano pieces and songs.[2] Scoring the Sixth Symphony was his main musical task during August, and on returning from his brief visit to Hamburg on 12 September (and now precise dates begin to become important, for the narrative will become more detailed), he discussed with Modest the possibility of an opera on the subject drawn from George Eliot, as well as making plans to revise completely both his earlier operas, *The Oprichnik* and *The Maid of Orleans*. On 19 September he was in Moscow for two days, then visited Anatoly at Mikhailovskoye, near Nizhni-Novgorod. He delighted in his brother's new home and his good spirits, and returned to Moscow on 29 September only because Modest's new play, *Prejudice*, was to receive its premiere at the Maly Theatre. Next day he visited Taneyev to hear some new piano pieces by the twenty-year-old Rakhmaninov, whose 'delightful' opera, *Aleko*, he had heard at its premiere earlier in the year, and whose exceptional talents he was quick to recognize. (Rakhmaninov's most famous piano piece, the C sharp minor Prelude, would follow within months of the opera.) Tchaikovsky decided to remain in Moscow for a further ten days because at Klin Alexey's wife was about to produce a second baby, and he did not wish to be there until after the birth. On returning home he scored the Third Piano Concerto, completing it on 15 October. The cellist Anatoly Brandukov arrived to run through the Saint-Saëns concerto he was to play under Tchaikovsky's direction in St Petersburg, and the two men journeyed to Moscow on the 19th to hear a Conservatoire concert, and for the trial rehearsal of Tchaikovsky's new Sixth Symphony. On 21 October Tchaikovsky set out on his final journey, an overnight one to St Petersburg. A week later he conducted the premiere of his *Symphonie pathétique*. A further week, and he was dead.

The question of how Tchaikovsky came to die so suddenly, unexpectedly and mysteriously has long been a bone of sometimes vicious con-

---

2 As I noted in my prefatory material, I decided, very regretfully, that there would not be room in this book to take account of either Tchaikovsky's songs or his shorter piano pieces. However, for readers wishing especially to investigate the songs, I would recommend this last set, the Six Romances, op. 73, on poems by Daniel Rathaus: the final song in particular is a masterpiece of economy and, for me, particularly moving. Also (or instead) – and because the songs have the advantage of being on French texts – readers might acquaint themselves with the Six Romances, op. 65 (the 'Artôt' songs). As for those who would wish to investigate the shorter piano works, I can recommend this last set, the Eighteen Pieces, op. 72 – a very varied, and sometimes surprising, collection. There is a stunning performance of these by the Russian pianist and conductor, Mikhail Pletnev.

tention. The essence of the one 'official' story is that he committed suicide to prevent a particularly sensitive homosexual relationship he had entered into becoming public knowledge. Let me state here categorically: there is no proof that Tchaikovsky's death was not from natural causes but from cholera caught through drinking unboiled water, though there are numerous threads, often spun by more than one witness, that seem to indicate clearly that *something* did occur, and attempts to argue that, since none of these can be proved, therefore none of them could have happened, simply will not do. The most significant trail begins with a meal on 1 November in Leiner's Restaurant in St Petersburg, and is opened by Tchaikovsky's nephew, Yury Davïdov, younger brother of Bob, who was one of the party. On arrival at the restaurant Tchaikovsky had asked for a glass of water. When the waiter had reported that they could not provide water because they had none that had been boiled to kill any cholera bacteria, Tchaikovsky replied, despite protests from the others, that he would drink cold, though unboiled, water. The waiter duly fetched it as Modest entered. Modest instantly forbade his brother to take the glass. But, as Yury recorded:

> Laughing, Pyotr Ilich leaped forward to meet the waiter, and Modest Ilich pursued him. But Pyotr Ilich outstripped him, pushed his brother aside with his elbow, and succeeded in gulping down the fateful glass at one go. Modest Ilich reproved him angrily – and then the merriment began.

Among the party, incidentally, was Glazunov. He left no personal account of the meal, but he must have seen what happened and what ensued, and he later told at least two quite independent people that this incident had occurred, and that Tchaikovsky's death was suicide.

Next morning Tchaikovsky, who was staying at Modest's flat, was already showing symptoms. Modest left a very highly detailed account of what happened from this point until his brother's death five days later. Its details sometimes make for very unpleasant reading, but Modest was obviously determined that it should be the more persuasive by loading it with very precise data. The problem is that Lev Bertenson, the very eminent doctor who attended Tchaikovsky, also wrote a detailed report of the course of the composer's illness, and the two simply do not match – and not only in details, for when Bertenson chronicled it in print after Tchaikovsky's death, it must have instantly been clear to some readers that, according to this,

Tchaikovsky had died on 5 November, not the 6th. Modest's account appeared five days days later, and 'restored' the missing day – which, of course, would only have served to fan the debate. Both men had closely observed the dying man. So how could this discrepancy have arisen? Who was telling the truth?

In fact, it is difficult to believe that the doctor would have printed anything other than the facts – but why in such detail? The only conclusion I can reach is that Bertenson feared Modest might massage events when published, and he was determined, in order to protect his own professional integrity, to forestall this with a detailed account that would crowd out the possibilities of manipulation by Modest. If this is the case, then Modest's account contains an invented day, as well as other discrepancies. But there is a further curious statement. Although Modest gives an account of the evening meal at Leiner's Restaurant, he makes no mention of a glass of water, but alleges that the fatal drink was taken at his apartment at lunch the following day. This is extraordinary, not only for such a potentially lethal supply being available to drink, but also because the symptoms of cholera appeared only four hours later, whereas the normal incubation period was twelve to twenty-eight hours. In addition, during Tchaikovsky's illness bulletins had been posted on the apartment's outer door, and Modest's record is sometimes inconsistent with these current reports. Further, the regulations required that the body of a cholera victim should be removed in a closed coffin immediately after death, but instead Tchaikovsky's remained in Modest's apartment on open display, and requiems were held round the corpse. As Rimsky-Korsakov, one of the visitors, noted in his memoirs: 'How odd that, though his death was the result of cholera, there was free access to the requiems. I remember that Verzhbilovich, who was completely drunk after a drinking bout, kissed the body on the face and head.' Nor were these the only inconsistencies and oddities in Modest's record.

There has been extensive and often acrimonious argument over these and other matters, and the only possible conclusion is that we are unlikely ever to know for certain what actually happened or – even more important – why it happened. But in 1979 one story emerged in the West that may provide a pointer to the mystery. Alexander Voitov had been a pupil at the School of Jurisprudence before the First World War and had amassed a great deal of information about some of the old boys of the school. On meeting Voitov, the Russian scholar, Alexandra Orlova, wrote down the following story from Voitov's dictation:

> Among the pupils who completed their studies at the School of Jurisprudence at the same time as Tchaikovsky there occurs the name of Jacobi. When I was at the school I spent all my holidays in Tsarskoye Selo with the family of Nikolay Borisovich Jakobi, who had been Senior Procurator to the Senate in the 1890s, and who died in 1902. Jacobi's widow, Elizaveta Karlovna, was connected to my parents by affinity and friendship. She was very fond of me, and welcomed me warmly. In 1913, when I was in the last but one class in the school, the twentieth anniversary of Tchaikovsky's death was widely commemorated. It was then, apparently under the influence of surging recollections, that Mrs Jacobi, in great secret, told me the story which, she confessed, had long tormented her. She said that she had decided to reveal it to me because she was now old and felt she did not have the right to take to the grave such an important and terrible secret. 'You', she said, 'are interested in the history of the school and in the fates of its pupils, and therefore you ought to know the whole truth, the more so since it is such a sad page in the school's history.' And this is what she told me.
>
> The incident took place in the autumn of 1893. Tchaikovsky was threatened with terrible misfortune. Duke Stenbok-Fermor, disturbed by the attention which the composer was paying to his young nephew, wrote a letter of accusation to the Tsar and handed the letter to Jacobi to pass on to Alexander III. Through exposure Tchaikovsky was threatened with the loss of all his rights, with exile to Siberia, with inevitable disgrace. Exposure would also bring disgrace upon the School of Jurisprudence and upon all the old boys of the school, Tchaikovsky's fellow students. To avoid publicity Jacobi decided upon the following. He invited all Tchaikovsky's former schoolfriends [he could trace in St Petersburg], and set up a court of honour which included himself. Altogether there were eight people present. Elizaveta Karlovna sat with her needlework in her usual place alongside her husband's study. From time to time from within she could hear voices, sometimes loud and agitated, sometimes dropping apparently to a whisper. This went on for a very long time, almost five hours. Then Tchaikovsky came headlong out of the study. He was almost running, he was unsteady, and he went

out without saying a word. He was very white and agitated. All the others stayed a long time in the study talking quietly. When they had gone Jacobi told his wife, having made her swear absolute silence, what they had decided about the Stenbock-Fermor letter to the Tsar. Jacobi could not withhold it. And so the old boys [of the school] had come to a decision by which Tchaikovsky had promised to abide. They required him to kill himself. A day or two later news of the composer's mortal illness was circulating in St Petersburg.

Is this story true? I doubt we shall ever know. Does this matter? No, not really, for Tchaikovsky's reputation rests not on the more sensational incidents and aspects of his life, but on his prodigious gift of great music to his own people and to us, and on not only the gratitude of his compatriots, but on the love and veneration they had conceived for this towering genius who was also such a generous, modest and – which comes through so clearly in the writings and memories of so many people – lovable man. The evidence of this was apparent immediately after his death became known. People crowded to Modest's apartment to pay their respects, by the next day over three hundred wreaths had arrived not only from Russians but from abroad, from opera companies and private citizens. The state paid for his funeral, the arrangements were assigned to the Imperial Theatres, and Russian opera companies, branches of the RMS, various institutions, and Russian cities asked to be allowed to send representatives. The funeral service, during which the Imperial Chapel Choir sang music by Tchaikovsky, would take place in the Kazan Cathedral, the first time this had been allowed for a commoner. The building could hold six thousand people, but sixty thousand applied for tickets, and finally eight thousand were squeezed in. Members of the royal family attended the service and the Tsar watched the procession, observing, it is said, 'We have many dukes and barons, but only one Tchaikovsky.' Traffic had been diverted to enable the funeral cortège to proceed smoothly, but the silent crowds were so large that it took four hours to arrive at the cemetery. Here Tchaikovsky was buried near Glinka, Borodin and Musorgsky. In 1897 a monument with bust was erected over his grave, and in the next year a seated statue was placed in the St Petersburg Conservatoire.

Such memorials were sincere and fully merited public tributes to a revered genius, but to those who had known the man, they were of secondary importance. So how shall I finish this book, which has been as much a tribute to the man as a celebration of his music? I hope I may be excused for returning to the words with which I ended my four-volume study of Tchaikovsky – the words of Hermann Laroche, his lifelong, often difficult friend, but who had perceived, perhaps more than any other critic of the time, the clues to his creative greatness, and who had known the man so well:

> You can analyse the technical merits of a score, you can indicate and enumerate the moral qualities and talents of the person in question, but it is not technical qualities – at least, not they alone – that embody what is fascinating in his music, nor do his talents and virtues impart to his personality its magnetic power. As in artistic creation, so in human personality: when all analytical and critical efforts have been made, there remains something undiscovered, something secret, and it is the very secret that is the most important element, the true essence of the subject. While making no claim to have explained the phenomenon, we still have to recall that phenomenon: we cannot forget that Pyotr Ilich, through his presence alone, brought into everything light and warmth. And if Europe mourns in him a major artistic force, one of the greatest of the second half of the nineteenth century, then it is only those persons who had the happiness of knowing him closely who know what a *man* has been lost through his death.

Appendix 1

Brief Descriptions of Musical Forms

Sonata Form

Sonata form is also sometimes described as 'first-movement form'. Readers unfamiliar with matters of key should ignore mentions of these as they are not crucial for understanding what follows.

Sonata form is a musical structure established in the second half of the eighteenth century, especially by Haydn and Mozart. It was normally used for first movements in nineteenth-century symphonic works (not only sonatas, but symphonies, concertos [though here considerably modified] string quartets, etc.) and frequently in finales; it could also, for instance, be the basis for symphonic poems and operatic arias. Its use was extended into the twentieth century, and it is still sometimes employed today.

The form comprises three main sections: exposition, development and recapitulation. There is almost invariably a coda (literally 'a tail') as conclusion, and sometimes an introduction, which is usually slow and musically independent of what follows. The following diagram outlines the form:

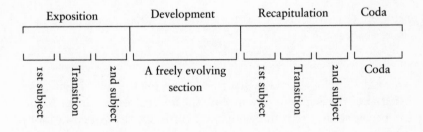

The exposition consists of two 'subjects', the first a section sometimes built from one or more motifs (i.e. small – sometimes *very* small – thematic ideas), the second more broadly melodic in Tchaikovsky's works, and almost always containing two distinct tunes. The first subject will be in the work's main key (its 'tonic': for an explanation of key, see Appendix 2), the second in a different key; between the subjects there is almost invariably a passage (the 'transition') during which the shift to the new key is made. In earlier sonata-form movements the exposition was usually repeated, but while, for instance, Schumann and Brahms sometimes followed this practice, Tchaikovsky rarely did. The development section is entirely free, usually focusing on the materials of the exposition and travelling through a variety of keys, and often building to a powerful climax. The recapitulation, where there is a return to the tonic, retraces the general design of the exposition, though perhaps with a good deal of variety. With both subjects now in the tonic, the exposition's transition requires at least some modification. The coda rounds off the movement.

Rondo Form

There are three types of rondo:

Simple Rondo

Based on three musical ideas spread across five sections to make an ABACA structure. The A sections (called 'ritornelli') are in the tonic key; the B and C sections (sometimes called 'episodes') are normally in a new key (often not the same for both). The A sections may be absolutely identical. Simple rondos are rarely met in the pieces by Tchaikovsky discussed in this book.

Rondo

An ABACABA structure. A more ambitiously scaled piece, based now on three ideas.

Sonata Rondo

An ABAC–development–ABA structure. Whereas the two rondo types listed above are structurally unsophisticated pieces, a sonata rondo can be a very large structure with more musical variety and transitions between sections. It quite often provided the finale in (especially) classical-period symphonic works. However, the development section is, relatively, nothing like as extensive as that in a sonata-form movement. The initial B and the C sections are in different keys, but the recurrence of the B section is usually in the tonic. This brings the piece closer to sonata form itself; hence the designation 'sonata rondo'.

Fugue

Fugue was a fundamental form of the late baroque period (the earlier eighteenth century; its greatest exponent was Bach), and it thus predates the emergence of sonata form, with its particular aesthetic aims and attributes. A fugue's texture is contrapuntal – that is, it is made up solely of two or (usually) more melodic strands called 'voices'; all are of equal importance and interest, but are disciplined so that the underlying harmony their combination will produce conforms to that of normal baroque and classical practice.

A fugue is based on a single thematic idea (the 'subject'). At the fugue's opening the voices enter in turn with the subject (those already in continuing freely), after which the composer will decide how he or she will shuffle the recurrences of the subject between the voices. Unlike in classical pieces, there is no sectional, prescribed structure, the composer being entirely free to explore the single expressive world encapsulated in the subject, and to judge how long the fugue should be. To generalize: for the composer the fugue's subject is the nucleus from which can be created not a drama, as in sonata form, but an organism.

Appendix 2

Explanations of Key, Modulation and Ciphering

Key

Think of a piano keyboard:

The black notes are arranged in alternating groups of two or three between the white notes, but this is simply to make playing as practicable as possible; as far as sonority is concerned, *all* notes are of equal importance, and the pitch space between *all adjacent* notes (whether black or white) is equal. If you are puzzled by every thirteenth note (counting both white and black) having the same alphabetical designation, then reflect that if a note is played, and a man and woman are asked to sing that note (say, D), they will not both sing at the same pitch: the woman will sing higher, but it will sound (correctly) like the same note. In fact, they will probably sing two octaves apart (an 'octave' is the distance between a note and the next identical note, either above or below).

If you play upwards or downwards incorporating every note, both black and white, you are playing a 'chromatic scale'. Western music, however, has almost invariably been composed on 'scales' that use only seven of the twelve different pitches contained within the octave. In the music we normally listen to, two seven-note scales have overwhelmingly predominated:

The Major Scale

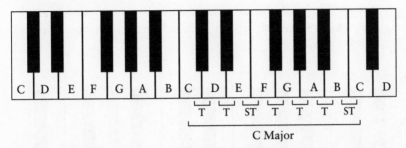

C Major

Starting on the note C, play only on the white notes up (or down) to the next C (five pitches – in this instance the black notes – have now been excluded). This is the 'major scale', which is the pitch basis on which the greater part of Western music has been composed. The interval between any two notes separated by a third note is called a 'tone' (T), between any two adjacent notes a 'semitone' (ST).

The Minor Scale

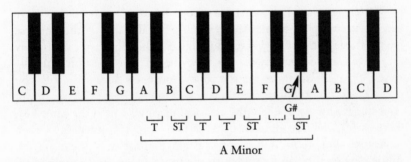

A Minor

Now starting on the note A, play all the white notes up (or down) to the next A. This is the minor scale – *except* that the note G, especially if the scale is upwards, is almost invariably replaced by the black note immediately above, 'G sharp'. (Black notes are labelled according to their position in relation to one of the two adjacent white notes: a black note above a white note is 'sharp', the one below 'flat'.[1])

---

1 The designations 'sharp' and 'flat' can seem to have confusing applications. Thus, for example, the black note between, say, D and E can be both D sharp and E flat, and, for instance, in certain contexts the white-note pitch F can be notated as E sharp, or the white-note pitch B as C flat. Whatever the individual instance, 'sharp' always means a semitone higher, 'flat' a semitone lower.

So far only scales with C as the 'tonic' (the term for the key note) have been considered. But major and minor scales can start on any pitch; what is inviolable is the tone–semitone structure of the scale. If, say, a composer wanted to write a piece in D major, this would involve two black notes:

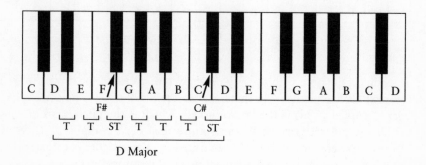

D Major

Modulation

In Western music of the past (say) four hundred years, pieces have been written 'in' all available keys, but have also during their course passed through other keys (i.e. 'modulated'), though almost invariably they have ended in the key in which they began. The question naturally arises: does modulation matter to the ordinary listener? Will you notice? Yes, it does matter – and yes, you will, even if you cannot put your finger on why. If a lengthy classical piece was all in the same key, there would be the danger of a certain sort of sameness – even monotony. But, more important, a passage in a new key can have a subtle new quality, and a return to the tonic does bring, after a tonal excursion, some sense of resolution. That may be something experienced only by the well-practised listener who may still, nevertheless, lay no claim to special expertise. But if your doubt remains, try a simple test. Everybody, I suspect, knows that great, but so simple theme from the last movement of Beethoven's Ninth ('Choral') Symphony (it is the anthem of the United Nations). It is as short and simple as any hymn tune and, like so many hymns, has four phrases. Run through it in your head, and stop at the end of phrase three. Does that sound like a plausible ending? No – because, with the harmony Beethoven gives it (and we only ever hear it with its harmony), it is in the 'wrong' key.

Only with the final line does Beethoven return us to the tonic, and the piece gains a true ending.

Be patient about modulation. Music, exactly like a spoken language, is itself a language with a vocabulary, a grammar, and a variety of structures of its own. If it did not have these things, it would be incoherent, and most of us have absorbed the basics of this language unconsciously, simply by hearing lots of bits of music – just as we learned to speak our own language simply by hearing it spoken. But like any language, to get beyond the basics requires attention and experience. It is my hope that, especially for the new listener who has had little or no experience of classical music, patient and attentive listening spread over a period of time will bring not only a growing enjoyment of classical pieces, but an awareness of other things in these pieces that the ear at first missed – and that from this will come an added enjoyment.

Ciphering

Ciphering is the process whereby the letters used to identify each white note on the piano are translated into a chain of musical pitches. To give a simple example: the word CABBAGE (containing only letters between A and G) can be converted into a series of seven pitches to make a tiny seven-note tune, and composers who have wanted in a particular piece to pay tribute to some person have often, where possible, devised a musical cipher out of that person's name or initials. Unfortunately, of course, English usage has only the first seven letters of the alphabet (A to G) available, but the Germans have a rather different system which gives the black note immediately above A the label B (not B flat, as we have it), which means that the next white note (our note B) has lost its label – so they assign that note the letter H. As a result, the name BACH can be ciphered (B flat–A–C–B), and many works incorporating this cipher have been composed in tribute to the German master. Because both France and Italy also have variants in their systems of note-naming, they also can cipher words that English cannot. There seem clearly to be instances in Tchaikovsky's music where, employing mainly the German system, he has used ciphering, and I have drawn attention to a few of these.

Appendix 3

Glossary of Musical Terms and Non-English Words

Musical Terms

ANTIPHONY: where a composition requires the performers to divide into two or more independent, and often spatially separated, groups who may perform sometimes in alternation, at others jointly

ARIA: a composition (especially operatic) for a solo voice

BAR: a piece of classical music is almost always composed in regular metrical units of either two or three pulses (or multiples of these). These units are called bars and are marked off in the score by vertical lines

BEAT: the basic pulse of a piece (usually the crotchet; see note values below)

BINARY FORM: a musical structure in two sections, each of which may be repeated

CADENZA: a (usually) brilliant solo passage, normally set towards the end of an aria or a concerto movement; in classical music a cadenza may sometimes be composed, or even improvised, by the performer

CANTATA: a work for one or more voices accompanied by instruments

CANTILENA: a 'flowing' song or melody

CHORALE: a hymn (-like) melody

CODA: a 'tailpiece' – the stretch of music that rounds off a composition

COUNTER-MELODY: a tune heard simultaneously against another tune

DIVERTISSEMENT: a set of decorative dances

DOTTED RHYTHM: a two-note jerky rhythm

444

FIGURE: a short, distinctive melodic fragment that is much used in a piece

FUGATO: a brief passage in the style of a fugue

MODULATION: the process of moving from one key to another (for a fuller explanation, see Appendix 2)

MOTO PERPETUO: 'in perpetual motion' – a piece or section marked by unbroken impetus

NOTE VALUES: every composition is made up of a complex of notes which have a fixed relationship in terms of their duration. The longest is the breve and, in the following list, each note is one half the length of its immediate predecessor: breve, semibreve, minim, crotchet, quaver, semiquaver, demi-semiquaver. (Clearly there is a vast difference in duration – a ratio of one to sixty-four – between the breve and demi-semiquaver). If a dot is placed after a note, then its length is increased by one half. In notating the beat itself (see beat above) the note most commonly chosen is the crotchet

OBBLIGATO: an important solo instrumental part against another tune

OCTAVE: the distance between a note and the next same-named note either above or below

OSTINATO: a brief melodic idea (or perhaps a rhythm), repeated many times at the same pitch

OVERTURE: the orchestral prelude to an opera, though it may also be an independent orchestral piece (usually descriptive) for concert use

RECITATIVE: a declaimed style of singing in which the pitches are specified, but in which the singer delivers the words at a more spoken pace, on occasions almost in a 'patter' manner

RITORNELLO: a passage that returns more than once (e.g. in a rondo movement)

ROULADE: a florid passage of runs, etc.

SARABAND: a leisurely dance (mostly pre-1750) in triple time

SCENARIO: the outline plot of an opera or ballet

SCHERZO: literally a 'joke' – a lively, capricious piece

SCORE: the manuscript or printed text of a piece of music

SCORING: the process of setting out in detail the final text of a composition

TERNARY FORM: a musical structure in three sections, the first and last identical

TRIO: either a composition for three instruments, or the central portion of a minuet or scherzo

VOCAL SCORE: the score of a vocal piece (e.g. an opera, cantata, etc.) in which the orchestral part has been arranged for piano

Non-English Words

Adagio: very slow
Allegro: fast
Andante, Andantino (semplice): moderate speed (simply)
Cantabile: singingly
Con fuoco: with fire
Crescendo: get louder
Diminuendo: get quieter
Flebile: tearfully
Funebre e doloroso: funereal and sorrowful
Giusto: at a suitable or reasonable pace
Maestoso: majestic
Ma non troppo: but not too much
Molto: much, very
Molto espressivo: very expressively
Piano: quiet
Pianissimo: very quiet
Più: more
Pizzicato: with the strings plucked
Pointilliste: a term used in painting of 'crowding a surface with small spots of various colours which are blended by the spectator's eye'
Presto: very fast
Prestissimo: as fast as possible
Quasi: like, as
Tempo: speed, time
Tutti: all, everybody
Valse triste: a sad waltz
Vivace, Vivo: lively

Index

Figures in bold type indicate discussion of individual works. 'T' indicates Pyotr Ilich Tchaikovsky; 'NvM' indicates Nadezhda von Meck.

TCHAIKOVSKY

– String Quartet no.3 in Eb minor,
op.30 xiv, 56–7, 80, 106, **107–8**, 127,
238, 396
– String Sextet: *Souvenir de Florence*,
op.70 xii, xiv, 56–7, 382–4
Choral
– All-Night Vigil, op.52 185
– *Cantata to Commemorate the Bicente-
nary of the Birth of Peter the Great* 104
– Coronation cantata: *Moscow* 255,
256, 374
– Liturgy of St John Chrystostom, op.41
183–4, **184–5**, 253
– *Nine Sacred Pieces* 185
– *Ode to Joy* 23–4, 35, 77
Operas
Cherevichki (*Vakula the Smith*) xii, 10,
86–7, **87–93**, 100, 141, 195, 198,
282–3, 301, 303, 305, 320, 321
– *The Enchantress* 117, 195, 302–5,
305–312, 313, 315, 320, 321, 326, 363
– *Eugene Onegin*, op.24 xii, xiii, xiv,
61, 68, 87, 90, 106, 117, 152–5,
155–67, 174, 177, 198, 199, 216, 223,
231, 234, 241, 244, 282, 284, 299,
300, 317, 322, 337, 339, 343, 344,
359, 360, 367, 368, 369, 372–3, 374,
399, 418, 430
– *Iolanta*, op.69 90, 400, **400–402**, 430
– *The Maid of Orleans* 5, 117, 193–5,
196–201, 222, 234, 244, 245, 253, 282,
431
– *Mazeppa* xii, 117, 243–4, **244–52**,
255, 257, 258, 268, 275, 282, 307,
316, 317
– *Oprichnik* 46, 61–2, **63–8**, 70, 85,
292, 307, 431
– *The Queen of Spades*, op.68 xii, xiv,
61, 87, 117, 155, 244, 256, 344, 367–9,
369–79, 381, 382, 391, 399, 413, 430
– *Undine* 47, 61, 72, 114
– *The Voyevoda*, op.3 22–3, 36–7, 46, 47,
63, 64, 67, 116, 224, 225, 388–9, **390**
Orchestra
– *Characteristic Dances* 22–3, 44, 384
– Concert Fantasia for piano and
orchestra, op.56 279–80, **281–2**, 331
– *Coronation March* in D 394
– Fantasy Overture: *Hamlet*, op.67a xii,
xiii, 143, 335, **340–42**
– Fantasy Overture: *Romeo and Juliet*

x, xii, xiii, 47–50, **48–54**, 55, 56, 70,
72, 77, 96, 126, 281, 289, 295, 297,
317, 322, 329, 330, 340, 341, 390
– *Fatum* (Fate) 46, 67
– Festival Overture: *The Year 1812*,
op.49 30, 37, 81, 223–4, **224–5**, 251,
256, 328–9, 330
– Festival Overture on the Danish
National Anthem 30, 36, 255
– incidental music for Ostrovsky's *The
Snow Maiden* 75–6
– Italian Capriccio, op.45 220
– *Manfred Symphony*, op.58 xii, xiii,
40, 105, 289, 291–3, **293–8**, 301, 302,
315
– *Nutcracker Suite*, op.71a 191
– Overture in F 23, 28, 29, 30
– *Pezzo capriccioso* for cello and orches-
tra 326
– Piano Concerto no.1 in Bb minor, op.23
xii, xiii, xiv, 93–5, **95–100**, 101, 103, 106,
143–4, 178, 179, 216, 218, 220, 281,
328, 330, 345, 346, 392, 394, 395
– Piano Concerto no.2 in G, op.44 xii,
xiii, xiv, 95, 190, 214–15, **216–18**, 222,
281
– Piano Concerto no.3 in Eb, op.75
281, 414–15, **415**, 419, 430, 431
– *Sérénade mélancolique*, op.26 xiv,
100
– Serenade for Strings, op.48 xii, xiii,
225–6, **226–8**, 317, 328, 330, 331, 345,
395
– *Slavonic March*, op.31 123, 124
– *The Storm* overture, op.76 22, 23, 32
– Suite no.1 in D, op.43 187, 190–91,
191–2, 214, 220, 228, 327, 345, 346
– Suite no.2 in C, op.53 **258–60**, 266,
268, 275
– Suite no.3 in G, op.55 xii, xiii, 258,
269, 270–75, **276–7**, 278, 283, 328,
331, 345, 346, 392, 394
– Suite no.4 *Mozartiana*, op.61 191,
323, 326
– Symphonic Ballad: *The Voyevoda*,
op.78 xii, xiii
– Symphonic Fantasia: *Francesca da
Rimini*, op.32 xii, xiii, 124, **124–6**,
126–7, 289, 293, 326, 329, 331, 335,
340, 341, 390, 427, 428
– Symphonic Fantasia: *The Tempest*,

458